The Road Back Home

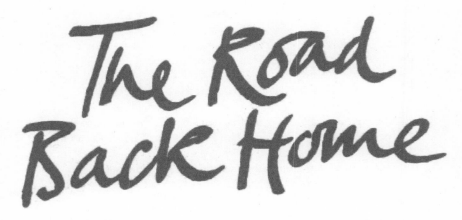

The Road Back Home

The bittersweet memoirs of a
Geordie coal miner's son

SID WADDELL

EBURY
PRESS

1 3 5 7 9 10 8 6 4 2

Published in 2009 by Ebury Press, an imprint of Ebury Publishing
A Random House Group Company

The Random House Group Limited Reg. No. 954009

Addresses for companies within the Random House Group can be found at
www.randomhouse.co.uk

A CIP catalogue record for this book is available from the British Library

The Random House Group Limited supports The Forest Stewardship Council
(FSC), the leading international forest certification organisation. All our titles
that are printed on Greenpeace approved FSC certified paper carry the FSC
logo. Our paper procurement policy can be found at
www.rbooks.co.uk/environment

Mixed Sources
Product group from well-managed
forests and other controlled sources
www.fsc.org Cert no. TT-COC-2139
© 1996 Forest Stewardship Council

Printed and bound in Great Britain by Clays Ltd, St Ives PLC

ISBN 9780091932220

To buy books by your favourite authors and register for offers visit
www.rbooks.co.uk

*I don't know why Mam is looking so merry up Granny's backyard.
I had glowered and screamed non-stop for the first
eighteen months of my life.*

CONTENTS

ACKNOWLEDGEMENTS

Many people have helped make this book a portrait of a mining clan and a way of life rather than one Geordie boy's unusual personal journey.

I have to thank Andrew Goodfellow at Ebury for expanding my horizons on the scope of the book and for encouraging me to balance the laughter with the tears. His colleagues Ali Nightingale and Justine Taylor have also made valuable contributions to the end product.

In the Lynemouth and Ashington area my memories have been jogged by several friends. Historians Neil Taylor and Mike Kirkup served up a wealth of detail on pit life and local lore. And my old grammar school pal Keith Lister opened my eyes to some of the harsher sides of life in Dalton Avenue. Thanks to all of these.

Now to the immediate clan, the Waddells and their offshoots. My brother's ex-wife Iris Longley, my cousin Elsie Snowball and my Auntie Jean Cullingworth have provided me with photographs dating back to the 1920s. But most help in this and other areas of our family history has come from my cousin Robert Waddell and his wife Gladys. They were Bob and Martha's best pals and loved them dearly. Robert was also my ear-smacking mentor when I went off the rails. I could not have written this 'saga' without these folk and I hope they think my efforts are fair.

Finally, my wife Irene has monitored this project for many years. She has bullied and cajoled me to be honest about my motives and not to hide my failings in the warm mist of humorous nostalgia or cocky self-esteem. She also suggested perspectives on strong wilful women like my mother Martha and my granny Mary Jane that would not have occurred to me. She frequently dammed the torrent of my gushing prose.

I must take full responsibility for any errors or exaggerations in the story and any harsh portraiture of the cast. In this respect, I have tried to make it clear at every turn that I myself was no angel.

Sid Waddell
Pudsey
West Yorkshire

Prologue

In 1954 we moved from a pretty bungalow in a leafy village to the drab rows of Lynemouth. But I soon found under the soot and muck the warmth of a real community.

I have not lived in the former pit village of Lynemouth since 1961 but the winding road north from Newcastle will always be the same nostalgic highway, each twist charged with vivid memories and powerful emotions.

On a bright, gusty day in March 1999 I got on the bus at the Haymarket bus station in Newcastle in a very sombre mood; there would be tears aplenty before the day ended. I was to clear out the contents of 102 Dalton Avenue, the cottage where my dad Bob grew his leeks, Martha, my mother, ruled the roost and my brother Derrick made us all laugh, despite the daily fears and hardships of life in a mining community.

After leaving the posh suburb of Gosforth the land becomes less rich, the trees somehow less green and the houses definitely poorer. The only thing worth turning a sod for out here was to get at the rich seams of black gold, best gleaming Geordie coal. To the east large clouds crowded over the North Sea and I spotted the odd unnatural man-made grassy mounds where once there was a serried line of pit heaps, blazing red like Etna and spewing out fumes, but in their own way as awe-inspiring as the Swiss Alps. In the towns of Bedlington and Ashington there are still the garish fronts of workingmen's clubs and beer palaces, but nowhere near the bustle and sweaty throb of the life that I remember as a lad in the 1940s. Mrs. Thatcher put paid to all that. She picked on our lot as the 'enemy within'; the miners had to be put in their place for giving pain to a succession of Tory governments. 'That woman', as Martha always spat out, killed all our pits, and the people who walk round here now, pushing prams and killing time on corner ends, do so like ghosts; they have little substance in their lives and no hopes at all.

Beyond the barracks streets of Ashington the land looked less welcoming than ever. The pewter grey swirl of the North Sea framed the coast and the scabby hawthorn trees all bent inland, crippled by the nagging east wind. Then the bus rumbled past the hulking rusty gantries of the now defunct Lynemouth Colliery, once the pride of both the NCB and the local pitmen who cheered the raising of flags to announce record tonnages clawed from under the pounding waves. In the end, all the slogging, sweating and cheering counted for nothing. Then I saw the smudge of tiny houses to the north and we were in the village of Lynemouth and a lump came into my throat.

I got off the bus and looked up at the 'Hotel', a mighty brick beer palace where Derrick and I had roistered, a place Bob had scornfully avoided and Martha and I had faithfully attended Catholic Mass – at an altar built of beer crates. Memories of trying to feel holy while the cleaning women in the corridor told dirty stories of last night's sex and thirsty boozers hawked up last session's phlegm on the wall outside brought my only real smile of the day.

My only reason for being in my home village that day was nothing to do with happy memories. I was there to clear things up after three deaths.

For years I had let my fertile imagination conjure up my dad's death and my likely reaction. My morbid moments always figured an accident in the pit and him dying under a fall of jagged rock. I knew I would cry and certainly swear at God, Jesus, the National Coal Board – whoever. But when Bob did die it was how Martha took it that knotted my guts and made me sob and punch and kick the coal house door.

It all happened in late November 1989. I was sitting in my house in Leeds when I got a phone call from my brother Derrick. He was never one to exaggerate, nor was his tone ever far away from humorous.

'Bob's in hospital. The angina's got a bit worse. They've got him on a breathing thingy – but he's eating like a horse. He says the food is shite but he's yarking it down.'

I didn't like the sound of 'a breathing thingy' so I packed a bag quickly and headed for Leeds City Station.

As usual in time of crisis, I called on the booze to help, a cosy conduit to turn the dark skies blue. I sat on the train and slurped a couple of cans of lager and let my mind slip down memory lane. Bob was 83 and had worked down the pit for 48 years despite having a weak wheezy chest. He was a small man with spindly legs but very big in the shoulder. For nearly 15 of those years he had been a coalface and then salvage drawer – pulling the roof down by sheer muscle and hoping the resulting torrent of rock and rubble did not cover him. He used to fall on the settee at the end of a shift, curl into a ball and sleep the sleep of the knackered before rousing himself for dinner. Not surprisingly, the heavy graft took its toll. He developed angina around 1956 and had a mild heart attack in 1972. As I opened another can, I recalled that scare. I'd grabbed the train, got pissed on beer and whisky and bawled my way to Lynemouth. I raced up Dalton Avenue, sure there would be an ambulance with flashing lights at 102 and a stretcher being hauled out with a covered body.

He was sitting in his armchair by the fire supping tea, face ruddy and eyes twinkling. I cuddled him like he was a kiddie's toy, tears streaming. 'Did you think I'd be deed, Sidney?' he jested warmly. 'Tough lads, the Waddells,' he added as he banged the angina point, just below his heart. Soon we were in the Hotel all together – Bob, Martha, Derrick, me and a bunch of pals – and knocking back plenty. Derrick and I got hammered on beer and whisky, and Martha, sitting in her pearls and her ocelot coat, did justice to half a dozen double gins. Her lined face glowed and she tossed her still-dark curls. She was basking in the Christmassy glow, and having her menfolk round her 'aal wi' smilin' faces' was better than the gin or the wall-to-wall Woodbines.

'I'm surrounded by bloody alcoholics,' said Bob, toting his second half of shandy.

As the train pulled into the Toon I hoped against hope that this time we would end the day just as merry. It was raining as I trotted up Station Road in Ashington, past the former billiard hall where I had hung out with Screw, Bubbles and the gang of wide boys, and the Buffalo cinema where I had snogged and groped my way through my early teens. Then I went to the modern reception block of Ashington Hospital and asked for the ward my dad was in.

The four cans of lager had schmoozed me into an edgy, almost chirpy mood. The first thing I saw when I entered the side room off the ward was the 'breathing thingy', making Bob look for all the world like a pig with a see-through snout. His eyes were closed, his face was grey and his breathing hardly raised the blankets. Time for being tough, I said to myself, but I could not stop the tears. Martha ran and hugged me and Derrick gave me a grin through gritted teeth. 'His heart is very weak,' said Mam, speaking like a child who has just memorised a difficult lesson.

I leaned over and kissed his forehead. I took a crazy joy in how cool it was. Hurrah, no temperature. His eyes opened and he smiled, the warm glow that always came when he greeted his grandchildren. He slid half-upright and pulled off the piggy mask. 'Can some bugger get me a cup of tea and a biscuit? I'm warkin' wi' hunger.'

The words broke the pall. Derrick ran out for the stuff. Martha plumped his pillows and I began stroking the veins in his left forearm, trying to make the blood flow better. Suddenly he grabbed for the 'thingy' and sucked in more air. For a second his eyes glazed over but then the grin flicked back.

The staff nurse came round a few minutes later and took his pulse. She told us he needed sleep. I could not read from her face if this was good or bad. 'He's looking much better,' said Mam. 'He was looking real shabby yesterday.'

That was good enough for me. I dragged Derrick to the Hotel after tea and we had a good drink.

I was sleeping downstairs on the settee. The phone rang at about three o'clock in the morning. I trembled as I picked up the receiver.

'Is that Mr Waddell?' said the voice of a young lass.

'Yes.'

'This is Ashington Hospital. I am afraid I have to tell you that your father has died…'

My heart was crushed. I put the phone down. I began chewing my lip to keep control and walked upstairs. I opened the bedroom door and the landing light fell on Martha's face. She was sleeping the sleep of the exhausted, fragile and curled up like a child. On the wall above her head a sacred heart plaque glowed, flickering ruby red. The shiny white rosary beads handed down to her by my granny, Mary-Jane, were pressed to her lips by blue-veined hands. She had gone to sleep praying that Bob would be soon well. For a second I looked across the bed at my dad's place. I shook her shoulder and her eyes opened. Bleary, eye-rubbing surprise turned to pure dread.

'My dad has died.'

She smashed her face into the pillow and began to keen, an animal noise of sheer wretched agony. 'Why oh why don't they tell you the truth? Why do they let you think he's getting better?'

I threw my arms over her and cuddled her as tight as I could. Derrick came and held us both. He sobbed too, but his grief was throaty and quiet.

Then my mother broke my heart completely. She sat in Bob's tatty maroon velour-covered armchair nursing a cup of tea and raking the dying embers of the fire. 'We had such fun together, such fun,' she sighed in a hoarse broken whisper. I mumbled something about coal and ran into the backyard. I began banging my fists and feet against the

My parents were a great team and shared some great verbal banter.
Here they are in the parlour of 102 Dalton Avenue in 1955.

coal house door. I hurled back my head and screamed to the dawn-streaked sky, 'You're not fucking there!' My fury was aimed at the protective Catholic God that Martha and Granny had begged me to believe in. I smashed the shovel into the neat rounded pellets of smokeless fuel.

There was more drama over Bob's burial. And in this particular saga Derrick the jester became the joker who went wild. All my dad's family had been buried in the beautiful old churchyard at Cresswell, nestled on a green hill overlooking the white sandy sweep of Druridge Bay, washed by the pewter-grey North Sea; a fitting spot for a life spent nobly, digging coal for the nation. But there was a problem. Recent rules had been drawn up that only people living in Cresswell hamlet could be buried there. Our local undertaker came and told us that the vicar was adamant: Bob could not be buried near his father and mother. He would have to go to the tatty ill-kept field that was Lynemouth's burying ground. Derrick, stone-cold sober, threw an enormous wobbler. 'Me dad had fuck all for all of his life and I'm not burying him amongst condoms, beer cans and dog shit. Suppose I have to carry his body around in a fucking black bin liner, he's not going over there to that tip.' I had never seen my brother so passionate – and it worked. Our undertaker looked at plans of the plots at Cresswell and eventually found that there was room for Bob to be buried directly above his father.

On an overcast day we had to hold my mam back from flinging herself into the grave on top of the coffin. At the last moment she was given a single rose by the undertaker. It did the trick. Martha stood stock still, kissed the flower and gently dropped it down into the earth after her man.

The death of my brother Derrick in the summer of 1996 was even more traumatic.

While I was a school swot and a sports star, Tadger, Bob's nickname for him, was the family court jester. Derrick only wanted to make people laugh, even before he got to school. It was the same in his 18-year stint in the Royal Air Force. Geordie Waddell, as he was known, lit up bars and barrack blocks from Belize to Belfast with his cheek and sarcastic one-liners. But when he got divorced and began living with my mam at 102 Dalton, the trouble started. He could not find work, so took to spending too much time sinking pints of LCL lager at the Hotel and other watering holes. And when the pubs started opening all day, things went beyond a joke. He was spending up to ten hours a day on the beer and the fags and he stopped eating.

Derrick started arguing with Mam, and there were often frantic tearful calls from Martha when a row exploded. I raced from Leeds to Lynemouth one afternoon in 1994 to find the pair of them spitting insults across the room like a pair of wild cats. I was appalled to see two people I loved snarling and swearing at each other. Derrick was very drunk but I managed to calm him down. Martha did her best to wind him up again.

'I don't know why you cannot get a job – it's not that you're not intelligent!'

'I had a fucking job with the RAF for 18 years, or have you forgotten, woman?' was the riposte.

Then, as I brewed up in the kitchen, they started laughing and sharing Mam's pack of Silk Cut.

'We have 50 fights a week, Sidney,' said my mam by way of explanation.

No way to live, I thought to myself; 47-year-old bloke drinking heavily, only solid sustenance a couple of bits of toast in the morning and having constant verbal aggro with his ageing mother.

Then, two years later, I got a phone call from my mother that was quiet, concerned and totally rational. She told me that Derrick had been taken into hospital with 'something like jaundice'. Bells rang. Jaundice? Heavy drinking? It was probably much worse than they were letting on to Martha. I headed for Leeds station.

At the Haymarket in Newcastle I scrunched into a seat on the bus and tried to busy my worried mind with the *Evening Chronicle*. Suddenly there was a heavy tap on my shoulder. I did not know the bloke by name but he was a Hotel regular. His face was creased with concern.

'I seen your young 'un a week ago at the Hotel and he was bright yellow. Like a bloody no-parking line up a street. We persuaded him to drink lemonade but he was back on the lager afore closing.'

My gut twisted. Bright-bloody-yellow. That was more than just jaundice.

Just before one o'clock I ran into Ashington Hospital and was directed to the Intensive Care Unit. I found the ward and was surprised to see an empty bed. I asked a nurse where Derrick was and she laughed. 'Holding court with the rest of the smokers on the patio.'

I was gobsmacked. I was sure he would have been full of tubes and at death's door. He was in fact entertaining an audience of three people: two fellow patients and his 24-year-old son Robbie. He was wearing a dressing-gown and slippers and his face was in fact yellow. Not 'no-parking' bright yellow, more the browny yellow of wet sand. Holding a fag like Noël Coward, he stopped mid-joke and gave me one across the bows.

'Oh, I must be right shabby if Golden Bollocks has come here tappy-lappy.'

I didn't know whether to kiss the sod or clout his ear. Off he went as if in the NAAFI with his RAF buddies or entertaining the bar flies at the Hotel. The jokes came out thick and fast; self-mocking stories of winding up Italians with his RAF friends and being a 'Jungle Fighter' in Belize. Then suddenly the laugh was bang on Geordie Waddell himself. Two of the barmaids from the Hotel came bearing flowers for him and a clanking carrier bag. There was a hush as he delved inside the carrier and pulled out four litre bottles of Kia Ora orange squash.

'It'll do you good, Derrick,' said one of the lasses as we all dissolved in hysterics.

An hour later there was no sign of tiredness, but a nurse popped out to tell him he needed to get back to the ward for some pills and a kip. He sat on the bed and flipped a carrier bag of dirty clothes to Robbie. Then we both hugged him and danced down the stairs. Soon we were supping pints in the Grand Street Social Club and I was brimming with relief. Robbie's chubby boyish chops creased in mirth as he told me of his dad's exploits. On the doctor's advice, Derrick had gone into hospital for treatment. They had given him drugs to wean his body off alcohol. Wide-eyed, Robbie went on, 'But you know what me dad's like. One evening he fancied a pint so he put a cardigan over his pyjamas, put his slippers on and fucking escaped!'

I laughed so much I knocked my pint of lager over.

'He did, Uncle Sid. He walked down the path through the fields and along the pit road past the windmill. Then he only walked into the Hotel cool as you please, sat on his stool and asked for a pint of LCL lager. They refused to give him booze. They gave him a glass of orange, rang Cousin Robert and he drove him back to the hospital. He was dead calm about it and the staff didn't even bollock him.'

We laughed into our ale. But we laughed too soon.

Four days later, at about five o'clock, I went to the White Cross pub in Pudsey for a few pints of Tetley's and a game of pool. I played well against my friend Jon Greenwood, a retired teacher, and felt good telling him about my brother's recovery.

Just after six I went home. I knew there was something very wrong when I saw the flashing red light on the phone's answering machine. When the recorded voice told me there were five messages I blenched.

The first message was from Dick Longley, the husband of Iris, my brother's ex-wife. From his opening words I knew what the news would be. 'This is Dick, Sid, and I'm sorry to have to tell you that Derrick died in hospital this afternoon.'

Two large whiskies on the train north did little to stop the flood of tears and the avalanche of guilt. I should have stopped the little bugger drinking. I should not have sat in his company and bought rounds of drinks and pretended his problems would disappear in the boozy bonhomie of the Hotel and Lynemouth workingmen's club. I should have been more of a brother to him.

All this self-flagellation was stemmed a bit by my wife Irene. She was working in Newcastle and she drove me from the Central Station to 102 Dalton. 'Get a grip, Sidney. Cut out the self-pity and think of your mother,' she said.

It was nowhere as difficult a job as I had imagined. Martha was sitting in my dad's chair by the fire with a strained but calm face. There was a chair placed to her right for me. I hugged Cousin Robert and his wife Gladys, and Iris, who had raced to Lynemouth from Lowestoft. Then I sat down and put my arm around my mother. She clutched my hands and her gaze drifted to the fire. Gladys opened the door of the kitchen to go and make tea and Roger came bounding in with a mad, frothy-mouthed rush. He was Derrick's daft, half-house-trained mongrel, steak-fed and totally neurotic. He slavered all over my face and Martha yelled, 'Doon, Roger, doon! That bloody dog.'

A vision slashed through my mind of a very merry Derrick wrestling on the fireside mat with Roger, one of the last beings he really connected with. And then I wept.

Half the village turned out for the Jungle Fighter's funeral. As I escorted Martha down the broken concrete path of 102 past Bob's leek trench to the hearse, I saw people lining the street three deep. Young and old, people who had known Derrick as a bright-faced kid and others who had only seen him in boozy decline, were standing solemnly, showing respect. It is only about 500 yards to the church down by the shop where my mam and Derrick bought their fags, and people lined the whole route. There was standing room only when the priest said his bit. I was glad that he chose to set Derrick's death in the context of a region whose lifeblood had been stopped when the pits were closed. He spoke openly about the lack of jobs and the lack of hope. I was glad he was the one to say it, because coming from me it would have been pure verbal savagery, and would most likely have detracted from the dignity of the occasion.

I doubt that I would have got as far as the socio-political diatribe. I started by making the people laugh with a couple of stories about what a rip my brother had been as a kid. I made them smile for a minute or two, then after a few yarns about Derrick in the RAF, I filled up and had to get off.

But the Jungle Fighter had the last laugh. As the service ended, the priest announced that Derrick had wanted a certain song played at his funeral. So my daughter Lucy switched on a cassette tape and the strains of 'A Good Day Today' by Neil Diamond filled the church. It is a country and western song about a bloke whose wife has left him, whose dog has died and his car has been repossessed. Derrick's son Robbie gave me a thumbs up from across the aisle and I had to smile.

My brother Derrick, on the left, travelled the world with the Royal Air Force. He was very proud of his time as a 'Jungle Fighter'.

In the Hotel after the burial 200 folk drank to my brother's memory and recalled his joke-telling prime, but my mother refused to enter the place.

'It was that place that helped ruin Derrick with its bloody lock-ins,' was her verdict.

Martha went downhill rapidly after Derrick's death.

In an odd way, the rows and ructions with my brother had been a stimulant. But within a year of his death she was struggling to manage at 102 Dalton Avenue. She could not get upstairs unaided and a bed had been set up in a corner of the living room. A home help, Beryl, was visiting every day but even she could not cope. Martha was so weak in the legs that she needed help to get to the toilet in the night. On a visit in early May I was told in private that my mam had to go into care immediately.

It was arranged that, until a suitable old folks' home could be found, she would be looked after at the Cottage Hospital, six miles away in Morpeth. She was not happy; her legs might be dodgy but there was still life in the venomous tongue.

'I wish I'd had lassies – lassies look after you.'

At going on 82 she could still hurt with the best of them. I could do nothing else but shrug and button my lip. I could not up sticks and leave my wife and family in Pudsey to become my mother's nurse/companion, and she would not countenance living with us.

I had moral support on the drive to the hospital in the form of my cousin Robert and his wife Gladys, but it did nothing to brighten up the atmosphere in the car. My mam sat in the front with Robert driving. Her face was set like a calf being sent to market. We checked her in and went to sit in the hospital garden. Robert cracked jokes and Gladys did her best to praise the place. I plied her with fag after fag, but the eyes stayed as dead as a snake's. I felt like a guard at Belsen.

It was worse, much worse, a couple of weeks later when we took her from the hospital to stay at Avala Park old people's home in the village of Widdrington. It was the afternoon of the18th of June, and her 82nd birthday was the next day. It was cruel, but I had been advised by the experts that it might be extremely traumatic for her to go home first, or even visit 102 Dalton. Martha's room was smart, clean, bright and on the ground floor. After unpacking her clothes we went to the tearoom. I was boosted no end when two lady residents I recognised as Lynemouth people waved to her. She blanked them with a stony gaze. Then a man in a cardigan walked towards us, helped by a member of staff. Mam and I recognised him at the same time as Billy Chatt, always smart and heavily Brylcreemed and once her regular dancing partner at Lynemouth club.

'Is that you, Billy?' Martha managed a pale smile.

I froze as the stooped head looked up, and the dribbly bottom lip sagged. Billy's eyes were glazed; no contact at all. He shuffled on. I could not look at Martha. Welcome to your new home, Mrs Waddell.

Next day my mother's birthday dawned with a cold wind blowing black clouds and spitting rain from the North Sea. I led a birthday posse to Avala: Robbie, Cousin Robert and my pal Richie Stafford. It was tough holding back tears as the car followed the twisty road, skimmed with coal sleck from opencast workings. This was the route my mam and I took in her prime on our weekly pilgrimage by bus to Alnwick to see her mother Mary-Jane. She would be tarted up in lipstick and rouge, sometimes her ocelot coat, and always at the Woodbines. She always managed to start up a cosy natter to while away the journey. She loved company.

The rain got worse as I led the lads with their birthday cards and parcels into Avala. One of the staff showed us to Martha's room and my mouth was dry as I opened the door. Richie and Robert gave her cards and she sat on the bed and opened them. She made a show of being pleased. Robbie lit up fags for himself and her. I did not give her Richie's parcel; it contained a series of glasses that spelt out D-E-R-R-I-C-K. It was a gift from the football team at the Institute. Bad timing, I reckoned. Too evocative; keep it till Christmas.

We stayed for an hour, chatting on the porch outside. She had about three fags and was distant to say the least. I asked what photos or ornaments she wanted me to fetch over on my next visit. There was a note of near derision in her reply. 'Don't bother. I've got all the memories I need in my head.'

Over the next few weeks her mood became a little more positive. On one visit she said that she'd like me to get a picture. I thought it would be a religious one.

'I want a picture of Lady Di to go over the flowers on the table.'

I was gobsmacked. This was the woman who was egalitarian to her marrow; the Queen herself would have been lucky to get a bap and a brew from Martha if she was starving.

By the end of August we had persuaded her to dress up a bit and step out. Twenty yards along the road from Avala was Widdrington Station workingmen's club, Fully affiliated, and we got Martha made a member. She sat with a gin and a fag while Robbie and I played pool. Some nights she would go with a group of other oldies and play bingo. She remained feisty till the end. I had great trouble trying to get her pension money paid to the home by the Ashington branch of the DSS. It took Martha one harridan phone call to get it sorted. A young man was sent to see her face to face, had his ear bent and her just deserts were paid up soon after.

Thankfully, my very last memory of my mother was a very happy one.

In the middle of February 1998 Robbie and I made a visit to Avala. It was freezing cold and there was frost on the scraggy hawthorn bushes. We took Martha to lunch at a local pub and she had her favourite: prawn Marie Rose. She looked very frail but still swallowed a couple of gins. Then suddenly she said she wanted to go back. We got out of the taxi and she was fighting for breath. So we sat down on the veranda. I pulled up the hood of her coat as the east wind howled around us.

'Give us a tab, Sidney.' She coughed deeply.

She had emphysema as well as a very weak heart, but what pleasure had she in life now but Silk Cut? Robbie tried to light their fags with his lighter but the wind kept blowing it out. Mam laughed throatily. At last we got her fag going. When one inch of ash was showing she tried to

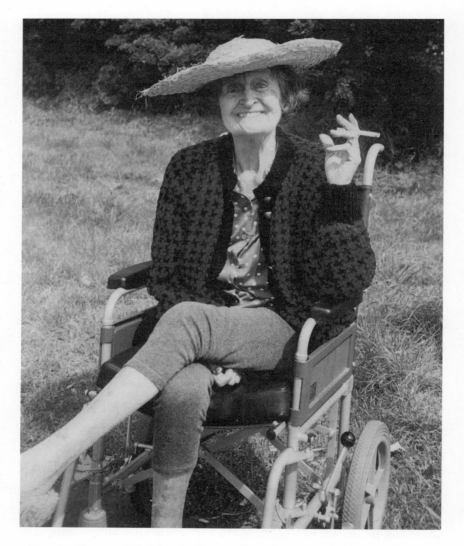

*Even at the age of 82, Mam had a twinkle in her eye and a fag in her hand.
She even joined the workingmen's club next to the old people's home.*

grip the fag in her fingers but failed. Her strength had gone completely.
So I held the fag while she sucked it, wind whipping her still-dark curls
and smoke watering her eyes.

One week later I was getting dressed at the house of my brother and
sister-in-law in Boston, Massachusetts, where Irene and I were holi-

daying. Irene came in the bedroom with a sombre look. She had just taken a phone call from my son Daniel.

'I'm sorry, love. Dan's just had a call to say that your mother died peacefully in the night.'

At Martha's funeral ceremony, in the same church where Derrick's coffin had lain, the same priest spoke of the woman he had known. He spoke of her happy, laughter-packed life with Bob. He spoke of the great religious faith that had been such a source of strength to her and Mary-Jane. Till it was replaced by Lady Di, I thought unkindly. Her favourite hymn, 'Make me a channel of your peace', was played as a climax to the service. As the coffin was carried out, a slice of silver light broke through the dark clouds outside and bathed us all. The sunlight was still splaying down on Woodhorn churchyard where we laid her coffin on top of the Jungle Fighter's. Somebody cracked an apt joke about Derrick, Martha and St Peter sharing a couple of jars and a couple of Silk Cut.

At 102 Dalton we had a wake and happy memories of my mam, dad and brother were recalled. The priest was a drinking man and he kept pursuing Gladys for a top up of his wine.

'Is there any left?' asked the priest.

'Aye,' said Gladys.

'Praise the Lord,' came the reply and the priest raised his glass to heaven.

This caused Cousin Robert to kink with laughter. 'Holy Joe's enjoying hissel,' he whispered. I looked around the happy throng, an atmosphere of fun and warmth that had been the essence of this little house.

Next day there was a small article about her passing in the *Newcastle Journal*. It was headlined 'SID'S MAM DIES'.

Irene smiled when she read it out to me. 'She would have liked that.'

Now, in the summer of 1999, it was time to pick through the memories.

I walked away from the Hotel and over the railway bridge where once we had daringly swung over and breathed in the smoke from tankies hauling coal away from the pit. I walked past the parade of shops that had once formed the Co-op and Martha had ticked on our clothes and shoes till divi day. Then the usual lump formed as I turned up Dalton Avenue, with its yellow-brick cottages and wide gardens, all glowing in summer sunshine. The air as usual tasted of coal and gunk from the nearby aluminium smelter.

Outside 102 was Iris's car and she and Robbie and my niece Regan stood solemnly waiting for the ritual to begin. I walked past the estate agent's 'Sold' sign – I had got £6,000 for the house – looked down at the weeds and broken jam jars in Bob's leek trench and opened the door for the last time. The smell of home was still strong: coal, Woodbines, dog hair and lavender furniture polish.

Our team started picking out things we wanted to take away. It was going to be thirsty work so I went down to the shop for a bottle of wine and some beer. Four young lads in black hoodies and jeans blocked the doorway, and a quick polite 'Excuse me' got me nowhere. I pushed past and got some bottles. The youths quite clearly heard the Pakistani lady commiserate with me over Martha's death, but they did not give a toss. I was just some greying old giff marching on their turf. My carrier bag bumped a leg and I shot them a hard glance. Poor ignorant bastards, I thought, no respect for owt. In the old days, parents, aunts or uncles would have clouted their mucky lugs.

Back at the house, I worked swiftly. Of my brother's stuff I took a framed pastel photo of him as a three-year-old, all merry eyes and Fauntleroy curls. I also packed a silver hip flask in the shape of a petrol can that his RAF buddies had given him.

I found some mock pearls that my mam had been fond of and a handbag containing some of my uncle Sam's military medals. I also found her rosary beads and light-up sacred heart. These I tossed in the skip in the back lane along with the old pots, pans and furniture. She'd kicked such gee-gaws out of her life and they had no place in mine.

Finally, I took an old cloth cap of Bob's. I found his loose-headed work axe and binned it and then got a real bittersweet laugh. It was an illuminated scroll given to my dad on retirement from Ellington Colliery in 1968. At the top were two gryphons rampant and the NCB motto: *E tenebris lux* (Out of darkness light). Underneath, in letters of blue, red and gold blared 'Certificate for long and meritorious service, in recognition and appreciation of 48 years loyal and efficient service to the Industry and the Country...' Great words to describe one of the 'enemy within'! Then the bitter bit – 'Presented to Robert WEDDELL'. As he said wryly at the time, 'You'd think after 48 years they'd know my bloody name.'

The four of us went for lunch at the Hotel and it was a big mistake. As we sat eating and drinking, four scruffy blokes, unshaven, in greasy jeans, and all well pissed, walked into the lounge. They loaded up the jukebox with Irish singalong songs like 'Seven Drunken Nights' and ordered the lassie behind the bar to crank the volume right up. As the raucous growls of the Dubliners swirled round they glowered at me in challenge and began playing pool. They smashed the balls at random then pretended to sword fence with the cues, swishing and stabbing the wood ever nearer to us. They were looking for bother.

I quietly asked the lassie if they were locals.

'They are now,' she whispered. 'They're sea-coal wallahs who used to doss in caravans and huts down at the shore. Now the council's given them houses here. Radge bastards.'

The drunkest man, aged about 50 and lurching with the drink, sat on a buffet a few feet from Iris and Regan. With a slack-jawed leer he leaned forward and tried to look up their skirts. He would have been brayed to bits if he had tried a stunt like that with Derrick or Cousin Robert. We left our drinks and quit the premises.

I'd had enough of the road back to my erstwhile Geordie home. It was now well and truly 'in the hands of the Philinstines', as Mam used to say. And the bastards were welcome to it.

CHAPTER ONE

Two Families

March 1922

Bill Waddell was known as a cock bird to everybody in the straggle of cheap miners' cottages that made up the hamlet of Ellington Colliery.

At home, down the pit, on his third pint at the club or kicking lumps out of an opposing football team, Bill did things his way with an arrogant challenging smirk. He was packed with lean muscle and his hawkish features and small glinty eyes exuded violence. Yet there was a streak of jokey self-awareness in the 25-year-old. He had been known to say, 'I'm a canny lad, alreet – as long as I get my own way.'

On the late afternoon of a blustery March Sunday in 1922 he was doing just that – lording it over the Waddell household.

'I'm having a bath whether yee like it or not.' Bill dumped the tin bath down in front of the fire as his sisters Elsie and Mary protested.

'But Dad will be back from the pit any minute and he'll be needing a bath. He'll be all hacky.'

Elsie was only 11 but already had a gob on her that would grace any fishwife. 'I'm not fetching no watter for you,' she added. 'There's not enough in the set pot.'

'Bloody well put more in then,' rasped Bill, pulling off his football boots and his strip. Clad only in his shorts, he began parading round the parlour flexing his muscles and muddy legs and singing 'My Brother Sylvestre', a risqué song about a randy, well-endowed weightlifter that he would not have sung if his father Thomas had been present. Bill had learned the song in the trenches in France during the war. He had won a medal for bravery – some would say madness – for single-handedly attacking a German machine-gun post that had killed some of his fellow soldiers. For his pains he had received a chest full of shrapnel.

Mary, always the family pacifier, tipped hot water into the bath and Bill dropped his shorts and got in. He put his tongue out at Elsie who sat sulking on the settee next to her brother Bob. He too was looking anything but happy. Bob had the traditional big nose of the Waddell clan and he kept stroking at it with his eyes cast down as if seeing pictures in the tatty old mat.

Bill knew full well why his 15-year-old brother, normally a quiet lad anyway, was positively solemn this evening. He was sure that Bob had no fear of going down 'Auld Betty'- named for a daughter of Francis Priestman, coal owner – as the locals called Ellington Colliery, the pit at the end of their row. It was the family mongrel Swank that was causing the lad to be down in the dumps.

'I tell you he'll come yapping at that backyard door any time noo,' said Bill. Then he let out a roar as Elsie sneaked up behind him and hurled boiling water from a basin all down his naked belly and private parts. He stood up in the tin bath and roared.

'Stupid effin lassie nearly got me back wet, silly ched.' Like a lot of coalface workers, Bill did not ever wash his back, reckoning the daily coating of black grime kept the strength in.

After a few minutes sloshing about, Bill dried himself, almost caressing the welted red scars from the war on his chest and the midnight-blue scars from the pit on his face. Bill was second to his father Thomas as the chief breadwinner for the Waddell family of 16; eight males, eight females; 17 if you counted Swank. Two of the eldest girls, Bab and Alice, had moved out but still the three-bedroomed cottage was home to 14 folk.

Bob was rapidly becoming known as a hard grafter, just like Bill and their father Thomas. He'd been working on the screens at the pit for a year now, sorting coal from stones on a windy gantry and putting seven shillings and sixpence a week into the family kitty. Within the next 48 hours he would go down in the cage to the pit bottom and start life as a trot laddie, hitching up full tubs of coal. It would be yet another string to the lad's bow: Bob was a dab hand at driving the Waddell's two-wheeled trap that took local rich people to the railway station at Widdrington and Morpeth. His soft voice and lumps of sugar kept the family's highly strung horse, Tomma, well under control.

Bill was once more trying to cheer up Bob by flicking the wet towel at him and inviting him to wrestle. But Bob was having none of it.

The back-door sneck rattled and the head of the household entered. Thomas Waddell's arrival was heralded by a hacking cough that seemed to start at his hobnailed boots. He stepped round the bath and spat phlegm at the fire. He missed and the blob of mucus stuck to the fender and sizzled. Bob looked down and noticed dark blood in the spit. All the Waddell men had weak chests, and father's wheezing and coughing were getting worse. Thomas went into the scullery where his wife Maria was peeling potatoes for the dinner. She kissed his blackened face and took off his helmet. Quickly Thomas took off his boots, knee pads, hoggers, shirt and vest. He walked through to the parlour and tested the mucky grey water that Bill had used.

'We told Bill you'd be needing the water,' smarmed Elsie. But Thomas only smiled. It was unusual for him to have to go to the pit all day on a Saturday, but being a 'slave of the lamp', a deputy, he was always at the beck and call of the colliery management. As if five and a half shifts a week was not enough, if there was the slightest hitch he was expected to dash to Bessie any time day or night. The pit was enough bother to Thomas, without his family having squabbles.

'Just hold your tongue, Elsie, and bring me some watter.' With that, he dropped his combinations and got in the bath. 'That's a lovely smell, hinny,' he shouted to his wife. 'What are we havin'?'

'Bit of boiled ham, dumplings, tetties and cabbage,' came the reply.

My dad is second from the right in this group. The year is 1937. He even got dressed up and sported a buttonhole to exercise his Bedlington terrier.

Thomas looked at his children. 'Remember, them that eats the most tetties gets the most meat.'

It was a ploy that never failed; the family got potatoes and vegetables first, then came the meat. The younger ones gorged so much on the stodge that they often passed on the meat. This meant that the males got the protein they needed.

Half an hour later, Bill was feeling full of the bull. He had put on a pair of flannel trousers and a clean shirt. As usual, football and food had given him a mighty thirst.

'Howway doon the lonnen with me, Bobla.'

He ignored a harsh look from his father.

'Divvent worry, father, I'm not planning on sneaking beer oot the Plough's back door to the bairn. We'll have a quick deek round the dene banks where we lost Swank.'

Bob got to his feet eagerly. He pulled on his boots and made for the door. In the tiny scullery kitchen his mother Maria was shouting out the back door into the yard. 'Come in, Sidney. Come in or I'll skelp your lug.' With a rush a skinny wild-eyed boy raced past his elder brothers, socks round his ankles and blood leaking from one grubby knee.

'We've got another Bill here, I tell you, daft as a brush.'

As they walked up the back lane in the twilight, Bill jumped on to his favourite hobby horse. Spitting with passion, he told his brother why the past months had been so miserable for the coal miners. 'The Ashington Coal Company is a gang of greedy bastards just like the rest of the bosses. They pay you fuck all to dig the bloody coal, risking life and limb every minute you're doon the bloody hole. Then they dock the fucking wages every time trade slumps a bit. They even lock yee oot of their rotten pits. But the union will fight them. Even if we have to go on fucking – I mean effing – strike again.'

Bob winced at the blue language which he himself never used but he agreed with every word. The strike of 1921 had been called when the Durham and Northumberland owners posted new wage rates of six shillings and ninepence a shift, cutting the wages of workers like Bill by nearly half. And, to add insult to injury, this callous action came soon after the government had accepted the recommendations of Chief Justice Sankey's Commission: state regulation of the pits, shorter hours and increased wages. It seemed that the bosses regarded the miners as slaves, to be slung any scraps they fancied. So they had to provide for their own any way they could. The Waddells, with their hard grafters, horse and trap business, large allotment and Swank keeping them in rabbit meat, were very lucky. Others were starving.

The two men turned westward at the end of First Row and saw the mighty silhouette of Betty framed by a wind-rippled bronze sky. The black headgear and pulley wheels rose upward like the towers and turrets of a modern cathedral. Smoke plumed from the tall brick chimney and twisted eastward over the pit heap. The heap looked like a glob of hell spewed up from the earth; it reeked of sulphur and runny splotches of it glowed red and purple like a burst boil.

'If I didn't have to go down the twat every day God sends, I'd say that bastard pit looked bonny,' said Bill.

As soon as the pair entered the dene Bob was off into the undergrowth yelling for their dog. 'Swank! Swank! Come on, Swank.' Bill shook his head sadly. Despite his protestation that the dog would be back directly, he was not optimistic. It was now five days since the dog had gone careering after a rabbit up over a knoll and disappeared. Swank had scrabbled down into rabbit warrens before and was now probably stuck – and probably dead. Bill spent a few minutes running about and shouting, but then it was time for a couple of pints and a game of dominoes.

'Divvent stop oot too late,' he shouted to Bob, cuffing his ear gently. 'You've got real work the morn.'

Watching his tearaway brother run off, Bob felt like weeping. But he didn't; he merely began calling out over the dark, sleck-filled water of the river Lyne. 'Swank! Swank! Where are you, Swank?'

When the putters and hewers started drifting past him at four in the afternoon next day, Bob Waddell knew he was a real coal miner.

His mother had got him up at seven, filled him full of bread and dripping and strong sweet tea, and shed tears as he left the house, whistling. On the short walk to the pit his cast-off boots had started to chafe, his new helmet had fallen off and he had dropped his bait tin. Then he had almost vomited up his breakfast as the rackety cage had dropped him and a dozen other men down into the bowels of the earth. It was pitch black as he walked along the main shaft and it was odd stepping in shoals of dust that came over his ankles. After one mile of dry plodging on he got to his workplace, the High Main seam, although 'High' was a misnomer; the dripping roof was a mere four feet above the floor. A deputy showed him how to hang full tubs on to a trot – an endless metal rope – and left him to it.

After two hours Bob had snagged his fingers a dozen times on the heavy couplings but other than that he felt fine. Odd human noises squeaked from the face and occasionally the roof seemed to shudder. But then he felt the need to do his business. He moved to where a couple of putters were working and asked where to do 'it'.

'Go behind the waste pile,' he was advised. He did, but how to wipe his arse? He decided not to worry and pulled up his hoggers, resolving to bring two sheets of the Cresswell parish magazine in his bait tin next day to do the job. After four hours he had his bait, jam sandwiches and cold water; his dad and Bill had advised him on the 'Pitman's Diet' since it avoided belly cramps.

When he walked out at four he was exhausted but proud. Maria, his mother, put a full plate of beef, potatoes and cabbage in front of him but he was too tired to do it justice. Halfway through the meal he flung himself on the settee in his work clothes and went to sleep. His father shook him awake after a few minutes and pointed to the tin bath by the fire, full of steaming hot water.

'Get in that and you'll feel loads better, son.' It was true. Bob rubbed at the black sleck on his face and felt the water soak his aching arms.

The noise from the backyard was more a bleat than a bark, but it electrified the Waddell clan. Thomas raced to the door and rattled the sneck. Bill flung down the racing page and Maria began to weep. In the tin bath Bob froze. His mouth went dry. His father carried in a mud-caked, blood-spattered bundle. Swank had returned.

Bob stood up and grabbed the dog to his chest. One eye was glued shut with pus. He sat down and used his bathwater to bathe the eye and the scarred body. Swank's skeleton legs pathetically kicked as if he was trying to swim. Bob kissed at the scabby eye. He washed at the dried bloody scars.

Bill gently felt at the scars. 'No rabbit did this. I'll bet that big old fox we saw in the dene got him. Teach the mad bugger to gan diving doon holes.'

The Waddells laughed, mainly out of relief.

Christmas 1922

Most seven-year-old little lasses in Alnwick, the picturesque county town of Northumberland, did not spend the night before Christmas doing what Martha Smith was doing. Some would be wrapping presents for their parents and some would be going to parties. Nothing so indulgent for Martha; at six o'clock she still had half a dozen bundles of kindling to sell at tuppence a time. She had been up and about since dawn scavenging old wooden beer crates from the brewery yard near her home. She jumped on the boxes to break them and then chopped the debris down to size. She wrapped the bundles with odd bits of wire. She was going to have that vital shilling if it killed her.

Martha was a full-faced stocky lassie with jet-black wavy hair and she was dressed for the sleety weather. Though her boots were second-hand and down-at-heel and her wool coat was a five-bob job from the local Paddy's market, she was warm. But what made her feel really good on that night was the goodwill she knew was abounding in Oaky Balks, the poshest part of town. There were fairy lanterns hanging on bushes and even the odd Christmas tree decked with wooden angels and gold-painted pine cones in some of the gardens.

She hefted her soggy potato poke even though the sticks inside raked her spine and clawed her hair straight as she went up yet another winding drive. She stepped onto a welcome mat and rang the bell. A shadow came into the light beyond the door and a tall woman looked down at her.

'Kindling, madam? Ah'm asking only tuppence a bundle.' Martha pulled a sample out.

The woman smiled and tugged at the lapel of Martha's coat. She stepped into the hall onto a polished wood floor. She looked down and could almost see her face in the sheen. From inside came the sound of carols on the wireless and kids playing. The woman went into the kitchen and came out with her purse.

'Tuppence seems a very fair price. How many bundles have you?' The word came out as 'bondles'.

Martha swallowed with excitement. 'Six – er – modom.'

The woman pulled out a shilling. Then added a sixpence. She put the coins into Martha's trembling hand. As Martha burbled thanks, the woman's eyes scanned her tatty coat and boys' boots.

'Have you any brothers or sisters?'

Martha said she had two brothers, aged five and two. 'Wait there a minute,' said the woman. She turned and ran upstairs and Martha goggled at the paintings on the walls and the long plush curtains. There were electric lights everywhere, even little ones in shiny brackets over some of the family photos and paintings. This was a far cry from the Smiths' tiny gas-lit parlour up the dank gloomy close at Clayport Street.

The woman came downstairs clutching a bright cardboard box. On the cover was a toy train.

'My son has been given two of these,' the woman said, handing the gift over. She also pressed a string bag of mixed nuts into Martha's arms. The gifts were accepted gratefully; in Martha Smith's world one person's charity was somebody else's Christmas present.

'Thank you,' said Martha, stashing the booty in her poke. 'Merry Christmas.' She ran up the cobbled streets to the rough part of the old town, boots clashing merrily and face aglow.

Knowing that little Sam would most likely be asleep, Martha let herself into the house quietly. She shucked off her boots and tiptoed up behind her mother Mary-Jane who was busy at the table. Her mother turned her pale, craggy face to her daughter and kissed her. Mary-Jane put down the paint brush she was using to chamfer up an old rocking horse that had a tatty mane and only one eye. It was to be five-year-old Sonny's main Christmas present and it had been given by a good-hearted Romany rag-and-bone man. Also on the scrubbed table was a large brown bag full of damaged apples and oranges – more charity, this time from Phyllis who worked on a fruit stall in the market.

Mary-Jane pointed to Martha's poke.

'Put what you've got left of the kindling on the fire; we've only got enough coal to get one going tomorrow.'

Martha shook her head and crossed the room to where the fire was on its last legs. She picked up the bucket they kept the coal in and chucked the entire contents on the fire.

Mary-Jane was aghast. 'What are you doing, lassie?'

Imp-faced, Martha tipped the contents of her poke onto the table. Her mother picked up the box containing the toy train. She kissed the bag of nuts, tears coming to her eyes.

'Your dad loved nuts. Nuts meant Christmas to him. He loved packing them in your stocking.'

They looked at the pastel-tinted photograph of Samuel Smith that hung in pride of place over the black kitchen range. The man of the house had served proudly in France with the Northumberland Fusiliers and his Kitchener features looked down on his family, uniform spotless, eyes of jet, waxed moustache framing a firm mouth. He had died six months before of kidney cancer, a skeleton relic of the soldier he had once been.

Martha bucked up quickly. She placed the three shillings and sixpence that she'd got for the sticks on the table. He mother hugged her.

'Run down the yard and order a bag of coal for first thing tomorrow.'

There was a clatter of boots in the close.

'That'll be Sonny,' said Mary-Jane, scrabbling at the stuff on the table. 'Don't let him see his presents.'

Martha picked up the coins and barred the door. She slid outside and grabbed her brother by the arm.

'Come with me, we've got messages to do.'

The hooked-nosed, deep-eyed boy protested but she dragged him down past the Clay Hills to the coal yard near the brewery. There she booked the Smith family's latest surprise present – Christmas coal.

Just after noon the next day the family sat down for Christmas dinner. They had chicken with potatoes and tinned peas. For afters there was 'damaged fruit', dreg ends from Willis's fruit stall, and the three kids were allowed to pick wrapped sweets off the Christmas 'tree' – a thick branch of evergreen donated by the garden nursery where Mary-Jane worked. It was decorated with home-painted tinsel and blobs of cotton wool and on top of it stood a cardboard Santa. Then, in the glow of a roaring fire, Martha played with a nearly new rag doll, Sonny ran the wooden train round the oilcloth and little Sam sucked on a stick of barley sugar. Their mother indulged herself in a rare treat. Her cousin Johnny, who often acquired bits and bobs that 'fell off a lorry' and had spent the odd stint in Durham jail, had given her a bottle of Alnwick Brewery 100 per cent rum. She mixed herself a toddy and was half asleep from its warmth when there was a rap on the door.

Martha opened the door and in came two regular visitors, sisters Marianne and Theresa from the local Convent of the Sacred Heart. The sisters kissed the children and Mary-Jane herself. The nuns admired the presents the kids had received and had brought some of their own. Sister Theresa went outside where one of the convent gardeners was standing with a wheelbarrow. The man took a tarpaulin off his load and carried in a three-foot-high plaster statue of Joseph and a similar one of Mary. He placed them by the Christmas tree where Sonny took one look at Joseph's sad stary eyes and began to cry.

Sister Theresa picked him up and comforted him.

'Sure, we heard you Smiths could not make it to Bethlehem this year, so we have brought Bethlehem to you.'

Mary-Jane turned to Martha. 'Give the sisters a drop of the rum, lassie.'

Both nuns nodded and turned down the offer of hot water.

'To Mary-Jane, the saint of Clayport,' said Sister Marianne, raising her glass. Martha raised her warm Vimto. The nun was right. Before the death of Sam Smith, her mother had certainly been a devout Catholic, but over the past six months she had started going to Mass twice a day and her rosary beads were rarely out of her hands. Her rock-solid faith, her prayers and the votive candles she lit by the dozen had pulled the family through the hard times following her husband's death.

As the two nuns left they placed an envelope under the tree. Her mother nodded and Martha opened it. She pulled out an orange ten-shilling note and waved it at her mother. She ran to her mother who had her eyes closed and her hands clasped in prayer. 'Pray, lassie, for the most kind sisters and the Good Lord who looks after us. Pray for a most beautiful Christmas.' Mary-Jane's voice lowered to a whisper. 'And pray for the soul of your dear daddy who is with the angels.'

Martha Smith knelt, bowed her head, fought against the tears and prayed for all she was worth.

Summer 1926

Andra Brown was a kindly outgoing old bloke but he was having deep qualms about letting the young Waddells loose in his fishing coble. Bob was older and had a bit of sense but Jack and Sid were treating the fishing trip as a joke. They were up at the prow playing pirates and twice they had slipped and fallen into the boxes of wet thrashing mackerel. It was a good job that Andra was out in Druridge Bay for fun today; normally he'd have skelped the lugs of any crew that were mucking about. But, as a good friend of some of the Waddells over the years, he was indulging the lads in a joy ride. He knew the big strike was hitting all the local mining families hard, and there were few pleasures in life for their bairns.

'Pack it in, you two,' shouted Bob from the stern seat.

His voice was not really harsh since his mind was elsewhere. The spinning line was jumping and twisting over the waves as more fish jumped at the flashing lures and got hooked. Sid took a running dive down the boat, snagging his legs on the oar in Andra's left hand. The boy grabbed at the line and jerked it sharply. Bob laughed and pushed him away gently.

'Tek yer pipe, young 'un. Sit and watch how I do it.'

The pair calmed down. As Andra rowed northward up the bay, Bob took the fish from the line and flung them into the boxes. He took a carrier bag from under his seat and dished up tomato sandwiches and cherry pop to his brothers. Then he pulled off his shirt, lay back and drank in the day. The North Sea sparkled as the sharp prow of the blue-straked boat cut forward, the sun streamed down, he sucked in air with no foist or coal dust in it and the smooth sands gleamed a pale gold off to his left. Like every one of the million coal miners in Britain, he had been locked out by the mine owners for more than two months. This time the greedy bosses wanted to chop the wages by nearly a quarter and increase the hours, so putters like Bob would be slaving for about thirty shillings for a six-shift week.

He pushed his anger to the back of his mind and looked on the bright side. The weather had been marvellous. He and his pals had been camping at Cresswell most weekends and had been living like Apaches in between skirmishes and buffalo hunts. His hair was cropped to the bone and his skin was black-brown. He knew there were soup kitchens on the go for serious cases of hardship and people were burning their hands scrabbling for coal on pit heaps – but all things being considered, the Waddell tribe were gannin' pretty canny. At least none of their lot was going hungry.

Bob felt guilty at this craven sensual enjoyment of the elements and the fun his brothers were having. Still he lay back against the strakes. Though it was only a couple of months after his nineteenth birthday, he was the head of the household in 10 First Row. His father Thomas had died four years earlier; chronic bronchitis had weakened his heart till it gave up. Bob's two elder brothers Bill and Jim had moved out, Jim to be a publican and Bill to be a free boozy spirit. Of his three elder sisters, Bab and Mary were married to miners and Alice was in service in Durham. There was the odd trickle of strike pay for Bob and 16-year-old George, and this was augmented selling vegetables from their allotment. They also still made good money from taking better-off people to the local markets and railway stations. Bob's married sisters were always coming round with gifts of food and money and Alice was a gem, saving like mad and tipping up cash to her mother. Some of this Maria passed on to Bab who had the Midas touch, particularly in investing in pigs to fatten up for slaughter.

Bob was wakened from this reverie as the coble rocked noisily. He opened his eyes and found old Andra pulling at his shirtsleeve. The old man was pointing with his unlit pipe at Sid who was lying squirming in the bows.

'I think the young 'un might be seasick.'

With the oars stowed, the boat was rocking from side to side as Bob moved to his brother. He noticed the lad was punching the flesh behind his right ear, eyes slitted in pain.

'What's wrong?' asked Bob.

He put his hand on the spot, but Sid batted it away.

'It's nowt. I banged me lug on the side, that's all.' This through tears – though it took a lot to make Sidney Waddell cry. A vision of Sid rubbing fiercely at his ear on more than one occasion flashed across Bob's mind.

'Is he alreet?' asked Jack.

Bob nodded as Andra took out the oars and began pulling back to Cresswell beach.

Once on the sand at the tideline, Andra left the lads to push the boat up onto a cradle with car tyres and haul it onto the dry sand near the dunes. He was back in a jiffy with some carrier bags. He smiled as he reached down into the boat and began loading mackerel into the bags. Bob thought the old man looked like Santa Claus; white beard, kind face, shiny eyes. And indeed the old man was in the present business. Andra held up two of the bags and gave them to Sid.

'Hold them tight or the crabs will get out.' Sid started but the old man winked at him. The four bags full of fish he pressed on Bob and Jack.

'Give these to your mother and anybody else you like. It'll keep you away from those bloody soup kitchens up Ashington.'

'Thanks, Mister Broon,' said Bob.

'Nay bother, son. Tell yer daft uncle Billy I'm asking after him.' With that he walked off towards a big gaunt house near the lifeboat station.

'He must know wor Bill,' said Jack.

'Everybody in Northumberland knows Billy, even the bloody Duke hissel,' said Bob, half-laughing, half-sighing.

The deep concern of the old fisherman for his fellow human beings struck a chord in Bob Waddell. Though usually a solid serious lad, he was given at times to sudden impulse – and this was one of those times. He and his two brothers had run through the woods round the ruins of

Cresswell Hall and up the back lane to their house. Bob had the phrase 'soup kitchens' screaming in his brain, and he was determined to do something about it. Swiftly he chucked a few crabs and mackerel onto the scullery slab, then picked up the rest of the bags.

'Tell mam I might not be back for dinner – I'm on an errand of mercy.'

Jack looked at him as if he was daft.

'Where are ye gannin'?' asked Jack.

'Ashington.'

An hour later Bob was sitting with the reins in his hand as Tomma jig-jogged into the Top End of Ashington. Behind him on the cart were the bags of fish and crabs, two dead rabbits and a hundredweight sack of potatoes, the latter part of the 'wages' of the young Waddells' potato picking for a local farmer. To his left were the tiny rows of cottages built for the influx of miners 60 years ago, doors no higher than five foot six. The gaffers knew we'd never grow bigger than that working doon the hole, Bob thought bitterly. Beyond the houses were the still-silent pulley wheels of Ashington Colliery, framed by dozens of conical pit heaps like an Alpine village minus the snow. As he passed Hiller's Penny Bazaars he turned his head to see Ashington's main beer palace, the Grand, all fancy stonework and stained-glass windows. He could not believe his eyes; slumped on the pub step was a familiar figure in floppy cloth cap and dusty clothes. It was his brother Bill.

Bob drove up to the iron railings by the pub and tied up Tomma. Five yards from his brother he could smell the stink of beer on his breath. He bent down and shook Bill by the shoulder. With a cough and a lurch the figure came to life. Bill jumped to his feet, eyes goggling and fists raised.

'I'll have you, you bastard...' He coughed and hawked noisily.

'No, you winnit, you silly bugger.' Bob pantomimed boxing and Bill laughed. He had a thick growth of stubble on his chin and dry cracked lips. It was obvious he'd been on a bender.

'Dusty and me had a win on the horses. Had a spree, like,' Bill offered by way of explanation. 'I haven't been home since yesterday morning.'

Bob had no idea where Bill lived or with whom. Bill saw the puzzlement in his face.

'Evie won't mind. She knows what I'm like. I gave her half the winnings so she'll have had a sup or two hersell.'

Bill eyed the contents of the cart. 'Where are ye gannin' with that stuff?'

'Old Mr Broon the fisherman mentioned the soup kitchens, and I thought I'd fetch summat for the poor buggers.'

Bill's ravaged stubbled face split in an almighty grin. He jumped up alongside his brother and shouted at Tomma. 'Giddup, you mad Galloway. Straight aheed.' Bill tugged at the reins and they slapped on Tomma's rump. He broke into a sharp trot. They headed past some new brick houses then turned right into the Hirst, lines of cheap yellow-brick cottages in rifle-barrel straight rows, a spartan barracks for the foot-soldiers of industry.

Bill told Bob about the place they were going to, the place local wags were calling 'Squatters' Paradise'.

'There's dozens of families in the old park living in bloody tents, sheds made from fish boxes, lean-tos, owt. Evicted by the owners, making fires with fences and being fed by charity. Bloody disgrace. When there was a bloody war to fight they ran the pits for the country, said we were the salt of the earth – but now we're rubbish and just hoyed on a scrapheap. The other day I hoyed all them bloody medals they gave me onto the midden. Mind, what can you do with folk who are locked oot by the owners, buggers who are half starving and then help the bosses' lackeys to build football pitches? Loonies. I wouldn't dig the bosses a bloody grave.'

It struck Bob how logical, eloquent even, his elder brother was when in the throes of a raging hangover. Five minutes of chat and not a single effing. Bob was impressed.

The cart drew into the gates of the park and Bob got a shock. Before him was a scene straight out of the cowboy pictures he'd seen at the Buffalo cinema up Ashington's main street. Dirty old boy-scout tents

A group of Ellington Colliery blades get all dolled up for the weekend around 1920. My wild uncle Bill is second from left in the front row.

were pitched; with clothes lines streaming raggy clothes. Bearded men in vests smoked pipes around brushwood fires, cooking cauldrons of broth hanging from wooden struts. Half-naked dirty bairns ran about wild with bands of feral dogs. One crazy-eyed boy with buck-teeth jumped up at the cart and pulled off one of the carrier bags full of fish.

Bob roared out, 'Stop, yee little sod.'

Bill just laughed. 'One less bag to dish oot to the needy.'

The Waddell brothers made their way to a brick shelter that had been part of the park in its heyday, an oasis in the mining desert full of flowers and shrubs, where two well-dressed women had a table set up. The posh-spoken women gladly accepted the food and assured Bob and Bill that they were 'angels'. But when they went on to mention their nearby church Bill dragged his brother away.

'They're not getting me listening to no bloody Holy Joe with his collar on back to front.'

Bill grabbed the reins and got Tomma into a fast jog with a slap on his rump. In a minute or two Bill called the horse to a halt outside a door in the back lane of Pont Street, just about the roughest in all of Ashington. He tied the cart to a lamp post and led Bob up a tatty yard. From inside the cottage came a rough voice singing 'Galway Bay', not in tune and with a definite slur. Bill winked.

'Evie cannit sing, but she can cook – and other things.'

As they went in through a dirty scullery the smell of cooking and beer was overpowering. Evie was a big lassie; heavy breasts hanging half out of a blouse and arms like a wrestler. She had curly black hair and gaps in her teeth. A pint bottle of beer was poised at her lips.

'Oh, yer back. I got the dinner gannin' cos ah knaa that you'd be hungry after a session on the pop.' She kissed Bill and he reddened.

'This is me brother Bob.'

Evie put down her bottle and kissed Bob on the cheek. She opened two more bottles of beer and offered one to Bob.

'I don't drink – I don't like the taste,' he said politely.

'Fucking Billy makes up for that no bother,' Evie said.

A few minutes later a meal was dished up on the bare boards of the kitchen table. Evie began mashing the potatoes with a beer bottle and Bill set out some rusty knives and forks. Bob ate half his food and then, as Bill began to rant about 'the bloody railwaymen and Jimmy Bloody Thomas selling us aal doon the river', he left. When I get married it won't be to a blowsy foul-mouthed drunkard who mashes tetties with beer bottles, he vowed.

Back at the little cottage in Ellington Colliery he was shocked to be told the doctor had been called for Sid. The pain at the back of the boy's ears had become chronic.

Over the next few months, the Waddells and their like suffered. In December the miners of Britain were forced back to work for less money and longer hours. It made a mockery of the proud slogan of May: 'Not a penny off the pay, not a minute on the day'. And a few weeks after, Fate dealt a crueller card; Sidney Waddell died at the age of 12 from mastoid trouble. He had been the family mascot and had never once cried even though at times his pain must have been excruciating.

October 1933 (Mischief Night)

The cakes lined up on the shelves of Foster's bakery in Alnwick looked scrumptious. There were shiny brown fruit loaves, slab cakes layered with marzipan and icing and some sponges oozing thick streams of jam. Martha Smith and her pals twitched with anticipation; Friday night was when the boss Mr Lenny Foster let the lasses have 'free habbins', their choice of the leftover cakes from the day. Martha had her eye on the slabs, since her family played hell with her if she took home the sponges that she made so well. The Smiths always said her sponges were far too sickly.

'Get cracking,' shouted Lenny, and the girls dived in. Phyllis Willis, Martha's pal but a pushy lassie at the best of times, elbowed in and began grabbing at the slabs. 'Greedy guts!' yelled Martha, only to redden up when Phyllis pushed the cakes into Martha's bag.

'I know Mary-Jane and the lads like them. See you later, outside Bella's.'

Phyllis turned back to the cakes and Martha smiled. Bella the Crit was a simple-minded lady who lived up Stamp's Yard, next door to the Smiths' close, and the local kids made her life purgatory.

An hour later Martha was ready for mischief. The cakes had gone down a treat with her brothers Sam and Sonny, but her mother had only had a sliver with a cup of strong tea. It was a gala night for Mary-Jane and she was a bundle of nerves; she was singing the lead in an adaptation of *Velia* with the local amateur dramatic society and was worried about her hands. For years now she had worked at the plant nursery near the brewery and the damp soil had made her hands rough and calloused. She hoped the wardrobe people had been able to rustle up some gloves along with the rusty feather boas and cast-off hats. The latch of the door went and Nancy McFall came in. She was going to babysit the boys while Martha sat and watched her mother perform in the spotlight.

'You get off to the show, I'll follow on soon,' said Martha. She fielded her mother's querying look. 'I've just got to see Phyllis about summat,' she muttered as she dashed out the door.

The 'summat' in question was shit, specifically human shit.

It was a tradition around Halloween for Alnwick kids to do nasty tricks to their neighbours and Bella Angus was a natural target. She was old, ugly – a scabby face and warts – and lived alone with some cats. She talked in a high-pitched spitty screech and was rumoured to be a witch. She went to the Bird and Bush pub every night at six for beer.

'Smell this,' shouted Phyllis. Martha reared away from the stick waved under her nose. 'Got it from the lavvy.'

Phyllis sniffed at the brown turds smearing the stick. She led the way further up the close and stopped at Bella's door. The only light was from the street end of the close where there was a bleary gas lamp. Phyllis daubed the shit all over Bella's sneck and the two girls giggled their way to the bushes further up the yard.

Soon there was a clank as Bella the Crit banged her beer can against the wall. 'She'll be canny peevy already,' said Martha.

The dark figure reached for the door sneck and a cry rattled down the yard.

'Ooh for ladge, wee's put shite on me door?' Bella screeched and dropped her beer, scraping her shitty hand on her door. 'Bloody shite.'

The two girls raced past her, heads ducked, shouting, 'Shit the sneck, shit the sneck.' They vanished off towards the pub and the Clay Hills.

'Ah knaa wee ye are. Bugger you,' cried Bella.

Three hours later Martha was wreathed in smiles as her mother's beautiful voice rang out to be appreciated by Alnwick's finest. The cast took three curtain calls and Martha shed tears to see her mother's face light up just like it did at Mass. There were few pleasures in the meagre world of Mary-Jane Smith. And they did not stop at the assembly rooms. Mary-Jane had insisted on walking home through the cobble streets and up their dank close in her costume with picture hat, feather boa and gloves. Dame Nellie Melba could not have improved on the performance and it got a round of cheers from the topers outside the Blue Bell Inn.

With Sam and Sonny sleeping, Martha tipped a tiny amount of coal on the fire and poured her mother a rum and water. She mixed herself a glass of beer shandy. Then Mary-Jane took out a clay pipe with a peculiar claw-shaped nipple under the stem, lit it and began puffing. 'A pipe as made in Knockcrockery over the water by one of our relatives – the finest pipes in Ireland.'

Martha drank quickly. She was anxious to get to bed so that she'd be ready to play for the local lasses' football team the next day. It was run by Roly Jobson, a local butcher, and went by the name of Jobson's Bullocks, an accurate description of some of the team.

Just as she was letting down the bed that she and her mother used, there was a banging at the door.

'For ladge, wee's that?' cried Mary-Jane, knocking out the pipe and pushing it under the coal bucket.

'Is that swine of a lassie that torments old women in there?' It was the screeching voice of Bella the Crit.

Martha raced to the door and bolted it. 'It's just daft Bella. She's drunk—'

'Plastered me sneck with shite, she did. So I'm cursing you, Mary-Jane Smith, and all yer kind.' More screams and bangs, then the clash of a door.

Martha had never been able to fool her mother. She hung her head as Mary-Jane lit up the pipe again, brow furrowed over her hawk nose.

'She might be radge but some say she's a witch. Ye put shite on her sneck and she can make bad things befall us, ma lassie.'

It crossed Martha's mind that a devout Catholic like her mother should not be setting store by mumbo-jumbo, but she said nothing.

At half-time next day a red-faced Martha was sucking an orange and laughing. Phyllis had scored two goals for the Bullocks against Warkworth and Martha had been giving her opposing halfback a bruising time. She looked up when she heard a voice yelling her name. It was her brother Sam and he was weeping.

'You gotta come now. Sonny fell into the rain barrel, landed right on his head, screaming blue murder. He's at the infirmary.' Sam dragged at Martha's hand as her pals clustered around her, cuddling her.

Bella's curse, was all she could think.

Fifteen-year-old Sonny Smith never got over the accident. The blow to his head left him a slavering, grunting cripple: a helpless creature who could not utter a clear word except 'Mammy' and who had no motor control over his head, arms or legs. He had to be lifted everywhere, dressed, fed and cleaned.

To her dying day Martha Smith blamed herself for what happened to her little brother.

CHAPTER TWO

Bob and Martha

Summer 1937

Bob Waddell looked up at the purple tops of the Cheviot Hills and drank in the pure air that was as cool as burn water. He sucked on a Woodbine and tapped the ash with a calloused finger. He looked down at his right hand and casually burst a couple of blebs, letting the sticky fluid run out over his palm. Shovelling tons of coal a day onto a conveyor in a low wet seam did nowt for your limbs, but it certainly put cash in the bank.

Now that his younger brothers were working at the pit, Bob had a chance to think about his own future. He was picking up a steady two pounds ten shillings in a good week and he was banking half of it. The rest he tipped up to his mother, all bar the five shillings he shelled out weekly on his pride and joy – a second-hand 500 cc Norton motorbike. Now he sat on the shiny monster, rubbing at the chrome on the raked handlebars with his hankie. He gripped the bike with his legs and felt full of the proverbial bull. It was a Saturday morning and Betty was a million bloody miles away.

Two of his pals, Billy Chatt and Jim Snowball, revved up their engines and the trio pointed their bikes into the soft wind blowing from the North Sea.

Two hours later the three lads were eating ice creams and mingling with the crowd at Amble Feast. It was the big day in the year for the folk of the small fishing port of Amble, with a funfair, fancy-dress competition and one of the biggest foot-running handicaps in Northumberland. The running was the main reason that Bob and his pals had made the trip; they were part of a 'school' whose champion, a mystery man known simply as 'Raymond' to the bookies, was supposed to be ready to beat all comers. Each member of the school put in a few bob to keep Raymond while he took a few weeks off work and trained hard, and today was payback day. A lot of money would be put on Raymond by Bob's pals to win the handicap final, but Bob was playing things canny. He felt that their champion would 'take the water in' at the death, in other words, he would choke. So Bob reckoned he would have a shilling or two on Raymond in the heats, but not the later stages.

The heats were a doddle. Raymond's long pale legs flew over the ground in a blur, his green plastic bib, just like the ones whippets wore, dipping to the tape in slick rhythm. Chatty and the rest of the school flashed their wallets, pulling off folding money. Bob held back. Chatty pushed him towards a florid bookie in a bowler hat.

'Gan on, Bobla, get in yer poke. Yee've got plenty. Wor lad's a cert.'

Bob felt in his pocket. Raymond had so far won him thirty bob, nearly a week's money. Bob imagined how many back-breaking shovels full of coal his winnings represented and he shook his head. He left the eager throng and bought a beetroot sandwich and a cup of tea from a stall. He found a place near the tape and watched the runners line up for the final. For 90 of the 120 yards it was all Raymond, head straight, arms angled nicely, knees high. Then a little burly Jock came up to his right shoulder and Raymond smelled defeat. His head went back and his arms flapped like a frightened ostrich. His attempt at a dip turned into a rolling stagger. He lost by two clear yards. Water in the veins, said Bob to himself.

There were some pig-sick faces in the pub shortly after. The school had lumped large on Raymond who was now sitting in the back of Jack Snowball's car in tears. Bob felt for them all and resisted the temptation to gloat. Instead, he bought a round of drinks.

And then he did something he had never done in his life: he touched alcohol. Just to make the lads feel better, Bob Waddell raised a glass of beer to his lips for the first time ever. The pale Vaux ale made him gyp and its bite in his virgin throat made him wince. He nursed the rest for a good hour, by which time the lads had eased their sorrow and were thinking of other things – lasses and the Saturday night dance at the Northumberland Hall in Alnwick.

The pit lads had more beer in the Crown pub opposite the dance hall and Bob toyed with a shandy. He did not really like dancing; he could just about shuffle round the floor to a quickstep or a Bradford Barn Dance but mainly he was very shy when it came to asking lasses to dance. He knew that many girls turned lads down on principle to get laughs from their pals and glory in the jeers as the lad went back to his jeering mates.

At eight o'clock the group moved over the road, checking their motorbikes, which were parked in the ancient Shambles. Inside, as his pals surveyed the bright throng moving in the last of the sunlight through the big windows, Bob went to the toilet and smoothed down his thinning, windswept hair.

Back inside, the band started up 'The Black Bottom' at full bouncy pelt. Not many of the dancers seemed to fancy the pace of the number, but one couple went at it all hammer and tongs and style. The man was a lounge lizard: rusty black dress suit, long black hair and pencil 'tash, patent leather pumps. He held his arms high and stuck his arse out like Groucho Marx. The lass had a chubby red-cheeked face and long black curly hair. Despite her heavy bosom and strong legs she glided and bopped smoothly over the floor. She was wearing a blue and white polka-dot dress and her face glowed with the exhilaration of the dance. Bob knew he could never meet her dancing standards – but he was completely smitten.

The music stopped and the couple unclasped near Bob. The lounge lizard pointed at his 'tash and the lass gave him something from her pocket. She laughed as the man sashayed off to the gents'. She turned and saw Bob ogling her. She pointed after the man. 'It's always the same. Johnny sweats up so much doing that that he has to borrow my mascara to freshen up his 'tash.'

The image of the lounge lizard applying make-up made Bob laugh. 'I wouldn't want my fellow using my make-up,' said Bob.

'Oh, he's not me fellow, he's Black Bottom Johnny. I'm the only one here he thinks is good enough to do it with. Do you want this one?'

Bob swallowed hard. The music was 'Charmaine', a slow foxtrot. You had to glide carefully and watch your partner's toes. The lass did not wait. She grabbed him and set off round the floor. He did the sensible thing and followed her, eyes rooted to the floor trying to miss her feet.

'Look at me or over my shoulder,' she commanded. He did and it worked better. She led him past Chatty and the lads and they grinned their appreciation.

'What's your name?' she asked, full-voiced, not just politeness.

'Bob Waddell. From Ashington way.'

'Martha Smith. From Clayport. I bet yee've got a motorbike.'

'How did yee guess?'

Martha ruffled his hair. 'Sticky up hair and oil on yer sneck.' She tapped his big nose and he reddened. 'Just joking,' she laughed and tossed her head. Her body moved naturally to the music. Bob too moved more confidently.

Later he took her home to her close up Clayport Bank on the back of the bike. She got off, gave him a prim kiss, jumped over a smelly open drain and said she hoped he would be back at the dance next week.

Bob gunned the Norton through silent black summer lanes by the sea with a light heart. 'Charmaine' sang in his ears as his headlights lit up high hedges and startled the odd rabbit. What a day: his first pint of beer and meeting a lass with a face full of laughter. He was charged with a new kind of happiness and he knew full well he would have to improve his foxtrot. But ah'll never master the Black bloody Bottom, he thought.

Martha Smith was developing strong feelings for Bob the coal miner. He was now riding his shiny Norton the 20-odd miles from Ellington to Alnwick a couple of week nights and every Saturday. It pleased her that, even if they were not going to the dance or the pictures, Bob always looked smart. He usually wore a sports coat and flannels, always a tie and often a waistcoat. He was clean-shaven and the only blot on his copybook was the odd skim of coal dust under his eyes. Probably rushes his shower after his shift to get to see me, she thought jokily. Martha liked the fact that her lad was not a talkative bloke and that most things he said were carefully thought out. She openly admitted that she, like her mother Mary-Jane, could blether for England.

On a bright brisk Saturday afternoon the couple were walking arms linked along the pure white sand of the beach at Alnmouth. To their left were the rainbow facades of fishermen's cottages and to their right whitecaps tufted the rolling North Sea. Bob, for once, was being chatty. He stroked the wen of his big nose and frowned in concentration. 'Ah'm on steady enough money now. Ah'm drawing over three pounds a week. Not bad till you think aboot the profits the owners, the Priestmans and the Milburns, are getting.'

Martha liked the fact that her man knew his worth but was not riddled with the bitterness she had heard from some coal-mining lads. She sensed how proud he was of the job he and his family and mates did. Bob's mentioning money made Martha suddenly blush. She was planning to take Bob to meet her family for the first time and she hoped he did not think his big attraction was the size of his wage packet.

'Ah hope you're hungry, Bob, because me mother has got some special stuff in for tea,' she gabbled.

His deep frown struck her to the core. He does not want to come, she thought.

Bob looked hard at her, smoothing down his thinning hair. He pulled at his collar stud.

'You do want to come and meet me mam?' Martha's voice trembled.

Bob put his arms around her and kissed her on the forehead. 'Of course ah want to meet your family. But you should have telt us. Us lot are better off than yee. I'd have brought some eggs or bacon or summat.'

Martha kissed him hard on the mouth. She mumbled through happy tears. 'Bob Waddell, you are a good man.'

Tea with the Smith family was surprisingly substantial: salad, pease pudding, boiled ham, pork pie and home-baked bread with Martha's special jam sandwich cake for afters. Strong tea was poured and Bob and Martha lit up Woodbines. Mary-Jane was speaking to Bob as if he was an equerry to the Duke of Northumberland, rolling favourite words like 'beautiful' round her mouth like gobstoppers. But something in the old lady's eyes told him she could be a monster. He wondered why she kept fumbling at a pocket in her dress. Mebbe young Sammy gans dipping for sweetie money, he thought. Sammy was up on the tatty grass patch at the top of the close with Sonny, Martha's crippled brother. Sonny had squealed and smeared snot on Bob's best jacket when he had carried him outside like any workmate injured down Auld Betty. Poor bugger, Bob thought, just a bloody bairn but crippled for life.

Bob and Martha began drinking Double Maxims and when Mary-Jane was halfway down her second Mackeson's stout she scraffled in the cushion of her high-backed chair and brought out a set of ivory-coloured rosary beads. She bent her head over them and kissed the cross with her thin lips. Now we get the sermon, Bob thought. Martha had told him several times that her mam was known as the 'Saint of Clayport.'

'This house that has been blessed by Our Lord and Our Most Beautiful Holy Mother...'

Them two must have a canny sense of humour, thought Bob, as he looked round at the greasy oilcloth covering the table and the raggy home-made mats. Mary-Jane was rocking gently, fiery green eyes rolling and falcon nose pecking for emphasis.

'The holy sisters of the Convent of the Sacred Heart are my light and my guide.'

Martha shot him a pleading look. Bob looked at the machine gun on the beer bottle label and maintained a solemn look. He remembered the hard times this family had had since the man of the house was taken.

The green eyes were now open. They locked on to Bob's.

'I go to Mass when I can and so do my bairns.' The lines on the pale face tightened. 'Is worship of the Lord part of the life of the Waddells?'

Bob carefully tapped the ash off his cigarette in the low-burning fire. Vivid thoughts of his brother Bill consorting with tarts at the Grand in Ashington and his sister Bab mocking the vicar as 'Holy Bloody Joe' ran in his mind. He spoke softly.

'Us Waddells do not go to church. Where ah work, down a wet dark hole, I see accidents that mek me wonder if there is a God.' He paused and he could sense Martha's fear. 'If he's up there it strikes me he doesn't give a baccy chow about pitmen.'

The words hung in the smoky air. Martha jabbed at the fire, eyes bright with imminent tears. Mary-Jane seemed eager to crank up the row. She edged forward and something fell from her pocket. Bob bent down and picked up a well-used clay pipe. The old lady reddened and snatched at it. Bob handed it over. My Waddell aunties frowned upon cigarette smoking, he thought, so God knows what stick they would give Martha if they found out that my saintly granny Mary-Jane was addicted to a dirty old clay pipe.

'It belongs to Bella's man, who got us the ham,' she burbled. Bob aborted a smirk and slipped Martha a wink.

Raw noises burst in from the close. There was a throaty scream of pain and Sam's shrill voice.

'Get away from him, yee bastards.'

Martha raced to the door and Bob followed her. By the crumbly stone wall at the grassy end of the close Sonny sat on a chair. He had his hands clasped round his withered legs and he was crying. Sam was kicking and punching at two lads who were swiping at Sonny's legs with pieces of tarred rope.

'Daft Sonny! Daft Sonny!' shouted the bigger of the lads, a stringy kid with buck-teeth. He lashed Sam across the knees.

Bob tore the rope from the other lad as Martha clawed at the chops of Buck-Teeth. She drew blood, shouting, 'Shite, yer nowt but shite, hitting a cripple.' Bob fetched the back of his hand to the ear of the smaller lad. The pair ran off.

Bob put his arms around Martha who was shaking with emotion. 'Effin' Saint Thomas's Closers,' Sam hissed. 'Twats the lot of them'.

Bob lifted the poor emaciated frame of Sonny Smith from the chair, snot smearing his face and a sour smell of sweat in his nostrils. He followed Martha and Sam into the tiny dark rooms.

'Mammy, Mammy,' whined Sonny like a whipped pup. Bob laid Sonny in an armchair and the Smith family crowded round, all weeping. Mary-Jane dabbed holy water on the boy's legs and brow, praying through tears, 'Oh, most blessed Mother of God, take care of my bit laddie...'

The pathetic family tableau struck Bob Waddell to the core. Damp-eyed himself, he resolved to do his level best to bring whatever happiness he could to this bonny lassie and her frail people.

December 1939

By dint of hard graft, frugal living and thought for the future, Bob Waddell now had a tidy sum in the bank. He reckoned that he had paid most of his dues to his family at 10 First Row, Ellington Colliery, and he was now thinking of laying down new roots. Specifically, he had his eyes on a smart bungalow in Cresswell Road, a mere ploughed field away from Auld Betty. Bob had made up his mind to marry Martha Smith if she would have him. So, with a mind full of fear, doubt and edgy hope, he met her in Alnwick marketplace on a Saturday at noon. There was a nip of frost in the air and she was looking radiant. She had on a red wool beret and matching scarf and glowed with pleasure as he rolled up on his Norton.

'Where today?' she asked, kissing him gently.

'Mystery tour,' said Bob. 'I want you to shut your eyes and keep your pretty little gob shut for half an hour.' She looked at him half slighted, then jumped aboard.

When they zoomed past the railway crossing at Widdrington Station, Martha's voice piped in for the first time.

'You're not taking me to meet your sisters again, are you?'

There was tension in the words; the last couple of meetings between the daughter of Alnwick's Saint Mary-Jane and the heathen Waddell lasses had been frosty and forthright.

Bob laughed. 'No, today is not about arguing the toss about religion, it's about housing.' He left her to stew on that one. Ten minutes later he turned left at the stone schoolhouse in Ellington village and eased the bike down a wide road with large trees on one side and about 30 semi-detached bungalows on the other. Bob stopped the bike at number 16.

'What do you think of that … for me and yee?'

The chubby cheeks blenched. Martha put her lips against Bob's neck. He got off the Norton but she didn't. She looked past him at the house.

'What kind of proposal is that for a lass! "*What do you think of that … for me and yee?*" '

Bob looked perplexed. 'Why, what are you saying?'

Martha pondered. 'Ah'm saying aye, Bob Waddell.'

Bob kissed her so hard she nearly fell off the bike.

He took a key from his pocket and led the way up the drive. Martha followed him like a child at a Christmas pantomime being asked on stage to meet Prince Charming. The back of the bungalow had a small lawn and a long vegetable garden. He'll grow his leeks here, thought Martha. Bob opened the back door and they entered a smart kitchen. Martha stared like a stookie. Bob switched on electric lights. Martha beamed; she was a long away from sputtering gas mantles like they had up Clayport Street. But her heart truly swelled when she saw the bathroom and toilet. No more morning swilling in a mean sink or trips up the yard on cold nights to a communal netty with no flush. Where you had to sit and whistle to let the neighbours know you were settled in for a Number Two. Even empty of furniture, the parlour, with nice pinkish tiles round the fireplace, the master bedroom and the best room, looking north over rolling fields to a small dene, all added up to a royal palace to Martha.

Bob put his arm around her and her eyes glowed as she pushed at her black curls, her cheeks flushed with delight.

'I've got enough in the kitty to get a bit of new furniture but we might have to go the salerooms up Ashington for some things,' he said.

Martha shook her head. 'Nowt else matters, hinny, it's just perfect.'

'Ah'll pay the deposit next weekend,' said Bob. 'Now, about your mother. When are we ganna tell her about us tying the knot?'

Martha frowned slightly. '*We* are not. I have done right by my family for years now. I will tell mother alone and face to face what I want to do. What I am going to do.'

Bob hugged his lass with a hidden sigh of relief; the fearsome Mary-Jane put the wind right up him at times.

But as it happened the old saintly lady knew a boon when it came on a plate and she accepted the inevitable. Her darling 'most beautiful' daughter, breadwinner, skivvy, nucleus of the Smith family, could marry Bob the coal miner with her wholehearted blessing.

CHAPTER THREE

Pigs and Prayers

*My very first baby picture. I was well over eight pounds at birth
and Mam paraded me round like a prize whippet.*

I was born in my granny Mary-Jane Smith's dingy parlour up a dirty
close in Alnwick on Wednesday 10 August 1940. Martha had spent a
week waiting for me impatiently while Bob looked after himself at home
in Cresswell Road. It would be the weekend before he could see his son.

Bob's eyes filled with tears when he held me for the first time. 'Oh, the
bairn, the bairn,' he said softly as he gave Martha a kiss. 'You've given
me an angel.'

I certainly did not look like an angel. I was over eight pounds in
weight and had a giant bulging forehead. I was coughing and
sneezing when I came into the world and I am still coughing and
sneezing to this day. Bob tried to comfort Martha, reminding her that
all the Waddells were 'chesty'. But he suspected that it might have

something to do with my mother smoking 20 Woodbines a day during her pregnancy.

The following weekend Bob arrived in Alnwick to bring home his wife and son. I was swaddled in blankets and taken proudly in my carrycot on the bus to Cresswell Road and our cosy bungalow, which would be my home for the next 14 years.

The first thing my mother saw when she arrived home was the shining white Silver Cross pram, with a midnight-blue hood. It had come from Auntie Bab and I would be the third Waddell family baby to use it, but it had been treasured and looked after and it shone like new. Martha forgot how tired she was and insisted on a walk round the village to show off her precious son. From now until I was 19 years old Martha would be showing me off in one way or another.

The miners did not go to war; they were in a reserved occupation because digging for coal was vital to the war effort. But the war came to us occasionally. On a night in February 1941, around ten o'clock, there was an air-raid alert and my mother led the way to the shelter at the top of Cresswell Road. My dad followed with me in a carrycot as a basket of brilliant coloured flares, dropped by a German plane as a targeting aid, exploded above us like Bonfire Night. My dad was so shocked by this that he stumbled and tipped me out into a ditch. He did not realise the cot was empty till he staggered into the shelter. He raced back along the dyke, weeping and swearing at his own stupidity, and picked me up. Red-faced, he ducked into the shelter and put me in my mother's arms. She almost suffocated me in sheer relief.

'Bloody stupid man,' said Martha 'Hoying the bairn oot so the bloody Jerries could hit him.'

This was much to the delight of the other pit folks huddled in blankets in dim candlelight.

There were tales of dogfights by planes over Ashington and a bomb dropped on Dalton Avenue in Lynemouth, demolishing two shops and several houses. Seventy-four people were injured and one lady was killed. But for the rest of the time, the community followed the war in the newspapers and made the best of food shortages and rationing like everyone else in the country.

My dad was not one for indulging in 'the pleasures of the mind'; when he was not out under the North Sea getting coal, he was crouched out in the garden, cloth cap pulled over his nose in concentration, eyes riveted on his prize leeks. He told great bedtime stories about cowboy heroes like Hoot Gibson and Tom Mix, but in all of my life the only book I ever saw him read was the *Up North Combine* pigeon annual. Mam, on the other hand, always had a book from the Silver Library on the go or the latest copy of *Red Star* magazine, packed with slushy tales of romance for housewives. But her big treat was to wrap me up and take me to the pictures with her.

Twice a week we would go to the end of Cresswell Road, hop on the bus and go to the cinema at Lynemouth Welfare Institute. The Institute, a fine Georgian-style building, had been built by the Ashington Coal Company in 1925, and by 1927 hosted dancing, roller skating and a cinema. In 1934 there was a change; the Institute would now be financed by a miners' levy, supervised by trustees from the unions and the coal authorities. The cinema section was open seven nights a week and was by far the most popular activity. The films were rented from local entrepreneur Walter Lawson who owned the five cinemas in Ashington. In the earliest days the reels were brought the three miles from Ashington to Lynemouth by a man on a bike. By the early 1940s they came by van, but a bike and bike lad were kept on standby in case of breakdowns. As it was, if the van was delayed the crowd showed their feelings by stamping, booing or throwing ice-cream wrappers at the blank screen.

I remember the excitement of being in a noisy queue waiting for the first house to start at six. Over the road early boozers would be making their way to the Hotel, a giant fake-timbered beer palace, built in the 1920s for colliery bigwigs, but now a magnet for every roisterer and randy lad within a ten-mile radius. Mam would open a packet of guddies and feed them to me. Through the steamed windows of the games room of the Institute I saw the swooping shadowy figures of the village's star snooker players in action, silhouetted against smoky green light. I felt cocooned, warmed by the eager bustle around me. But sometimes the rougher side of Lynemouth life impinged. Gangs of lads guzzling Tizer from big bottles, or eating chips from greasy packets, would shove to the front of the queue, daring the mams and old folk to react. Martha never failed to rise to such bait.

'You lot are just ignorant,' she would shout. 'You should wait your bloody turn.' It did no good but I sensed it made her feel better.

We never sat in the cheapest seats, the wooden rows at the back that looked like a coconut shy. We always sat in the middle of the stalls. There I would munch on jelly babies as Martha's chubby face with its shiny cheeks registered delight at Laurel and Hardy or tensed up at Errol Flynn swinging a cutlass at a villain.

Casablanca made my mother cry. She dabbed at the tears that were dribbling into her rouge. I thought she was ill. I started to cry too.

'Don't worry, Sidney. The film is making me sad, that's why I'm bubbling.' She leaned down and whispered to me, not wanting to spoil the enjoyment of others. 'But I'm very happy at the same time.'

Over the years my mother never missed *Casablanca* on the television. And each time Bogart and Bergman played out their tender farewell, Mam cried all over again.

A couple of weeks after my third birthday I sensed that something special, an occasion like Bonfire Night, Christmas or Hogmanay, was in the offing. My mother had been excited for a whole week, sharpening big knives known as 'gullies', and she had also been scouring giant saucepans, which had been gathering dust at the back of the cupboard. When asked about these activities she told me that we were going to kill one of my Auntie Bab's 'guffies'. My mam never said 'pig'. Mary-Jane's Irish ancestry had bequeathed a whole set of quirky superstitions. If a bird flew into the house that meant a death in the family was on the cards. The bird should not be yelled at or clouted with rolled newspaper. Doors and windows had to be opened so the bird could fly out, and holy water had to be sprinkled around, all the while offering prayers to Saint Anthony and the Mother of God to keep all safe. Likewise, my mother and my granny censored all Christmas cards. Any with birds on – even the ubiquitous robin redbreast – and any featuring the colour green would be tucked away in a cupboard and later quietly burned. Shoes and boots must never be put on tables, since that meant a sacking for some of the menfolk and hence destitution. 'Pig' was a word that must never be uttered, or bad fortune would occur, but 'P-I-G' was acceptable, as was the colloquial 'guffie'.

Either way, hearing that a pig was going to be killed, I began to cry; I had grown quite fond of the snuffling monsters at the Lynemouth allotments. They let me scratch their backs as we kids leaned over the fence round their sty.

'Divvent cry, pet,' said Martha. 'We need bacon and pork and sausages for you to grow big and strong. And there'll be the bladder for you and your pals to play football with.'

The fatal festive Saturday dawned hot, bright and windless. Normally, no matter the season, an east wind raked our isolated world, blowing in freezing from the North Sea. But today it was mild; and thin cloud threaded a pale blue sky. It was a perfect setting for death in the afternoon.

My dad had sold his motorbike before I was born and we could not afford a car. So we walked the mile and a half from Ellington, dad pushing his wheelbarrow full of knives, pans, old brown carrier bags and Martha's pinnies. It would be loaded with every form of pig meat on the return journey. Mam wheeled me in a pushchair. We walked past Auld Betty's giant dark pulley wheels and an eerie white concrete water tower that stood on skinny spiderlegs like an alien before arriving at my auntie Bab's house in Lynemouth. This was a new 'barracks' pit village flung up by the Ashington Coal Company in the early 1920s. It had 800 miners' terraced

My auntie Bab had a sharp tongue but a heart of pure gold. My uncle Jack Snowball, her husband, rarely disagreed with her.

cottages to start off with and 400 redbrick council houses appeared later. The village was split by a railway line that carried the giant wagons of freshly hewn coal. On the one side were three short streets of shops that included a post office, a chip shop, Cochrane's the barber's and a big Co-op. You could get anything from groceries or clothes there on tick, settling your bill and getting 'divi' quarterly – you settled up twice a year and were paid 'divi': the more you spent, the bigger the dividend. At the western end were the bigger houses usually allotted to colliery officials. And my auntie Bab, a real wheeler-dealer, and her husband Jack Snowball, a pit deputy, had managed to wangle one.

My aunt's parlour was set out as though it was New Year's Eve and she and her hubby were expecting first-footers. The tables groaned with sandwiches made with ham from home-fed guffies, sausage rolls, pickled onions and beetroot. My mother proudly added her contribution to the spread – three sandwich cakes oozing cream and strawberry jam. Uncle Jack Snowball, as always in a pinstripe suit and sporting a racy black fedora, played host. He had a pinched pale face and the demeanour of a depressed butler – thanks to Bab's nagging – but dispensed beer and cups of tea to order. There was a party atmosphere, with all the women flushed and excited. Even Auntie Jean, normally a mournful soul, sharpened knives with a ghost of a smile on her narrow chops.

I was feeling peckish, so I asked my mam if I could have a piece of her cake. She cut me a large slice and I began eating it, cream squirting as far as my nose.

'Ye'll ruin that bairn's teeth feeding him your Alnwick cakes.'

It was just like my auntie Jean to pee on the chips on a day when all the family were supposed to be pulling together. In one sentence she had insulted my mother's home town as well as her role as a parent.

My dad was out in the backyard or else he would have chastised his sister. But Martha did not need him. She could fight her corner. She'd had spats, mainly over religion, with Jean before.

'If ye could mek cakes as good as mine then maybe Norman would come out of that garage more often.'

The jibe brought smiles from the other women. It was well known that Auntie Jean's acid tongue meant Uncle Norman spent a lot of time in his garage in his overalls pottering about with car batteries.

Jean clattered pans, nerving herself to make more bother, but Auntie Bab was abreast of the tension. She pushed out her mighty breast, narrowed her dark eyes and hissed: 'Ye two keep yer barneys for Cresswell Road. This is my guffie killing and naybody's ganna spoil me fun. Mind you, the guffies might hev summat to say aboot that.' My mam led the laughter and Jean took her bile out on another pan.

Around one o'clock, two of my cousins ran in the back door. They were Robert Waddell, a well-built lad of 13 and his brother Tot, a couple of years younger. Robert had clean-cut bony features and a jolly demeanour. Tot was a big, gangly lump with shaggy black hair and the crazy smile of a kid who would rather smack you in the teeth than offer you the time of day. He already had a reputation as a champion scrapper. 'Howay,' he shouted. 'The pig's ready.'

I noticed my mother wince at the use of the taboo word.

Tot picked up one of the sharp gullies and began swishing it like a pirate.

'I'll gut the bugger mesell,' he yelled. He narrowly missed piercing a wing of the settee. Nobody told him to stop.

The women took off their pinnies and bits of lipstick and rouge were hastily dabbed. Then off went our cavalcade through Bab's backyard as if to a funfair or a day of picnicking at Cresswell beach. Cousin Robert took my hand and we followed Tot. Behind us came my parents and aunts and uncles. We went over the railway bridge, blackened from smoke and duff from coal wagons, and along the River Lyne to the allotments. Tot swiped at nettles with the knife and I grabbed a stick and did the same. We ran on the baked rutted clay of the path, sun streaming down through ash trees. A snuffly screech echoed from up ahead. Tot turned to me and winked. He mimed cutting his own throat with the gully. My mouth went dry and my belly rolled. What was about to happen hit me hard – the pig was going to be murdered.

The sty was surrounded by people. Among them was my granny Maria in a wheelchair. She had on a black cloche hat and an Otterburn tartan rug was draped over her legs. She was 73 and suffering from heart trouble but she was not going to miss the fun; she was in the front row. She blew a kiss at me and I smiled back thinly.

I was lifted up by my dad so that I could look into the sty. A big fat pig that I had tickled many a time was rolling in panic in the mud. Two ropes had been lassoed over its neck and around all four legs. Two grim-faced men in overalls and wellingtons opened the gate and walked into the sty. One had his hands behind his back. At the same time Robert and Tot and three men pulled on the ropes. The pig stood up and peered at the oncoming men. In a flash one man brought a hammer and a sharpened chisel out from behind his back and hit the pig between the eyes. There was a scream, blood flew everywhere and the pig crashed into its attackers. It burst through the sty doorway, chisel implanted in its head. Only young Tot could hold on to the rope and he was dragged along behind the pig. It veered up a dyke and knocked over my granny Maria's wheelchair, tipping the old lady into the dust. Her hat rolled off towards the river and my auntie Elsie ran after it as Bab, poise gone and screaming like a banshee, helped her mother. Men raced after the ropes and my uncle Jack Snowball ran for his Sunbeam car. I remember my granny's keening screams as well as those of the pig as my granny was bundled into the car and driven off to hospital.

We did not worry about Granny too long. The pig turned on its heels and pathetically staggered back towards its sty. The ropes were looped round the gatepost as the pig flopped squealing in the mud. One of the men produced a big mell hammer and battered the chisel into its brain. It flopped, shitting and snorting out one last squeal. Another man cut the pig's throat and held a pan to collect the blood – an essential ingredient of black pudding. I vomited in some nettles. My father held me. I saw how shamefaced he and most people were by the blood frenzy. But not the butchers, Robert, Tot and the lasso party. Daubed in pig's blood, they looked like a winning football team or the last men standing after a boozy brawl outside the Grand Hotel in Ashington.

An hour later the mood had changed – from charnel house to hoedown.

Auntie Bab's house was a hive of activity as Martha and the other women chopped, carved and minced. Men drank beer, but not Bob; he stuck to tea. Tot and Robert were walking round with bottles of Double Maxim, reliving the pig stampede.

On the radiogram 'The Runaway Train' screeched and somebody kept replaying it: 'The runaway train came down the track and she bleeeeew-eeeew...' My mother was sipping neat gin, always her celebratory tipple, and Bob kept wagging his finger at her in playful warning. Mam raised her glass and said loudly: 'Here's to yon brave guffie.'

Auntie Jean put down her glass of lemonade. 'Guffie? Guffie? Why cannit ye Alnwick gadgies call pigs *pigs*?'

There was pure venom in her tone. Martha flushed. She poised the glass as if to fling the gin at Jean. 'She winnit let me alone, the spiteful sod,' screamed my mam.

My dad stepped in. He put his arm around my mother and glowered at Jean. 'That's enough. Remember this is my wife and she is a Waddell.'

The moment passed.

Suddenly Auntie Bab banged on the dining table for order. She held up the pig's bladder, inflated and tied with string. It looked like a greasy scabby coconut.

'Jump for it, ye laddies,' Bab cried.

Tot hurled himself highest and caught the trophy. We followed him out into the back lane and used the bladder as a football. The big lads crushed and bashed me for fun as they played shooty-in with the netty door as goal. Scruffy, dirty lads I did not know muscled in on our game. They elbowed me down on the pavement, scraping my knees but I didn't care. This was as good as Christmas. And then all the fun stopped.

Uncle Jack Snowball came out of the house, his fedora crushed in his hands, a solemn look on his face. 'Granny Maria has died,' he announced, almost in tears

The pig's bladder was forgotten. My cousin Robert put his arms around me and his tears drew mine. In the heady turmoil of the day we had forgotten about our granny. Knives, sausages, blood, bladders, family feuds ... and now death. It was all too much; I howled for my mammy.

Apart from the villages of Ellington and Lynemouth, where the Waddell clan were centred, the other axis of my early life was my granny Mary-Jane's tiny one-bedroom flat in the close off Clayport in the wrong end of Alnwick.

For the past ten years, since his accident, Mary-Jane had been looking after Uncle Sonny. At the age of 25, he was not able to walk, talk, or feed himself. Her only respite came in the few hours she worked at the local garden nursery. Then her friend Florence Burnett would sit with him until Mary-Jane came home. Uncle Sam helped out in the evening but in 1940, aged 22, he had gone off to fight the Japanese wearing the proud scarlet hackle of the Royal Northumberland Fusiliers. Within days of landing he had been captured.

My mother took me to Alnwick almost every weekend and dad did not like it at all. After a hard week down the pit he would have preferred a family weekend in his own house. It was a constant bone of contention between them. When we stayed over on a Saturday night the bottom of a big cupboard with mirrors was let down in the parlour and Mam and I slept in it. It felt odd getting up in the night to use the 'pittle pail' and being watched by sombre flat-eyed plaster figures of Mary and Joseph. It was comforting that I was being watched over, as Granny never ceased to tell me, but it was spooky too. Looking at the lovely colours, the azures and silvers of the icons, I could not help feeling slightly guilty. I had been taught a list of people to pray for by my granny, but often opened my eyes in mid-chant, to look at the plaster saints.

'God bless Granny and Sonny and Sam. God bless Mam and keep Dad safe down the pit.'

Granny always kept her eyes tight shut as we prayed but I looked for signs of acknowledgement, particularly from kindly Joseph with his droopy beard and put-upon expression.

One night my dad paid one of his rare visits to Alnwick and we were all sleeping in Granny's parlour. Suddenly there was a commotion in her bedroom. Sonny was screaming and Mary-Jane was trying to soothe him. My dad leapt from the bed and made for the bedroom door.

'No, divvent gan in there, that's my job,' screamed Martha.

Bob turned, looking shocked. Martha rarely raised her voice to him in Mary-Jane's house. My mother got out of bed and opened the bedroom door. Granny was wrestling with Sonny.

'Come on John, me bairn, you've got to go to the toilet.'

Sonny screamed and shook his head in defiance. Then a damp stain appeared on his pyjama trousers. My mother and my granny dragged

Sonny to the pittle pail, dropped his pyjama pants and forced him to sit on the pail. He waved his arms and screamed.

'Can't you let the laddie up now?' asked Bob, as I hid my head under the bed covers.

'We have to hold him in case he wants more than a pittle,' explained Martha as Granny took the wet pyjama pants to the kitchen sink. 'This is what Mother has to put up with every day God sends. Believe me, I don't come here every Saturday for a bloody holiday. If I'm here for a few hours she can slip down to church and pray for us all.'

She spoke in a flat matter-of-fact voice as Sonny began to shit in the bucket.

Mary-Jane went to St Michael's church even when there was no Mass, and often took me with her. One bleak Saturday afternoon in the winter of 1943, the clash of the giant sneck on the church door announced our entry into a frightening calm. I tried tip-toeing behind Granny as she led me down the empty church, but still my feet echoed. There was the acrid smell of candles and pollen-like swirls of sweet incense. The Stations of the Cross were painted on the walls, a racked array of souls lamenting the persecution of Our Lord. Matching the very holiest was my granny's sculpted hawk face, rosary to her lips, damp eyes raised to the great blood-coloured east window.

Mary-Jane's grip on my shoulder was tighter than it should have been as we stood under the life-size statue of a twisted, naked bleeding Jesus clutching a royal-purple shift to his wound. Jesus's skin was yellow, tanned by candle smoke. Granny's voice was low but harsh.

'Kneel, laddie. Kneel and pray.'

'What for, Nana?' I asked.

'Pray for your uncle Sam. Pray that he will soon be delivered from the Japs' hands.'

I repeated the phrase 'Japsands'. For three years now hope and prayer had been punctuated by strange typed letters on brown card. They said 'I am well' or 'I am being well treated.' They were stamped with red

Japanese writing. There was mention of a giant railway. The paucity of detail was frightening. 'Japsands' locked into my psyche; I thought it was a place, a bit like Whitley Bay beach with palm trees; a place with bad, bloodthirsty natives.

Granny bent forward in the pew. All that stuck out from her head-scarf were the sharp nose and chin. She clutched her beads and her voice tore my young heart.

'Please bring my bonny Sammy back to his home. Please hear a poor woman's prayers.' Then her dry, beseeching intonement continued into the Apostle's Creed.

'Please bring my uncle Sam home safe.'

I offered my own prayer up in a reedy whisper. I did not know the standard prayers and offerings, so I solemnly vowed to be a good pure little laddie if God answered my prayer.

Our final call was at the small font on the way out. My granny dipped her fingers into the holy water and crossed herself. Then she cupped her hand, dipped deep and made a dripping cross all down my face. I licked holy water from my nose as we pushed pennies into black tin cans and lit long white candles. I interspersed the noise of the coins dropping and my own sneezing with my Japsands mantra.

The next part of my granny's Saturday ritual was very different from her holier-than-holy conduct at the church. We walked towards Alnwick Castle and I looked up at tall wind-buffeted towers with sculpted stone archers round the north-facing battlements, set there in the olden days to fool the marauding Scots that it was permanently guarded. We passed the busy salerooms where my mam and granny often went looking for bargain bits of second-hand furniture. Next was the Dirty Bottles, a famous pub with pebbled windows showing old filthy wine bottles, which if touched, legend said, would bring death to the defiler. Opposite the pub was a gaunt tenement that my granny always put the evil eye on, the former workhouse. Ever since her sudden widowhood 20 years earlier Mary-Jane had lived with the fear of destitution. Even though the 'workie' was now closed, it symbolised jeopardy to the Smith family.

Then we entered the busy bright premises of John William Allen, high-class grocer. Mary-Jane had shopped here for many years and, yet another firm hawser binding Martha to her roots in Alnwick, we got our family 'rations' here every Saturday. Everyone at this time in the war had to register with a particular shop for butter, cheese, tea and sugar and our ration books with their coupons were on the books of John William Allen.

The shop smelled of strong cheese and exotic coffee. It made me sneeze but I did not care; to me it was Aladdin's cave and a Persian bazaar all rolled into one. There were scrubbed wooden chairs for aged customers to take rest. There were brass pots full of change that whizzed round on a rail above my head. There was a whirring bacon slicer that looked like a piece of torture equipment from the Spanish Inquisition. Best of all, there were biscuit tins with glass tops racked at a child's height. As I nosed round the chocolate finger section I happened to turn towards the shelves of chopped pork, baked beans and tinned peas. I was shocked to see Mary-Jane stuffing tins directly into her shopping bag. By instinct I glanced at the proprietor, all shiny white coat and ruddy cheeks. He nodded and half winked at me, very definitely smiling. As my granny collected the rest of her rations and paid for them, smiling like a Mother Superior, I realised that John William Allen was on the same humane wavelength as the kindly nuns: Mary-Jane Smith, saint of St Michael's parish, poor widow woman, with a crippled son and lad a prisoner of war, was allowed to snaffle a few treats under the noses of the better off. Being a little sneak, I wasted no time in telling my dad of Granny's clumsy pilfering. 'Aye, wey it's not ganna harm anybody, son. Everybody in Alnwick knows your granny is a good woman who's had a hard life. Mind, I don't want you to help her with any pinching.'

Apart from my uncle Sam, the war spawned another unlikely hero in my childish imagination. I developed an odd love/hate relationship with the great war leader Winston Churchill, master of pure purple prose, theatrical V-signs, large whiskies, foot-long cigars and gravelly upper-crust voice. Around March 1945 I went to the Miners' Institute cinema at the nearby pit village of Linton. I was with my friend Eric Appleby, who was my age and lived three doors away, and some older boys. We were sitting near the front of a packed audience scoffing ice cream and brain-freezing limeade. The *Gaumont British News* came on with a raucous fanfare and suddenly there was Winny, in his plush overcoat with a fur collar, black homburg, his cigar poised like a bandleader's baton. He was waving to a crowd from a shiny open-topped car. The unctuous soundtrack was immediately drowned by 300 people booing, jeering, feet banging; some even tossing ice-cream cartons at the screen. The outburst lasted till Churchill's self-satisfied chops faded from the screen. I had no idea why there had been such a reaction.

When I got home I asked my father why the deep hatred of this man. Surely he was leading our fight against the Nazis and the Japs? Surely he was a key figure in getting Uncle Sam and Tommies like him home, and out of wicked hands? Surely this made him a good egg, in the parlance of my storybook heroes Biggles and William Brown.

My father's gentle eyes narrowed and he spat the words at me. 'He hates the working man, that fellow. He especially hates us pitmen. When he was Home Secretary in the 1920s he sent the troops into Wales to shoot striking coal miners. He's a Tory swine.'

Despite my dad's wholesale condemnation of the prime minister, I developed an admiration for the oratorical skill of old man Churchill. He was always on the wireless and I began mimicking his portentous tones. In the bathroom at our bungalow I would sit on the pot, often with my pal Alan Robinson as audience, declaiming, 'Nevaah in the field of human coooonflict...' I practised my delivery whenever I could.

A few days later I was playing in Auntie Bab's backyard with a wooden toy sword. I was imagining myself as Robin Hood holding at bay some of the Sheriff of Nottingham's men and was warning them in my Churchill voice to give in.

'Down, doooown, I say with those arms, vaaaaarlets.'

I had been warned not to play in the shed where my aunt kept sacks of potatoes to feed her growing flock of pigs. But the imaginary varlets took shelter in the shed. So I followed, jumped on sacks full of potatoes and swished my sword. Then I had a disaster. I slipped and three cans of paraffin – like the spuds, probably obtained on the black market – toppled off a shelf and onto the spuds. The smell drenched my nose and throat. Coughing and wheezing, I scrambled out of the shed.

Auntie Bab had a blue fit. She clouted my ear and used bad words. Even though I understood only a little of what she was saying, it appeared that she was accusing me of wilfully condemning a dozen pigs to death by starvation because I had ruined all their food.

What to do? I brooded till my mother and I went to my granny Mary-Jane's at the weekend. After Mass on Sunday I lit candles and prayed fervently that Uncle Sam would soon be out of the Japsands after over four years and, silently, that God could send half a dozen bags of potatoes to Auntie Bab to make up for the ones I had ruined. I hoped Mr Churchill would be on the same wavelength as our Creator and would do his bit to help bring about the miracle.

Next day I sat on the steps of the ancient Market Cross in Alnwick doing my Winny act. As my mam and half a dozen folks gossiped and waited in a queue for the bus to Ashington, I sucked on a clothes peg and frowned.

'Mooore tanks. Mooore ships. More tetties for my auntie Bab's pigs,' I growled and offered V-signs in all directions.

Three days later I was back with my mam at Auntie Bab's. I was a bit disappointed that she was not smothering me with kisses and Blue Riband chocolate biscuits. My mam went up the back lane to see my auntie Mary, leaving me alone with Bab.

'Have the tetties for the pigs come yet?' I asked, all bright-eyed.

My aunt turned puce. She sneered at me, stood on a chair and opened a high cupboard. Sweets for my miracle, I was sure. Then sheer terror gripped me. Fiend-eyed, my aunt swung down at me with a silver

*My uncle Sam cuts a fine strapping figure in the middle of this army
photo of early 1940. Soon after, he was imprisoned by the Japanese
for over four years.*

hammer. It crashed into my forehead as I screamed, then it bunched up
harmlessly like a dead snake. It was made of rubber.

'Cheeky little sod,' hissed Bab.

There was, however, one happy ending to the whole saga of my early
prayers.

One day that summer I had run myself stupid on the sands at Alnmouth where my parents had done much of their courting. They had pointed out a spot where a swarm of giant rats had gathered round them as they picnicked in the dunes. Back at Clayport I had collapsed in a heap on my granny's settee.

I was shaken quite roughly from my sleep. My dad's stubby strong fingers tousled my hair and I smelled beer on his breath. Not like him, I thought. I looked beyond my dad and saw Granny and my mother, with drinks in their hands and tears in their eyes. Then a tall figure swooped and kissed me roughly on the brow. There was a shock of black wavy hair and a blur of khaki. A strip of coloured medals jingled on the man's chest. He plonked a beret with a hackle on it on my head.

'Hello, wor Sidney. Do yee knaa who ah am?' More beery breath. I began to bubble. So did Uncle Sonny, tears and snots running down his face. Sam hugged him roughly. The prayers of me and my granny had worked; the Japsands had given up Uncle Sam.

Sam tipped out one of his kitbags. He pulled out some Lion chocolate bars. I had never seen so many sweets. Then he swooshed an aeroplane at me, a foot-long ivory model of a Mitsubishi fighter. Wrong side, but who cared? Then the gaslight flashed off a genuine Gurkha kukri, just like I had seen in my comics. He let me hold it. I thrilled with anticipation. Just wait till Eric and Alan saw this treasure. And just wait till I waved it under the nose of Auntie Bab. Her and her rubber rotten hammer.

CHAPTER FOUR

A Good Scholar

Ellington County Primary school was at the top of the road, only 150 yards from our house. It was a small, pretty sandstone building with three classrooms, a small sloping school field and an ugly yellow-brick air-raid shelter behind it. It taught around 70 children, who came from the fishing families of Cresswell, the farming families of Ellington village and the mining community. I would watch the children go to school every morning and would stand entranced watching them in the playground. The boys kicked a ball around and the girls played skipping games and I desperately wanted to join them. I pestered Mam all the time about when I could join them and she would explain patiently that I had to wait until I was five. But she always had a warning for me: 'It's not just for fun, wor Sid, you've got to buckle down and do book learning and writing.'

Book learning did not worry me. My mother had already taught me to read from comics. Every week the *Beano, Dandy, Film Fun* and *Radio Fun* were delivered to our house and I would wait like a hungry puppy as they dropped through the letterbox. I loved Desperate Dan and his insatiable appetite for cow pie; Corky the Cat; and above all Lord Snooty and his Gang. And, until I could join the children in the playground, I had my own gang and it had to be run my way. I was the Lord Snooty in charge of my best pals Alan Robinson and Eric Appleby when we played games in the street and the fields.

Alan was a quiet, small, tubby boy who lived in one of the posh pebble-dashed semis at the village end of Cresswell Road. I occasionally went to his house for tea and remember antimacassars and deep, enveloping settees. But Alan was more often at our bungalow, where we played football or cricket in the drive between our house and the Dowsons'. I insisted that I had to be centre forward, first to bat or the captain if we played pirates. I also devised a very strange ritual called 'Plan Time'. Whenever I needed to go to the toilet I solemnly led Alan into our toilet and locked the door. Then, as I strained away, I outlined our next game in detail. 'Tomorrow we will go to the Swing Field with bows and arrows and I will be Robin Hood. You can choose who you will be.'

Alan danced to whatever tune I called.

My relationship with Eric was much more complex. He was no spear carrier and a keen rivalry symbolised our relationship for the next few years. Eric was a pale-faced freckled kid, with a stammer and bad hearing.

This last feature Martha put down to Eric's mam Edna clouting his lug at the slightest provocation. Edna Appleby did have a tongue like a viper and lashed out at her kids at times, but I reckon my mother had it in for her because her husband Stan was a deputy at nearby Linton pit – a rung up the social ladder from a mere 'labourer' like my dad. Status meant a lot to my mother. On the bus to Alnwick on our regular trips, my dad was always described to strangers as a 'supervisor' rather than an everyday pit yacker.

The Appleby bungalow was only four doors away from us and I spent a lot of time there. It was as spick and span as a new pin. First, you had to take your shoes off at the door. Eric's dad Stan was a handyman, unlike Bob, and had made all sorts of little wooden tables to put coffee and pop glasses on. Eric used to gloat over the fact that he had a 'Plusogram', an electric state-of-the-art record machine, while we just had an old second-hand tatty wind-up job.

On Christmas Day in 1944, I ruined the festivities for the Applebys.

I made an early visit to their house because I had received lots of sporting and comic annuals as presents and I was eager to show them to Eric. I remembered to take my shoes off in the glassed-in porch, then I raced into the living room. Soon Eric and I were comparing books happily and guzzling Tizer, while Eric's younger sister, Sheila, bustled around us trying to join in. I flopped down on what I thought was a pouffe covered with a white rug. There was a crunch of splintering wood as my bum landed on Sheila's star present, a handmade doll's cot. I sprinted home and locked myself in the toilet. Soon, outside the door I heard Edna and my mother going at it like fishwives.

'You have got that laddie ruined,' screamed Edna. 'He does what he likes. My bairns know what discipline means.'

'If yee call discipline hammering a kiddie's lugs till he cannit hear, then I'm pleased to God I have none of it in my house,' Martha countered.

As usual my mother found it easier to start a row than to see reason, especially where her darling son was involved.

It was a few weeks before Eric spoke to me again, and months before I was treated to more tunes on the Plusogram.

On my first day at school I was scrubbed and sparkling, my light-brown hair pudding-basin trimmed. I was dressed in matching grey flannel short pants and jacket, new Fair Isle pullover and even a tie, wool with black and grey lateral stripes. My tie got some funny looks from the other kids, including my friends Alan and Eric. Huh, I thought, I'll show them, I'll be top of the class and win the egg and spoon race on sports day. I was trembling with excitement as Mam left me at the door of the classroom.

The euphoria lasted for all of three hours. I loved Miss Vardy, all tweeds, thick glasses and soft maternal voice, and I loved sitting at a proper desk rather than the polished-top table at home. But by the noon break all the expectations and exertions of the morning had made me tired. Martha came to take me home for dinner and I almost went to sleep after my egg and chips. I settled down on the settee with a comic and did not want to go back. She dragged me up Cresswell Road for the second half.

Miss Vardy turned out to have a dark side, raising her voice at stupidity and banging her ruler at naughtiness. Carefully I worked my way into her good books by whipping my hand up first on all occasions. I rarely got answers wrong and usually got full marks for sums and spelling. In fact, not only was I a voracious reader, I also discovered that I had a photographic memory. This was to stand me in good stead later in my education, and it made me Miss Vardy's blue-eyed boy. So good was my first report at Christmas 1945 that my parents bought me a real scholar's desk as a present. When I saw it I cried with pleasure. It was varnished yellow, had proper inkwells, and a lid that when raised revealed partitions for books, pencils and rubbers. The cost to my parents must have been at least two pounds. The war had pushed up miners' wages dramatically and in 1944 the underground minimum weekly wage was set at five pounds, Bob had a piecework job as a filler shovelling coal onto a conveyor belt so, in a 'good' back-breaking, hard-grafting week, he could place five pounds seven shillings on the table after offtakes. That two pounds represented 40 per cent of my father's weekly wage, and it could have gone on fags, drink, nice clothes or into the kitty for a seaside holiday. That desk was the beginning of my family's investment in my future, and I was just five years old.

It was around this time that I first began to understand just what my dad endured every working day to support our family. One weekend early in 1946 I stayed with my dad at his family's house at 10 First Row in Ellington Colliery. Since my granny Maria's death, my auntie Elsie had become the lady of the house that had once crammed as many as ten people into its two bedrooms, a best room with antimacassars, sideboards and vases that nobody ever used, and busy kitchen with a giant black range. Now Elsie looked after my uncle Jack, who was 35 but showed no intentions of getting married.

It was early on a Saturday morning. Mam had gone to Alnwick alone and my dad had gone to Ashington. I came out of the old-style netty – no flush and old newspapers to wipe your bum – and was scraffling around in the shed. I found two small battered wooden stools and a small torn harness.

There was a rattle outside and I blenched. Auntie Elsie would clout my lug if she caught me in the shed; any excuse for Elsie to vent her quick temper. But it was only my uncle Jack. He was holding his left hand under the yard tap and it was in a mess. In fact, his thumb seemed to be hanging off.

'What happened to your hand?'

He grinned like a little lad who had never grown up.

'Just a bump, son. I was filling alongside your dad and I was trying to smash a big lump of coal. Clashed me hand instead.' He kissed the crusted wound. 'But it'll be alreet cos I had a quick piss on it. Works wonders.'

I gasped and this was a cue for Jack to let rip with a hair-raising story of a filler's life. 'Last week me and your dad went doon Blakemoor drift and halfway to the Dogger Bank.' My eyes rolled. 'It was a two-foot-six seam and we were down on our sides with the harnesses and crackets,' he pointed at the gear in the shed. 'We were in a foot of watter aal day. Good job we had them thick ganseys wor Mary knit for us. When you're sweating like a pig like we were the wool gets real warm. You feel like a pig lying in its own shit.'

My dad occasionally brought home a tatty wool jersey from the pit for a wash. He told me and my mam he used it to dry off the pit ponies. I gave an icy shudder as I realised what that tatty old jumper meant: twisting about shovelling coal under the sea, with other water swilling all round you. The images stayed with me for ever. I prayed every night for all the Waddells and the Smiths, but I prayed hardest of all for my dad in his daily battle down Auld Betty.

On a spring morning in 1946, I was called out in front of the whole school – babies, infants and juniors – because I had been chosen to unveil a seat for the old people of the village. Also called out to partner me in the ceremony was a cute, gobby, dark-haired little girl called June. She was not very bright, nor was she a teacher's pet, but she always wore nice clean clothes. She was forever chatting me up and suggesting going for walks, but I always turned her down. As we stood at the front that day, I prayed that nobody thought we were romantically involved just because we had been paired up to pull a Union Jack off a bench.

The day we unveiled the bench June shook hands and dropped curtsies with the elderly people who had been wheeled out for the ceremony just as if she was in training for the position of lady-in-waiting to the Queen. I shook hands and smiled for the camera, but I was aware of one man glowering at me. He was the father of the local vicar and made it his business to know who was who in our village, and what was what. He had his eye on me because I was a Catholic. He could not fail to know this because Martha bellowed it to the heavens on a regular basis in shops, on buses, anywhere. I didn't like the look, it was as if he had already marked me down as a troublemaker.

In the summer of that year Eric Appleby and I had been playing football in the vicarage paddock after the other kids had gone home. I had copped the big green apples over the small wall in the vicar's orchard. I suggested to Eric that we go and pinch a few apples. Concern flared over his freckled chops.

'B-b-bu-but wha-wha-what if we get cau-cauc-aught?' he stammered.

'We run like billyo,' I replied.

I climbed the biggest tree and Eric stood at the bottom with his pullover stretched out to catch the apples as I began to fling them down. Then there was the clang-clash of the bolt on the orchard gate. Eric froze, no doubt thinking of yet another slap from his mother.

'Run like hell!' I yelled.

He did and I dropped the last ten feet from the branches, my knees jarring into my ribs. The vicar's dad saw us both clearly. His eyes swung from Eric to me and he waved his fist. 'I know who you are,' he shouted.

Huh, I thought. What's he going to do about a few cooking apples?

On the Monday morning there was, as usual, a full school assembly. I was about to start back to my classroom after the hymn when the headmistress banged her desk for attention. 'I have an unfortunate announcement to make about a raid on the vicar's apple orchard. Sidney Waddell, step forward please.'

I blushed, gritted my teeth and walked to the front. I looked at Eric who was two shades of scarlet brighter than me. The head continued. 'Up till now, Sidney, you have been a credit to the school, but you have brought shame on yourself and the rest of us. You will go to the vicarage later today and apologise to Reverend Ridley.'

I was fuming. The reason I was called up and not Eric was because he and his parents went to the Protestant church every Sunday and the Waddells did not. Still, I said nothing to Eric, his parents or mine. I did not get to unveil any more seats. But, next time I had the chance I vowed to get wimpy Eric for not coming clean. I did apologise to the Protestant vicar, head down and in a whisper. He accepted gracefully and I went home hoping the nuns at Alnwick would never hear that I had risked hellfire by talking to a prominent member of the opposition.

I was in general a very honest little boy. I did not tell my mam and dad about the apple saga, the public humiliation at school or my apology to the vicar because it would upset them. They thought the sun shone out of my backside and there was no need to disillusion them. But I had to react strongly at times to Martha's over-protectiveness. She always made me wear a thick woollen vest because the Waddells all had bad wheezy chests. And she made this worse by layering me with Vick Vapour Rub whenever I coughed. Kids often sniffed at me as I passed. On top of this she begged me not to play near the stagnant ponds in the Swing Field across from our house by the river Lyne – a favourite for catching sticklebacks in jam jars – or to venture near the sea at Cresswell.

I was only six years old and would never have gone the two miles to the seashore, but everybody, even kids still in nappies, went to the ponds and the river. With Alan and Eric I played cricket near the ponds, then, when we got sick of that, we played jumping over the ponds. So I often fell in and played on, soaked to the very vest. The river was much more exciting. It wound through the valley near Todd's farm and the best place for little fish was under the road bridge. Sadly the underside of the bridge was slimy with weeds and I fell in on a regular basis. To cap it all I went on a raft made of railway sleepers and old car tyres with some bigger kids and it sank in six feet of water. I could not swim but was pulled out by a lad called Billy Hallowell. He wanted me to go home but I said no. I lay in the sun under some ash trees till my clothes were dry.

Next morning I was coughing green lumps and had a temperature. I got worse over the next 24 hours and Dr Skene, an old Scottish buffer in tweeds who smelled of pipe smoke and whisky, was called. He took my temperature, sounded out my tubes and declared that I had pneumonia. Martha was completely distraught. What had we done to deserve this? Weakly, and gobbling pills, I confessed: I told her that it was not heeding her warnings and falling in pools and rivers that had brought illness down upon me. I felt so bad about letting her down I wore a vest until I was well into my twenties.

My illness and convalescence were the occasion of a state visit to our bungalow by Mary-Jane, with Uncle Sam in tow. It was only for the weekend, so my crippled uncle Sonny was looked after by my granny's neighbour Phyllis, who lived up the same close.

Granny walked in with the bag full of rations from John William Allen's, wearing a shabby old black fur coat and a 'Paddington' suede hat; the poor old holy-rolling widow had real style on occasions. She then proceeded to do what she always did on her rare visits to Ellington. She sat in an armchair pulled right up to the fire, opened her legs showing her bloomers, and began to rub her hands as if freezing. 'Put some coal on that fire, laddie,' she pointed at the roaring coal fire.

It was early September and the sun was shining, but my granny was in the land of free coal and she wanted her fair share; back in Alnwick coal was hellishly expensive and used sparingly. My dad nodded. I went out to the coal house to fetch it and chucked two shovelfuls of best nutty slack on the fire. Within five minutes we were all lathered with sweat and I heard Dad mutter to Mam, 'If it gets any hotter in there, we'll have to go and sit in the garden.'

Martha put her finger to her lips and whished him; 'Mother' was not to be upset on her visits. She had a poor crippled mentally retarded son at home, Mam was always reminding us, and needed some respite. At least she had the good grace not to bring her smelly old clay pipe with her.

Uncle Sam also had a regular ritual when he hit Ellington village. It involved Lynemouth Workingmen's Social Club and pints of Federation special ale. One Saturday night Bob, Martha and Sam went to the club at about seven. Martha did the waltz and the quickstep with her regular partner Billy Chatt, Bob sipped halves and played a frame or two of snooker and Sam got plastered. He had to be half carried home. Even then he wanted more drink. Despite Bob's protests, Granny gave Sam a glass of Alnwick Brewery 100 per cent dark rum with a dash of pep to end his day of 'recreation'.

He was sitting on a pouffe by the fire rambling drunkenly about the Japs when Martha remembered I needed to take a pill. I refused point blank, saying they tasted horrible. So Mam had a brainwave: Would I take the pill if Soldier Sam took some? I nodded. She rattled out two pills into Sam's palm and winked at him to pretend to take them. With a goofy smile, Sam swept his hand to his mouth and followed the move up with a swig of rum. Two minutes later he toppled forward onto the mat, out cold.

During the two weeks I was housebound with pneumonia I spent the days reading and being read to by Martha. As well as the *Beano* and the *Dandy*, I devoured the detective skills of *The Hardy Boys*, two preppy Yankee lads who were smart at sleuthing, and I became obsessed by Mark Twain's *The Adventures of Tom Sawyer* in which generally good moral egg Tom is constantly upstaged by the louche and worldly wise

Huckleberry Finn. In fact, when I started courting – at age seven – I modelled my tactics on Tom's advances to Becky Thatcher, the local judge's pretty daughter. For 'heavy relief' I turned to the 20 volumes of Arthur Mee's *Children's Encyclopaedia*, bound in red imitation leather, having been purchased from a door-to-door salesman on the never-never; again, money aimed at improving my prospects in life.

But the deepest roots of my infant psyche were grown when Cyril 'Squiggie' Dowson introduced me to the boys' story-papers *The Wizard*, *The Adventure* and, above all, *The Hotspur*. Cyril was about four years older than me and was a brilliant footballer. He lived next door in a house that was always untidy and smelly. His mother Hilda was a chubby, curly-haired lady who had let herself go to seed. She seemed to swear whenever she opened her mouth. Cyril always had knots in his hair and dirty collars and cuffs on his shirt, yet he was like a ten-year-old uncle to me.

Cyril read to me till I got the hang of it. When I got going myself, I could not get enough of William Wilson, the 200-year-old bloke who ran the mile in three and a half minutes because a steam train was up his bum. Then there was Baldy Hogan, going on 50 but a demon half-back, forever bundling Fancy Dan dribblers off the ball. But my absolute favourite was the accounts in *The Hotspur* of dorm feasts, fagging, ragging and derring-do at the footer and rugger of the boys of Red Circle boarding school. I was so impressed that I actually joined my own private branch of the school. And it got me ragged, scragged and almost killed.

My mother, as well as being a member of the Co-op, also had 'tick', a credit account, at a couple of men's stores in Ashington. So when in the autumn of 1946 I went for my new 'rig-out', the world was my sartorial oyster. I had always worn horizontal striped ties, usually black and grey, but now we trolled the shops for a Red Circle tie in red and silver-grey. In the end we found one at Doggart's in Ashington and – wonder of wonders – we found a red and grey hooped cap that more or less matched. To top this, I got some new grey socks trimmed with red bands.

The following Saturday morning, as usual, I got on the bus at Ellington with my mam to make our weekly pilgrimage to Granny's. I had the lot on: cap, tie, socks, grey jacket, grey short pants and a red and grey checked pullover. I got a couple of funny looks but stared out of the window oblivious. Martha sat in front of me and immediately got into a 'clash' with a posh female stranger. Soon she was waving a Woodbine in the air and had taken a dive into her own fantasy pool. Our family name Waddell, pronounced 'Waddle', had become 'Wadd-ell' – stress the last syllable – and Bob had been upgraded from 'coal-filler' to 'overman'. Mary-Jane had been born in County Roscommon in Ireland – in fact, she had been born up a close in Alnwick just like me. I waited for her to say that we would probably have time to drop in on the Duke and Duchess of Northumberland for a cuppa and a chinwag.

After these hour-and-a-half journeys, with most of the adults on the overheated bus smoking, I had to get a breath of air. So, as Martha and Mary-Jane got up to speed over tea, I went out to the Clay Hills next to the brewery. For a while I talked to a little lassie who was about my age. She had a strong Scottish accent and took me to see her pet rabbits across the busy road behind the fire station. But as I was returning home, I sensed danger. I had seen him before, and he had seen me. He was the most malevolent kid I had ever clapped eyes on. He was a nine-year-old Jimmy Cagney, with a bit of Bill Sykes thrown into the mix, and the dead eyes of a desert lizard. That was Chalky, leader of a gang from the notorious St Thomas's Close. He had shouted at me before, hurled stones and made rude gestures, and that was even before my new plumage.

He wore boots with no socks and they clashed the ground as he began to run after me. 'Jessy! Big soft Jessy,' he screeched. Two of his henchmen were with him, flinging stones at me. I was directly opposite my granny's house with an open drain and a major road in front of me. Chalky jumped at me, trying to get my cap. I held onto it and blindly leapt the drain, legs pumping. I caught one foot in the swirling water but scrambled onto the tarmac of the main road. I ran blindly for my granny's close. The young man driving the MG sports car had no chance of stopping. His left front fender smashed into my right arm and sent me splashing back into the streaming piss and shit. Chalky and his pals ran away quickly. Uncle Sam came screaming out of our close and carried me indoors.

The local doctor was called and he looked at my bruised right arm. He got me to move it in several places and then impatiently told my mother that there was nothing wrong with my arm. A few days later I was in the Swing Field at Cresswell Road with my pals, skimming stones over the pools, when Uncle Bill, passing by on his bike, saw me playing and joined us. Suddenly he asked me why I was throwing the stones side-on, almost underarm.

'Because my arm hurts when I chuck properly,' I replied.

Bill took me home and reported back to my mother. Next thing I knew I was in the X-ray department at Ashington hospital where they diagnosed a fracture. Martha made a special trip to the doctor in Alnwick to tell him exactly what she thought of his expertise.

CHAPTER FIVE

Betty's Brood

There was plenty to celebrate at 16 Cresswell Road, Ellington village, as the festive seasons of Christmas and New Year came upon us at the end of 1946.

Demand for coal was at an all-time high because of the war and its aftermath, and at last miners were getting a fair day's pay. The national union had been formed, from a federation of regional unions, in 1944, and it symbolised the collective ethos of the men who had done their bit to win the war. A minimum wage was introduced that pleased the leaders of the National Union of Mineworkers. Still, my father was not rolling in clover. A five-and-a-half-day week brought him a minimum of five pounds, and if he shovelled coal harder, piecework rates meant he would take home just over six pounds.

But what made our celebrations extra special at the end of 1946 was the nationalisation of the coal mines. The pits had been run in the national interest and that of the workforce during the war, and on 1 January 1947, the blue and silver flag of the National Coal Board was raised over Betty and every other colliery in Britain on Vesting Day. Outside Betty was a sign saying that the NCB would manage the pit for the nation. All this meant that the pits belonged to the people; that after all the years of strikes and savage wage cutbacks by the old coal owners, the value of coal miners and their dangerous job for the nation were recognised. It also meant that the Labour Party, created by the trade unions, had done the right thing by the miners. The build-up to this glory day was something never to be forgotten.

Preparations started on Saturday a week before Christmas. Soon after breakfast Mam began making an enormous pan of broth. From somewhere she had acquired a great ham shank and she slung this into the simmering vegetables. I asked who the broth was for and was told that my cousins Robert and Tot were on the way 'to do a bit of work'.

When I heard the two lads walking up our path I ran out to greet them. Robert, as usual, had a warm grin, but Tot, loose-jawed and manic-eyed, greeted me with a clout on the ear. He was only joking but it hurt. I wiped away my tears and followed the pair as Bob led them to the chicken coop at the bottom of the garden. I did not realise what was about to happen until Dad started pointing at certain of the pullets and Robert and Tot took off their jackets. Dad opened the coop door and I was dragged inside by Tot. Robert started the festive cull. He grabbed a pullet, clutched its fluttering body under his right arm and with his left hand broke its neck like a corn stalk. He tossed the body to Bob. Tot grabbed another bird and gave a twist with his enormous hands – and the head came right off. Blood squirted on me from the neck and the still twitching body flew past, slung to my dad.

'It's wor Christmas dinner,' explained Bob.

Not wanting to poop the party, I accepted a pullet and tried to strangle it. The bird pecked my hand savagely as I failed to get the gist of it. More blood on my pullover. Tot the Strangler took over.

After about eight birds had been killed Tot and Robert went inside for the broth. My friend Alan Robinson joined us and was not surprised when told I was hopeless at chicken strangling. 'I could have telt yer that,' said Alan through a mouthful of gristly ham and squelchy carrots. 'It was the same when he killed the sparrow with the 'pult.'

He went on to tell everyone the tale. That spring I had been proudly showing Alan and Eric my prowess with a new metal catapult. I had bought it from the model shop in Alnwick, where I went for model aeroplane kits with my saved-up pocket money, and I was really gloating. Alan and Eric's weapons were self-made tat, made out of twig branches and knicker elastic; mine was shaped like a knight's shiny spur and the elastic shone like jet liquorice. I was shooting off lead pellets like a cross between David of Goliath fame and Billy the Kid. Suddenly a fat sparrow went skimming past us and into a leafy hawthorn bush. I let fly at the bush and got the shock of my life when the spuggy tumbled onto the grass, flapped its wings weakly and died.

'Great shooting, Sid!' yelled Alan.

Even Eric, usually grudging with any approval of my actions, nodded his freckled nose.

I was totally devastated. I had coldly killed one of God's creatures. My granny Mary-Jane was giving me a kind of pre-Catholic morality coaching course after our church visits before I got started on confessions, communions and all that business. Killing an innocent sparrow was definitely a venal sin. I shed hot tears. Eric and Alan were crying as well – with laughter. I found a stick and scraped a shallow grave. I laid the warm soft body in the hole and heaped grass and dock leaves on it. Then I sank to my knees, closed my eyes, clasped my hands and began reciting a bit of the Catholic confession ritual I had picked up. 'Oh, my God, because thou art so good, I am very sorry that I have sinned against you and I will not sin again.'

I made an oath to myself to confess the sin when I had been trained up in the Faith enough to make my first proper confession.

When Alan finished the story, Robert and Tot laughed long and loud. They were continuing the Waddell heathen tradition.

On Christmas Day the first couple of chickens cooked up nicely and were well appreciated by all of us. The others became the centrepiece of our New Year celebrations a week later. Because Vesting Day coincided with New Year's Day 1947, my parents had a Hogmanay that was higher on the hog than usual. At that time – and to this day – New Year was celebrated more than Christmas in the towns and villages of Northumberland. The Scottish traditions of heavy drinking, feasting, open house and first-footing were observed for several days. My granny

Mary-Jane and my uncle Sam came to stay, leaving Uncle Sonny in the capable hands of friends. For the first time in my life I was allowed to stay up till midnight 'to see the New Year in'.

All day long Martha and Granny baked cakes, pies and sausage rolls. Dad and Uncle Sam went out and brought in bottles of beer and two bottles of whisky. A bottle of 100 per cent Alnwick Brewery Rum and a giant wedge of Cheddar cheese – probably stolen by Granny from John William Allen's shop – were put in pride of place on our sideboard. Then at about eight on New Year's Eve, Bob, Martha and Sam got dressed up and went off to Lynemouth Social Club. After supper I watched Granny sup sweet stout and smoke her clay pipe while I drank Tizer and tried to make a model plane. This always got messy because I used a razor blade to cut out the balsa-wood bits and kept nicking my knuckles. My planes never flew, but looked good painted silver with dark blood-red trim.

Then, just as I was starting to yawn, all hell was let loose. First, Uncle Sam, curly hair flying, legs akimbo and eyes ablaze, fell through the door. He kissed me with breath that stank of beer and Woodbines. Martha staggered in after him, bleary-eyed and bouncy with high spirits. She kissed me and laughed, then kissed her mother and wept. Bob was stone-cold sober and I sensed his disapproval.

'Peevy,' said Granny, hiding her pipe in the coal bucket, 'They are weel peevy.' Soon my uncle Tommy Chester and his wife Elsie arrived. Tommy was well gone with drink and Elsie was not pleased. As his chatter became faster and louder, her face scrunched up as though she had been eating raw gooseberries. Cousin Robert came just before midnight, red-faced and shirt-tail hanging out, and was allowed to drink shorts, even though he was only 16. Then came more jolly revellers, in the form of my wild uncle Bill and his girlfriend Olive. Bill had a demob suit on and a scruffy white silk scarf knotted at his throat. His eyes were red and he had not shaved for a while. He kissed everyone, including the men. Olive was in a black fur coat that seemed to have come off a ragman's cart and her scarlet lipstick started at her nostril and reached nearly to her chin. She smearily kissed me and made tracks to the gin.

A few minutes before midnight the back door was opened and people went quiet. Then there was the sound of Big Ben booming from the radio and the pit buzzer began its hoarse rhythmic whooping. Every light in Ellington Colliery over the fields seemed to be blazing. To the right of the colliery rows even the smeared black silhouette of Betty looked magical in the frosty, starry glow. The crowd began kissing each other and me. Then they formed a rocky, stumbly ring and sang 'Auld Lang Syne'. Uncle Sam had to be supported and kept from falling in the fire.

Martha grabbed me and began rubbing my face with coal. She painted my brow and cheeks like I was an Indian brave going off after his first scalp. I was handed a bottle of whisky and pieces of coal – for warmth and comfort – then pushed outside to re-enter as the First-Foot. I was no tall, dark stranger but instead a little mousey-haired familiar. I was hugged and kissed stupid. And even though I was only six, New Year became my favourite night of the whole year. Our little village became for a short time as warm and cosy as any in my storybooks.

The celebratory mood continued the next morning. Again Mam and Granny began baking and, at around 11.30, Bob and Uncle Sam started to get ready to go to the club. Sam put on a Northumberland Fusiliers tie and a smart jacket, while my dad went out like a schoolteacher – tie with tiny knot, Brylcreem, best suit, waistcoat and watch and chain. They would have a bit of 'jollification', a few pints and a game of bingo like always, but this New Year's Day was one of celebration and history in the making.

The dinner was ready at half past two but there was no sign of the menfolk. Granny and Mam were having a glass of shandy each and their faces were tight as they avoided each other's eyes. The door clashed open just after three and Sam barged in, singing and unsteady. He tried to give Martha a hug, but she shrugged him off. Bob shuffled in behind him, face sagging, tie loose, thin strands of hair sticking up. 'Sorry, pet,' he slurred.

It was the one and only time I ever saw my father drunk.

Halfway through the now ruined meal, Sam tried to laugh off the lateness and the drunkenness. They had been persuaded to go to a pitch and toss school behind Ellington vicarage. When Mary-Jane and Martha expressed shock at them chucking the family money away, Sam blew his top. He poured more Double Maxim and began swearing. 'Can't a man have any effing fun?'

Bob tried to take the glass off him and there were nearly blows.

The meal was finished in silence, with my mother sniffling through tears. Bob himself started to cry and he put his arm around my mother. Through the heavy silence the fire popped merrily. Suddenly my dad went to the coal bucket and chucked the lot on the flames. 'There, Mary-Jane, that should keep you happy. Gan and warm yer arse if you like.'

I was shocked by my dad saying a rude word, but it broke the gloomy mood and faces brightened. Even Granny nearly smiled. But Bob was not finished. He went to the window and pointed over the fields to Betty and the new National Coal Board flag fluttering over the pulley wheels.

'I hev to gan doon that bugger every day. And today of all days is no time for arguing. That pit and all the pits now belong to us. The greedy buggers who wouldn't pay for safety or more mechanisation and kept cutting wor money are not our bosses any more. The sods will be getting 66 million pounds in compensation, and some of them Portlands, Londonderrys and Priestmans will still be there on the new Coal Board committees. But I'm a happy man today. We've got good men like Jim Bowman pleading our case. When I'm doon that black hole now shovelling me pluck oot, arse scraping the roof and watter soaking me legs, I'll tell myself, "Betty, dee yer worst, cos now you're aal mine."'

My mam, Granny and Uncle Sam were not looking at him. They were staring at the tablecloth. He was not finished.

'And ye knaa who did this? It was Hugh Dalton, Clem Attlee and Nye Bevan – the Labour government – *wor* government. So next time the Duke of Northumberland puts it in the *Alnwick Gazette* that you should vote for the Tory candidate tell him to gan and pelt shite. Now who wants a cup of tea?'

It seemed then that this was one of the most significant moments of my young life. Within an hour I had seen my dad maudlin drunk, eloquent, profane and with political convictions he usually kept well hidden. Bob did not often say much, but when he got going he gave it both barrels.

It was typical of my father that when he began considering a new departure – a very dangerous but highly paid job down the pit – he said very little about it. He did not want Martha and me to get knotted up with worry.

Bob and Martha had high hopes for me, they did not have a clear idea of where I was going but one thing was dead certain: whatever my future held, it would be nowhere near Auld Betty. So hard-earned money was spent on books, encyclopaedias, desks and, later, other glittering inducements for me to 'stick in at school'. In another of Bob's favourite aphorisms, I was to 'Make every post a winning post.' They even gave me a little red diary to record my marks in spelling and arithmetic tests. I remember it had weekly mottos like 'Keep your nose to the grindstone and your eye on the road ahead.' My favourite was 'Moderation is the silken string binding the pearls of all virtues.' Sadly, that went down the tubes – particularly as regards the demon drink – well before my sixteenth birthday.

Then in about February 1948 there was another good reason to boost my dad's earnings. My mother was pregnant. It did not seem to be cause for celebration in our house and I do not remember either of them talking about it to me. With a new baby leaking money, the family coffers had to be topped up and that meant more danger for Bob and more worry for Martha.

The 1,450 men who went down Betty every day were entering a savage environment. Six miles out under the North Sea there were some high seams of well over four feet, but in 1948 they were still working two-feet-six seams, and men had to lie in water to cut coal. In fact, Betty was only kept workable by constant pumping out of water – one million gallons per day. There was very little gas in the pit, so explosions were not a problem. But random falls of stone from the top of shafts killed on average one man per year, and in the seven years up to 1948 there were 14 deaths this way. Certain jobs in this environment were very hard, like face-work and hand-filling. But Bob's new job of coalface drawing was the most dangerous down Betty, so it was no surprise that he kept very quiet about it to Mam and me.

The first time my curiosity was stirred was in June 1948 when Bob brought home his pit clothes for cleaning during the two weeks' annual holidays. He had been coalface drawing for a few weeks. We had a small shed outside our bungalow for spades and the wheelbarrow and that's where I went rummaging in the summer of 1948. There was a pile of dusty, mucky clothes; a blue zephyr vest, thick woollen shirt, moleskin 'hoggers' – knee-length trousers – thick long socks and heavy studded boots. By the pile was a carbide lamp that I'd seen before and a black helmet with several dents in it. But now several new items of gear appeared. I was fascinated by them but they sent a shiver of fear up my spine. There was a sharp pick, an axe with a wobbly head and a sharp steel ratchet device attached to a chain. To my young mind it was as if Bob had gone into the torturing business like some of the villains I read about in my pirate books

I was half right; my father's new job, started a few weeks earlier, was sometimes violent and always very dangerous. But the only torture would come if he and his mates weighed up the job wrongly.

The drawers worked in pairs and it was their job to move the conveyor belt forward when a new coalface was to be worked. This was the easy part. The danger came after the hewers – and later mechanical coal cutters – had finished getting the coal from a face and the roof supports – wooden chocks, props and steel planking – had to be pulled out. Pillars of coal had been left to help keep the roof up, but when the girders and props were ratchetted out by chains and brute force, the roof

This is coalface drawing, the very dangerous job my dad did for many years. The drawer is removing a prop and hoping not too much of the roof falls down.

caved in. If the drawers got it wrong, or Auld Betty was in a bad mood, they could be trapped, injured or killed in seconds. In worked-out faces the timber props were twisted at crazy angles and the metal ones bent like reeds in the wind. In this black jungle two sweaty men heaved and writhed like serpents, tools seemingly part of their very bodies, with the roof only inches above their heads. They were pitting every sinew against the living earth. Bob did this job for the next ten years and the biggest pay packet he ever brought home in that time was eleven pounds ten shillings, and that was as late as 1958.

I did not mention my deep fears that my father would be killed in the new job to anybody. Not to my parents, my pals Alan and Eric, nor to Uncle Sam or my granny Mary-Jane. But my newfound zeal for religion should have been a giveaway. I went to Mass with Granny and always ended our private prayers at the end with 'and please, God, keep me dad safe down the pit'. It was also the punchline when I kneeled at the end of my bed saying my private prayers. Because my mother was pregnant and restless at night, she was sleeping alone in our best room while I snuggled up each night with Dad in their big bed. I hugged to him very close as he told me bedtime cowboy stories of Hoot Gibson and Tom Mix and Swank, the brave rabbit-chasing Waddell dog.

I also went for an each-way bet: to Christian prayers I added a host of eccentric pagan superstitions. When I went to the Corn Exchange or Playhouse cinemas in Alnwick on Saturday nights I always sat in the same seat – right in the middle of the very front row. I always walked along exactly the same streets on the way to my convent instruction, counting off railings in multiples of three, and never stepping on cracks in the pavement. When I went to the little font in church I dipped in exactly three fingers to bless myself. Whenever I entered my granny's I genuflected to the plaster Josephs and Marys and turned three times anti-clockwise.

But it was all to no avail. What I feared and had tried to protect my

The year is 1948 and I am in front of our bungalow in full Red Circle gear. Note the second-hand girl's bike.

father from happened, and I don't know what sin of mine was to blame. It was not sloth, as I was doing well in school. Covetousness was a distinct possibility. I had a bike but I was ashamed of it. It was a shiny cherry-red job and went well with my Red Circle gear but it had no crossbar; it was a girl's bike, handed down by my cousin Brenda McLawrence. Eric and Alan had made a couple of smart cracks about a 'lass's bike' and I was eager for a birthday replacement – with drop racing handlebars, derailleur gears and a saddle skinny enough to slice slivers off your buttocks. I broke my own rules and added a request for a new bike to my prayers.

I used to get home from school at half past three and quite often my mother would be noticeably tense. She would be smoking Woodbines one after the other and looking out of the window at the pit. Her belly would be jutting out of her pinny and she would suddenly hurl herself into cooking or making cakes. Then the pit buzzer would go, meaning that the back shift was over. This would signal a dissolving of tension and she would ask me about my day at school. If the buzzer went earlier it meant that there was an accident, possibly a serious one, at the pit.

One warm July afternoon I was kicking a ball around our small lawn and thinking of running up Cresswell Road to meet Dad. His hair would be wet from a shower at the pit baths, but coal dust would still smear the hollow of his eyes. He would sit me on the handlebars of his old bike with its squeaky chain and sing us home, 'Clap hands for Daddy coming doon the wagon way, a pocketful of money and a cartful of hay.' As I was deciding whether or not to meet him, suddenly the buzzer began its throaty whoop and I heard my mother scream. I ran inside and saw her goggling at the sideboard clock. It said that it was only twenty minutes to four. Accident!

I ran next door and pulled at Hilda Dowson who was reading a magazine and smoking in front of her fire. She had her stockings rolled down her fat blue-blotchy legs. She ran after me into our house.

'It could be Bob. It could be Bob!' My mother was hysterical. She was tugging at her hair and banging gently with clenched knuckles at the bulge under her coloured pinny.

Hilda made her sit down, gravelly voice intoning, 'Yee divvent knaa, Martha. It could be summat serious or it could be nowt. It could even be just a deed pony.'

That concept made my mother cry even harder. Hilda made strong tea and lit up comforting Woodbines for her and my mam. I went into my parents' bedroom, got down on my knees by his side of the bed, clutched at the sheets that had been covering him just hours before, and began praying. 'Please, God, mek me dad alreet...'

By twenty past four my mother was frantic. The latest Bob was ever home was ten past. Then there was a knock at the door. Hilda went to open it and she led a colliery deputy in pit clothes into our parlour. He looked solemn but not devastated.

'It's Bob, isn't it? He's deed!' My mother's scream cut to my very quick.

The deputy bent over her chair and took her hand. 'There has been a fall of stone, Mrs Waddell. Bob and his marra are trapped. A bit more of a roof in the Fourth West than they expected came away. It's just gravel and shale, we think, not big stones. There's been banging with picks and shovels from their side, so we assume they're not too bad.' By way of further consolation, he added, 'It happens aal the time with the drawers.'

It seemed to calm Martha but it did nothing for me. I had visions of my dad gasping for air and calling out for me and Mam.

The deputy took my mother, wrapped against the shock in our best Otterburn plaid rug, out to his car. Hilda sat with me and gave me Tizer and Blue Riband chocolate wafers till I felt sick. After I'd had them I went into the bedroom and prayed, asking God to make my daddy all right and that for now he should forget about the fancy bike. Then Cyril came in and we made a camp from pillows and tipped-up dining chairs and played in it. I tried to set my lip and jut my jaw and be a big laddie. And I only cried a couple of times because God was surely on my dad's case.

They brought him home at about nine. An ambulance stopped outside and he was brought in on a stretcher. By now my auntie Bab, the sister closest to Bob, was with us and even her tough face burst when she saw him; it was a sight to make anybody weep. The stretcher men made to put him on the settee but he grunted 'No' and pointed to the buffet by the fire. I realised that even bashed to bits he did not want to cover the settee in muck, sweat and blood. He was propped against the wall, arms and legs flopped like a stringless puppet.

He was still in his pit clothes. His boots had new dents and the hoggers were ripped and bloody. Under his jacket there was blood on the vest. His face was like a turnip somebody had been cutting to make a 'miggie', a Halloween mask. There was coal and dried blood all down his chops and his eyes were glazed. I went over and tried to pull off his pit helmet. It would not budge; the fall of stone had jammed it tight. Auntie Bab, practical as ever, rubbed Vaseline round the rim and coaxed off the helmet. My mother began to scream when she saw the black and blue bruise along his hairline. I picked up his carbide lamp, which had fallen from the hat.

'I'll be alreet,' he whispered. Auntie Bab poured a shot of the New Year whisky and he sipped it.

Martha heaved at her pregnant belly and nipped out her Woodbine with her fingers. 'Run the bath, Sidney.' I did. The two women stripped Bob and helped him to the bath. I looked at the red welts down his back and the deep cuts on his knees. 'Ye'll nivvor gan back doon that bliddy pit,' screamed Martha. He kissed her on the forehead and gave her a look that said the opposite.

Nobody had seen fit to take my dad to Ashington Hospital to see if there was internal bleeding or any broken bones. He had walked out of the pit with a bit of help, hence he was okay. They would expect him back pronto. In fact, he took the next four days off. The weather was nice, so he spent a lot of time looking at his prize leeks. The big Leek Show was about eight weeks off and he thought he could get in the top 20 and maybe win a canteen of cutlery or some posh crockery for Martha. He had been given the seeds from a local expert grower called Joe Dixon, and he dished out no tat.

I watched through the window as he dug with a trowel and pulled tiny weeds from round the white barrels of the leeks. He felt at the bottle-green flags as if they were finest silk. It was like watching a master tailor weighing up his raw materials. He was in shirtsleeves and wearing his old battered cloth cap. If the cap peak was tilted to the side it meant he was puzzled: did the leeks need more water or urine or sheep's blood? If he pulled the cap down low over his nose to the Andy Capp position, it meant he was concentrating. When he was satisfied his leeks were flourishing he would tilt the cap back and let the sun hit his balding pate.

On this occasion he finally tilted the cap back and hunkered down like a kid about to chuck marbles. Then the cat from next door swooped at a little sparrow pecking for worms on the lawn and Bob went mental. He hurled his trowel like a spear at the cat, screaming 'Away wi' yee, you swine.' He missed but the beast raced off, spitting. He was always one for the underdog, was Bob.

CHAPTER SIX

A Right Holy Show

Just like I had eight years before, my brother Derrick Robert Waddell came into the world at my granny's tiny house in Clayport Street, Alnwick. The date was 11 October, 1948, and this time my father was around for the birth. He and I had been alone at our house for a week and Hilda Dowson next door had kept an eye on me before and after school until Dad came home. I didn't know how I felt about the arrangements; on the one hand I missed Mam, but on the other, it was good to have Dad to myself and the house was certainly more peaceful. As the day of the birth had drawn nearer Mam had been short-tempered and tearful and now Mary-Jane was bearing the brunt. But Martha had not left before leaving us with mountains of broth and home-made bread and cakes. She was not going to have the Waddell sisters accusing her of neglecting her menfolk.

Now Dad had taken a few days off from the pit and I was taken out of school for the momentous event. It seemed to me that there was a lot of hanging around in this baby-making job. Mam and Granny were talking with the midwife in the bedroom while I sat in the parlour with Dad. Occasionally Mam would emit a loud yell.

'What's Granny doing to Mam?' I cried.

'Don't worry, lad, that's just the baby coming,' said Dad, but he was looking a bit worried himself.

As Martha's cries became louder and more frequent, I burst into tears and would not be comforted. Bob told me to go out for some fresh air and I ran out of the house like a scalded cat. I hated the baby for hurting Mam and wished it would go back to where it came from. After half an hour of mooching around the streets I gathered enough courage to go back to the house of torture. I could hear the howls ten yards from the door and this time it wasn't my mother making the noise. My new brother certainly had a good pair of lungs. I ran into the bedroom to find my father holding up what looked like a skinned rabbit. The new arrival had thick curly black hair. There were still streaks of blood on him. My mother lay on the bed exhausted but triumphant. She had a celebratory Woodbine – she had never stopped smoking during her pregnancy – and a cup of tea.

Later on I was sent to Baines's corner shop for my granny's messages and as I came out, a tall cadaverous man in a suit grabbed me by the arm. He told that he was the man from the local school board and he demanded to know why I wasn't at school.

'Ah'm not from here. I gan to school over at Ellington. I'm on holiday because my mam has just had a babby.'

He did not look convinced, so I led him to the end of Granny's close and he heard Derrick screaming at full pelt. He believed me then and went about his business.

The baby provided an extra catalyst for my granny Mary-Jane to extend her emotional blackmail of my parents. It had always been understood that I was to be brought up as a good little Catholic, despite the fact that I went to a Protestant school. Hence the regular visits to St Michael's church for Mass, with Granny showing me the ropes. But a couple of weeks after Derrick's birth, Granny came up with a wheeze that locked me, my brother Derrick and my mam into a Saturday ritual that over the next few years became a tedious and hated chore.

I remember playing cricket on my own up the end of the close with the lavvy door as a target for my strokes with the bat, and hearing odd bits of the debate inside Granny's parlour.

'So I will get to see bonny little Derrick every week,' she cooed. 'And

Sidney will spend every Saturday morning at the convent with Sister Theresa, learning the Catechism.'

Every Saturday morning? The words were a death knell to my weekend social life. Up to now our Saturday visits to Alnwick had been sporadic, but now they were to be set in stone. Martha liked the idea, since her mother could help with the new baby, and she could help Granny look after Uncle Sonny. Bob went along with the idea because it made Martha happy, and he had got his way about my not being sent miles away to a Catholic primary school. But nobody asked me. Maybe they knew that I would go along with anything that might make God look after my dad down the pit.

So it began, the tedious weekly ritual that would last well into my second year at secondary school.

Just after nine on Saturday mornings Martha, the baby and I would walk up Cresswell Road, me carrying a large holdall for the 'rations'. Eric and Alan, my best pals, would be on the swing in the Swing Field or trying to catch frogs in the ponds. They would call out to me and I would grunt a muted greeting back. Their day would continue at the pictures in Ashington – maybe the weird scary futuristic world of Flash Gordon, or the dafties Abbot and Costello or the glossy heroics of Roy Rogers and Trigger at the matinee – or they'd picnic at Cresswell beach, or go with their dads to watch football at Portland Park in Ashington or even travel all the way to Newcastle to watch the Mighty Magpies, Newcastle United. Fun and frolics all the way. But I was off like a junior John the Bloody Baptist to learn about God, Jesus, and all sins mortal and venal.

With a puff, a wheeze and a rattle a tired old single-decker United bus would pull up at the green bus shelter in Ellington village. We would push our way down the bus full of lady shoppers and families visiting relatives and Mam would joyously greet a few regulars. She'd settle the baby and light up a Woodbine, happy as a P-I-G in parsley when she got a clash going with somebody. Meanwhile, I sucked in the smoke of a myriad fags and looked out the windows at the tatty colliery rows of Widdrington and Red Row, the latter made up of ochre-coloured corrugated-iron cottages in the shadow of a fume-spewing pit heap. My spirits would rise as the view to the east became the golden sands of the fishing hamlet of Alnmouth but then travel sickness would kick in and I would sometimes have to get off the rattler to be sick. It was no fun with a couple of dozen people gawking out the bus window, sniggering at a little boy in 'Red Circle' clobber projectile puking.

Then there would be the relief of gulping in fresh air at the market-place in Alnwick. We would hit Louie's café for brilliant creamy ice cream. Then we would go to the butcher's and get a couple of rabbits, hanging ready-skinned. Just up the street was the baker's shop where we would buy delicious Scotch mutton pies. We would have these later with Oxo gravy for lunch.

This was my patchy preparation for my first piece of 'instruction', which happened in January 1949. At noon on a cold grey Saturday I walked down Bondgate and knocked on the big black door of the convent. In a couple of seconds the door was opened by a bright-faced novice nun, cheeks ruddy like my mam's and wearing a wooden cross a foot long on a string round her neck. I told her I had come to see Sister Theresa and she quietly let me in. There was a tangible silence in the place and a hint of incense. I tippy-toed along a corridor behind the nun; I was scared of blotting my copybook with the venal sin of clumsiness. I was shown into a white room like a cell with two chairs and a table. The only jot of colour was a sacred heart picture with a glowing red candle in it.

The figure who came in after a few minutes added no colour at all to the scene. I had last seen Sister Theresa sipping a small rum at Granny's a few years before, cheeks faintly blotched with goodwill. But now the marble-sculpted face was drawn with concern – presumably for the welfare of Mary-Jane's grandson who must be saved from the wiles and ways of the heathen Waddells. Her grey eyes were calm glittery slits, her purplish lips thin as razor blades. When she spoke, it was like specks of hailstone rattling on a glacier. It was clear that this lady was with me to do business – God's business.

'Your grandmother Mary-Jane is one of the holiest women in Alnwick, Sidney. She wants you to follow in her footsteps. And I am here to teach you how.'

So that was the score right from the kick-off. Goodbye Roy Rogers. Goodbye Trigger. Goodbye Abbot and Costello. Hello sackcloth and ashes. From outside filtered the Saturday sounds of happy kids on their way to the Pastures, the grassy banks below Alnwick Castle. Traffic swooshed past on the Great North Road, taking young folk to pleasures of the flesh like football or beachcombing. And here was I, just eight years of age, taking the first step on a road that could lead me to becoming a priest, or even Pope Sidney I, a move that would have sent Martha and Mary-Jane into raptures.

Sister Theresa outlined her master plan, fully discussed with Martha and Mary-Jane, for my path to the heart of holiness. Over the next two years I would be prepared to enter the Faith, climaxing in a glorious Confirmation in Granny's 'home' church, St Michael's, next door to the convent. I would have a holy sponsor, wear a suit and white carnation, even carry an ivory-white Bible. In echoey solemn words I was told that when I was sufficiently schooled in the tenets of the Catechism – knowing 200 pages off by heart – I would have my first Confession and Communion. These rituals would continue weekly till I could parrot on all the creeds, responses, prayers and know when to kneel and when to stand up during Mass. Meanwhile, in the alien heathen world I lived in, I was to live as clean and pure as I could.

In the top class at Ellington primary school a buxom, sporty lady called Connie McKintosh, the headmistress, was grooming a bunch of us to pass the 'Scholarship'. The Scholarship, or '11-plus' exam, was the big watershed in one's young life. If you passed you went to the grammar school and on to a career as a teacher, perhaps, or white-collar work such as a bank clerk, or on to a mining college to be taught a skilled trade that would lead you to become an electrician or engineer in the pits. Failure meant a few more years at school, then a job in a shop or factory for girls; for boys farm labouring, council manual jobs or unskilled pit work.

Eric Appleby was one of my best pals and it was generally accepted that he would pass the Scholarship. He was better in the crawling-to-'Miss' stakes than I was, he even put apples on Mrs McKintosh's desk in the morning. His dad was a bit of a gardener and the apples were green cookers, but apples were apples. I would do anything to upstage Eric.

One day I moved from my desk in the back row and sat next to my girlfriend Joy Taylor. There was a murmur of shock. Eric looked peeved and Joy blushed. But 'Miss' merely nodded warmly. It had been a struggle to claim Joy for my own. Since Joy's best friend June and I had unveiled the bench together a couple of years back, June had kept giving me google eyes. But I preferred pretty, sweet quiet Joy to her brazen gobby pal.

Joy was lovely, though she sometimes smelled a bit of horses. Her dad was the chief horsekeeper at the pit and Joy often helped him feed and groom the ponies. But on the night I escorted her to the First Linton Wolf Cubs' Christmas social and beetle drive she exuded only beauty. Eric, with no escort, could only look at us with an envious snarl.

Now dibbing and dobbing with the cubs should have been a positive moral influence on me. Sadly, Eric and I disgraced the woggle, lanyard and the rest of the uniform. One evening after cubs we went into the phone box next to the vicarage at Ellington and tried out a trick some older lads had taught us. They said if you stuck a knife in the slot and pressed the A and B buttons the money would flow out. I had found an old jackknife and presto! ... it worked. We put the loot in our cub caps and ran off, chuckling.

Two days later as I arrived at school I noticed that the Sunbeam car of Mr Bennett, the man from the school board and a ringer for Boris Karloff, was parked on the road outside. A cold knife stabbed my spine. In the five minutes before the bell rang I stood near the wall, tight-lipped. I saw Eric but said nothing. On the bell we went into the top class. Mrs McKintosh caught my eye and turned away damp-eyed. Mr

Bennett, in a dark suit, looked around like Dracula biding his time. Eric's freckles were standing out like currants in snow.

'A pupil of this school has done something very serious, involving money from a phone box.' Mrs McKintosh's voice contained half a sob.

A pupil? There were two of us, I wanted to shout out.

She continued, 'Sidney Waddell was seen poking in the slot with a knife and taking the money.'

All eyes turned to me. I gritted my teeth and glowered back.

Miss beckoned me to the front. I walked out with my eyes on the floor. Mr Bennett looked down his nose at me as though I was vermin. I stopped, half-turned to the class and shouted, 'I wasn't on my own. Eric Appleby was with me, Miss'.

Eric's face went from white to beetroot to purple and he started to cry. He walked forward and stood beside me. Miss's eyes flared with pure disappointment. Mr Bennett took his cue and launched into a well-practised sermon about what happened to bad lads. They would be taken away from their homes, locked up in 'reformatory schools' – my mind boggled with visions of Dotheboys Hall – or sent on the training ship moored at the nearby port of Blyth. Eric wept buckets at every detail and I nearly made my bottom lip bleed with biting it. I could distinctly hear Eric sniffling about his mother. She would belt his much-abused ears for sure. But neither set of parents ever heard about our dishonour. I think 'Miss' persuaded Mr Bennett to let it slide.

I walked home alone that day. Eric had seriously fallen out with me and so, it seemed, had all my classmates. I thought it was because of the 'crime' until Alan Robinson came up behind me, yelling, 'Telly pie tit! Telly pie tit!'

I had broken the most important rule of the playground: do not sneak on your friends. My Catholic instruction was turning me into a vindictive, judgemental prig.

At this time I also started to give vent to alarming outbreaks of uncontrollable temper. One of my dad's most treasured possessions was a punch ball, a battered leather contraption that was suspended on thick elastic that hung in the doorway of our bathroom. We also had a pair of lumpy boxing gloves and Bob had shown me elementary forms of jabbing and upper cutting. This was a very practical skill; it might lead to the pro-boxing ring or help on Saturday nights up Ashington if you chatted up the wrong lass. One night I listened rapt to an exciting fight on the radio with Dad – a posh-voiced bloke named Barrington-Dalby commentated – and afterwards I started lacing into the ball. I got carried away and hugged the ball as if it was a wrestling opponent. I was screaming 'I've got you!' and jumping off the ground. Then, with a clatter, the elastic snapped and the whole set-up crashed to the floor. White-faced, my father dragged me bodily into the front room and smacked me hard with his hand on the back of the thighs half a dozen times.

'You have got to behave,' he muttered, near to tears himself. He turned to my mother and said, 'You spoil him too much. He's got to learn to behave.'

Martha could not bear to watch, but her silence confirmed that she agreed with my father.

The brick-and-wall incident, however, was much more serious.

Some pals of Bob's had just finished building us a new brick wall outside our bungalow. It was about four feet high and six feet long and it stretched from our coal shed to the Dowsons' garden. One afternoon Cyril Dowson's friend Sort Whalley, a lad of about 11, came to see Cyril. I was with my friend Alan Robinson and as Sort leaned his bike against our new wall I saw red.

'Get that bike away from our new wall,' I yelled.

Sort sneered, as much as to say 'Piss off, kid!'

I picked up a jagged half brick the builders had left and held it high. 'Move that bike or yee'll get this.'

He started to laugh. Alan waved his arms at me, begging me to back off. Instead, I let fly and hit Sort with the brick on the left cheek just under his eye.

There was blood everywhere. Cyril ran out, saw the damage and began calling me all the daft bastards. My father came out of our house and Sort calmly told him what had happened. This time my dad did not cry. He told me to take down my short trousers and underpants, got a belt and thrashed my bottom soundly. Alan watched. Then I was gated, nobody was allowed to come to visit me. I was ordered to hurry home from school each day, and I was confined to the sitting room, only used for special occasions, after tea.

The wild Waddell blood, a torrent in Uncle Bill, and later a flood in Cousin Tot, was in my veins. There would be more times in the years ahead when I let fly with no thought of self-preservation or consequences.

Despite my dad making good money at coalface drawing, and a take-home pay of about six pounds ten shillings a week when the national average wage was about five pounds, we never took a real 'annual holiday' like some other Ellington mining families. In the two-weeks miners' holidays in June some folk went to Blackpool or Butlins at Filey. We did not have a car, so went to Alnwick for the odd few days on the bus. Mam and Dad were saving hard for my future and that of my brother Derrick. I remember my dad once looking at me doing my junior school homework and saying, 'Stick in, Sid. You're a good scholar and I want you and the bairn to get good jobs. There's nee way you two are gannin' down Betty.'

It was the deep moral imperative of my parents. For my brother and me, there was to be no drudgery, danger or stark poverty like Bob and Martha had experienced. It ranked above my mother's vow when anybody talked of another war: 'I'll dress wor Sid up as a lassie in ringlets and ribbons before I let them take him for a soldier.' Despite her misgivings, years later, she did let Derrick sign on with the Royal Air Force.

During July of 1949 we spent a few days at my granny's. On the Saturday night Mam, Dad and Uncle Sam went off to the Crown pub at about seven. Derrick was asleep in his cot and Uncle Sonny, getting worse year to year, was in his room, occasionally moaning softly, 'Mammy, Mammy.'

Granny would put down her clay pipe and go and talk to him as though he was still in nappies. A few minutes later Granny came back to her rocking chair and her Mackeson sweet stout. About an hour later she lit the gas mantle and put half a shovelful of coal on the fire. Then I stopped making a Sabre jet model plane and asked for the money for pop and chips. She stumped up and I ran to Jack Carlisle's chipper and got us both fish and chips, with a bottle of American Cream Soda for me.

I was on my third glass of pop when Granny said, 'That's enough pop, my laddie.'

With dumb greedy insolence I drained the glass. 'I want to go to Baines's shop for sweets,' I said flatly.

'You've had enough sweets this week. No more.' She pointed the pipe at me menacingly.

'If you don't give me the money for sweets, I'll tell Auntie Jean about that pipe.'

As soon as the words left my mouth and I saw the hurt look on Granny's face, I was mortified.

'I don't think Sister Theresa would like to hear that,' said Granny, reaching in her purse nevertheless.

I took the money and bought the sweets, but I did not enjoy them. I had blackmailed the holiest woman in Northumberland and it burned in my mind all the way to the convent the next Saturday. I was going to see Sister Theresa for my last instruction before my first Confession and Communion. I intended running a carefully generalised list of venal sins, of the flesh and of the mind, past her after we'd done the 'parrot session'.

Things started well. I rattled off the early bit of the Catechism, no bother.

'Who made you?'

'God made me.'

'In whose image and likeness did God make you?'

'God made me in His own image and likeness.'

For half an hour I regurgitated the dos and don'ts list of a good little Catholic laddie, finishing with a recital of the Apostle's Creed and a tricky prayer that starts 'Hail, Holy Queen, Mother of Mercy...' Sister Theresa's lips loosened momentarily in a shadow of a grin. She patted me on the head. I told her that my first Confession, due at five that evening – the pictures at the Corn Exchange started at six – would feature a bit of disrespect for my parents, some impure thoughts and some mild dishonesty. No mention of malice against my pal Eric, semi-erections in dark cinemas or blackmail against my saintly granny. She nodded.

But then I put my foot right in it. I told her that I had been affirming my faith in my religion in debates with Eric and Alan – both Protestants. A flare of passion coloured her pale face and she hissed like the Wicked Witch of the West. 'Never do that again, Sidney. The Protestants are poor misguided people. Avoid them. Never discuss our faith with them.'

Five hours later I entered the Confession box at St Michael's church. People kept coming out and bustling to a pew, kneeling in prayer and rattling off penances. I had one big terror; that the priest would give me as penance several repeats of a prayer I did not know. Soon I was in the darkness, kneeling. Through the grille was a bowed eerie shape. I tried to stay calm.

'Bless me, father, for I have sinned … this is my first Confession.'

There was a slight intake of breath, then a sonorous soft indication that I should spill the beans.

'I have … er … been disrespectful of my parents. I have sworn. I have … er … had impure thoughts.' No reaction. 'I have told lies...' Nothing. 'I have missed Mass, morning and night-time prayers.' Now the crunch. 'I have been selfish and unfair to friends and relatives.' I remembered the pop and sweets. 'I have been a glutton. And I have wilfully murdered one of God's innocent creatures.'

He took my pause as the end of my list.

'Say ten Hail Marys and ten Our Fathers, my son. And go to your first Holy Communion in a State of Grace.'

I danced out of the box, past the bleeding statue of Jesus and knelt in the row before the altar. This was a doddle. I knew the prayers and half sang them off. Then I ran out into a rainy night. I slipped and tripped against the railings on the church steps. 'Shit!' I yelled. My state of grace had lasted only a matter of minutes.

I avoided gluttony at the movies, having only a packet of fruit pastilles.

I then stayed pure and had only water and a dry bread crust before making my first Holy Communion the next day at ten. I nearly choked when the holy wafer clagged to the roof of my mouth. I wanted to claw it out with my fingers but that seemed no way to treat the body of Christ. At least the priest had a slug of wine to wash his down with. So I went back to my pew between smiling Martha and beaming Mary-Jane and used my tongue as a cement mixer till I swallowed the crumbled host. I reckoned that that was a venal sin at the very worst.

After two years of instruction, and conscientious attendance at Masses, Confessions and Communions, the great day came when Mother, formerly Sister, Theresa announced to me in the spring of 1950 that my struggles had not been in vain. With tears in her eyes she kissed my forehead and announced that a sponsor had been found and I would be Confirmed in the Faith at St Michael's in Alnwick in one month's time. My granny cried, my mam hugged me and even my dad seemed impressed. My uncle Sam was so overcome he had to go to the Bird and Bush and get blotto. I was taken down the street to a tailor and measured up for a charcoal-grey suit. It would come with a waistcoat and would cost nine pounds and ten shillings – a week-and-a-half's wages to my dad. He rationalised that it would keep Mam and Mary-Jane happy. Generosity to the Catholic cause would also be ammunition for him when the debate came about which grammar school I would go to;

would it be with the Catholics at St Cuthbert's, Newcastle, which was 20 miles away from Ellington, or with the Protestants at Morpeth, only six miles away?

Over the next two weeks there was talk of little else but my Confirmation. But a bombshell landed in Clayport. We did not have a telephone, so Mary-Jane could not get the bad news to us. We walked into her house on the Saturday and her face was set like thunder.

'Father bloody Mullarkey has written to Mother Theresa saying that because Sidney lives outside the parish of St Michael's he cannot be Confirmed at my church. He says he will put him on the list for Ashington.' She paused. 'I'm not having my laddie Confirmed in a bloody brick shed!'

St Michael's looked like a church, with crenellations and spires; Ashington's Catholic church looked like a jerry-built fire station. Granny was not finished.

'If Father bloody Mullarkey does not change his mind I will go down to the pant on Sunday and sing with the bloody Band of Hope!'

What a threat this was. It might even make its way to the pope himself. Saint Mary-Jane Smith of Alnwick, the Holiest Woman in Northumberland, shaking a tambourine and singing with a bunch of teetotal Prots!

My granny was true to her word. On the next Sunday evening at six, my granny, dressed in her Paddington hat and a second-hand coat with black fur collar, stood with the 'Bandies' and sang her heart out. And it did not do one jot of good.

Three months later, I went to my Confirmation at the 'brick shed' in Ashington. In support were Mum, Dad, baby Derrick and a few Prot Waddells, who looked puzzled by all the standing up and kneeling down. I had my new suit on and a white carnation and my Alnwick sponsor was at my right hand.

Mary-Jane boycotted the ceremony. On our next visit she sat with her pipe and pronounced the entire episode 'a right holy show', her words for a complete farce. And I noticed that Mother Theresa and her mates called at Clayport much less often. And as a result of this betrayal the name 'Father Mullarkey' became a byword for high treason and perfidy throughout the Waddell and the Smith clans.

CHAPTER SEVEN

The Real Red Circle

*My ten-year-old head was full of tuck-shop fun and scrapes with
rotters, but I found Morpeth Grammar School more earthy
than the ivory towers of my comics.*

From the early summer of 1950 the question of whether or not I would
pass the Scholarship dominated my life, even though the decisive exams
were almost a year away. I woke up in the night sweating about it and it
was added to the litany of my regular morning and night prayers about
the welfare of our family.

'...and please, God, let me pass the Scholarship and go to Morpeth
Grammar.'

I was a bookish kid by nature, so swotting was no problem. As well as
reading stories of high adventure and poring over the boys' papers, I

loved opening my children's encyclopaedias and looking at lists of butterflies or foreign stamps or drowning in passages about dramatic deeds from English history featuring the likes of Robin Hood, Boadicea and King Alfred of cake-burning fame. I was obsessed with the heroes of the boys' papers *The Wizard, The Adventure* and above all *The Hotspur*.

We sometimes went to Morpeth on Market Day and I goggled at grammar school pupils who wore black caps with a badge, a gold tower with red and white stripes, and blazers with gold sports badges on them. I will never know whether I was seduced by the plumage or whether the miner's brat had deep yearnings to mix with the sons of shopkeepers, farmers and doctors. I just knew then that it was the most important goal of my life to make it to that school. And Bob and Martha had their own psychological input at the time; their method of getting me to aim high was pure carrot and stick.

I was the last of my trio of friends to get a real racing bike. Eric had a boring black Raleigh racer. Alan had got a new, unbranded machine courtesy of the Co-op tick system. I still had to make do with the shabby red girl's bike, handed down to me by a cousin, that I'd had for two years. So, on our trips to Cresswell, I would make up a pathetic third 'racer'. Alan would pedal madly and smash on the brakes in the gravel outside Brown's ice-cream shop, flinging up shale like a speedway star. Eric would match this by riding no hands down the last of the hill. And I would putter in in third place and fling my apology for a bike against a fence.

All that changed at about half past seven in the morning of 10 August 1950, my tenth birthday. I was hoping for the usual books with a chemistry set as my 'big' present. My mam called me downstairs, kissed me and so did my kid brother Derrick, who was nearly three. Then, out of the sitting room, Dad wheeled out a bike I had lusted after for years. It was a Rudge racer, frame sparkling in silver-speckled gold. It had drop handlebars, fancy gears, racing caps on the pedals and more chrome work than a Rolls-Royce. It must have cost all of £15. I nearly cried as I got on the saddle, Bob holding the bike for support.

Martha looked at me hard and said, 'Now we want you to stick in and pass that Scholarship.'

I vowed solemnly to both of them that I would stick in harder at school.

The bike was slightly too big for me, even though I had the racing saddle at its lowest setting. That did not stop me leading our trio off round the lanes near Cresswell as if we were in the Tour de France. Eric, Alan and I would pack our saddlebags with tomato sandwiches, Scotch mutton pies and Tizer and shoot off. Quite often the bag joggled so much that the flavours of the pop and food mixed. I was so proud of my new bike that I often raced home from school at dinner time, swallowed my egg or sausage and chips and had a quick spin to the shops for Martha's messages. I got so cocky that within days of getting the bike I came round the curve and down the gradient to our house using no hands. It was bound to end in tears – and it did.

Jimmy Foster was a well-loved local character. He was a chubby, cheery bloke sporting a greasy brown trilby and a khaki smock, who had a travelling shop. Once a week he would show up with his van full of groceries, and local housewives, including my mam, would spend half an hour inside the big van choosing cans and packets and sharing local gossip.

So this day I was in top Tour de France mode. I had just passed Ellington pit and decided the straight half mile to the school was a time trial for the yellow jersey. Up on my toes I went, belly muscles sucked in, arms like whipcord. Jimmy was just giving Patricia Charlton's mother two pounds of new potatoes and asking after her hubby Bill, when there was a bang. Jimmy threw open the back door of the van to see me lying in a heap in the road, blood pouring from my forehead. Worse, the front forks of the glossy bike I'd had for only two weeks were now bent back six inches out of kilter and the front wheel was buckled completely. Bob and Martha were not impressed. And for weeks after, whenever Jimmy came to our door he looked at me quizzically and said, 'Still got that bike?'

My cockiness, reckless bravado and my Red Circle outfit often landed me in trouble with older lads. And there was definitely one place where it was asking for bother to strut your stuff or step out of line. That place was Lynemouth, branded 'Little Chicago' by a local paper because of its gangs of wild youths, some urged to fight at the drop of a hat by dads who had been hard men in their heydays. The top gang, I had been told, was headed by Les Dunning, who was 15, had tight curly hair and a cheeky smile, but was a killer. Les and his brother Ronnie were fearless and often took on much older lads in fights in Ashington and the rough fishing village of Newbiggin. Nearer home, blood had flown under Lynemouth railway bridge when a champion chosen from the Dunning/Batey gang had fought it out with Friar Tuck-type staves against the toughest of the Tunn/Shears gang. I often had to visit Lynemouth to see my cousins and aunties but they lived in the north end of the village, nearest my home, not the south, where the hooligans rampaged.

Nevertheless, one Sunday afternoon while my parents and my brother Derrick were at my auntie Bab's, I ventured out to visit the Welfare sports ground, in the heart of 'Apache' country, where a mass 30-plus per side football game was a tradition. I was wearing an old jersey, black shorts and black plimsolls.

I stood on the sideline and watched as some heavy tackles went in from big lads on little titchy kids. Some kids were eating Mars bars and others jam sandwiches brought out by their mothers. Bottles of pop littered the touchline and swigs were taken regularly. 'Which side am I on?' I shouted.

I was waved on by a big lad pointing south. I took up position on the right wing. Every time the ball came my way I was bundled off it roughly. I drifted into the middle to shoot and was flattened by one of my own team, screaming, 'My ball! My ball!' The mayhem descended to farce when a local character called Chick Charlton, a skinny gangly boy of about 13, was kicked up the bum. Chick raced after his assailant, holding his arse and shouting, 'You should have some human sense!' and a fight ensued.

The game surged on around the punch-up.

Despite the fouls and the fights, there was some real class evident in the match. One of the few lads wearing proper boots was a solemn-looking lad called Jackie Herron. He could well have stepped from the same pages as Baldy Hogan of *The Adventure*. Jackie was 11 but had the physique of a 15-year-old. He dribbled brilliantly, called confidently for crosses and the thwack of his head on the ball was like a rifle shot. Later, in 1956, Jack went to Leeds United to be groomed as the new John Charles. And a few fields away in the pit town of Ashington Bobby and Jack Charlton took part in similar impromptu matches.

The only real violence directed at me personally that day came from Jos Hanson, a stocky lad with wavy dark hair and thick lips. The Hansons were of Norwegian stock and had arrived in Lynemouth via America in the 1920s. Like the Dunnings, they had notoriously short fuses.

'Stay away from wor Stella,' he hissed in my ear as he elbowed me off the ball.

Stella Hanson was the local Lynemouth beauty and she knew it. She was 11 and had given me the glad eye several times. I had taken to sitting next to her uninvited at the local pictures. It did not happen again.

A few days later Alan, Eric and I were playing football with an old caser ball in the Swing Field when some Lynemouth lads approached us. They were led by Jos Mitchell, a tall 14-year-old who was at Morpeth Grammar, his brother Billy who was my age, and a couple of Jos's mates. In no time they had pinched our ball and were playing with it. I ran and grabbed the ball, then tried to escape home with it. Jos grabbed me and I called him everything I could lay my tongue to without offending my extremely moral code of conduct. 'Bugger! Sod! Blighter!' I yelled just like Billy Bunter having a go at the bullies of the Remove.

Jos grabbed me and yelled, 'Let's teach this gobby twat a lesson.'

He and one of the other big lads held me down. They ordered a reluctant Billy to sit on my chest and slap my face. He did, but not very hard.

Then the Waddell cavalry turned up. My cousins Tot and Billy, both with fearsome reputations as battlers, heard the fracas as they were passing on their bikes. They chased off the older lads but pinned Billy Mitchell to the grass. Tot handed me the heavy caser ball. 'Stot it on the fucker's nose,' he ordered.

'But he just slapped me,' I bleated.

'Stot it and dee it hard and the Mitchells will never bother you again,' said Tot.

I did as I was told, making sure the lace landed square on Billy's nose. Blood flew all over and he almost choked on it and pouring snot. My rock-hard cousins just laughed. On future visits to Lynemouth, whenever I got mean looks from the Dunnings, Hansons, Bateys or Hindmarshes, I tried to put on the tough Waddell mask, and prayed the hooligans knew I was one of the clan.

After the fight with the Mitchells, my cousin Tot told me the latest Uncle Bill story. Nobody could keep tabs on Bill's movements, job, if any, or indeed current woman or place of residence. He was like a loose fiery comet in zany orbit round East Northumberland.

'Bill stopped us outside the Hotel and said he'd heard we'd been gannin over to Amble for the dance,' said Tot. 'He said he'd hire us his horse Silver and his big cart. He said it was a snip at ten bob. So me, Billy, wor Rob and a few others took him up on it. We had a canny night and when we got back we unyoked the horse and opened the stable door. Bugger me if there's not a geet scrafflin and Bill and Olive bollock naked on the job in the straw.'

I forced a laugh. But I blushed hard. I knew what 'on the job' meant. It was what bad lads did with racy girls in Ellington farmyard on dark nights. I had heard that the vicar's nubile daughter was involved; these Prots were capable of anything. It was dirty and sinful. Both my granny and mother constantly warned me about girls, 'fast lassies' who could lead me astray and stop my golden progress at the grammar school and beyond.

One of the delights of my mother's life was ballroom dancing. By the time I was ten she had taught me the rudiments of the quickstep, the foxtrot and the waltz. She would put a record on the gramophone, set my arms around her and sashay me round our living room. But that was not enough. She decided that I should be properly trained in tap dancing. Without telling anyone she enrolled me in 'Bert May's Academy of Modern Dance – Ballroom and Tap', in the shadow of Alnwick Castle and within smelling distance of the brewery. We could not afford the proper footwear, so my mam took my second-best black shoes to Basil Morris's cobbler shop in Lynemouth and had metal taps fitted, heel and toe. Basil accepted the job with a smile; he often put studs or bars on normal boots for footballing lads who could not afford the real thing.

The following Saturday morning, in my Red Circle gear, and wearing my newly adapted shoes, I walked the 300 yards from my granny's to Bert's place. The class consisted of three lads and four girls, all about my age. I was the only novice so, as the rest practised to music, I stood in a corner doing a stamp-shuffle-stamp with alternate feet. Bert occasionally left the main group and encouraged me to flick my knees and ankles harder and wave my arms about like aeroplane wings. One hour later I was very bored, but cheered by the fact that Bert promised me a more testing workout with music next week. I stamp-shuffled out on to the street.

They came down on me like moonshine-crazed Comanches on a wagon train. There were four of them and they were led by Chalky, who I had last seen glaring down in triumph at me as I lay with a fractured arm in an open sewer. I began to run, my taps echoing on the cobbles. Chalky kicked at my legs and I tripped over the kerb. He sat on my chest, spitting on my face. I could smell stale piss on his dirty trousers.

'Sindy is a muckle Jessy. Sindy is a rotten Cath!'

He tore at my striped tie, trying to throttle me. I noticed his pals had handfuls of stones ready for pelting. I bucked my hips upward as violently as I could. Chalky was quite skinny and he flew off me. I raced off over the Clay Hills and into the backyard of the Bird and Bush pub, Uncle Sam's main watering hole. Chalky was about ten feet behind me and stones were raining on me. Should I run in the pub and get Sam? No, I decided, a man who defied the Japs for years would expect me to fight my own battles. I had a brainwave. In mid-flight I dropped in a heap on the tarmac. I had used the manoeuvre in the odd scuffle with Alan and Eric. It meant you got the drop on your assailant. Chalky tripped over me and fell against a beer barrel. I was on him in a flash, kicking at his knees and belly with my taps. I was about to start calling him all the bastards when I saw some men come out of the pub. One was my uncle Sam.

'You are nothing but a complete rotter,' I yelled, this being the top insult at the Red Circle.

Sam put his arm around me and Chalky got up. His ratty face was all red and he rubbed at his bruised knees. 'Yee divvent fight fair, Sindy.'

I had to laugh; the nastiest kid in Alnwick lecturing me on Queensbury rules. He slunk off with his cronies and I was never bothered by him again. Uncle Sam showed his pride in me by taking me into the bar of the pub. He bought me a glass of beer shandy and spent the next ten minutes demonstrating a commando elbow smash that I should use next time louts set about me. Nobody seemed to find it odd to see a ten-year-old boy drinking beer and wearing shoes with silver plates on their soles. And the occasion was in fact a double wake; I never went back to Bert May's Academy and I never again fought completely fair.

I had few nerves when I sat the Scholarship exam. We did trial papers for a few weeks before the big day and I had performed well on these. My only qualms were with a few logical aptitude tests that came as a surprise and I found puzzling.

Then came the day when some of us were called out to the front by Mrs McKintosh and handed letters to take home. I never opened a school report in all my six years at Ellington school, and I was not tempted to rip open the brown envelope now. Instead I raced home at dinner time. Martha opened up the letter, told me I had passed and patted me on the head. Egg and chips never tasted better.

At half past three I went home, picked up the letter and ran like the wind to Ellington Colliery. I slowed to a trot as I entered the pit yard.

High above me the giant wheels in their steel cage began to whirr and spin and the buzzer blew for the end of the shift. Suddenly the doors of the double-decker cage opened and a straggle of dirty black-streaked men holding lamps made their way towards me. Two called greeting but there was so much muck on their chops I did not recognise them. I panicked. Which one was my dad?

He came towards me spitting on his hands and wiping the area round his eyes. He smiled when he saw the letter.

'I've passed, Dad. I've passed the Scholarship.'

He patted me on the head. 'You've done well, son. You worked really hard and I'm very proud of you.' It showed in his eyes.

'Ah'll be going to Morpeth, not St Cuthbert's, won't ah, Dad?'

'Aye, that's for sure,' he replied. 'Whatever your mam and your granny say ah'm not having you trekking to the Toon every day. Morpeth is the granny school for you.'

I laughed at the pun.

We walked to the tally cabin and he handed his tokens in. Then he led me into the baths. What a sight! Long ropes dangled from the ceiling with the men's clothes on them. All around naked black-and-white patched bodies wandered, buttocks and bollocks dangling free. Bob announced my success to the world as he stripped off.

'Wor Sid has passed the Scholarship.'

I went pink with embarrassment. Two or three of Dad's pals came over and shook my hand; one man gave me a half-crown and another a florin.

It was the same tune all the next week. We went to my uncle Tommy's smallholding and even crotchety Auntie Elsie gave me a kiss and two big bars of Cadbury's chocolate. My uncle Jack, who lived there, pressed an orange ten-bob note into my hand. I could sense the family and community pride in my achievement.

Sadly, in the middle of our rejoicing a massive black cloud came over our little community. One sunny afternoon I was playing cricket with Alan, Eric and some other lads when an older boy called Billy Hallowell joined us. His father was a miner like ours and Billy, a tough lad who was a good footballer, was sobbing. We dropped our bats and clustered round one of the dustbin lids we used as wickets. He told us that there had been a terrible disaster at Easington Colliery, 40 miles away down the Durham coast. In a great underground explosion 83 men and youths had been killed. We all rushed home in tears. We passed people at garden gates hugging and weeping. It was as if the disaster had occurred over the field at Auld Betty.

In our bungalow my dad, fresh from his shift, sat hugging Derrick. My brother was two and a half, had the Waddell big nose and he was his jolly self, tweaking at Dad's rapidly disappearing quiff. This was in sharp contrast to the tears held back in my father's face and Mum's hysterics. On the wireless was more news of the disaster. The cause of the explosion was thought to be sparks from the picks on a coal cutter igniting firedamp gas. I hugged at my mother, begging her not to cry.

'Could summat like that happen doon Betty, Bob?' Mam asked. I had wanted to ask that question but wasn't sure I wanted to hear the answer.

He spat into the fire and watched the sizzle. 'It's not very likely. There's a bit of stythe in some areas of the pit, but we know them well.'

He was not looking at us when he said this. I felt he was giving us flannel.

The pall over our little villages lasted for weeks. So many people turned up at the funeral service in the church in Easington that they had to put the overspill into the Welfare Hall. Wreaths, flowers and cards came from South Wales and Scotland. The tragedy united the whole British mining community. But it was the photos in the papers that moved me the most; a big cross on the church altar made from real mining picks; old pitmen with bent shoulders and grey heads, gripping their caps in homage outside the church, and, worst, the women of the victims in dark shawls keeping a hopeless vigil as the rescue teams went in. Two of the rescuers died in the operation.

I asked my dad why he and the men of Ellington and Easington had to go down the pit.

'Because it's all we know, son, and it's for you, your mother and the bairn, it's so we can all have a decent life. Mind, yee two will never gan doon bloody Betty.'

He looked at my mother for agreement and all she could do was nod and cuddle Derrick to her breast.

My passing the Scholarship was great news for our friends and family. But it managed to cause a mammoth ruction in my granny's new council flat in King Street, Alnwick.

There was much more room in her new house, so my parents took Derrick and me there for weekend stays more often. A few days after my good news we were sitting in Mary-Jane's kitchen on a sunny Saturday afternoon having sandwich cake after a tinned salmon and cooked ham salad tea. Neither my lot nor my granny had a phone, so she was given the news by Martha over mugs of hot strong tea. She nodded sagely, hawk nose and eyes aimed into her cup. Mam's voice reeked of concern and my dad looked wary. And then my mam said, 'So some of his pals will be going to Morpeth Grammar and that's where he wants to go.' Mam sat back and waited for a reaction.

Granny licked her lips and looked up at the sacred heart on the wall.

'Bob, and you, Martha, promised me that Sidney would be brought up a Catholic.' The words were almost hissed. 'There is a Catholic grammar school called St Cuthbert's in Newcastle and it would be better for his immortal soul if he went there.'

The word soul hung in the air. Mam's face dropped. My dad leaned forward. There was no rapprochement in his eyes.

'That Catholic school is in the west end of Newcastle. To get there means Sidney would have to get on a bus at half past six in the morning, then get two other buses. He'd not get back into wor house till well after six at night. Then he's got homework to do. Don't be daft, woman. He can be at that Morpeth school in less than an hour.'

My little brother Derrick came in chasing a ball and Martha clutched at him and put him on her knee. She looked pleadingly at my dad. His face slackened a bit and his voice became quiet. He pointed at me and Derrick. 'Look. I have to gan doon a bloody pit every day. I divvent like it but ah dee it.' He pointed at Derrick and me. 'Them two will never gan doon Betty or any other bliddy hole in the ground. Wor Sid is a good scholar. He'll mebbes be a teacher or a bank clerk, I divvent knaa. But he'll gan to the best school. That means Morpeth, not a bloody slog aal them miles to Newcastle every day.'

The subject was over. But the hard stares between my dad and my granny carried on all weekend and I knew what they conveyed. Granny was thinking, 'That heathen pitman with the gander's neck' – he did indeed have a skinny neck and big Adam's apple – and Bob in turn thought, 'Bloody old witch'. I had heard each call the other these names under their breath during previous bouts.

So that was that. King Edward VI Grammar School, Morpeth, was informed that Sidney Waddell would like to become a pupil and he was duly accepted. A letter came to our house with a mighty list of what I would need. First, the uniform of cap, tie and badged blazer should be bought from the approved shop in Morpeth. I would need a stout satchel – *not* an ex-army khaki haversack – big enough to take games equipment. Then came a list of bits and bobs for certain subjects: a set square, protractor, ruler, pencils and a fountain pen. I would also need a Bible. This hit Martha hard; they meant a Protestant bible. For the moment we put the problem to one side. I would need a pair of white plimsolls, a pair of rugby boots and two pairs of white shorts for PE and games. A 'house' sports shirt should be purchased when a 'house' was allocated. 'House shirt': no knight's gear of cloth-of-gold ever sounded more glamorous! This was the real Red Circle and no mistake.

My dad was bringing home about seven pounds ten a week and the list added up to over twenty. So off went Martha to Auntie Bab's for a cuppa and a cash loan. We could pay her back when we could afford to. Bab's exterior was harsh but underneath she was the Waddell family's financial reservoir, and she would always err in our family's favour when it came to paying back her money. It was years later that I found out exactly how much Auntie Bab helped us out. I have no doubt others went to her for loans, but I was a special case.

Two weeks before I was due to start the grammar we got everything but the uniform and the satchel at shops in Ashington. Then Martha and I got the bus to Morpeth. I paraded round the shop in the black blazer and cap, not wanting to take them off. We went to look at satchels. There were some cheap plastic ones on display, but Mam led me past them. Thinking about the 'games equipment' and the 'house shirt', I went for the biggest satchel – deep reddish-brown leather, with buckled smaller pockets on the outside.

Back home in Cresswell Road I ran into my parents' room and before the dresser mirror put on the cap, stripy tie and blazer. I was tempted to don the new satchel, but didn't. Then I marched out of the house and paraded up and down like William Brown of the *Just William* books. Thank God Alan and Eric, Scholarship failures both, did not come out of their houses, or else they would have clocked me. I had about as much self-awareness as a wild boar at a swill trough.

Day one dawned bright and clear. I was breakfasted, uniformed and satchelled before my dad left for the pit at half past seven. Playfully he pulled at the tight leather straps cutting into my shoulders.

'You could do with them being loosened a bit,' he said.

I sneered at him and stiffened even more. He patted my four-square cap and went off. The school special bus from the end of our road to Morpeth was due to leave at five past eight. I was there 20 minutes early, standing like a new guardsman outside his sentry box. Each time I moved, my pencils and protractors rattled hollowly in my satchel.

They came upon me like blasé anthropologists sniffing a new jungle species. Three pimply lads in crumply blazers, no hats, with army haversacks daubed with scribbles, sneered at me and giggled. A couple of lasses with green watch caps and pleated green skirts from Morpeth Girls' High yawned and mashed chewing gum. Red Circle? Bloody borstal, more like.

An ancient red United bus rattled up. Nobody cared that I was first in the queue. The scruffs jumped on ahead of me. There were a couple of jeers, at least three 'buggers' and definitely one 'fuck' in the badinage. I took one look at the zoo down the bus and sat down, still satchelled, in the very front seat. The chat behind began to feature 'cocks' and 'fannies' and I felt my neck turning red.

Then a lugubrious male voice began a monologue designed specifically for me. 'I canna wait to grab one of these new starters and ram his heed doon the lavvy and flush it.' Cheers and laughs. 'Or mebbe I'll drop his pants and rub axle grease on his bollocks.' More cheers, some female.

I fought back tears and the desire to rub my strap-seared shoulders.

My first day at Morpeth Grammar continued with a slow nervy trudge up the winding main street of the market town. After the scruffy specimens, both lads and lasses, I had seen on the school bus, I was not surprised at the motley lot I now beheld. Two or three lads I judged to be about 13 had their caps pushed so far back on their heads that you could not see the headgear from the front. Some of the older lads were snogging girls from the High. There were other pristine first years like myself, conspicuous by their new blazers and shiny satchels. What, I wondered, would I do if dunked down a toilet, had my privates roughly exposed or otherwise humiliated? I was as edgy as a half-blind baby hedgehog out alone amongst foxes.

I entered an avenue of pines and rhododendron bushes that framed the russet bricks, Norman arches and high slender turrets of King Edward VI Grammar School. I envisaged myself in front of the giant main oak door holding up the Victor Ludorum trophy for swarming photographers. To my right was a swathe of greensward and beyond that the elegance of the Headmaster's mansion. A tingle of warm optimism flooded my veins, balancing the gnawing fears.

Round the back of the Victorian facade, in front of two high wooden huts, the new boys milled. Three or four older boys in long trousers stood at the four corners of the playground, one with a lanyard and whistle round his neck. The whistle blew and the hubbub dipped. 'All new boys follow the prefects to assembly.'

He and his colleagues guided us like sheep through a high oaken door, down echoey stone-flagged corridors and into a large hall. This was more like it. It was very like St Michael's church in Alnwick without the incense and icons, but definitely Red Circle-ish. The prefects pointed and prodded us new lads, about 50 in all, down to the front. There was the noise of other, older boys piling in, and some of the rookies looked round, impressed but still showing high anxiety. Not me; I was on Cloud Nine. Above the stage were glass cases full of silver sports trophies. And, joy of all joys, there were ancient oak boards with golden letters listing captains of rugby and cricket and winners of scholarships to universities. I closed my eyes and pictured: 'S. Waddell – pity I had no middle initial – Captain of the XV, State Scholar.' I naively plotted a seamless road to glory. I would not swear when my temper erupted, be slovenly or engage in snogging.

A piece of wet chewing gum on the back of the neck broke my reverie. The scruffy rabble behind us new lads were letting rip with random missiles. They did not let up even when a phalanx of black-gowned masters swished down the central aisle and onto the platform. But then the most fearsome bloke I had seen in my life up till that time, the last man onto the stage, turned at the lectern and total silence reigned. He had the head of a Roman senator: marble-white wavy hair, sculpted from a centre parting, the nose of a bald eagle and hooded obsidian eyes. The rimless glasses sat at an angle that seemed to defy any smidgeon of disrespect. The voice seemed to come from the crater of a dormant volcano, dry, but exceedingly dangerous. This was the Beak, G.F. Howell, Headmaster.

I marked the Beak down as a man not to cross. But in the course of the next eight years I managed to do just that.

Half an hour later I was seated in the front row of a classroom already seething at a perceived slight, just like Martha might have done. I was in the front row of class 1B with 24 noisy lads, most of whom, as far as I could judge, came from the pit rows of Ashington and were about as uncouth as you could get. Many were turning and shouting matey abuse at each other. Through the wall there was an impressive silence from 1A – the sons of doctors, farmers and shopkeepers, I had no doubt. Within minutes, I was assured that no segregation was involved. Mr Chas Webster, groomed like a diplomat, forever picking at pieces of imaginary lint on his gown, was our form master and he explained that there was nothing in the class's designations, the division was random. He also explained the system: every fortnight there would be tests and the Top Boy would get to sit at the very back, with the class arranged in order to the plodders and wastrels at the front. And at the end of the year there would be a Form Prize for the brightest pupil; it would be handed out in front of the whole school and an audience of parents on Speech Day at the Coliseum cinema.

I imagined my mam, raven hair sparkling, lipstick and rouge in place, perhaps wearing Auntie Lily's fur coat, sitting amongst the well-off parents clapping her hands off and glowing with pride. Bob, of course, could not afford to take a shift off from the pit, but how his gentle eyes would shine when I showed him the book that was my first Form Prize.

Though it never crossed my mind at the time, I now realise how amazingly fortunate I was. If the Butler Education Act of 1944 had not come into force, abolishing fees for grammar school pupils, there would have been no Red Circle for me. If the coal mines had not been nationalised and wages made stable and fair by the Attlee Government in 1947, our family means would not have been sufficient to support my education. If Bob and Martha had been different people – feckless and selfish instead of frugal and generous – my story would have been vastly different. And God knows where we'd have got without the bottomless purse and good heart of my formidable auntie Bab. Bless her.

CHAPTER EIGHT

Golden Boy

After the initial shock of my first day, I took to Morpeth Grammar like a duck to water. But one very odd chord was struck, one more to do with Desperate Dan, cow-pie eating star of *The Dandy* than the sedate tuck-shop japes of Red Circle. In the second week of term I had just finished school dinner when I was caught up in a posse of lads running up the path to Top Field, our sports ground. I asked a lad what was up and he replied 'Butter eating', as though this was self-explanatory. We raced out of the woods and joined a yelling group of about a hundred boys gathered outside the cricket pavilion. I pushed to the front and saw two fourth-form lads poised over a beer crate on which were stacked a dozen half-pound blocks of best butter. This shocked me; butter, like many commodities, was rationed. What was going on?

Lynn Foreman, a chubby lad with a mighty quiff and crafty eyes wised us all up. He was known as a wheeler-dealer. In fact, during one assembly while the rest of us were singing hymns, I had heard him discussing horse racing. 'Right,' he said now, 'I lay even money on the Pole winning this. Who'll tek six to one against the other bloke?'

The 'other bloke' was a grocer's son, who had pinched the butter from his dad's shop. It appeared the contest was that if the Polish lad ate the most butter, he won three pounds of butter. If the grocer's son won, he got a ten-bob note from the Pole. Betting was brisk, with Foreman taking most bets on the grocer's son, shaking his head as if he knew something the crowd didn't.

Off went the pair. The grocer's son took tiny nibbles, swallowing with a grimace. But the Pole looked as though best butter was his staple fodder. He bit off great gobbets and swallowed them whole. He did the first half-pound in five bites. Lads with their money on the grocer's son yelled 'Snot' and 'Worms' in the Pole's face, but he just grinned through greasy yellow lips. The grocer's son began to vomit during his first pack. Foreman called it victory to the Pole, who finished pack two with a happy belch. I went back to 1B's classroom feeling very queasy.

Happily, other early experiences were more in line with my grand expectations. I had been looking forward to 'Physical Training' when our weekly lesson chart was issued. The master in charge was a short stocky man called Mr Duncan, nicknamed 'Bant' because he strutted like a bantam cock. He also tried to teach us Art. At Bant's instruction we lined up along the wall. 'I will now allocate you to houses,' he said, with real portent.

We all knew that Wright House, who wore red shirts, was the best. But how would we be selected?

Bant, chest out like a sergeant major, walked along the line. He had to look up since some of us – Ted Bowman, a gangly lad from Ashington, and myself for sure – were taller than him. I did a Charles Atlas-type pose and it worked. On Bant's second pass along the line he said 'Wansbeck' to some lads, 'Drysdale' to others, but 'Wright' to me. He put the biggest and brawniest in Wright. His motive became clear a couple of days later when we turned up in our new house tops for our first rugby session; he was the house master for Wright, the Mighty Reds.

Every Wednesday for the rest of that term Bant, Mr Tweddle, who taught French and wore a natty black beret, and Mr Stokoe, a dapper blond who sported a Carnegie College athletics tie, taught us the rudiments of rugby. I loved it. I was tall and broad-shouldered but not very supple. When I played soccer, I could run fast but could not manoeuvre my body with agility, which meant I could not excel at the game. But in rugby, where I played wing-forward, my straight-line rushes were ideal.

Soon I had a new idol to add to the good eggs of Red Circle. He was a ginger firebrand who could run like the wind on the wing. His name was Nigel Savage and he was also in Wright House, although he was a year above me. Whenever I tried talking to him he ignored me. But we often played touch rugby at lunch breaks and a couple of times he crash-tackled me into the schoolyard walls. I chose to read into this that he saw in me a future rival but the smirks on the faces of his friends as I pulled myself up told a different story.

I soon weighed up who I had to beat at lessons if I wanted to sit in the top seat of the class. My main rival was a skinny studious-looking lad from Bedlington Station called John McGinn. Every night after school I went into the bedroom and hit the books mercilessly. I never put on the gramophone and I told my parents to keep *What Cheer, Geordie?* down on the radio. It paid off.

Apart from our form teacher, Mr Webster, and the three masters who taught us rugby, I was particularly impressed by Mr Anderson, our elderly, patient, French teacher. He encouraged us to use our Geordie vowels and gutturals in our spoken French. In his early days as a pupil at Morpeth Grammar he had often walked to school and back from the village of Rothbury, ten miles away. I had ideas of becoming similarly dedicated to the academic life, wearing the gown and teaching here just as he had done.

So it was that I attended my first Speech Day at the grammar school. I sat in the dark of the Coliseum cinema next to Billy Mitchell of Lynemouth, once my enemy, but now one of my pals. On a stage rimmed with flowers sat the Beak and all the robed masters. One by one the prize-winners walked on, buffed up to the nines. Nigel Savage took a prize, massively applauded by his form mates.

At the 'Blackberry Week' half-term holiday of October 1951 I put on my oldest clothes and went potato picking. A local farmer hired schoolkids to bring along their own bucket and gather spuds flung up by a tractor-pulled digger. It was easy for me because the field was opposite our back garden. I'd wait till I heard the first cough of the tractor preparing to make its first run, put on my wellies and balaclava helmet, jump the dyke, shrug through the hedge and start scrabbling

It was hard work; you could bend with your bucket held in one hand or you could kneel in the wet soil and pick with both hands. Method one made you stiff and method two meant your legs from the knee down – I was still in short pants – would be freezing by the eleven o'clock tea break. That was when my mam and others came out with hot drinks and dripping sandwiches. We poured the buckets of spuds into sacks and men with a trailer took them away. On top of the wage – about five shillings a day – each picker was allowed to take a bucket of spuds home each day as a bonus. In addition to my bonus bucket, I popped home through the hedge for lunch and several toilet calls each day, each time taking a full bucket with me, my balaclava and pullover draped over the 'swag'. By the end of the week there were four sacks of spuds in Mam's back kitchen and we were gifting them to my aunties. Mam knew how I had acquired them but, just as with Granny's shoplifting, she turned a decidedly irreligious blind eye.

A few days after my return to school after the holidays, I walked into the house and found my mother in tearful hysterics. Hilda Dowson, hair tangled and pinny mucky as usual, was trying to make her calm down and have a Woodbine.

'The bairn is lost,' cried Hilda. 'Your mam came round about an hour ago and we got talking and your Derrick just wandered off. But we think the little Armstrong lassie is with him. Her dad's out looking now.'

'We need to get the police,' wailed Mam.

'I'll try and find him,' I said, sounding more confident than I felt. 'If I'm not back in half an hour, then get the police.'

I had a quick flash of where the little bugger would be. There were some deep pools at the top of the Swing Field and they had fascinated him on our last visit. In fact, though he was only three, he was sharp on his feet and he had run knee-deep into a mossy pool yelling 'Ploggies!' and tried to scoop up frogs with his hands. Little bloody nuisance, I thought. Derrick was a pain. As a baby, when I was forced to walk him in his pram, he flung rattles and dummies all over. Once on the bus to Alnwick he had scuttled under the seats and been attacked by a cocker spaniel. More than once he had scribbled on my immaculate homework. We now shared a bed in the big back room and he was forever kicking me in the groin. As I raced up the muddy ridges of the Swing Field, I was distraught.

At the most northerly pool I came across Jack Armstrong, our next-door neighbour. He usually had slicked-back Brylcreemed hair, but now it hung over his eyes. It was obvious he had been crying for his lost daughter. 'Any ideas where they can be, Sidney?'

As it happened, I had. Derrick had been fascinated a few days earlier when I walked in with some billycans of blackberries. I told him I'd picked them in Warkworth lonnen, a cart track just over the rise.

'Follow me,' I shouted.

We breasted a rise and headed for the bramble patches among some young pine trees. We heard the sound of kiddies crying, yelps of misery rather than pain. Derrick and Kay Armstrong were tangled in a bramble bush under a collapsed wire fence. Both were caught by the wire and Derrick's curls were snarled in briars. I lifted the wire and Jack pulled them out. Derrick squealed as the thorns scratched his head. He started to speak and I could hardly keep my laugh in. Both kids had blackberry juice all over their chops.

'She got stuck,' whined my brother. 'Then ah got stuck mesell!'

Then I saw my kid brother, not as a total nuisance, but as my own hero of the time, stout Tom Sawyer. Tom too would have dived bravely into a bramble bush to save Becky Thatcher, the judge's daughter. I even forgave him the berry juice on my blazer badge and the rip the wire had made in my best school pants.

Despite grumbles from my dad, my mother still dragged me and Derrick to Alnwick every Saturday on the wheezy old bus. My brother sat on my knee, wriggling and putting his tongue out at the folk behind. The ostensible reason was still the 'rations', our regular order from John William Allen's, but Mary-Jane had deeper motives. From the minute Martha walked into the flat at King Street, she was Cinderella. There would be a pile of dirty washing that she would see to and she would clean the entire place. But Mam saw it as her duty because she could take the strain of looking after Uncle Sonny off her mother for a while. While Mam slaved, Granny would take Derrick and me to the butcher's shop with its hanging rabbits, and to Jack Carlisle's chippie.

Just before Christmas 1952, we were coming back to Granny's with a fish and chip lunch when she tweaked my ear playfully. 'I've got a surprise for you, my laddie,' she winked, knowing the tweak had stung. 'I've got a real Bible for you to take to that school.'

I mumbled my thanks, shaking internally at the prospect of showing up at assembly at the grammar with a white Bible; what would Savage think, or Billy Mitchell, my new pal, or Bowman the class piss-taker?

The thought haunted me as I carried Uncle Sonny to the outside toilet. He smelled and slavered on me as I prayed he would not need a Number Two with bum wiping to follow. I was lucky this time, but it was bad enough pulling out his member and shaking the drips off it. Then I had to do up the buttons of his fly as his withered arms clutched at my neck for support. How I envied other grammar lads supping hot Bovril after a Newcastle United match or queueing for the first house at the Morpeth Coliseum.

However, things looked up as we prepared to go for the six o'clock bus back home. Granny produced wrapped Christmas presents and Mam shoved them in her bags on top of the groceries. Uncle Sam handed me a carrier bag and in it were six second-hand American comics featuring Superman, Batman and Spider-man. These were like gold to me; I dived deep and ravenously into their lurid world and then could use them for swaps. One Yankee comic, with its adverts for BB guns and real Stetsons was good for six *Hotspurs* or *Adventures*.

Three hours later Dad was snoozing by our home fire and Mam was baking. My kid brother was asleep in our bed. I had just eaten the best rump steak – courtesy of Granny's butcher, done to a cinder and with a fried egg on top – was on my second Blue Riband and was standing on a Bronx ledge with Batman as the Riddler shot at us with a ray gun. Then my bliss turned to angst. I remembered what Granny had wrapped in plain brown paper along with the bright presents. I took the package to the bathroom. It was white all right – gleaming ivory white, with a gold cross down the front and gold trim down the pages. And it was so thin. I looked inside my Catholic Bible and saw there was no Old Testament. I could just imagine what the wags of 1B would say. 'Oh, just look at Moses Waddell. He's come down the mountain with the *five* Commandments!'

The next day we had surprise visitors. We had just finished Sunday dinner and Dad was deep in the *News of the World* sports pages. Mam was finishing washing the dishes when my least favourite cousin came shrieking in the door. It was Enid Cullingworth, daughter of my auntie Jean, aged around nine and showing all her mother's crass social graces. 'Lily's at my house! She's been there an hour.'

This was trilled as a triumph, Enid meant that Auntie Lily, who lived in Ashington, favoured her house over mine.

'We've got no custard,' I said sarcastically, a reference to Enid's latest daft fad – a custard-only diet.

A few minutes later Auntie Lily walked into the room, followed by her daughter Brenda and Auntie Jean. Lily hugged my dad and started chatting to my mam. Jean, often referred to by my mother as Keyhole Kate, a beady-eyed Nosey Parker from *The Dandy*, went snooping around the house as usual, looking for dusty shelves or fag ends left in cups.

I was fascinated by the fuss that my dad, shy and undemonstrative as a rule, made of Brenda. She was about twelve, tall, pale, with dark wavy hair. My dad sat her on his knee and plied her with questions about school. He looked at her the way he looked at Derrick when he wasn't being a little sod. When Brenda replied she called Dad 'Bobert'. Why the pet name?

Suddenly Auntie Jean hurtled in from her tour of our house, clutching my white Bible. She had it open and was stabbing at the inside cover where I had written 'S. Waddell 1B'.

'You're never going to let that laddie tek this to the grammar school. It's more like a box of bloody Milk Tray than a Bible.'

Martha was on her like a lurcher on a rabbit. Eyes ablaze, she tore the Bible out of Jean's hands.

'You've got a nerve, Keyhole rotten Katie. Poaching round me house when we've got company and criticising my bairn's Catholic Bible. You're lucky I don't smack yer miserable chops with it, God help me.'

Brenda and Enid started to cry. Auntie Lily stood up to leave. I did not know which way to look. My mother was crying with anger. Dad began to rake the fire. Enid, half-smiling, led the way out. Brenda pecked us all a light kiss and whispered in my ear, 'Happy Christmas.'

My dad gave my mother a glass of sweet sherry to calm her down. Three hours, and three glasses, later, while Dad sang Derrick to sleep with 'Clap Hands for Daddy', Martha told me why my dad made such a lot of cousin Brenda.

'Your dad is a canny fella, Sidney, the heartbeat of the Waddells. When owt happens folks turn to him.' Her voice lowered to a whisper. 'Your auntie Lily fell pregnant to a man who did not want to marry her. Some in the family called her a bad woman for doing what she'd done. But your dad took her side. Your uncle Freddie McLawrence married her and took Brenda as his own daughter. Your dad thinks she needs all the love she can get, so that's why he cuddles her. He wants her to feel wanted.'

As I went to the bathroom I could hear my dad's tuneless voice singing to Derrick:

> 'Clap hands for Daddy coming doon the waggon way,
> A pocket full of money and a cart full of hay.'

This was the first time I remember thinking about my life and what it meant to have a mam and dad who loved and cared for me. I even began to appreciate the difference between my life and the insecurities that Brenda must be filled with.

A few days later Derrick and I sat under the Christmas tree ready to open our presents. For weeks Derrick had been writing letters to Santa and sending them up the chimney. As he went berserk in his new pedal car, I dug into a pile of comic and sports annuals. Then my dad called me out to the back kitchen. He had his back to me and when he turned I gasped. He was holding a state-of-the-art wooden sledge. Other kids had nailed-up kipper boxes and the like, but this was beautiful. It was done in lovely blue wood, all screwed and streamlined. The runners were shiny steel. I ran my fingers along them.

'One of the pit's blacksmiths made it, son. He reckons it will fly. Look after it.'

I called it 'Bluebird' and did it fly? Soon after Christmas it snowed hard for a couple of days, and on the afternoon of the second day there was a heavy frost. As the dark winter twilight settled my dad told me where I could get a good run.

'When I was a laddie, the best sledging place was the north side of Lynemouth Dene, on Crawford's Bank just down from the farm. There'll be a track already, I bet, and the frost will have made it lightning.'

I tied a hank of old clothes line on the front of the runners and ran to the Dene. Dad was spot on; beyond the curve of snow drifts was a swathe of sheer ice. I rubbed the runners with fresh snow. I ran to the edge of the slope and dived belly flat aboard. It was bliss. Bluebird glided over bumps and I shouted with pure joy. I thought the drifts at the bottom of the slope would slow us up, but they did not. Ahead was the thin ice on the river with only the wide-strung wires of a cow fence between me and a drenching. I dug in my toes to brake, grabbed the rope and hurled myself off the sledge. I rolled in snow and Bluebird skidded on top of me. The runner banged my brow. But I hugged my new treasure and rocked with mad laughter.

In my excitement I forgot that I had drifted from my own patch. Despite the cold I was working up a real sweat hurtling down the bank. Then I heard noises up near the main road and two lads came plodging through the snow. They ran up to me and I recognised them as Lynemouth lads – trouble. They were both about 15 and they had bother in their eyes. One began making snowballs and the other, a mean kid called Davison, who I had seen thumping younger lads at the mass football matches, bent down and grabbed my sledge.

'Ye'll not mind if ah have a go, will you?' He had a skinny ferrety face that frightened me. I nodded.

He jogged to the brow of the bank and belly flopped on to my sledge. At the bottom he dragged his toes to stop the sledge before the fence. Then he kicked at it and it slid into the icy river. I screamed at him.

I ran to the river and dived at the sledge rope. I pulled at it furiously as Davison bent over me and pushed wet snow down my neck. His pal pounded snowballs into my back. 'Think you're a smarty in that grammar school gear,' Davison sneered.

I wanted to let go the rope and smack him, but I feared a bashing. The pair ran off and I tugged my sledge from the frozen Lyne. I vowed that one day Davison would pay.

My big hero of the time was Alf Tupper, 'The Tough of the Track' in *The Rover* comic. Alf was a welder who was so poor he lived in the welding shop on a diet of fish and chips and strong tea. This did not stop him beating brash Aussies and bronzed Yanks at the mile and half-mile all over the world. My diet was a bit better, except for one item. From the age of six I had devoured my mam's jammy sponge cakes each night for pudding. I paid the price in the spring of 1952. I got violent toothache and had to be taken to Mitchinson's, the demon dentist, in Ashington. Horror stories were told about Mr Mitchinson and his blunt needles.

I arrived at his surgery one morning with a muffler round my chops –'to keep the cold out' – and with my mam in tow. I was shaking with terror when I went in and things got rapidly worse: I had to have four big fillings. Half an hour later I lurched back into the waiting room in agony. My mam looked aghast as I mumbled tales of cocaine wearing off and needles stabbing gum tissue. She warmed the scarf on the radiator and wrapped my jaws up.

Just then my day was brightened when a familiar figure walked into the surgery. White silk muffler, pock-marked face, demob suit – my errant uncle Bill. This was not the time to act the wimp. I bravely told Bill I was fine. My mother had shopping to do and Bill said he was early for his appointment, so I was left in his company while Mam went up the street to the shops.

I felt slightly awkward in the company of this exotic man whose lifestyle was the talk of the Waddell family. Nobody knew exactly where he lived or who was his floozy of the moment. Sightings were reported in low pubs in North Shields and at race meetings, and he sometimes turned up at family weddings, only to be bribed with beer money to bugger off. He had blue eyes like my dad but unlike his they were not kind. Uncle Bill twitched with constant nervy irritation, like Bill Sykes in a church eyeing up the collection box. He coughed all the time, clouting his chest with his fist. I wondered if I dared ask to see the shrapnel holes left by the German hand grenade.

'Are you getting on alreet at the grammar school?' he asked.

'Canny. I'm having trouble with algebra, but I'm top of the class.'

'Algebra! Is that near Cape Toon? I was never very good at geography.'

'It's not a place, Uncle Bill. It's like symbols you do sums with...' I stopped myself, realising he was joking.

He winked. 'Tell you what, this summer holidays I'll tek you poaching along with your cousin John and Mousey.'

And he was off on one of his vivid tales about his latest exploits. He, John Ferguson and Mousey Bell – so-called because he looked like a cartoon mouse – were just back from a salmon-poaching trip ten miles north on the Coquet river. They had parked their van at dead of night, taken out their long net and the two teenagers had swum over the river with it. The net was secured at either bank and they settled down to wait for the incoming tide to fill it with fish. Sadly, a couple of water bailiffs had come along and they had scarpered, leaving the net behind.

'Next time we're not ganna use a net,' Bill leaned to my ear and whispered. 'We're ganna hoy in a stick of gelignite. It'll be just like Bonfire Night for you.'

I nodded, but had visions of the Beak calling me onstage at assembly to answer a charge of blowing up the river Coquet. 'Maybe, Uncle Bill, but I'm planning to spend most of my holidays running up and down dunes at Cresswell to improve my stamina.'

His eyes lit up. 'No bother, there's a load of rabbit runs through them dunes. I can teach you how to net them.'

On the bus back home Mam asked me what Uncle Bill had talked about. 'Mostly nature study,' I replied, pulling the scarf tighter round my chops.

A few weeks later in the first week of June my mother took Derrick and me on a visit to our Lynemouth relatives. It was a Saturday morning and my dad was doing an overtime shift down Betty. Derrick and I were knocking heads off dandelions and Mam was pushing the pushchair. My brother rarely used it, but today it came in handy; Martha had let rip on a baking jag and was transporting loaves, sponge cakes, ginger snaps and even some early fruity Christmas cakes soaked in Alnwick brewery rum. There was a light breeze coming in from the sea and a trickle of smoke bleached the azure sky above Betty. I shuddered at a sudden mental flash of Dad toiling down there, but it was gone in a jiffy. My mind turned to presents: if we were dishing out food, surely a few coppers would come our way? When we passed Crawford's Bank, scene of my encounter with the bully, I had a pang of fear. I looked out over the dene, bursting with greenery despite the black coal-sludged water of the river, and figured that a day like this Davison would be down amongst those trees looking for frogs to inflate with drinking straws or little kids to belt.

We were just going under the bridge towards my auntie Mary's when a figure came towards us on crutches. It was my cousin Robert and he was hopping, putting no weight at all on his left leg. Despite the obvious pain, he was his smiling self. 'Hey up, Sid. Hey up, Tadger.'

My brother almost bowled him over. Robert always made a lot of Derrick. 'Canny on, kidda'

'What happened to your leg?' asked Martha.

'It was that mad pony I work with on the putting. He bucked sudden and a full tub came off the way. I was pushing it back on when the pony jumped again and the tub trapped my leg against the wall. I'm lucky it's not broken. Doctor said it's just badly sprained.'

Robert gamely put the bad leg down and took his weight on it. He grinned but it obviously hurt.

Robert insisted that we go to his house in Eden Terrace for a cup of tea. This was not part of Mam's plan. Robert's mother Mary Ross was not respectable and was a slovenly housekeeper. The house in Eden Terrace was a tip, particularly the kitchen. But Mam also knew it would be impolite to turn Robert down. Thankfully, Mary was elsewhere and Uncle Geordie gave my mam tea and me and Tadger had Tizer. Martha doled out cakes and biscuits. I noticed that Geordie, just like my dad, had the Waddell chest. He hawked constantly and spat phlegm in the fire. Like my dad he was a coalface drawer down Betty.

'You should see the doctor about that cough,' said Martha.

'I hev done. Emphysema, says Dr Skene.' Geordie laughed. 'All that dust doon Betty. Give us a tab.'

They shared a laugh and a Woodbine. The door clashed and in came a scruffy bundle, my cousin Sid, who was nearly six. He grabbed a ginger snap from a bag and a Woodbine. He pretended to smoke it. We all laughed; little Sid was tarred with the same brush as Uncle Bill. He wagged off school, went bird-nesting and already knew some very naughty words.

After fifteen minutes we went round the corner to Chester Square and the house of my auntie Mary. Halfway up the backyard we heard coughing, like an ancient tractor trying desperately to start on a frosty morning. The door was ajar and my mother tapped gently on it. Auntie

Mary, another of my dad's sisters, came to the door and greeted us with a faint smile. She had the pinched features of the Waddell women but generally she had a cheery attitude. Not today, however; she sighed at more ruttling barks and spitting noises. I followed the two women through the scullery and into the parlour. There was a bed under the stairs and my uncle Tommy Herron was sitting on it spitting into a bucket. He was wearing pyjamas over long johns. He was unshaven. But what made my brother clutch my leg in fear were the grunty gasps for air and the lines scarred into his ashen face. He looked at us like a drowning man in an empty sea.

Auntie Mary made him lie down, shushing him like a child. We had more tea and pop in the scullery. We got two rabbits and some fish in exchange for the food. As Derrick and I were ushered out to play in the yard I heard my aunt mumble through tears, 'He'll never gan back to that pit again. The dust has got him, wor Tommy. Tossed on the scrapheap at 54.'

That night I lay in bed and every time I heard my dad's occasional chesty cough, I winced. What would happen to us if my dad got the dust, had an accident or was killed down Betty? I hadn't said my prayers for a week or two, so I kneeled by the bed, blessed myself and started with, 'Please keep my dad safe down the pit...'

I did not need to pray for good results in the end of first-year exams. I had done every jot of homework all year and, during the exams, I sat up till midnight learning all my lessons parrot fashion. Mam plied me with cocoa and then pleaded with me to sleep but I bashed on.

When my parents opened my report they were, in the main, delighted. I had half a dozen As. History and English were my best subjects with science not far behind. But Bob frowned at the fact that I was only seventh in Maths. 'You've got to stick in there,' he groaned, meaning I was not on track to be a nuclear scientist.

But my worst result gave me a mean little bit of satisfaction. I was almost last in Religious Instruction, so my granny Mary-Jane would be livid. Maybe now she would stop thrusting God stuff down my throat all the time.

Meanwhile some very non-God stuff was lapping at the innocent shores of my boyhood.

CHAPTER NINE

Young Love

Despite having been at the grammar school a year now, I still spent much of the summer holidays with Alan Robinson and Eric Appleby, and one of our favourite spots was Cresswell beach. This was a magnificent curving swathe of white sand and there was a rampart of high grassy dunes. We played a game of racing to the top of the dune and jumping as far as we could.

The three of us were sweating cobs after half an hour of the game. Eric and Alan went to the rocks to look for crabs and I stretched out on the sandy side of a dune wearing only my woollen bathing trunks. I was half asleep when I felt a hand tickling my stomach. Thinking it was bullies again, I leapt to my feet with raised fists. In a way it was a bully – a female one.

Her name was Pat, she was nearly 15 and she was wearing a bikini. She had straight ginger hair cropped short. She was not pretty but she had startling sea-green eyes. On the school bus a few weeks earlier she had made her friends laugh by rubbing a rounders bat between her legs and moaning, 'Oh, Sid!'

She had a dreamy yet devilish look in her eyes which were fixed on my cossie. I tried to push her hand away but she kept stroking. I felt my manhood rousing. She had big breasts and she swung them shamelessly. She began fumbling with her bra strap. I remembered what Mam and Granny had said about fast lasses. 'Please don't, Pat,' I pleaded.

'Come with me to those bushes over there,' she whispered.

She stroked my thigh and bent to kiss me. I rolled away. I heard my friends' voices coming up the other side of the dune. She stood up and the dreamy grin vanished. 'Ta-ra ... little boy.' She ran off.

Like most 12-year-old boys I was very confused about all things to do with sex. On the one hand I got erections – usually at the cinema when watching dance sequences featuring the long flashing legs of Ann Miller and Cyd Charisse. But on the other hand I still thought girls should be wholesome princesses like Kathryn Grayson or June Allyson. When girls like Pat talked loudly on the school bus about 'cock skins' or 'fanny pads', I squirmed and buried my head in a book.

I was having a growth spurt in the early weeks of the new term and pestered my mam to let me start wearing long trousers. Money was not a problem, we had a 'tick' account at the Lynemouth branch of the Co-operative Industrial Society. On a bright September Saturday morning we got the bus the short ride to Lynemouth and walked down past Smail's the butcher's to the menswear part of the Co-op. My mam, as usual, had a bit of gossip with the assistants as I looked at grey flannels. A lot of the stuff looked like it was made out of horse blankets, but there were finer, almost silver, pairs that took my fancy. With my mam's back turned, I whipped into the changing-room – a cupboard full of shoe boxes – and sprannced out like Burlington Bertie, looking for a mirror.

'Ooh, what a lovely fit,' cried the assistant, sensing a couple of quid extra in the till.

Martha frowned. She bent and pinched at the pants in the knee area.

'I was thinking of something more sturdy. Remember, these are for five days a week at school.'

'I promise you faithfully, Mam, I'll look after them like they were the crown jewels.'

She caved in. We walked out with me holding the neat parcel containing the fancy pants. As we turned the corner heading for Auntie Bab's there was an echoey thud. A big caser football bounced off the Co-op's massive plate glass window. Ken Brown, a grammar lad, winked at me. I thought he had miskicked. He hadn't; again he volleyed the ball at the glass from four feet. The whole pane shuddered.

'I don't think you should be doing that, Kenneth,' said my mam.

'I dee it all the time,' came the reply. 'The window bends and the ball's only half blown up.'

He kicked even harder.

I couldn't wait till Monday. I put the new pants on on Sunday afternoon just after dinner. 'Just getting used to them,' I explained.

My pals Alan and Eric were playing on their bikes. They were both wearing short pants. They said nothing, but I thought I could detect envy in their glances. They started playing a bike game involving going as slowly as possible, wiggling the front wheel while pedalling gently. They offered me a go and I carefully tucked the cuffs of my new pants into my socks. I was wiggling great when I pushed the pedal too hard. The wheel was at a right angle to the handlebars and I fell over them onto tarmac. I banged my left knee hard. I stood up and looked down – at a four-inch tear in the silver cloth. My pals both began to laugh as I went into a complete panic. Rolling up both legs of the pants over my knees as if planning on going paddling, I ran home.

It was impossible to hide the damage from Bob and Martha. I had to stand there while Mam yelled and called me all sorts of idiot, and Dad angrily lectured me about 'money not growing on trees'. Then my mam got out her sewing kit and some white thread. Now, baking was Martha's forte but needlework was not. Her sock darning was like the pattern on a lattice sausage roll. The result was a black crease with white highlights.

I had not been at the bus stop more than ten seconds on the Monday morning before two girls asked, 'What's that on your knee?'

And at school cries of 'Tramp!' and 'Kneesy' began before lesson one. I could not help thinking that Mam had botched the job on purpose to teach me a lesson.

I was back in short trousers till the Friday afternoon. After school my mam took me back to the Co-op and bought a pair of the thick battle-ship-grey flannels. I vowed I would never wear them other than for school. Two weeks later some of my form went to the girls' high school just down the lane from our school to take part in square dancing. It was a laugh and when it finished I paired up with another lad and played doubles at tennis on a hard court against two girls. We won and, being the show-off I was, I jumped the net to shake hands. My right foot caught the net and my left knee slammed into the ground. The thick material split – a jagged tear this time. As I stewed over what to tell my mother, a thin pale girl with a June Allyson smile offered to repair my pants for me. She was called Sheila Gordon and she lived in Lynemouth. I had noticed her on the school bus wincing, like me, at the dirty mouths. She reached into her satchel and took out a needle case. Then, as I lifted my leg onto the seat to expose the tear, Sheila proceeded to sew it up – with yellow thread.

Even though I got the expected loud lecture from Mam, I detected an amused glint in her eyes. I may have been her precious boy but she was sure the double humiliation was good for my soul. This time she bought some glue called Noso and put a patch inside the tear. The darker shade of grey partially hid the damage and I was told that if I wore the pants till Christmas I would get yet another pair of new flannels. It was looking like a costly Christmas; my brother Derrick was growing fast and needed new clothes and I had been promised new rugby boots. This all meant that my dad had to put in loads of Saturday shifts to push his weekly take-home pay to over nine pounds. Some miners did take home over 20 pounds a week in 1952, but they were younger men who manned the new mechanical coal cutters and the fillers who worked like beavers beside them.

It was this need for extra money that took me into the wild waves of the North Sea at dead of night.

My uncle Tommy Chester was just about the most cheerful bloke in the whole extended family. Unlike Auntie Elsie, his wife, he was a chatterbox and a live wire. He was also very active in the National Union of Mineworkers and it was he who taught me the politics of the industry.

He was also a very sharp lad at turning a penny. He had a smallholding near Cresswell and he often went for 'sea coal'. With a fierce wind from the east whipping up six-feet waves, tons of coal from outcropping seams off the mouth of the Lyne river were washed up on the beach at Bog Hall. Locals had been collecting the sea coal by hand, bucket, sack and horse and cart since the 1920s. In the 1930s the coal became more plentiful as the Ashington Coal Company began tipping waste by Strawberry Hill to the east of the bay. There was even more booty when a coal waste disposal called the Flume was built in the 1940s to take waste into the sea from Betty and Lynemouth Collieries. It was all bunce for men willing to work hard, since the NCB never disputed ownership of the coal and there were always merchants from as far away as Newcastle ready to buy it from whoever piled it up and marked their 'claim' with a piece of driftwood and a nom de plume.

It was about nine o'clock on a Wednesday night that Ches came calling. I was sitting by the fire cleaning dried mud from my football boots, Mam was reading and Dad, braces still down his bum after a big dinner, was snoozing. The rap on the back door came as a shock. I could hear a jingling of harness as I went to the door. I opened the door and the wind swept in, loaded with wet splinters of sleet. Ches was there wrapped up in an old mac and scarves.

'Tell your dad she'll be waist deep in nutty slack doon Bog Hall,' he yelled. 'If he puts his gear on sharp we'll mek a fiver each, no bother. You can come wiv us if you like.'

I had done my homework. I could hold Tommy the horse while they shovelled coal from the waves. It would help the family budget. My dad nodded. He put on waders and I got old wellies and tucked in a pair of my stitched long trousers. We wrapped up with hats and scarves and went forth, with Bob chanting his foul weather mantra 'Caad blaaa the bleary bloody blast.'

We set away on the road to Cresswell at a fair clip, Uncle Ches giving Tommy his head. There were narrow single-plank sides to the flat cart and we held onto them. Behind us giant shovels and a pair of Tilley lamps bounced in the coal duff from Ches's last expedition. Tommy's hooves clattered on the road and gobbets of hail splattered us. We careered past Cresswell church, its tombstones casting long eerie shadows in the crystal moonlight. I felt like a new member of Long John Silver's reckless band intent on grabbing booty, which in a way I was. At the bottom of Cresswell Bank we saw and heard the sea, swirling madly and flinging foam up over the white cottages of Fisher Row.

I could sense the excitement of both men. My dad and Ches were bright-eyed, and it struck me that this was a holiday for them. Both were used to slogging their guts out for coal under the North Sea. A bit of shovelling at the waterline would be a doddle. Suddenly Ches hauled back on the reins and Tommy slowed to a swift trot as he was guided down a curving track in the dunes. The cart pitched in deep ruts and our shovels nearly fell off. Bright flaring lamps and harsh shouts pinpointed our destination.

The coal lay in thick swathes of up to three feet high, for all the world like a shoal of jet-black oysters. Around the clumps four-foot waves sluiced up more coal, then the tide tried to suck it back. Four other parties of sea-coalers were already in action; one man held the horse while others shovelled coal onto the cart, waves pounding their waders. We backed Tommy into the raging water and I was given his bridle to hold. I was terrified; he champed the bit and tried to bite my wrist. Ches gave me some sugar lumps to keep Tommy sweet but he nearly took my fingers off when I offered them. Finally I waited till he opened his mouth and flung the lumps down his craw.

My dad and Ches were filling up the cart quickly, but not as quickly as two lads aged no more than me who had the 'pitch' next to us. They were the Lister brothers, Ivan and Keith, sons of Tom Lister, a stoneman at the pit and a champion poacher, known to be able to net 60-odd rabbits in a night. I had heard that with the sea coal and the poaching, Ivan did not see much of Lynemouth school. Ivan had been able to yoke a horse and cart since he was six and now had the fastest beast on the beach, a tall long-legged mule. It brayed, bucked and screamed but it got from the waves to the dry sand faster than Tommy. No matter. We got the three cartloads that made a ton to our pile in less than half an hour. By three in the morning there was only duff and stone left and Ches reckoned we had about eight tons of best coal.

We stood around drinking tea from a flask and eating jam sandwiches. I was so pleased that Tommy had not bitten me that I gave him a sandwich. Ches wrote his name on a slate and put it on our heap. The agent would come in the morning with his lorry and collect all the coal, paying out later.

'I reckon we'll get thirteen quid for that lot, Sidney. Me and yer dad will tek a fiver. I get one for Tommy. So you get two pound.' Ches reached in his back pocket and gave me two pound notes. I did not want to take them. 'Go on,' he laughed. 'You should be buying that jock strap sooner rather than later. All that scrumming yer doing.'

'That's too much,' I said, offering a pound back.

'Give it to your dad, so he can buy Martha summat nice for Christmas.'

I handed the note over to Bob.

My love life started, not with anything as romantic as a kiss, but with a cheese straw.

In the middle of January 1953 I had stayed on at school after the bell to practise kicking a rugby ball. I sprinted across Morpeth bus station at half past four and just managed to get on the school bus for Lynemouth as it moved off. I pulled off my satchel with muddy boots tied to it by their laces and flopped in a seat. I crammed the satchel under the seat and felt the boots rub something. I looked up into a familiar pale face. It was Sheila Gordon, the girl who had sewn my ill-fated long pants. She dabbed at her long green school gabardine and I apologised. She laughed off the incident softly and took off her green bobble-hat. She had light brown wavy hair and freckles round her nose. She seemed breathless when she spoke and she was very pale.

'I tend to get very excited when its owt to do with rugby,' I said. 'I've just finished a practice. I'm in the Under-14s, you know.'

She looked about as impressed as if I had told her I breathed or that I drank Tizer occasionally.

'With all that exercise you'll be needing a bit of nourishment. Try these.' On her knees was a wicker basket covered by a tea towel. She held out a packet. I took out three or four yellowy flakey sticks. I ate them, chewing slowly because they were very dry and very salty.

'Lovely,' I lied. 'Just like my mam makes.'

'Good. I usually bake them too long and put too much salt in them when we have to do them for Domestic Science.'

She looked out of the bus window at the dark trees with flashes of the dull silver river behind them.

'It must be great to do sport. They say I might be allowed to play a bit of tennis in the summer if I'm better.'

The words, flat and soft, hit me like a punch. As the dull bus lights flickered and the engine heaved us up banks and along twisty lanes, Sheila Gordon told me one of the saddest stories I had ever heard. For the past six months she had been in Stannington sanatorium being treated for tuberculosis. She still went back for check-ups, but it looked like she was clear. There was a quiver of fear rather than optimism in her voice. In the space of a 20-minute bus ride I was smitten. As I picked my satchel from the floor at Ellington, I made sure my hand touched hers. She dipped her head but I could see the smile.

Though my young heart skipped whenever I saw Sheila in the next few days, I did not go overboard. I did not sit next to her on the bus for several days nor did I walk her up the street to the high school. Instead I bided my time till the following Thursday. After school that afternoon I got to the school bus early and sat on my own. She saw me and came and sat beside me. I was so nervous about asking for a date that I burbled on about playing wing forward and crashing opponents to the deck. She nodded dutifully at the right times. My nerves peaked at Ellington where I should have got off. But I stayed on – both of us tongue-tied – till her stop, near my auntie Bab's at Lynemouth. We stood looking at each other like idiots. She twisted her bobble hat.

'Do you want to go to Ashington pictures tomorrow?' I asked.

She nodded. 'Get on the twenty-five past five bus.' She kissed me primly on the cheek.

It was one and a half miles back up the pit road to my house and I ran it in about 12 minutes. In my ears rang a jaunty pop song of the minute 'A Gordon for Me', a rollicking Scottish song. I sprinted up our path and into the house and the smell of dinner. My dad and Derrick were already eating. Mam looked at me.

'Bloody old school honk, got stuck on the Whorl Bank.' It was the first of many lover's lies.

The first date was a success. Sheila looked wonderful in a long black skirt and white blouse. We went to the first house at the Wallaw cinema in Ashington and I put my arm round her shoulders just as the big picture started. I had liked the fact that she offered to pay for herself at the ticket office, but only rotters let girls pay.

We got the bus back to Lynemouth and at her stop she pecked my cheek and stood up. She was surprised when I followed her off the bus. 'Won't your parents wonder why you are late back?'

'Not the way I run, love. They'll just think the bus was late a bit.'

This became a weekly ritual. We found a cosy corner of the bus shelter near her house, kissed under the lamplight for ten minutes, then off I went in my school mac and scarf, hurtling past Auld Betty and up the straight road home. A red face and a touch of heavy breathing bothered nobody; I was known to run everywhere.

The pattern of Friday night movies and my road running went along smoothly for a month. I was besotted by Sheila Gordon and she gave me a small snapshot taken in the hospital grounds of her wearing a floral dress on a sunny day. Last thing at night, after saying my prayers, I kissed the photo and put it under my pillow.

One afternoon I returned from school to face the kind of broadside that only Martha could deliver. As my kid brother looked on sheepishly, she pulled the photo of Sheila out of her pinny pocket. 'Are you going to tell me who this is?'

I tried to play for time; see how much she knew. 'How did you find that?'

She pointed at my brother. 'The bairn found it under your pillow.'

Derrick shared a double bed with me and I glared at him. He stuck out a pet lip and began to sob.

'It's just a lass I've been to the pictures with a couple of times. It's nowt...'

'Do you kiss her?'

I was pretty sure that dry pecks could not make a girl pregnant nor did they constitute a mortal sin. So what part of my mother and granny's convent-approved moral code was I transgressing? She gave me no time to answer.

'I know about this girl. I showed Billy the fishmonger the picture and he said he sells her mother kippers.' Martha's eyes sparkled with hot tears. 'She has got bloody TB!'

I twigged. Here was Martha with a snotty-nosed asthmatic lad, who she wrapped in a wool vest and smothered in Vick even in the most sweltering August, only for him to go courting major lung disease.

'All right. I won't promise to stop seeing Sheila, but I will never kiss her again.' Later that night my dad came to me solemn-faced as I did my homework.

'We don't want you to see that Gordon lassie any more, Sid.'

'You can't stop me,' I snarled.

No reply.

The following Friday night it was thick with fog. Sheila and I were cuddling behind a garage near her house. I heard echoing voices a few yards away.

'We'll never catch them on a neet like this.'

It was the throaty tones of my cousin Billy. Then I caught the manic laugh of his brother Tot. My father was certainly on my case; he had deputised my cousins to be spies.

Just to spite Martha I kissed Sheila deeply. Then I took off like a whippet. My footsteps rang out on the wet pavement and the hounds began to howl. 'Hold on, Sid, we just want to talk to you.'

Their boots clattered down a ginnel as I eased onto the grass track round the dene. Now they could not hear me. I pounded on till I hit the Ellington Road. There was a frosty silence when I got home, but no mention of Sheila or my cousins.

Till the end of February I kept kissing and my cousins kept on red alert, but they never caught me. One black night in late February at the end of Eden Terrace I was trapped in a ginnel with one at each end. So I jumped a hedge and hurdled over six gardens, sending poultry skittering, ruining onion sets and leaving my cousins blaspheming.

The funny thing was that it was never discussed out in the open. When I saw my cousins in passing they were always friendly and my parents, who must have been getting reports of the fruitless chases, never mentioned Sheila again. Our courtship fizzled out when she went back into the sanatorium – no doubt reported back to Martha by Billy the kipper seller. I sent a couple of letters and got a couple back, but we both simply moved on.

By March 1953 I was well established in the Under-14 team and I now rubbed shoulders with my idol, Nigel Savage. Colin Danskin, our rugby master, turned me into a marauding wing forward. Just as I learned all my lessons parrot fashion, so I followed to the letter his simple rules for my position.

'Once the ball is lost, race at the opposite fly half and flatten him.'

I was so fit and fired up that several times I was warned by referees for hitting the man before he got the ball. So, with the coach and our captain patting my back, it was odd that my only critic was my dad.

Bob was my biggest supporter, even though he had never seen a live rugby match in his life before I started to play. Each Saturday morning we developed a ritual. I put Cherry Blossom on my new rugby boots as he shaved with a cut-throat razor and Brylcreemed up as if heading to the social club for the Sunday bingo. Then he would put on his best flat cap and an old gabardine mac and we would get the bus to Morpeth or the away venue. At the match my dad would never do much talking, only speaking to masters if spoken to. Bob was the only father to attend regularly; others came from time to time. Sometimes visiting masters thought he was a Morpeth master, then he would open his mouth and yell 'Git him low, wor Sid'. It was the beginning of a long, intimate quest by him to see me get the red rose of England on a jersey. But not at any cost; he wanted me to get caps without cheating. He told me off for tackling too early, 'You're fast enough to see the ball into the hands. Only lunge then.'

Playing rugby every Saturday in the winter months caused a big revolution in my life. I could no longer make the weekly pilgrimage to Alnwick with my mam and kid brother. The relief was enormous; the world was my oyster, I could go to the movies or take in a football match. I used the afternoon of one of these Saturdays to visit Frank Brennan's sports shop in Ashington to buy my first jock strap. My pal Alan Robinson came with me. I really did think that Frank, Newcastle's legendary centre-half, would handle the transaction personally, so I was flabbergasted when a doe-eyed young lassie said, 'Can I help you?'

Slowly and deliberately and looking at the ceiling I said, 'I would like to buy an athletic support.'

She turned and brought three boxes from a shelf. Alan was trying to kill a laugh. 'Small? Medium? Or large?' The glint in her eye was pure challenge. She held the white dangly objects with their limp pouches up in order.

'I'll take a medium,' I muttered.

Outside the shop Alan let his amusement rip.

'You should have topped the cheeky bugger by asking for a large one and then asking her for a date.'

I ended my second year at the grammar school on a high. I was told that I had a good chance of getting in the county rugby team next year.

There was also a bonus that I explained to my parents after they had opened my report and praised my efforts. A party of third-form boys was going to France in mid-August for ten days and it was suggested that I go as well. I handed over a letter from Mr Tweddle, my French teacher, saying that my route to university could well involve French, so gaining experience of speaking the language with actual French people would stand me in good stead. The trip would cost about £15, plus a bit of pocket money – two weeks' wages for my father. A look of apprehension passed between Mam and Dad but there was no discussion. A trip to Auntie Bab's for a cash sub was in order. While my dad, who had never been further than Darlington, 40 miles south, in his life, was lying twisted, heaving and straining under the North Sea, I would be visiting the Champs-Élysées and the casino at Deauville.

But it did not take a trip to la belle France for me to lose my heart again. It happened in a miner's cottage opposite the Regal cinema in Ashington – at a soirée. Being a ladies' man now, I had taken on a new Saturday night persona. I grew my hair long and pressed it into a ripple of deep waves that fell over my left eye. Despite it being a steaming hot July, I wore my dad's gabardine mac and a yellow McDonald tartan scarf. I got some funny looks standing in the cinema queue at 5.30 as lads dressed in white T-shirts and jeans mooched moodily past. But the gang I had joined were Ashington's bohemians, young grammar school lads and lasses. Nobody was actually 'going with' anybody. We all sat along a row at the pictures and then went to the cottage of a big lass called Enid for coffee and records on a Dansette. Enid's parents were members of a nearby workingmen's club and they were never home on a Saturday before ten.

Ella Renwick wore tight, long black skirts with figure-hugging white sweaters, and always a natty little scarf round her neck. But it was her voice that hooked me; it was like liquid smoke. When she said 'Sidney', never 'Sid', I'd have fought a dragon for her. Fortunately, it never quite came to that.

I walked her home one night and behind the Council Chambers, with soot from a coal train raining down on us, we kissed. She was two years older than me. Next Saturday I met her at the end of her street and she made me smell her neck.

'What do you think of my perfume?'

It honestly smelled more like battery acid than my mam's stuff, kept in stoppered bottles with tassels on her dressing-table, but I was diplomatic. 'Interesting. It has *frisson.*'

I was heading for France in a few days and thought I'd fling in a bit of the lingo.

'I made it myself,' said Ella.

I did not know what to say. I just nodded and began telling her how I was thinking of playing centre at rugby next season and how many folk thought I'd make the county team.

'I don't like sport that much. I only play hockey and tennis cos they make me.' I felt that this was a jibe.

At the Regal first house that night I put my arm around her and she looked at me as though I was daft. I kept it there for the whole picture. It was like cuddling the Venus de Milo, all marble and no life. On the way to her house we discussed the film. I expected a real Betty Grable kiss to see me through two weeks in France, but all I got was a pair of lips like a zip fastener. Mind, she did hug me very tightly.

'When you're in France, Sidney, could you visit a couple of dress shops and sketch the latest fashions for me?' Pure honey from the rock. 'I want to try making them myself.'

I nodded and was rewarded with our first proper kiss.

The visit to France was not very cultural. Les Invalides and the Louvre had massive queues and by the time we got in it was time to leave. My spoken French did improve, however, thanks to some French 16-year-old lads who were staying at the same lycée as us and who sang dirty songs after dinner. I also got a bit of a taste for a tangy dark beer called Geuze. Sadly for Ella, I could not find the fashion shops.

Nor was Deauville exactly packed with high art. We visited the casino, the race track and found a billiard hall when Mr Tweddle was off-guard. Then I had a Eureka moment. I found a little street full of shops with robed mannequins in the window. I sat on a pile of baker's trays and began drawing. I was busily sketching when a heavy tap hit my shoulder. He had epaulettes and a Foreign Legion peaked cap. He was not happy.

'Qu'est-ce que tu fais?'

'Je suis Anglais. Ici sur mes vacances. Ma femme est une tricoteuse et elle souhaite d'essayer les – er – latest fashions'.

He took my pad and for a moment I thought he was going to tear up my work. 'C'est interdit. Absolument PAS! La couture est privée.'

It made good sense: why fill your window with expensive clothes, then let a Geordie lassie knock up a copy for nowt?

Ella did not find my account of the saga in the slightest bit amusing. She took my sketches and nodded approval. She thanked me for my efforts and asked how the holiday had gone. I said it had been fine but I could not wait to get to Lynemouth Welfare and begin training. She said she could not join me at the pictures that Saturday; she was going to try making one of the French dresses.

The 'Dear Sid' was delivered by one of her friends as I walked up the street to the grammar a few days later. It was in a violet envelope and smelled of the dreadful scent. I didn't trust myself to read it in public. I went to the toilets before assembly. The key words were 'immature' and 'sport obsessed'. I was hurt. I had run the gauntlet of the gendarmerie for the bloody woman, and all I'd got was this mumbo jumbo. Better devote myself in future to red rose badges and Corinthian ideals.

CHAPTER TEN

Lynemouth Lad

A week into the summer holidays of 1953, I looked out of the window to see Eric Appleby careering down our path waving a piece of paper. 'I've got in, Sid, I've got in!'

Eric had sat the 13-plus exam at Linton Secondary School. He was a late developer and was obviously far too bright to languish at the local secondary modern.

'It'll be g-g-reat, won't it, travelling on the bus together. I can't wait till the h-h-holidays are over.' Eric's stammer crept in as his enthusiasm swelled.

I wasn't sure how I felt about Eric going to Morpeth. I think I was pleased but part of me was disappointed that I would have to share the glory.

'You'll be in the year below me, you know,' I said, ungraciously. 'And poor old Alan will be the odd one out.'

But nothing I said could blunt Eric's pleasure at the results. He went off skipping down the road to tell others about his triumph, freckled face all lit up.

Back at school in September, I saw little of Eric, except on the bus. For the first few days he sat with me, all shiny new uniform and stiff, leather satchel but then he slowly palled up with others from year two and our friendship slowly drifted.

Bob continued to be the sole parent who supported the Under-14 rugby team of which I was now the captain. But on the first Saturday of November 1953 my dad had to work overtime down the pit and he missed a dramatic development in my rugby career.

Up until that day I had played as a marauding wing forward, essentially a defender, bashing the fly-half with abandon. But that day at home to a Tynemouth school I played as a centre. At first I was nervous and kept looking at where my dad usually stood. Then a burly lad called Brian Carolin, a brilliant footballer, crashed through a tackle and passed to me. I wrong-footed the full-back and dived over for a try. In the end I scored three tries. On the bus back home I daydreamed of county honours, the badge of the Percies on my breast and maybe even that red rose of England.

I ran into the house, excited and shouting. 'Hey, Dad, you should have seen my first try. I swerved...'

I shut up in shock. I knew that my mother and Derrick were at Alnwick visiting Granny, but Dad should have been back from the pit an hour ago, slumped by the fire having a mug of tea and listening to sport on the wireless. Accident! The word screamed in my brain. I ran out of the house and jumped the fence at the bottom of the garden and ran over the ridges in the recently ploughed field. I sprinted to the pit office. A clerk there calmed me down and said that there had been a fall of stone. My father had been struck by a massive stone on the right leg and had been bruised a lot, but there was probably no break. He had been taken to Ashington hospital. I sprinted to the bus stop and was lucky; a bus came in five minutes. I kept my eyes shut on the 15-minute journey, praying that my dad was all right and that somebody would blow Betty up.

The hospital was only a two-minute dash from the bus station. I was shown to a ward and the first thing I saw was my dad's big nose. He was sitting up in a bed waving. I fought the tears. He was laughing and making calm-down gestures. I hugged him and he said, 'How did you get on playing in the centre?'

In sheer relief I bawled, 'Three fucking tries.'

He put his hand over my mouth. Grinning, he said, 'Canny. But divvent get yersell hoyed oot of the hospital, son.'

He showed me his damaged leg, tented under a cage contraption. The knee was very swollen and crusted with blood.

'They don't think it's broken, but I'll know better when the X-rays come back,' said Dad. He took my hand and pressed it. 'Now, you know what your mother's like. She'll have a wobbler and want to be fleeing in here tonight. I want you to tell her I'm going canny. She should bring yee and Tadger in tomorrow, alang with a few grapes, me tabs and a bottle of American Cream Soda. Right?'

Just before eight that night I waited for the Alnwick bus outside Barker's shop in our village. It was frosty and I banged my shoes and thwacked my chest to get warm. How to tell Mam the bad – but not terrible – news? I decided to be straightforward.

The bus clattered through the misty blackness to a stop, people rubbing steam from the windows to check where they were. The conductor lifted off a sleeping Derrick and I took him in my arms. Martha clanked down the holdall containing the rations and a full carrier bag. Her face blenched with fear when she saw I was alone; Bob's cheery face smiling from under his tatty cap was a bright beacon on her busy Saturday, a sign that she could think about herself and him for a change.

'Me dad's in hospital but it's alreet. His leg's not broken.' I said it loud above the bus's roar as it rumbled off into the night.

My mother's hand went to her mouth then to her brow, blessing herself and emitting a small keening noise. She forced my hands together as my brother wriggled to the pavement. 'Pray, Sidney, for your poor father!'

Derrick tugged at her coat, saying, 'Dad. Dad. Want me dad.'

I wanted to shout to both of them that he was fine, probably making the nurses laugh or reading the football paper. I was saved by the Lynemouth bus pulling up. We were the only customers and the conductress, a blonde called Sadie, knew my mam.

'Still making that trek to Alnwick, Martha? You are a right mazer.'

My mam made the effort and engaged in small talk. I quietly butted in to say my dad had had a mishap at the pit. It sounded better in the bright smoky warmth of the bus. The conductress twigged that I was trying to mollify my mam and she was quickly out with the Woodbines. By the time we got off at our stop I had Mam convinced that Bob would surely last till morning.

The sight that met our eyes, Mam, Derrick and me, in the ward next morning was as far from doom and gloom as you could imagine. My dad's right leg was heavily bandaged and still under a cage and he was laughing fit to bust. Two nurses were tickling the toes of his left foot. On hearing our steps both the nurses jumped and grinned at us nervously. One held a small red bottle and I saw that my dad's toenails were the same colour. He could hardly be at death's door if he was letting cheeky young lasses polish his nails.

'Eeeh, we are sorry, Mrs Waddell, but your husband's got such lovely feet!' said one of the lasses.

Martha's face told them that Bob would get 'lovely feet' all right when she got him home. She hugged him and then bent into a carrier bag. She pulled out a cough medicine bottle and flung holy water all over his brow, his poorly leg and his nail polish.

'Give over, woman, I've just had a bloody bed bath,' he moaned.

She also produced grapes, Woodbines, cracker biscuits, pork and stuffing sandwiches and some Blue Ribands. Derrick attacked the grapes.

A doctor came and told my parents the score on Dad's injury. The leg was not broken but the knee cartilage was badly damaged, so Dad would need an operation and have to stay in hospital for a few days. He would be back at work within two weeks. I saw the relief on my parents' faces. Sick pay was very small and our family could not afford a long lay-off. Then a man in a mac and old cap came walking down the ward.

'Hey up, Oliver,' Bob shouted.

The man, who looked very distinguished and had the calm pale face of a priest, smiled and joined us. He was carrying a flat brown paper parcel. He hugged my father with genuine affection.

'It's a good job that stone just got your leg, Bob' he whispered, but I heard it clearly. My mother did not. Bob gripped Oliver's arm and wagged his finger. Oliver looked panicky and began making a fuss over Derrick, now guzzling grapes four at a time. My dad introduced his workmate Oliver. They had grafted at conveyor filling for years before turning to salvage drawing.

'He doesn't gan to pubs or clubs at weekends, Oliver, he gans painting,' said Dad proudly.

Oliver handed the package to Dad and he opened it. It was a beautiful watercolour sketch of the ruin of Dunstanburgh Castle up the Northumberland coast. In the deep green of the grass was the signature 'O. Kilbourn'. There was a moment when my dad and mam just stared in awe. The pastel-blue sky and golden sandstone were light years away from the dark foisty bowels of Betty. I could sense that this man who grafted alongside my father was properly proud of his talent. It pleased me that such a fellow counted my dad as a friend. But Oliver's whisper about the stone made me shudder; it could have been the size of a steamroller and it could have killed Bob.

'I'll stock you up on grapes next time, Bob,' said Oliver as he left, pointing at the empty bowl.

Derrick had scoffed the lot.

The next few months I concentrated on sport. On the rugby field I emulated Wilson of *The Wizard* and in running, the Tough of the Track.

My dad used the knowledge he had gained with a school of professional runners in the late 1930s to become my coach. In the first couple of weeks of January he had me on a strict regimen to get rid of the effects of the plum duff and Martha's cream-filled cakes. Each morning at seven I would down two raw eggs in milk with a dash of dry sherry, then I would jog at least a mile before going to school.

I managed to get into the County Under-15 rugby team. Again the family kitty was plundered, this time for new boots and proper rugby shorts with pockets and buttons, not skimpy gym shorts held up with knicker elastic. When I lined up in the forest-green jersey at Newcastle against Cumberland, shaking like a novice greyhound, Bob was on the touchline and I did not let him down. I didn't score but I kicked well in defence. I was only 13 and the baby of the team. We narrowly lost the match, but the master in charge told me I had my position for the next three games, the last two against Surrey and Middlesex away.

After all the money shelled out on me since starting the grammar school, I was scared to tell my dad about the southern tour. But the chance came unexpectedly. He was so excited that he took me and Willy Charlton, our school captain, to lunch at the ritzy Eldon Grill beneath Grey's Monument, in Newcastle. The posh waiter took Dad's mac and put a hand out for the cap, but Bob shook his head. He put it in his pocket; at work, at play or in the garden with his leeks it was his talisman, and it would be a tragedy if he lost it. We had roast pork with all the trimmings and – big surprise – he had a bottle of Amber Ale. He almost never drank alcohol but this day was special. He even called for a half shandy for Charlie, who looked 18. I had Tizer.

During the apple crumble I brought up the tour, but was expecting my father to tell me that he couldn't afford it. So I was surprised when Dad beamed. 'Certainly you can gan on that, son. You've got to show them London folk how good ye Morpeth lads are.'

'But it's ganna cost…'

He held up his spoon.

'Never mind the cost. I've had my name down for a colliery hoose in Lynemouth, and I'm told we'll be hearing summat soon. So we'll be selling the bungalow and putting money in the bank.'

On the bus home we passed through Lynemouth. It was a dull February evening, made duller by clouds of steam and coal dust spitting from a railway line of massive trucks. Some dirty kids threw chip packets at the bus and did V-signs at the passengers. The serried rows of pit cottages looked like a barracks, all dull yellow brick. Some drunks got on at the Hotel, the notorious beer palace, and began arguing and swearing. Dad asked them to watch the language but all they did was swear louder. Even the river Lyne, swollen with heavy rains, was nothing but a torrent of black coal sludge. Then there were the tarty lasses like Pat and the vicious gangs and the bullies. Why would my parents want to leave Cresswell Road? I thought.

My dad loved his garden at Cresswell Road, especially his leek trench. It was about twenty feet by ten, boxed by thick railway sleepers and filled with rich thick black mulch. This was augmented by sheep's blood, horse manure – gleaned from the road when farmers' carts passed by. It was guarded carefully against the raids of crows and starlings. Bob had a catapult and would let fly with pebbles. Each individual leek shoot was surrounded by a jam jar with the bottom knocked out to stop beetles feasting. From early spring my dad would be watching his darlings as if they were whippets or pet rabbits. You could tell how the leeks were doing by the angle of his cap: over nose – worried; cocked to one side – new idea; flipped back, brow to sun – happy.

My mother loved a crack with Hilda Dowson next door and the string of tradesmen and insurance men who called. These always had a fag, cuppa or in winter a bowl of home-made broth with chunks of ham swimming in it. At Christmas and New Year this lot were also treated to a generous nip of whisky or Alnwick Brewery rum. But probably my mother's biggest social occasion was the laying out of the body when somebody died. Usually this involved a very old person, like Mrs Grundy who lived four doors along. I remember my dad coming into our house and telling me to take the gin bottle to number 18. I was terrified; I had never seen a dead body before. I banged on the back kitchen door and Hilda opened it. I saw the top end of the dead old lady, a bandage tied around her chin. Woodbines on the go, my mother and Mrs Appleby were washing her, all smiles and chat. The gin was for their own respectful little wake. I was shocked but strangely impressed, even though I had nightmares about the plastic-faced corpse for weeks.

I came back from the southern rugby tour aflame with sporting ambition. As part of the trip we had been to Twickenham to watch the England versus Wales schoolboy match. Starring for Wales was a brilliant centre called Richie Griffiths, brother of full international Gareth Griffiths, and I determined to copy his scything runs.

My dad had his own agenda. He had had me out running in the mornings during the rugby season, but his real ambition was for me to be an international sprinter. At the end of April 1953 he came home from the pit with a parcel. He opened it and proudly laid a pair of black running pumps on the table. Martha let out a shriek; it was one of her superstitions that shoes must never be put on the table; it meant the breadwinner would lose his job. So Dad took them off and helped me put them on my bare feet. They were sticky and battered but velvet-soft, with no sole under the heel part. And the sole itself was odd; it had a hollow panel in it. 'That's for the lead,' said Dad with a wink.

It was an old story about professional runners. They ran heats with lead plates in their pumps, fooled the handicapper and took the lead out for the final.

I couldn't wait to try the pumps out and went calling on Eric to show them off. He was surprised; we had not seen much of each other in the past few months, except on the bus. But he seemed happy to tag along. The thick cow pasture of the Swing Field was no good, but then Eric had a brainwave. He suggested the track alongside the gravel path over Linton Flats would be just the job. In rugby shorts and a hooped Sloppy Joe, I put the pumps on and jogged gently along the short springy turf. It felt magical; the pumps seemed to be working my legs. With Eric cheering me on I did practice racing starts and swoops to a make-believe tape. The All-England Schools Athletic Championships were to be held in Ashington at the end of July. Oh, to be in the team and march round the Hirst Welfare behind the county banner, waving at the crowd.

The reverie was smashed by a familiar nasal whine. 'Going to be a star runner, are we now? You couldn't win an egg and spoon race in them shitty pumps.'

It was Davison, the Lynemouth boy who had run my new sledge into the river. He spat on my pumps. Davison grabbed my ear and twisted it. It hurt but I did not let on. He was daring me to hit him. He was six inches taller than me. I'd lose a fight, I knew. He let me go and mooched off. 'Bloody coward as well as a big head, Waddell.'

'Why am I always the one who gets picked on?' I asked Eric after Davison had gone. 'It's not just round here. It's at school as well.'

'You're good at sport, you're good in class, and you don't mind telling people that either,' Eric pointed out. 'You think the sun shines out of your own arse. If you think that's going to make you popular, you're crackers.'

It was the longest speech I had ever heard Eric Appleby make, and he did not stammer once.

I became obsessed with track running. I devoured books from the library about great athletes like Jesse Owens, my dad's favourite, and Arthur Wint, the lean Jamaican quarter-miler. That was going to be my distance, a long sprint that meant tortured muscles and rasping breath. I even put on the new pumps and practised starts on the tiny patch of grass outside our front wall by the bus stop. I got some funny looks! During one of these sessions my dad came pedalling back from the pit. He jumped off his bike and corrected my hands, which he said were not far enough apart. Then he pointed back up the road towards the school.

'You're having sherry and eggs, now we'll add the final ingredient to make you fly. Jack Lucas has just had a load of manure delivered. Ye get a bit of the dry stuff at the edges and eat it before tea tomorrow.'

He winked and went indoors.

Horse shite! Full of vitamins or ace gardener Jack Lucas would not be putting it on his leeks, potato patch and flowerbeds. Trust my dad to never miss a clever trick.

Next afternoon I jumped off the school bus and dawdled down Cresswell Road. I sidled up to Jack's manure pile and grabbed some dry dottles of manure. At our gate I paused, checked the coast was clear, then put one lump in my mouth. At first the taste was of old Shredded Wheat, then it turned to slimy animal excrement. I fell into the back kitchen puking and retching. My mam had hysterics. I vomited in the sink and washed my mouth out with dandelion and burdock.

'I bet it's that semolina they mek you eat at school,' said Martha.

'No,' I gasped. 'It's horse shite. Me dad told me it would mek me run faster.'

She was making pastry for a pie when he came in. I thought she was going to hit him with the rolling-pin.

'What kind of father are you? Telling the bairn to *eat horse shite!*'

I heard him start to plead something about only making a joke as I locked the bathroom door and began my homework.

In the last week of April 1954 my dad announced that we had been allocated a colliery house in Dalton Avenue, Lynemouth. The advantages were obvious: we would live rent and rates free and the cash kitty from the sale of our bungalow would go towards my and Derrick's education and possibly even a family summer holiday, which we had never had before. I was asked how I felt about a move. I hid my fears of bullies and hooligans and said only that I would miss my friends Alan and Eric. My parents pointed out that it was less than two miles from Cresswell Road to our new house and that I would see the lads regularly. We would also be in the same cosy streets as my uncles, aunts and cousins, so cups of sugar and basins of broth would always be on hand. The last tenants of 102 Dalton had been less than ideal, so my dad's friend Billy Mann and his men were decorating the whole place from top to bottom. We would move in early May.

Normally I trained for my running in an old fisherman's sweater and shorts, but one day Martha came back from Ashington Co-op with a big parcel. In it was a dark-blue tracksuit. I was speechless with delight. I put it on, slipped on my pumps and wrapped a white towel round my neck just like Arthur Wint. I sat on the wall waiting for my dad feeling like I was on the Olympic podium.

Two evenings later after dinner my dad suggested a trip to the new house. He told me to put on my running kit, new tracksuit and to bring my pumps. The plan was to try me out over 440 yards at the Lynemouth Welfare sports ground. We cycled past the dene, now full of greenery, and along Dalton Avenue. It was very broad with big gardens. Men in shirtsleeves were working in them; faces red, caps flipped back and braces round their bums. Some called greetings to Bob. The two-storey cottages were in terraces and their yellow bricks caught the late sun.

We leaned our bikes against the hedge of 102. The garden was quite neat with a big potato and cabbage patch. There were some canes for sweet peas and then a patch of what looked like wet soot. It was the remains of a leek trench. Bob bent down and sifted the mulch.

'Bit of work and I can grow whoppers here,' he said.

The inside of the house smelled of paint and turpentine. Billy had installed a new tiled fireplace and above it had created a mock-oak effect in lincrusta with niches for nick-nacks. Upstairs there were two small bedrooms, one of which I would share with Derrick. At our bungalow our room was twice the size. I knew for certain I could not swot hard for exams here. The kitchen was very small with a pantry off it that contained a set-pot for boiling clothes. The bathroom was even smaller, with no place for a wash basin. We would have to wash daily in the kitchen sink where the dishes were washed. The yard outside had a shed, a toilet and a coal house. I looked in the toilet. It was very basic and it had a smell I didn't like.

Bob sensed my doubts. He pointed at the toilet. 'It's more hygienic to have the netty outside. And just think, with us all using pittle pails in the night, it'll be smashing for me leeks.'

I had to give a grudging laugh.

I opened the yard door and looked out into the back lane. Some lads were playing football with the doors as goals. They looked friendly enough. Then a man came down the lane on a rickety bike. He yelled at the lads to clear the way. They took no notice. The man swerved onto the path and a collie dog ran out snapping at his ankles. The bloke tipped off his bike and began kicking wildly at the dog, cheered on by the kids.

'You get him, Freddie,' they cried.

Roused to a frenzy, Freddie picked up his bike and hurled it at the dog. It missed, hit the wall and the chain fell off. A kid sidled over to me.

'That's Freddie Gray, he's daft as a brush.'

Great, I thought. Here's me worried about Lynemouth bad boys and the first adult I come across is the street nutter.

We moved on to the Welfare sports ground. This consisted of two football pitches, two tennis courts, a bowling green and a cricket oval that was one of the finest in Northumberland. My dad told me to warm up and I jogged round the grass edge. It was certainly very springy. I did a few starts and dip finishes, then joined him outside the brick pavilion. He was holding a big brass stopwatch.

'One of my marras has loaned me this for the season. He says give it back when you do the quarter in 56 seconds.'

I knew I would be lucky to get my time down that far. But I was excited to be running against a real clock, just like Alf Tupper, the Tough of the Track.

I got on my mark. Bob clapped loudly and off I went. The secret of the quarter mile was to sprint out for the first hundred, coast for two hundred, then give it your all to the tape. I started the last phase too early and hit a wall ten strides from home. I dipped, staggered and fell on my face. Bob bent down and showed me the time. The watch read 58.5. Our school record for boys under fifteen was 57.9. My dad laughed. 'Canny good, Sidney. Do you fancy a manure sandwich?'

We both knew that I had every chance of improving in the next ten weeks to make the All-England Schools meeting.

As we left the Welfare a very smart man, wearing his Sunday-best coat and oiled hair parted down the middle as if by a tomahawk, passed us with two big Alsatians. He nodded greeting to my dad and pointed at my tracksuit. 'Is your laddie gannin oot for the mile?' he asked.

'Not yet. Quarter, but ye never know,' said Bob.

'It's just come over on the wireless. That Roger Bannister has broken the world record for the mile and run inside four minutes. The race was at Oxford this afternoon.' He walked on.

Bob and I were speechless. The four-minute barrier broken by an Englishman. What an omen. I vowed to myself that I would train till I dropped in pursuit of an international running vest.

But for the minute I had to make do with a Co-op wool vest when I got down on my marks. Morpeth Grammar School entered a host of competitors in the East Northumberland area sports, but we had no special vest. Mam had a brainwave; she got some black tape and stitched 'MGS' in four-inch letters on my front.

I won the 440 by a street and anchored the relay team to victory. Two weeks later, in newly bought spikes, I came a close second in the county final in 57.0 seconds, good enough to book my place at Ashington for the national championships.

To say that all this went to my head would be an understatement. Martha almost got arthritis of the fingers sewing on my badges. I went

Aged 14 I was obsessed by athletics. Here I am about to break the school junior 440 record prior to going to the All-England Championships.

to school with three blazer badges – school, county rugby and county athletics. The last one was level with my pocket. I was teased mercilessly at school, and even some of the racy girls on the school bus called me 'Badgey'. I was impervious to their taunts, which I put down to jealousy; just wait till I had roses and lions to flaunt. I also had badges on my tracksuit and 'MGS' in white tape on the back.

The Lynemouth Gala was an annual event at the Welfare sports ground and started with a parade of floats, fancy dresses and brass bands round the village. Then there were pillow fights for the adults and egg and spoon races for the kids. I was there for the serious stuff – plaques, half-crowns and five bobs for running. I was just pulling on my new spikes when a bunch of lads came by. They were led by Geordie Hume, a burly dark-haired lad with red cheeks. He was about a year older than me and known to be a good fighter. He could also run a bit.

'I'm going to beat you even if I divvent train,' he spat.

Reports had no doubt come to his ears of my hurtling round the cricket pitch. I stripped off my towel and tracksuit and went to the start of the 100 yards. Geordie lined up next to me. I sneered at his football shorts and scruffy black plimsolls. He was with me till halfway down the grass track, then I breezed the run-in by five clear yards.

I offered to shake Geordie's hand but he refused. He just glared.

I did not bother taking my tracksuit off for the hurdles – not real wooden ones, only sweet pea canes balanced on metal stakes. I eased out of my mark, letting Geordie take the lead. To my consternation he made no attempt to jump the first hurdle, he just ploughed through them all. I jumped the lot and came in second.

He stood by the finish line with his mates, all of them red-faced with laughter. A fair section of the crowd was laughing as well.

Two weeks later I walked into the Hirst Welfare at Ashington for the All-England Schools Championships. It was the proudest day of my life. The sun shone brightly and the emerald turf, laid by striking miners in 1926, looked like sheer velvet. I walked proudly with the Northumberland team in white T-shirts and scarlet shorts. My mam, dad and brother Derrick waved from the crowd. As I pushed through the crowd to get ready for my heat, excited people patted my back. Suddenly a suntanned figure in a blue blazer with English lions on the pocket was in front of me, signing autographs. It was Bobby Charlton, now on the books of Manchester United and already a legend. Bobby slipped me a wink. I could have happily died at that moment. I loved the confident Olympian glow of Charlton, an innocent yet god-like aura.

I did not expect to set the track on fire. I had only been doing the 440 for a few weeks, I was a year under age and I was on a growth spurt. I came third in my heat with a time well inside 57 seconds and was eliminated. But there was some consolation: I was adopted as a mascot by two of the old hands in the Northumberland team. They were both 16, from the Duke's School in Alnwick and had been finalists at previous championships. Willie Parkinson was a tall gawky Geordie with buck-teeth who ran with all the grace of a camel. Frank Lauder, a Scot with bulging muscles, had narrowly failed to win the javelin the year before. These two were the wide boys of the team and they led the way to a pub, shouting, 'Jackie Milburn is the best centre-forward in the world.'

Few of the athletes from other counties chose to dispute the claim.

The pair made me and some other young team members hide behind barrels in the pub yard and they came out with bottles of Newcastle Brown Ale. We sang dirty songs, raised toasts to Newcastle United – perennial stars of the FA Cup – and, in the glow of all this camaraderie, I determined to make the county athletics team every summer.

By August we were settling as a family in the new house in Lynemouth. My mother made friends quickly with some ladies at our end of Dalton Avenue. One was Nellie Foster who was the local 'Mrs Cannybody', first to help when bereavement or other mishaps befell her neighbours. We were only a hundred yards from the parade of shops that included the butcher and the Co-op, so Martha's popping out for messages could take two hours, gossip included. My dad too did his share of socialising, leaning over the garden gate talking to fellow gardeners, taking their advice on getting his new leek trench right. He had transplanted that season's leeks from Ellington and was hoping he would get a 'stand' good enough to get in the top ten at Lynemouth Club show. I had ventured like an explorer up the Amazon the entire length of our street of over 200 houses. I had done it dribbling a tennis ball and aiming shots at coal-house doors. At every turn there were reminders of Auld Betty. Lads would be shovelling in heaps of coal for old miners, happy for a shilling a shift. In some yards there were old crackets, stools that hand hewers used in two-foot seams in the old days. Occasionally from a back kitchen would come the hacking cough got from 'cutter duff', dust spewed out by the new mechanical coal cutters. My dad often offered the opinion that these new machines with their whirring steel picks would put 'blood on the coal'.

One sunny afternoon I accidentally kicked my ball over a yard wall. I opened the door quietly and looked round. No sign of my ball. I bent and looked under the shed, then I heard a cough. The toilet door was ajar and it swung open and there was an old man with a beard, flat cap and a clay pipe, trousers round his ankles, newspaper on his knees, trying pathetically to kick my ball back to me. He connected and I picked it up. I beamed in thanks and the old eyes flashed. I noticed tell-tale blue scars of coal-dust in the ridges on his white brow. It was if he was an ancient piece of furniture, sat outside in the yard for an airing.

'He cannit wipe his own arse noo, but you should have seen him play for Lynemouth. Kick like a packing mule. And could he shovel coal.'

The man speaking to me wore no shirt. He was in his fifties and had curly red hair. He had a pitman's pale skin and enormous arms. His right arm was twisted inwards from the elbow and it had a long purple scar. He had the same craggy face as the old man. I thanked him for my ball.

On the way back to 102, I reflected that I was now as near the heart of my dad and his family's experience as I would ever be. Our idyllic life in leafy Cresswell Road was over. Now I was a Lynemouth lad, deep in the muck, sweat and work-gleaned pride of Dalton Avenue.

For my fourteenth birthday I was presented with a new charcoal-grey suit, a red paisley tie and a fancy maroon waistcoat with gilt buttons. This was what the smart man-about-Ashington was wearing. It was a joint idea of my parents. Bob thought I needed the suit when I went to represent the county rugby team – full of public schoolboys – while Martha was intent that I resume my dancing career. She encouraged me to go ballroom dancing at the Arcade on Mondays and Saturday nights. Bob did not like dancing, so her partner at Lynemouth Club Sunday dance nights would be me in a year or so. She made me put on the suit to quickstep and waltz round the living room with her while 'Ramona' and 'Tangerine' crooned out slushily from the record player.

Shortly after my birthday we showed off my suit and our nifty steps at a family wedding reception at a hall near Ashington baths. It was a Protestant wedding, so our party – me, Derrick, Martha, Bob, Granny Mary-Jane and Uncle Sam – had given the church service a miss. But what a night it was. Uncle Sam was drunk before seven and telling Japanese atrocity stories. Derrick, coming up to six years of age, plied Mary-Jane with Newcastle Brown Ale. My granny was really relaxing, knowing that Uncle Sonny was safe in the care of Florence Burnett, her best friend. She was flushed and weaving on trips to the toilet by nine o'clock. Suddenly my notorious uncle Bill, in a claw-hammer coat and a white silk scarf – but with three days' stubble – staggered in with a woman who looked like Olive, her make-up applied as if by trowel. They swished past the bride and groom and began hitting the finger buffet and the free booze. Bill put his arm around me and asked how my running was going. I told him it was going good but he was hardly listening. Soon Bill was taken into a corner by my cousins. After a short debate, he and the woman left as swiftly and unceremoniously as they had arrived. My cousin Robert told me the score.

'We've bribed Billy with a couple of quid to piss off back to the Grand.

Him and his girl can have a fight there and nobody will give a monkey's toss.'

Then all the Waddells were stunned to the core when the Saint of Clayport got slowly and delicately up onto the stage and sang 'Velia, Witch of the Wood' unaccompanied and pitch perfect. The audience went wild. Then Granny got back on the Broon and insisted on my drinking the oily Hooligan's Broth as well. 'Get it doon ya, laddie, it'll dee you good,' she said.

I stopped after four bottles and about midnight we got a lift back to Dalton Avenue. I was so drunk I kept falling in our hedge. I vomited on my dad's prize leeks and on my new suit trousers. As I retched, Granny held me by the waist, shouting slurrily, 'Get it up, my laddie – it'll dee you good.'

I had got stupid drunk for the first time. Even my dad saw it as a rite of passage rather than the start of the slippery slope. I purged myself for a week afterwards. I had raw eggs in milk every morning and ran two miles after breakfast and after dinner. I was due back at the grammar school in a few days and I was determined to be fit for rugby. It was sunny and I ran till I was red-faced, round and round the Welfare cricket pitch, kicking and chasing an imaginary rugby ball.

Two days before the term started I woke up next to my little brother. My chest was on fire and I was fighting to breathe. I threw the window open and tried to suck in air. I spat green phlegm into a hanky. My chest muscles were locked in spasm and I was getting air in only by sucking with my throat. Through my mounting panic I tried to work out what was happening to me. I knew it was something to do with moving to Lynemouth. I was now breathing fumes from two pits, Auld bloody Betty and Lynemouth Colliery, each only half a mile away. Added to that, our new house was 20 yards from the school field, where the grass had been cut the day before. The air was packed with clouds of grass pollen.

Next day Dr Skene visited and confirmed a serious asthma attack. I could breathe only by hugging my chest to an armchair and pressing the muscles loose. He gave me an inhaler and warned me only to have two puffs every twelve hours. If I had more I could have a heart attack. And no rugby 'for at least two weeks'. I was meant to be playing rugby against Newcastle Royal Grammar, our big rivals, in a week's time. I used the inhaler four times that night. My chest eased, but my eyes popped and I could hear my heart pound. I was too jangled to sleep and spent the night cursing the shitty lousy village of Lynemouth, where the very air could destroy you. Underlying this anger was blame, heaped on Bob and Martha for bringing me to the dirty yellow bricks and back lanes of Dalton Avenue.

One week later, still using the inhaler, I played rugby against the Royal Grammar and scored in a narrow victory. At half-time I was paying for it and in quite a state. I sat on the grass, hearing my heart thud like a mallet. My dad was almost in tears. But he knew that substitutes were not allowed and that I must play on. I sucked in more drugs and rejoined the action. On the bus back home I was still wheezing and cursing lousy bloody Lynemouth.

Barging in through the door, the first person I saw was Auntie Bab. She and Mam were sitting at the table drinking tea. Mam jumped up. 'You look terrible, son. You never should have played with your chest.'

'If we hadn't moved to this horrible place I wouldn't have a bad chest. I don't see why you dragged us all here. It's a bloody midden. We were happy at Cresswell Road.'

Martha looked like she was going to cry and Bob was thin-lipped with anger as he greeted Bab, who stood up and reached for her coat. 'I'm away home, now. Sidney, you can carry my messages for me.'

When Bab gave an order, you obeyed. I was ready to drop with exhaustion but I wearily picked up her bags of shopping and left the house, following her down the garden path.

As we went through the gate, Auntie Bab narrowed her eyes and gave it to me with both barrels. 'You ungrateful little snot nose. How dare you speak like that to your mam and dad? He's the hardest grafter in the whole family. The reason you're now living in Lynemouth is because they need money to keep you at that posh bloody grammar school. How many times do you think they've been getting subs from me? And it gets harder and harder for them to pay it back. So every time you go on your jaunts to France and down south, you just remember that.'

The tirade lasted right to Auntie Bab's door. I practically threw in her shopping and ran away. Walking back home I started to cry and I stayed out until I managed to compose myself.

When I arrived home Bob and Martha were obviously at the tail end of a massive row.

'Auntie Bab had no right to make you carry her messages,' cried Mam. 'Now get your clothes off and get into the bath. We'll have you with pneumonia again if we're not careful.'

Dad sat in his chair looking completely deflated and I wanted to give him a great big hug. But he would have been shocked at the show of affection and I was not about to tell them what Auntie Bab had said to me.

As I lay in the bath I promised to myself that I would show more consideration to my parents and not take their generous support for granted. I broke my promise again and again over the years, but now and then Auntie Bab's words would come back to haunt me: 'You ungrateful little snot nose.'

CHAPTER ELEVEN

The Sunny Side of Dalton

*My kid brother Derrick was never as competitive as me at games
and schoolwork. But, even at eight, give him an audience
and he could make them laugh.*

My brother Derrick flowered like a wild nettle in our new environment
in Dalton Avenue. He was just approaching six and had the sort of face
old ladies love to pinch. He also had a halo of tight light-brown curls.
Unlike me at his age he did not care for sport, books, drawing or ego-
tripping. He wanted to be outside with other kids and there was a touch
of the Marco Polo about him; show him a distant patch of blue yonder
and he was off rambling free. But as usual Martha had her bairn weighed
up and she had her ways of keeping tabs on his frequent disappearances.

She bribed one of Derrick's pals, a little dark-haired lad called Kaney who lived further up Dalton, with sweets and coppers to be her eyes and ears and alarm buzzer.

Mam's big fear was the dene just yards from our house, a warren of sloping paths through ash trees, hawthorn thickets and bogs that led to the dirty black water of the river. Birds' nests, rabbits, pirate camps under bushes – you name it – the dene was a paradise for kids. It got your clothes covered in crap, your feet sopping wet – and your blood rushing hot just being there. 'Dek's to the dene,' became a familiar piping cry. Little Kaney would be standing halfway down our backyard pointing the way with one hand and expecting his wages in the other. I would have to stop doing my homework and sprint off yelling for Tadger. Then I would have to drag him screaming back home for his tea. Mam would berate him for worrying her sick, but Dad would give him a cuddle and scoff at Mam's hysteria. This became family dogma: I was Mammy's boy because I caused her no bother; Derrick was 'Daddy's laddie', with the family big nose, Shirley Temple curls and puppy-dog eyes, who never needed charm or guile to get his own way. And increasingly Derrick's 'way' was the opposite of mine. I had a big head and Derrick had no ambition to excel. I was competitive; he was not. I hit the books hard; his energy went into being the class clown. At Lynemouth school he started doing impressions of the Big Bad Wolf to amuse his pals, rolling his eyes and huffing and puffing till his face went red. It got so bad that his eyes began hurting and Mam took him to Dr Skene, who ordered Derrick to stop the act or risk permanent eye damage.

My frustration at being my little brother's keeper came to a head one wet evening in October 1954. I had finished my homework – sitting in the empty bath for peace and quiet with Whisky our Bedlington terrier – and was just getting ready to go to Ashington on a first date with a lass called Jacqueline Harrison from Bedlington Grammar. I put on my new charcoal suit and was standing in front of the mirror in the parlour applying Brylcreem to my curly quiff. Dad was having his after-dinner kip on the settee and Mam was up the street gassing. Suddenly the back door clashed open, startling Dad from his sleep, and Martha came in screaming like a banshee. 'Me bairn, me bairn, he's lost good and proper this time.'

I made her sit down and tell me what had happened.

'I've just seen little Kaney and he says Derrick was ettled on going to the shore. He could have fallen in the river or got stuck in sleck at the Flume or be drowned at Strawberry Hill.'

She was sobbing her heart out. My dad got up and put his arms around her. I knew what I had to do.

'Suppose I run my guts oot till it's pitch dark, I'll find the little bugger.'

I pushed thoughts of Jacqueline standing at the Wallaw cinema corner, stood up and fuming, to the back of my mind

I did not have time to reach for a mac. I just raced out into the downpour. I clattered to the school end of Dalton and down the ginnel to the dene. I turned right on the cart track along the high bank and ran though bramble bushes towards the water. The east wind lashed rain into my face and soaked my suit. Why couldn't wor effin Derrick not get lost when I was wearing my tracksuit? I wondered unkindly. I began yelling, 'Tadger! Tadger! Can you hear us?'

My words echoed back mockingly from low grey clouds and deep sodden woods. It was now nigh on three hours since the little sod had been seen and I was terrified. Hot angry tears mixed with the rain on my face. I imagined carrying a sleck-smeared dead little body up our backyard to face my parents.

I was now at the end of the dene path. I could just make out the sand of Strawberry Hill beach ahead. Getting there meant jumping a barbed-wire fence and sprinting on through a water meadow peppered with cow pats. I stopped and tucked my trousers into my socks. The rain got harder, so hard I drank it in breathy dribbles.

'Help! Ah'm stuck!'

The cry was thin, weak and thready. But I knew it was Tadger. He had a foot caught in a 'rabbit hang', a metal noose laid by poachers. Trying to pull himself out had just made the thick wire tighter. My first urge was to clout his ear. I didn't. I prised the noose from his ankle and hugged him roughly. We both ran home.

Bob and Martha smothered Tadger in gluey affection. Dad stripped off his clothes and put him in the bath. Mam made hot cocoa for him. Both gave him a mild rebuke for wandering off and Mam cursed the poacher who had set the hang. When both my parents had settled by the television, I went into the bathroom and shouted at him.

'You never bloody think, do you? You're nowt but a selfish little twat. I'm ashamed to call you me brother.'

It made him sob deeply, holding a sponge to his quivering blue lips. Within seconds I felt a total swine; there was only one selfish twat in 102 Dalton, and it was not my little brother.

My suit was covered in muck and soaked through, so I put on my school blazer and flannels and re-Brylcreemed my hair. Laden with deep remorse for bollocking our kid, I sat on the 6.10 bus to Ashington knowing I was out of luck. Our date had been for 5.30, time for a quick ice cream and then settle down in the double seats at the Buffalo cinema for a hands-hold and a possible first snog. Fat chance. Jacqueline was nowhere to be seen. I mooched up the street to Docherty's billiard hall and sat with my hand over my school badge, in case the wide boys started mocking me. I watched some lads in T-shirts play snooker skilfully and with loads of banter. I did not offer to join in. I drank ice-cold ginger beer and ate a packet of crisps. Just before eight o'clock I went up the street towards the Regal cinema. The first house was just coming out and I thought maybe Jacqueline might have gone to the movies alone. She had not; she came out on the arm of my hero at Morpeth Grammar, Nigel Savage. They both looked through me with a nervous collaborative smirk.

I ran to the People's Park and did four helter-skelter laps, pushing every muscle to the pips, fuelled by anger and resentment.

You could not hold anger, bile or any grudge against our Derrick for long. The chubby face went from high glee to cartoon grumpiness in a flash. He never was really badly told off by my parents and never walloped. Not for him smacked legs or the belt like I had received at about the same age for hitting Sort Whalley with a half-brick right between the eyes. My brother's misdemeanours were never malicious; he just had a penchant for falling into mishaps. Take the night I took him to the first-house pictures at Lynemouth Institute. It was shortly after the soaked-suit incident and I was trying to make up for my harsh words. I paid for tickets in the ninepennies rather than the wooden seats in the 'cattle pen' at the back. I rationalised that sitting in a plush seat, he would be less likely to fiddle, kick his seat back or annoy the folks behind. Once settled, I dosed him with fruit pastilles, ice cream and weak orange juice from a carton.

The farce began halfway through the main feature, an eerie shadowy black-and-white film about a man pursued by a gremlin who sat at the top of lamp posts and leered down at him. As the man grew more frantic, my brother became more twitchy. He turned in his seat and watched the movie reflected in the big spectacles of a man behind.

'Sit still, you little bugger. Torn aroond and watch the bloody picture!' the man hissed.

My brother would not look at the gremlin. He began to wail softly. 'I'm scared. I wanna gan home.'

I patted Derrick's shoulder and made him sit properly. He bent forward and slowly slid head first on to the floor. There was no bump and he did not cry out. I pulled at his short pants. He did not budge. I flipped up his seat and there were cries of 'Quiet!' I tugged at both of Derrick's shoes. He shouted, 'I'm stuck!'

I bent down and pulled hard. This time he screamed and the lady usher came down the aisle, flashing her torch at us. By the rays I saw that Derrick's hair was stuck fast to the floor by old chewing gum. As he writhed, his curls got more stuck. I began laughing. His flailing legs bashed against the seat in front.

'I'm going to chuck yee two oot,' screamed the usher.

You'll be lucky, I thought, you might manage to shift me but not our

Tadger. Now the house lights had been put up and the film stopped. The hooligans in the 'pen' began banging their feet and booing. The usher was wielding her torch as if she was going to batter me. I pulled hard and with a sound like Elastoplast ripping off a wound, Derrick's hair parted company with the floor. He squealed and I laughed harder at the claggy grey blob on his hairline.

My parents did not laugh at first. They blamed me for the whole saga. Martha tried rubbing warm butter on the claggy gum and raking at it with a nitty comb but it would not come off. Then Bob got his electric shaver and attacked the area. The gum came off all right – and so did a half-crown-sized clump of my brother's curly hair. He had a bald patch high on his forehead till his dying day.

Even at the age of six my brother was defining himself in opposition to me. Not only did he play the joker whenever possible, but he scrawled graffiti on my athletics and rugby team photos. On a shot of my sprinting into the lead in a 440, he wrote, 'Wor Sid, the pillock, with skiny [sic] legs.' And on the back of my Under-15 rugby he wrote, 'Mam, Dad and Sid are all bigs [sic].' Whenever I tried to help him with home-work when he was about eight or nine, the whole thing collapsed as an angry shouting stand-off after only minutes.

In the first few months in our new street Derrick did more socialising than I did. It was not that I was scared to go to the top end of Dalton; in fact, my cousins Robert, Tot and 17-year-old Billy, another tough fighter and pit worker, all encouraged me to seek them out if I got lip or bother from anybody. But as their mother Mary Ross continued to act like a 'trollop' and was regarded as a disgrace, my mother told me to stay away from her. So, on trips to the west end of our village I avoided my uncle Geordie's house.

But, by a strange set of circumstances, I did find out how the folk on the 'unsunny side' of our street lived. One afternoon my dad walked in from work and asked if I could do a favour for a stone man at the pit called Tom Lister, who had a wife and six kids at 26 Dalton. Their son Keith was struggling with algebra at our grammar school and could I help him? I twigged who the lad was, a lanky quiet fresh-faced first year

My rough tough cousins Billy and Robert were feared by the gangs, and they were my bodyguards in our early days in Lynemouth.

who seemed terrified of the masters and prefects. And his problem struck a chord; algebra had baffled me in my early months at Morpeth.

A couple of days later Keith Lister called and handed my mam a parcel. In it were two skinned rabbits. Bob started to laugh. 'Your father is still Lynemouth's star poacher, is he?'

Keith blushed scarlet but glowed with proper pride. 'Aye. Him and me brother Ivan nabbed about 70 rabbits this weekend. Dad asked if yee like salmon. They'll be up the Coquet when the nights get warmer.'

My dad winked at me. 'Teach this laddie them sums and we'll feed like kings summer and winter, courtesy of the Listers.'

Number 26 Dalton had a yard totally unlike ours. It was chock-a-block with piles of coal, wheelbarrows and small carts. There were worn pieces of horse harness everywhere. I remembered seeing Keith and his brother Ivan with their mule when I had gone sea-coaling with my father and Ches. In a hutch slept a couple of white rabbits, kept for pets presumably and not for the pot. Inside, the sights and smells were even stranger. There were dozens of skinned rabbits hanging in the scullery and a stink was coming from the set-pot. Ivan was stirring a witch's brew of potato peelings and bacon rinds, gleaned from local dustbins, for the pigs. He winked at me. 'Divvent worry, Keith. I'll teck the crowdy to the pigs. Yee sit here and talk to yer posh new pal.'

Mrs Lister sat us down with bowls of broth and crusts of bread. I could hardly eat mine for the stink of the crowdy. Tom Lister, burly and with a strong Yorkshire accent, talked about poaching. His wife, florid and with beautiful long hair, spoke eloquent southern English. I learned later she had spent years working in London and France. The house was untidy, verging on scruffy, very like farmers' houses I had been in. There was no sign of posh curtains or the latest Lyncrusta. Martha would have had a blue fit and reached for the bleach.

'What are you going to do with all those rabbits?' I asked.

'Sell them door to door,' said Tom as though I was daft. 'My lads never miss a trick. Keith and Ivan were picking coal off the shore to sell to merchants when they were eight.'

Auntie Bab's hectoring voice played in my ears. *You ungrateful little snot nose.* I never helped my dad in the garden with his leeks and Mam polished my and Derrick's shoes every night. I washed the dishes only on her birthday as a special treat. I clumsily changed the subject.

'How do you kill the rabbits or are they dead in the traps?'

Tom Lister stood up. 'We don't use traps, we catch them in nets. Then...'

He ran out into the yard and came back with one of the white pet bunnies. He held up the fat struggling beast in his left hand and with the forefinger and thumb of his right hand crisply snapped the rabbit's neck. It was as easy as twisting open the salt in a packet of crisps.

'That's how you do it, Sidney...'

The broth came bubbling back up and I raced out into the yard and threw up.

I started training in April and Dad spent five pounds on new running spikes for me. He was now bringing home around nine pounds ten a week, after tax, union dues and national insurance, which meant he was paid 11 pounds 'top of the cheque'. The national average wage was about eight pounds and some coal fillers were taking home 22 pounds, but killing themselves shovelling to earn it. Miners were now the highest-paid industrial workers in Britain.

The rigours of coalface drawing were telling on Bob. He had a wheezy hacking cough and sometimes flopped onto the settee and slept the sleep of the totally knackered after his shift. Once or twice he was so exhausted that we had to shake him hard to wake him up for his dinner, which was always hot, always featured meat, and always on the table at five sharp.

Bob's investment of time and money in me paid off. We went to the Welfare cricket pitch five nights a week and he put the clock on me only very occasionally. He said running against the clock could make me stale. I trained hard for the All-England meeting at Manchester. There I won my heat in 55.9 seconds on a scruffy cinder track. I was eliminated in Round Two, but I was not downhearted. The Lynemouth 220 had convinced me that I was an out-and-out sprinter. I would do the 100 yards next season.

My focus was not exclusively on advancement, exams and sport. I was big for my age and had taken to slipping into the big back dance room-cum-lounge at the Lynemouth Hotel – alias 'The Jungle' (because part of the dance floor was a bamboo cane cage with plastic vines), as the Lynemouth Hotel was known all over Northumberland – for the odd beer on Saturday nights. The Hotel had been built in 1925 by the Ashington Coal Company to house visiting colliery officials at Lynemouth and Ellington collieries. But now its mock-Tudor portals, eaves, galleries and stained-glass windows were a facade for what was very like a saloon in Dodge City. It had cowboys aplenty. Twisty Medlen, lamed for life by a fall of stone down Auld Betty, used his crutches to trip up drunks for fun. Les Dunning would show up in his best Italian suit and fill up with beer till he fancied a fight. He would run home, change into old jeans and T-shirt, go back to the Hotel and smack the first bloke who looked funny at him. Another regular was Keith Lister's Uncle Harry who had several years as a top professional boxer in the 1940s. Harry trained at the Institute and had such a powerful left uppercut that he sometimes knocked sparring partners through swing doors. In his prime he fought 58 fights and lost only four. In mid-1955 he was back down Auld Betty by day and by night averaging 50-plus pints of bitter a week. Stories were told off him helping the Lister lads at the sea coal by strapping a kiddie's bath to his back and acting as a horse, hauling coal from sea to heap. Eventually the pints and the punches got to Harry and he began talking to trees and lamp posts. Later he lived in a tatty caravan down the shore and bashed all the windows out 'because I love the fresh air'.

These were the regulars at the Hotel. But on Saturday nights in summer, lads from Ashington, Newbiggin, Blyth and Amble came flocking for beer and women. Coach trips from Newcastle and Gateshead would pull into the car park that once was the stable yard and Toonie lads and lasses would pour out in their best clothes. Twice a year a coach full of bonny bouncing lasses from Haggie's Rope Works in Newcastle would arrive and all bets were off. The local blades like Les Dunning, Richie Stafford and Gordon Crawford would get all spivved up and were first to get a dance partner, since they knew some of the lasses from previous visits. The idea was to pour drinks down the girls, suggest a 'breath of fresh air' and try to make out in the stables or indeed on the coach itself. Indeed the branches of the Jungle were hung with scented letters from appreciative Tyneside ladies.

One Saturday night I was just thinking of leaving when a row started between one of Les Dunning's gang and a hard case from Red Row. The hard case had tried to break into the Bradford Barn Dance and the

Lynemouth lad objected. In seconds the locals were hitting out at strangers and glasses were being smashed on people's heads. I slipped out and headed home. I didn't fancy trying to explain a fat lip or a black eye to Bob and Martha.

The chat-ups and punch-ups were in fact taking place on hallowed ground; the dance room was where Mam and me went to Catholic Mass. At around ten to ten on Sunday mornings Martha would dab on a bit of lipstick and rouge, put on her ocelot fur coat and sling a head-scarf around her curls. We would traipse off to the Hotel, past the odd French letter in the stables and down a passage where the cleaning ladies would be mopping up the dregs of beer and blood. All the tables would be set out, chairs placed in lines and a dozen beer crates stacked to make an altar. The two altar boys draped a tablecloth over the crates and put the wine vessels and candlesticks in place. Mam would head for the front and I would drag her to the back. I always aimed to be down-wind of Stan Levison, a burly Brylcreemed cricketer, who knew when to kneel, when to stand up, when to bless himself and when to look extra solemn. Mum knew all the drill by heart and all the prayers, responses and creeds. But I just followed Stan. If Stan had shouted 'The Pope's a pillock' during a prayer I would have seconded him

My mind often wandered off. I would scan the heads of some of the women who always seemed to be showing off their best hats at Mass and wonder why Martha did not bother to wear one. I looked around and compared this place with Mary-Jane's elegant St Michael's Church in Alnwick, with its statues, icons and incense. But I always concentrated fully when the bells rang for the most solemn part of the service. We all knelt, bowed our heads and beat our breasts, chanting, 'Through my fault, through my fault, through my most grievous fault'. What had I, Mam, or for that matter the priest done to act so frenziedly penitent? It was hard to stay in a holy cocoon when the cleaning ladies were loudly describing their love lives or recent operations behind a glass partition. 'He just pulled me knickers to one side.' 'They gave me a bottle and told me to piss in it.' Amen. Mass was usually over fifteen minutes before pub opening time and some of the Catholic menfolk just went from kneeling and praying straight through to the main bar for beer, bingo, and free cheese and pickles.

In August of 1955 we took my brother Derrick to Mass at the Hotel; it was his first and his last visit. He got very bored about 20 minutes into proceedings and began to look around. In the chairs immediately in front of us were John and his family. John was a dour, thick-featured man who had a very cruel streak; a dog once chased one of his chickens and he buried the dog alive. The dog's owner and his pals gave John a good kicking. Today John was deep in prayer, possibly asking forgiveness for killing the dog. But his little four-year-old son was in playful mood. The laddie had angelic blue eyes and white-blond hair and he began making faces at Derrick through the slats in the back of his chair. Derrick replied by shaking the slats like a monkey. The little boy responded by shaking the slats like King Kong and making loud gorilla noises. John clouted his son's ear good and proper. Derrick and I kinked with laughter. Martha did not stay to gossip after the service. She tore into both of us for getting the kid clouted.

A few weeks later the priest, a young curly-haired Irish lad, six foot tall, called at our house at about four. Dad was not back from work and so there would be no cracks about 'Holy Joe' or 'him with his collar on back to front'. I was having a great row with my mam. I had asthma badly but wanted to play rugby the next day. I was drinking a foul mixture called Famel Syrup, using my inhaler and coughing phlegm into a bucket. Mam's eyes lit up when the priest dropped in. 'Tell him he must not play tomorrow, Father,' she whined.

A crafty look came over the priest's face. 'Sure now, Sidney, I have an idea. What do you say to coming out into the back lane and trying to leapfrog over me. If you can, you play. If you can't, you don't. Make sense?'

I agreed and out we went. A group of raggy kids watched us. The priest stood in the middle of the lane with his back bent. I took a ten-yard run-up and cleared him easily. He shook his head. He wagged his finger at me and stood erect with his head bent. I cleared him easily again, not even skimming his hair. He glowered at me and stood as tall as he could. This time my trousers riffled his hair but I definitely cleared him.

'I've passed your test, Father, and I'm ganna play.'

'Yes, Sidney,' he sighed, 'you passed okay. But for me and your darling mother please don't play rugby tomorrow.'

I could tell that he was fond of my mother and she of him. My mam still dreamed that I would become a priest like him, even though she knew it would be over Bob's dead body. And I had not seen anything in religious life that would make me want to join their numbers. I asked if he thought when he signed on for the priesthood that he would be boosting morale in mean streets like our pit village.

'I go where God's work needs me – even if that work involves playing leapfrog with a stroppy Geordie gurrier.'

I looked up the Irish word and it means 'a young fella with cute tenacity'. It would do for me. The next day I played rugby.

I gave up on religion a year later. I knew how important the Catholic Church was to Mam and Mary-Jane; it had sustained them through the tragedies of their early lives. But I had now come round to Dad's way of thinking and religion seemed irrelevant to the life I was leading. Telling Mam was going to be tricky and for a few weeks I deceived her by telling her and Granny that I was going to Mass but instead walked past St. Michael's church and the convent where Sister Theresa had trained me in the faith, to sit in the Duke's Pastures in the meadows under the castle. There I would read borrowed magazines like *Razzle*, full of white thighs, black suspenders and silk stockings with seams.

I was still making occasional weekend trips to Granny's flat in King Street, Alnwick, even though I dreaded listening to Uncle Sonny's cries for his mammy. Sonny was now 37 and declining. His speech was a series of grunts and animal screams. And though his body was withered and he had to be lifted everywhere, Mary-Jane would not have a wheelchair for him. She had tried him in a wheelchair years before and he had howled to be out. She had sacked the wheelchair, saying later after a few milk stouts, 'My bit laddie is not a cripple.'

But he was. One sunny Saturday afternoon, when Mam was doing the shopping, Mary-Jane and I carried Sonny out the front door and sat him on a dining-room chair. I was left to mind him. For a while Sonny sat looking at the sun, then he wriggled and fell off the chair. I lifted him back on but he would not stay still. He fell on the pavement again and I struggled to lift him up. As I bent I was pushed aside by Uncle Sam, fresh from a boozy afternoon in the Bird and Bush. Roughly Sam hauled his brother upright and began to shake him. 'Behave, you bastard,' cried Sam and Sonny began to slobber and weep.

I was aghast. Sam continued to eff and blind. Granny ran out and heard him. 'Get your hands off my laddie, you swine,' shouted Granny, hot tears welling in her eyes.

Sam and Mary-Jane tugged Sonny as if he was a rag doll, each trying to be the one to take Sonny inside. Neighbours came out at the commotion. It was a holy show and no mistake. Sam backed off and I helped Granny take Sonny indoors. I blathered something about it only being the drink, but Granny was not buying that. Thankfully, Sam went back to the pub. As Granny laid Sonny on his bed and tried to soothe him, I better understood Mam's visits to Alnwick and realised too that Sam ran to the pub to escape from the strain of looking after Sonny by drowning in a warm pool of Double Maxim.

The highlight of my dad's year came in September as the leek show at Lynemouth and District Social Club loomed. The days before the 'howking', the ritual digging up of the best leeks, were always tense, and always laced with elements of sheer pantomime. Bob would come home from the pit, snatch just half an hour's sleep, then bolt his dinner. Then he would roll up his sleeves and set his flat cap to the 'business' angle, down low over the eyes. He would squat on his haunches by the trench and inspect each of the two dozen leeks. He would prod at the white butts and caress the green fronds, looking for blemishes. The leek show was a beauty pageant. You had to put in a 'stand' of three leeks and size was important. In fact, in 1952 Fred Brough, who worked down Auld Betty, broke the world record with three leeks each measuring 74 cubic inches round the base. But size was not the only criterion. The white of the butt must not be tarnished by streaks of yellowy brown decay and the fronds had to shine emerald green.

In September 1955, the Friday night before the show, my brother and I looked out of the window and were happy. Dad's cap was stuck on the back of his head – the pleased signal. He was stroking six of the leeks and nodding vigorously. There had been rumours of leek slashers destroying likely winners and he had sat out in the garden with an old double-barrelled shotgun – not loaded – till two in the morning one night. Now he called us out to begin the 'howking' ceremony. We went into the back kitchen where Mam had laid out clean fluffy white towels, jugs of milk and pans of hot water. We got a towel each and went into the garden. Bob carefully dug with a garden fork and prised out two monsters. Carefully he flicked soil from the white spaghetti-like roots. Derrick and I carried in the leeks as if they were the most delicate china.

A bed sheet was laid on the floor of the parlour and Mam looked down on the final six chosen leeks. She washed them with warm water then stood back as Bob, with a touch like Tintoretto, 'painted' the butts and roots with milk. When he finished, the six wedging leeks looked as though they had been varnished. He did not take his hat off till the leeks were covered with another pristine bed sheet. 'Top ten or me name's not Bob Waddell,' he whispered, twisting his cap nervously.

Next morning we took the prize leeks to the club in the wheelbarrow. Bob pushed and Derrick and I walked sedately and proudly like two pages assisting Sir Galahad to a joust at Camelot Park. We joined the joshing gang of other leek fanciers queueing to put their stands in the show.

'What have you got under that sheet, Bob? Pit props?' said one of the Taylor family.

'Better than them scallions yee've got there,' replied Bob.

Underneath the banter was a nervy competitive edge. It was alien to my dad's usual matey nature.

Inside the 'Big End', the concert room, officials logged the entries and put markers on each man's stand. Bob had a quick glance round at some of the competition and seemed happy that his leeks were well up to par. Then we were ushered out. Nobody was allowed to get too near the array of leeks for fear of tampering. Only the judge and two officials were allowed in the Big End after the last leek was entered. First prize was a full suite of furniture – two armchairs and a settee – worth a couple of month's wages. This was a very serious day indeed.

At seven Mam was all gussied up in her best frock and Dad was suited and Brylcreemed. Martha polished our shoes and dabbed water on my brother's wild curls. We set off in silence for the club, my parents puffing tensely at Woodbines. We walked into the main door of the club and my nose twitched at the rich smell of beer and nearly one thousand leeks, with a sideshow of marrows, turnips and cabbages. Bob led us to the twentieth stand, and then we moved upwards. It struck me he was cruising for a bruising if it turned out he was going the wrong way. Suddenly he let out a gentle roar that started at his navel. 'Whaaah! Me little beauties.'

The lights sparkled off the butts of his best three leeks and the card read, 'Stand Number 10. Robert Waddell'. Behind the leeks was the prize: a kitchen cabinet, cream with red trimmings and red handles inlaid on the glasswork and with a let-down table for light snacks. I had never seen my parents look so pleased.

All next day the smell of leeks in our house got stronger and stronger. Dad kept the best six for seed and the rest of the trench formed our staple diet for the next two weeks. That evening we had leek and beef dumplings for dinner and Mam left a chopped pile of leeks for frying. Then they went back to the club for bingo, a dance and a modest bit of gloating.

Two hours after dinner Derrick said he felt peckish and I fried the mountain leeks in butter and made loads of sandwiches with doorsteps of bread. We washed the lot down with American Cream Soda. Then I had a bottle of Vaux's Double Maxim while Derrick ate two Blue Riband biscuits. Within minutes we were both vomiting and laughing in unison in the netty in the backyard. It was one of the greatest closest moments we ever had together.

If you believed what Cousin Robert said, his prize leeks were like tree trunks. This lot look to me like scallions.

CHAPTER TWELVE

Satan's Citadel

Back at Morpeth Grammar School in the autumn of 1955, at parents' evening, the new headmaster, W.L. Elsworth, a Cambridge man, told Bob and Martha that I was 'Oxford or Cambridge material'.

But I had other things to distract me from school. I was becoming keener to get a proper girlfriend. In this area I had a very unusual guru, Billy Mitchell. Mitch had become one of my best friends at the grammar. He lived in Boland Road in Lynemouth, near many of my cousins, and had been very unfortunate. In 1955 he developed serious chest problems and was in and out of hospital for nearly a year. He was a jokey, gobby lad with dark bushy hair and mad eyes, so the nurses made a lot of him. When he came back to school he would tell anybody who would care to listen tales, obviously embroidered, about being tossed-off under the blankets and shagging nurses while they were supposed to be giving him bed baths. I found myself horrified yet excited by his yarns, often recounted at full voice and in lurid detail on the school bus, where kids of 11 coloured-up and covered their ears, much like I had at that age. Mitch could also sing 'Rock Around the Clock', just like Bill Haley. I envied him his crooning voice and all the attention it got him.

But it was my dad who set me on the primrose path to the billiard hall in 'Satan's Citadel'. This was the name given to Ashington in 1955 by a local vicar in a newspaper article. At that time Ashington was known as 'the biggest pit village in the world'; 'village' because it had no town hall. There were five collieries in the Ashington area – Auld Betty, Lynemouth, Woodhorn, Linton and Ashington itself – and they employed around 10,000 workers. Some lads 'got away' by boxing or football, or joined the forces or the merchant navy. However, most males went down the pit and took what 'recreation' they could. And with full employment in the mines some lads had money to burn and went 'on the hoy' at the weekends. The disappointed vicar deplored the fact that many of Ashington's population of 29,000 spent a lot of precious time and hard-earned money in the town's 23 workingmen's clubs, two billiard halls, seedy dog track and three beer-palace pubs – the Grand, the Portland and the North Seaton Hotel. It was the vicar's view that many people in Ashington were, to use a frequently heard phrase, 'Heading for Hell like shit off a hot shovel'; not his words exactly, but certainly the sentiment.

Now my dad Bob did not mean to send me down the slippery slope but it was he who set the ball rolling. Behind the cheap wardrobe in my parents' bedroom was a long black metal tube with a locked cap on one end. Inside was a beautiful billiard cue that Bob had won a few weeks before meeting my mother in 1936. It had never been used. Occasionally he would take it out and slide it lovingly through his battered fingers, smiling in nostalgia. I persuaded him one night early in 1956 to take it to the Welfare Institute in Lynemouth and show me a few shots. I thought Bob would just stick on an old pullover but I was wrong. A visit to the hallowed billiard room was, like the Leek Show, a solemn ritual. He put on a clean shirt, tie and waistcoat and slotted a watch-chain with an old Booth Cup football medal – Uncle Bill's, I think – hanging on it, and pasted down his thinning topping of hair with water.

We had to wait to get a table and we sat like devotees of a religious cult in the smoky shadow as one of the high priests did his stuff on the spotlit green baize. He was called Campbell. He was cadaverous and high-browed and dressed like a bank manager. The knot in his tie was the size of a pea and he had a starched collar. He moved gracefully round the table, stopping occasionally to wipe his specs on a hankie. He swooped elegantly to manoeuvre the balls, cannoning spot white to red and plain white. It was pure angular science, plus a smidgeon of show-business arrogance. When his break hit 100 we all gasped and the maestro dabbed his head daintily with his shirtsleeve.

'He's got more edge than a broken pisspot,' said a voice behind us.

'Ssssh,' hissed Bob with a wide grin.

When we got a table my dad tried to drill the basics of cueing and positional play into me. He said never to use power unless you needed it. But I was not listening. I couldn't wait to get to Docherty's billiard hall in Ashington, a wide boy's mecca, and strut my stuff like the great Campbell, give or take a slather of Brylcreem and a waistcoat. My parents, like many, deplored the new Teddy Boy outfits: lurid purple and green drape jackets, long hair with sideboards, skintight trousers, brothel-creeper rubber-soled shoes, these were to them signs of total dissolution and immorality. I was told that they were all taboo. What I was allowed to wear didn't come close to the true Teddy Boy style: my mam's mate, Jean Bone, knitted me a canary-yellow jumper and I got some purple socks and patent leather black shoes with suede front panels on her 'tick' account at Arrowsmith's department store in Ashington. What with this lot, a crew cut that showed off my sticky-out ears and patches of volcanic acne, I was a ringer for Tab Hunter's geeky kid brother. But Jimmy the Screw, Bubbles, Joe Morris, Stan the Battler, Cliff the Para and Tom Cowan adopted me as their mascot. The draw was less affection and most probably the seven shillings and sixpence pocket money that Bob doled out to me at five o'clock on Friday nights and the pool-hall gang had in their pockets by eight.

I made my first sortie to Docherty's on a cold misty February night. I knew an overcoat would get me scoffed at as a softie, so I shivered my way up Ashington's main street in the yellow jumper and baggy old blue denim jeans and turned left past Keith Cazaly's shop window full of ladies' undies. I went up the dim stairway, checked the warm coins in my pocket, and felt my mouth go dry with fresh adrenalin as I heard the magical click of balls and hoarse fag-raked voices. I slid twitchily into one of the main dives in Satan's rip-roaring Citadel.

There were about 12 tables in the room. In front of the glass-paned kiosk near the door was the 'match table' where local stars would play for pride – stakes were often involved but never admitted – and that was the stage where Docherty, the lean world-weary owner would deign to show his silken cue gifts now and then. On it that night the big match was a clash of Black Hat versus White Hat; hook-nosed swarthy Galley took on Scotty, pale-faced and worried-looking. I watched as Galley boasted to the onlookers,

'Even Houdini could not get out of that snooker.'

Scotty did but made no cheap riposte. He whistled softly as he chalked his cue. They were like a pair of henchmen in a gangster movie: one an introverted fretter, one a bighead blusterer.

The other tables were a motley selection. Some had good naps and others were threadbare. At the outsides were the most tatty, some even with holes in the pockets. That's how I met Joe and the gang. I was buying some crisps and pop when there was a noisy clatter on the bare floorboards and something hit my right heel. It was a white cue ball. I picked it up and looked over at the table. A lad with curly black hair and prominent teeth waved at me. 'Can we have our ball back, mister?' one called with a sarcastic grin.

I took the ball over to them. The curly lad smiled and held out his hand.

'You're Waddell, aren't you? At Morpeth Grammar? Some of my mates have run against you. I'm Joe Morris. I gan to Saint Cuthbert's in Newcastle. That's Jimmy the Screw.'

Jimmy was dressed in a sharp black Italian suit and sucking on a fag. He twisted his pretty freckled face at me. He noticed the query on my face.

'I got me name cos if it moves I'll screw it.'

He took the cue ball and set up a shot. Out of the shadow near the toilet came a figure straight out of a teen rock movie. He had a black curly quiff, and wore a white T-shirt, black leather jacket, tight black jeans and basketball boots. If only Martha would let me wear let half that gear, I moaned inwardly. He had crafty eyes and thick lips. He did not walk, he bounced. 'Hey up. Albert Buttles. You can call me Bubbles.' He looked hard at my sweater. 'I'll bet your mother is a champion knitter.' He looked round for applause and Joe and Screw laughed.

Joe bent near my ear. 'If Bubbles teks the piss out of you, it means he like you.'

Soon we were playing a game of Crash, a shortened version of snooker where you leave off the reds and get points for cannons, for one shilling a time. By eight o'clock I was skint and had to borrow my bus fare home. But by then I felt I had passed a test. I told stories about me and Derrick getting sick as dogs on leek sarnies and how Granny held me while I puked on Dad's leeks. I even used the f-word for effect. 'Fucking Ella Renwick nearly got me put in clink by the fucking gendarmes.'

'I hope you shagged it,' said Jimmy.

My sudden silence and beetroot chops gave the game away.

'V-I-R-G-I-N – I can spot 'em,' said Jimmy 'We'll mek certain yer wick gets dipped, son.'

'Hurry back, Sidney,' shouted Bubbles so the whole hall could hear. 'And tell yer father to up yer pocket money, cos we need it for beer, bookies and dirty women.'

So began my dual existence for the next few years; grammar school student by day and apprentice wide boy by night. I hit the billiard hall at least once a week after my costly baptism.

At home my mam went about the rest of her chores unaware of the rebellious route my life was taking. My dad did not like some of my tales from the billiard hall, but said nowt, even when the odd curse word slipped into my chat. And that's what we Waddells did all the time; we talked. There was a constant stream of visitors to 102 Dalton, and my mother was the perfect hostess. As if to make up for the lean hard times she had experienced as a young woman, she played Lady Bountiful to friends, family and a host of tradesmen. They never got away without a fag, a nip of hard stuff, a bowl of her home-made broth or a slice from one of her gooey cakes. We had a veritable Dickensian parade of regular tradespeople. Joe the milkman always had fresh eggs for my mother and the latest gossip from the streets of Ashington. Mary the baker parked her van outside in the back lane and sometimes was there for an hour as she and Martha put the world to rights over Woodbines and strong tea. Then there was Jimmy Perfect of Newbiggin, fish salesman extraordinaire. Jimmy would sit sucking a Woodbine and tell tall stories of his ancestors taking small cobles halfway to the Dogger Bank or chasing the mighty shoals of herring. Then he would sell Martha his best kippers or succulent cod at a knock-down price. She would reply with tales of the poverty and fun up Clayport Street. Sometimes she would crank up the

Like myself and Uncle Bill, Robert was a tearaway in his youth. Then he met and married the lovely Gladys. They became Bob and Martha's best pals.

gramophone and get Jimmy, in his smelly fishy khaki overall, to join her in a quick foxtrot round the parlour.

Generally, my mam was much less at loggerheads with folk in Dalton Avenue than she had been. She only saw those of my dad's sisters who did not snipe about religion, and she was very friendly with my cousin Robert's wife, Gladys. Gladys came from a mining family in Ashington and her lot had known hard times, so she and Martha sat for hours swapping stories of hardship.

In March 1956 my mother and I were invited to experience at first hand what my dad went through for his family every day. We were to go down Auld Betty to take a look at Bob's bleak world. The trip had been dreamed up by my cousin Robert and my uncle Tommy Chester. Both were very active in the local branch of the National Union of Mineworkers. They persuaded the management of Auld Betty to let me, Martha and Robert's wife Gladys make a trip down below. I got Billy Mitchell to take a letter to the grammar school saying I'd been struck with asthma, and on a sunny morning Martha, Gladys and I were led into the tally cabin in overalls by Robert and given a hat lamp, battery and a brass token. I wondered why my mother kept patting her bulging pocket but, knowing Martha, it would be sandwiches for elevenses.

We entered the lower section of the double-decker cage and a bell clanged. I was terrified. We rumbled down for about three minutes. Then we got out and the blackness was unbelievable. As we fiddled with the lamps Robert led us towards the mothergate, the main road to the working faces. We walked through black spongy dust. Odd noises of men talking bounced off the dimly lit walls. I lasted about ten minutes. I began coughing and wheezing and went into asthmatic spasm. It was not just physical; my Catholic imagination had kicked in. This must be retribution for sending a lying letter to school. Martha turned and, by the light of my lamp, I saw the panic in her face. Suddenly she dropped to her knees and pulled something from her pocket. It was a bottle of holy water. She began splashing it on my head and blessing herself with it.

'Oh, most holy Father and blessed Virgin Mother, bless my laddie and his poor father who has to come to the godforsaken place every day.'

Cousin Robert could not stop himself laughing.

So my one and only trip down Auld Betty resulted in my being helped back to the cage and up to bank. They let me shower in the pit baths, my clothes lassoed and strung up on a pulley, and I was too ashamed to wait for the group photograph. Martha never made it as far as the Fourth West section, way out under the North Sea, where Bob worked, but she did see men tending the evil-teethed cutters and she did feed sandwiches to some ponies. And she was in her element later as she told florid tales of the visit to the 'black tunnels of Hell'. 'Good job Wor Sidney's a canny scholar, cos he only lasted ten minutes doon Betty.'

There was concern in the family about a mystery wasting illness that had hit my uncle Jack. He was my dad's next-to-youngest brother and aged 45. Jack had been an ardent fishermen and co-owner of a fishing coble at Cresswell. Like my brother Derrick, he was a laugh-a-minute person. As a young man he had been a horse-racing fan and had gone on many bus trips to Redcar and York. On these he had always taken squares of newspaper in case he was caught short, and once he had taken a chamber pot along to Wetherby Races in his haversack! He claimed that toilet facilities at the courses were bad, so: 'Wherever I go I take my poe. And a good supply of paper.'

In mid-March 1956 uncle Jack had to stop work as a filler at the pit because of weakness and depression. My dad took it upon himself to visit his brother as often as he could. Jack was a bachelor and lived with my aunt and uncle, Elsie and Tom Chester, on a smallholding near Cresswell. One evening I went with Bob on a visit. We walked slowly along a lonnen that led from Auld Betty to the sea. A pleasant breeze blew in our faces. My dad was very solemn. He had his eyes on the path as he walked. I began to worry.

'Has anybody any idea what's wrong with Uncle Jack?' I asked.

'No, son. The doctor reckons he's always been bad with his nerves. He's high-strung just like yee are. Mebbes a nerve's trapped or summat.' My dad spoke with hope rather than conviction.

I did not like the worry that imbued every word. My mood of dread deepened when I saw my uncle; his usually bright eyes were dull and staring and a big vein throbbed in his left temple. He was sitting by the fire on a buffet and when he got up to take a cup of tea he doddered. He dug in his pocket and gave me an orange ten-shilling note. 'Keep stuck in at school young 'un,' he mumbled.

I wanted to refuse the gift but a motion by Dad indicated I should take it. Bob helped Jack into a big Crombie overcoat and the pair went for a slow walk up the meadow to the stable.

I was on the verge of tears myself when I heard a sobbing from the kitchen. My auntie Elsie was normally a toughie – she had once rubbed my neck red raw with a scrubbing brush after seeing me skimping the task – but now she was crying as she washed the dishes. The sight of her crying was powerful: Elsie had a face that only a mother could love, and seeing it scrunched-up with pain cut me up properly. I put my arm around her.

'When you're next at that Catholic service pray for your uncle, will you, Sidney?'

I had not the heart to tell her I was now a non-believer and was only going to Mass in the pub occasionally to please Martha.

'Aye, I'll dee that,' I said.

My dad held his head high on the walk back home. But he said very little. I was too unnerved by what I had seen to try and force conversation, so I unconsciously walked faster to get the journey over quickly. I stopped and looked around. My dad was trying to match my pace and was holding his right hand to the centre of his chest. He was gasping.

'What's the matter, Dad?'

'Just me manky old wheezy Waddell chest,' he joked. 'Bit of a nagging pain. Take a spell and I'll be canny.'

It is March 1958 and I am proudly holding the ball as captain of Morpeth Grammar first team. I will not isolate which members of the team drunkenly disgraced the school at Barnard Castle.

He wasn't. A few days later he went to the doctor and angina was diagnosed. The doctor said Dad should think long term of taking on lighter work than humping conveyor tracks and wrestling with chains and props. It would mean less money, so Bob dismissed the idea. Next time I went with Martha to Mass at the Hotel, I prayed from my heart for both my dad and Uncle Jack, and hoped God and Jesus and Co. would take an errant soul back on board.

It was not just the wide boys at Ashington billiard hall that were pointing me down the primrose path; the scions of the grammar school first XV had been doing their bit too. The captain, Joe Elliot, often lit up fags after training on Top Field and so did his deputy Ewan Dawes, who was rumoured to have sex with his girlfriend the night before jumping and grappling in the line-out. Our scrum-half, Brian Underhill, spent a lot of time at the local bookies and organised three-card brag schools behind the cricket pavilion. It was these lads who showed Brian Carolin and me what the 'character-building' aspect of rugby was really all about. We had just enjoyed a draw in a late season match against Newcastle Royal and, still wet from the showers, were led down a ginnel to the Greyhound, a scruffy pub frequented by tarts and hawkers.

We were told to go and sit in the pub backyard while the older lads went in the main door. After five minutes Underhill opened the back door and we entered low-life heaven; dartboard, greasy linoleum, rude calendar, streaked spittoon, foxed mirror advertising Bell's Scotch Whisky and the wonderful debauched smell of dead beer. At a battered old piano with fag-burns and wonky bratiches sat Brian Reid, one of the RGS team. He had a fag on the go and was squinting as the smoke hit his eyes. He was wearing a yellowy silk cravat – the first I'd ever seen outside the movies. Reid did a few fancy trills then played 'When the Saints Go Marching in'. All of us sang along and some tapped raucous time with tin ashtrays.

At the end of the song, the RGS lads called on Morpeth to give a song. Ewan Dawes led the way with 'The Ball of Kirriemuir' – a graphic description of the deflowering of 24 virgins, most of it anatomically impossible – followed by 'In Mobile' – every line containing a different swear-word – and 'Dinah, Dinah, Show Us a Leg' – in which Dinah reveals much more than her stocking-tops. Despite my convent training, high moral stance and upwardly mobile ambitions, all I wanted to be that Saturday afternoon was a dirty song leader.

Two hours, three pints of ginger beer shandy and several extra-strong mints later and I was watching *Grandstand* on a flickery television in our parlour with my dad. As usual the curtains were drawn to make the picture better. I told Bob the highlights of my day; a try and some good tackling in the match but nothing about the Greyhound.

He punched at the coal fire with a poker, cleared his throat and spat into the flames. 'I think you're fast enough now to go for the hundred yards. You could win the England schools if you train hard. I reckon you should play no rugby at all next season, just work on stamina and speed. What d'you think?'

Immediately I thought: no. Miss all the dirty-song singing? Miss the adulation as I sold a dummy or dropped a goal? I gave a properly weighed answer. 'If I wanna be captain of the first team in two years, I cannot take a sabbatical.'

He heaved a hefty sigh and phlegmed into the fire again. 'The way yee chuck yersell into tackles you'll get crocked good and proper.'

He turned back to the rich Northern tones of Eddie Waring yodelling 'ooohs' and 'aahs' as northern bruisers thumped seven bells out of each other. My dad had never seen a live rugby league match, but he had an uncanny knack of predicting the winners of games. Even with my knowledge of rugby union, I could not outguess him. I didn't know it then, but Bob would also turn out to be a soothsayer in a different matter.

Dad and I set about the moving on in my running career. At the far side of the Welfare sportsground was a long 150-yard swathe of lush grass, wide enough to take four runners abreast. This was to be our 'field of dreams'; other lads might be thinking of Wembley or Twickenham, but that strip of grass, sandwiched between Lynemouth's tatty cemetery and the colliery manager's mansion, was where Bob and me could dream.

Bob was my coach and he did a thorough job. In the late 1930s he had studied the styles of all the professional runners his school had come across. He had also recently been to foot-racing meetings where the legendary Albert Spence of Blyth had been star man. So my dad took me step by step through the art of sprinting. First, I got down on my marks and came up and out gradually, taking 20 or 30 strides before running upright. Then the knees had to get high and the arms pump. It was rumoured that the heavily muscled Spence got the knee-lift perfect by strapping wooden splints to his legs, but we only tried this once. It was like doing a three-legged race solo. Finally, a controlled dip to the tape with the shoulders completed the technique. After two weeks and six outings, Dad put the watch on me over a measured 100 yards and I did a respectable 10.8 seconds. The county sports were just six weeks away and I knew I was in with a chance.

However good the coaching was that I got from my dad, I was determined to gild the lily. I stood in front of my mam's dressing-table mirror one night clad only in white skimpy running shorts and posed like Charles Atlas. I was pathetic; my biceps looked like sparrow's kneecaps and my thighs were very puny. I had a brainwave. Some lads were walking around Lynemouth with massive lats, pecs and quads bulging out of tight T-shirts and jeans. They'd got pumped-up thanks to the gym run at the Institute by Colin 'Tashy' Neil. Colin was a top gymnast, a flamboyant bloke with jet-black hair who looked and spoke like a mafia don.

'So, Sidney, you've come decided that a proper series of exercises with the weights will improve your running?' Concern was poured on like treacle, then a harsher tone. 'Well, let me tell you. Weights will not only improve your speed over grass, but will improve your whole life. Even your sex life.'

The last bit was added as a joke, but I saw fit to tell my leotard-clad guru that the last was way down my agenda. So it was that I started doing squat thrusts for my thighs and bench-pressing up to 230 pounds for my arms and belly muscles. The result was a shock: after two weeks on the weights my time dropped to 11.1 seconds flat-out.

'Bloody Tashy and his bloody weights,' yelled Bob, looking at the watch. 'The daft bugger's med yer muscle boond!'

He was dead right; I had overdone the weights, but after another two weeks I got the balance right and did 10.6 seconds.

A few days later my dad came home in tears. My brother Derrick thought he had been hurt in the pit and hugged his legs, weeping. My mother was hysterical, throwing holy water all over his ancient cap. I knew something terrible had happened at Auld Betty. Bob sipped hot tea from his favourite mug and looked at me like a man who had sinned massively. He had not showered properly after his shift and there was coal dust round his eyes, streaking down to his mouth. Our dog Whisky lapped at the muck round Dad's wrists.

'I could yark me bloody tongue oot me heid.' He spoke low and hoarse and never took his eyes off me. 'Calling Tashy Neil aal the stupid sods for showing you how to gan on with them weights. The poor bugger got caught in a coal cutter today. It chewed up his right arm and shoulder. If he hadn't been a strong man with the weights, gymnastics and things his neck and heid would have been sucked in. He pulled hissel oot by sheer guts. There was blood spurting aal over. His marras say they've seen nowt like it.'

My dad began sobbing and I could not hold it together. I began to cry. Mam got her old rosary beads out and I prayed with her. I prayed bloody Betty would flood or go on fire and be closed down. Then Bob could get a job as a bus driver or a farm labourer. Living in the deadly shadow of Betty meant living with jeopardy; everything else was a temporary respite, be it sport, lasses, passing exams or my new pals at the billiard hall.

The next day Mary the baker had more news of Colin. She had been delivering bread to neighbours in the Neils' street and they were filled with horror. Colin's wife had gone to Ashington Hospital to see him. He was lying under a red blanket and when she sat down, Colin, heavily sedated, had told her not to worry. This as her shoes filled up with fresh blood from his injuries.

Colin was back at the gym about a month later. He said that the surgeons had talked of amputating his lower arm and hand. He told them that physical fitness and gym work were his life and they had managed to make a thin bridge of bone knit together. Now he sat flexing the arm; massive biceps mocking the puckered stitched area just above the wrist. It was heart-breaking to see him in subsequent weeks working the bad arm with light weights. Being the man he was he tried heavier and heavier weights – and the bone bridge snapped. Still he sat doing 100-pound curls with his left arm and glaring daggers at the plaster on his right.

I was second in the Northumberland County Senior 100 yards to a good runner from Newcastle Royal Grammar. I got a medal for my efforts and the first man I showed it to was Tashy. 'Well done, Sidney, I'm proud to have done my little bit to help you, son.'

The baritone voice was husky with emotion, but the jet 'tash bristled proudly. And I was proud to get this praise from one Lynemouth lad to another.

CHAPTER THIRTEEN

Reading, Writing and Fighting

One aspect of my fifth-form year had delighted my uncle Sam. He was now working in Alnwick at the Drill Hall as storekeeper for the Royal Northumberland Fusiliers. He had proudly served the regiment as a young man and wore his medals and tie on ceremonial occasions. Given this proud connection, I had no alternative when told I had to choose army or RAF for the school's Combined Cadet Force. I signed up for the Fusiliers, and every Friday climbed aboard the school bus in cheesecutter cap with red hackle, khaki jerkin and pants and bulled-up pit boots. Some cadets added puttees and belts, but I thought that a step too far even for a show-off like me. We could choose which one of the forces to join and there was a class divide. In the main the miners' sons went for the army and the shopkeepers', farmers' and teachers' sons went for the RAF.

I really enjoyed the parading. On Friday afternoons, muddy and sweaty from a football kickabout, we would line up on the Head's lawn and be inspected by Mr 'Nit' Parry and Mr 'Monty' Williams. Both masters took the parade very seriously, Mr Parry adding a proper shiny-peaked cap and medals to his uniform, and at least one boy each week was told to 'get your hair cut'. Sadly, our other military activities left much to be desired. Stripping a Bren gun for servicing turned into dropping it on the gym floor and hoping it came to bits, and cleaning a .303 rifle was no more than sliding a few pipe cleaners down the rusty barrels and shaking them out. If they stuck it was tough.

This lackadaisical attitude was very prevalent when, in June 1956, we went on 'manoeuvres'. The day before the event I was walking past the staffroom and happened to see a piece of paper on the floor. It was a map of the area of Northumberland between Morpeth and Rothbury. A red ring had been drawn around the hamlet of Dyke Neuk, about six miles due west of our school. I pushed the map under the door of the empty staffroom and went off.

Next morning, a Friday, about 60 lads in uniform were paraded and divided into platoons of six, each under a prefect. I was in the team of Bill Charlton, a fellow first team rugby player. Each prefect was given a map, a compass and a couple of map references. The idea was that two coaches would take us off to the western wilds and we had to find our way to the secret rendezvous. I pulled Charlie to one side and said I knew the location. I told him it was Dyke Neuk and he told one of his pals who was leading another platoon.

Off went the coaches, echoing to naughty songs, down winding lanes with dancing streams, then into the dry yellow heather tracts to the south of the market town of Rothbury. At around 11 o'clock the first coach stopped in the middle of nowhere and chucked out the first platoon. Charlie's team were set down a few minutes later by a stile under a purple crag. We scratched our heads and looked puzzled till the coach was out of sight, then we fell about.

Charlie had a plan. 'First we have our pop and sandwiches. Then we run around in the bushes to get muddied and burred up. Then … we get the bus!'

A wheezy old battered bus did come along and we got tickets to the Dyke Neuk pub. There was one dodgy moment when we passed a platoon of our schoolmates, sweating and frowning at the map, but we hunkered down in hiding.

Charlie, tall for his age and loud of mouth, went in the pub with another 17-year-old and came out carrying pints of scrumpy, a doddle at seven pence a throw. We sat on benches behind the pub supping and sunning ourselves and laughing like drains at the thoughts of our brave colleagues plodging through bogs and sheep shit. This was certainly better than double French or aeroplane identification like our RAF counterparts would be indulging in. Soon Charlie's pal and his team showed up and more cider was ordered.

The rest of the cadet corps arrived at the Dyke Neuk pub roughly two hours after our two parties. Despite much sucking of mints by our platoon and the other cheaters, Mr Parry sensed a rabbit was off. It was clear that some of us were pissed, and both the prefects were in big trouble. Then a whisper went round about the bus. I had been spotted by the platoon we had passed. I was called to the staffroom on the following Monday. Not only Mr Parry but also Mr Williamson, who would be my English teacher, and Mr Anderson, French, were also in attendance. The marked drop-off in my behaviour all year was noted. The Dyke Neuk incident was cited as designed to sap school morale. I was sent away to stew, swot and try to pass ten 'O' levels. It was obvious already that I would not be destined for big responsibility when I hit the sixth form.

The masters stressed that last-minute cramming was almost a sin; there should be no burning the midnight oil on the eve of the exams. But I took no notice and I went at swotting like a bull at a gate. From two weeks before my first 'O' level exam I took my books and notes to our tiny bathroom at seven every night and did not go to bed till I had learned every fact.

I would sit at the end of the bath nearest the cistern on a bed of dirty clothes. My only distraction would be Whisky licking at my face or needing to go in the yard to do her business. Martha would bob in with cocoa, pop, sweets and bacon sandwiches. Now and then I would get her to quiz me on my mugged-up facts. Around midnight Mam would plead with me to sack the books and go to bed, but I'd plough on some-times till after two. Then I would walk through the dark parlour with the fire smouldering under coal dross – it was never allowed to go out, and had become a talisman for our family, like Mary-Jane's glowing sacred heart. I would tiptoe up the narrow stairs, avoiding squeaky boards, hearing soft snores from Bob and Martha, and slip into bed beside Tadger. I would drift off to sleep with Lynemouth Colliery's orange misty halo of light coming through the curtains, the eerie soft scream the pulley wheels and coal wagons made and the gritty whiff, so strong I could taste it, of my adopted village up my tubes.

I kept up this monotonous regimen for almost a month. The exams started in early July and the weather was very hot. Some lads unwound by going swimming or cycling; not me. I would jump on a bus and go to Morpeth. I would run to the Black and Grey pub and play darts with town lads for a couple of hours. The mindless competition and the hot lights relaxed my bulging brain. Then I ran to the bus stop and went back to Dalton and the books. Only one night did I really panic. I found I had left my Religious Knowledge notes at school. Bob and Martha said I should trust in what I already knew, but once a crammer always a crammer. I got the bus to Morpeth at about six, sprinted to school, got the notes, and went to bed at three in the morning.

If anyone had asked me one hour after the exam who the king or queen was or what was Boyle's Law, I could not have told them. I had turned myself into a piece of factual blotting paper. Early in August I got the 31B bus to Morpeth at ten on a Wednesday morning. I wandered up the school drive, as lads – some laughing and others almost weeping – came back from seeing the results boards. My pal Alan Pearson was flashing his prominent teeth and combing his quiff. 'Got the entire *web*, all the lot,' he bragged.

I pushed through the crowd and scanned the lists. I'd passed with distinction.

'Very good, Sid.'

I turned in shock.

Masters were not supposed to call boys by their first names. It was Mr Parry in his weekend pullover and cords, sucking his bendy pipe. He shook my hand. 'Glad your best mark was in History.'

He mimed swilling a pint. 'Take it easy on the scrumpy down the Joiners.'

I gulped; he knew the pub and my tipple of choice. It was like he had his own secret service dogging my every move.

'I'll tek it easy, er, Norman.'

He winked and turned away.

'By the way, I've prevailed on them to make you a prefect. Don't let me down.'

By noon on results day Pearson, Brian Carolin, John Whalley, a soft southerner who had drunk and joked his way into our company, and I were in the back room of the best boozer in the world. The Joiners' Arms is tucked up a narrow street just over the road from Morpeth Castle. Back then it was the second clubhouse of Morpeth Old Edwardians, the grammar school's old boys' rugby team. It was where the coach left for away games, and many a pre-match pint was sunk here. The front bar was a boozing shrine to boozing life. A gaslight effect shone on pictures of great runners at Morpeth Olympic Games; moustachioed men in leather jockstraps, flexing waxed muscles. In glass cases were stuffed hawks that had once swooped from eyries in the Cheviots and giant salmon poached from the dancing Coquet. The landlord Joe was an old boy of the school and knew fine well we were well under 18, so he passed our drinks through a hatch to the back snug. We started on scrumpy at eight pence a pint and soon added Guinness to the mix. The singing stopped at about three but the boozing did not. Wednesday was Market Day and traditionally farmers sold their beasts, then went on the bevy. Several roistering old boys of the grammar sent rounds of Black Velvets through the hatch for us.

I don't know why the argument with Carolin started. I think he got me wrong when I questioned him about leaving school and not aiming for university. He said something about my 'having my tongue up Mr Parry's arse'. We argued and he invited me outside. There was a hush. I shook my head and said I would not fight him. I knew he was stronger than me; I'd have been mashed to bits.

'So, Weddell,' he got my name wrong deliberately, 'you're a coward as well as a big-heeded arse-licker?'

I went red and was about to change my mind about fighting.

'Will yee write that doon as a reference on his application for Oxford, Calor?' Pearson's quip defused the situation. Carolin sneered at me for the rest of the session. But the 'coward' tag rankled with me for a long time.

At about six Pearson and I made a move. We rolled along the riverbank and heard the notes of 'Blue Suede Shoes' blaring out from the funfair outside the Coliseum cinema. The 'shows' as we called it, came twice a year to Morpeth, and the local lasses dressed up for it. We strolled past the penny rolling and darts at cards stalls to the hub of the action, the Speedway. Just walking up the springy planks made me excited. There were lads in jeans and T-shirts and girls in blouses and shiny skirts with layered petticoats posing and preening like crazy. You could almost smell the sexual possibilities in the hot, throbbing petrol-scented air. A bunch of giggling lasses wended through the crowd and sat in one of the long seats. Pearson pointed at one of the girls, big chested and flashing her stocking tops. She was wearing red knickers.

'That's cock-teasing Katie – knows a thing or three,' said Pearson.

One of the show lads came for the girls' money. He leaned over and whispered something in Katie's ear. She laughed and pushed him away. He nodded to his mate in the kiosk and the ride started to move slowly. The roustabout took a few more payments, then stood up on a motorbike like a circus act. He was about 20, looked like Jack Palance, with black Elvis hair and tanned face. He had on a red lumberjack shirt and tight jeans. He put his hands on his buttocks and ground his hips. All eyes were on him as the Speedway moved to top speed and the lasses screamed.

'Go on, Nicky,' yelled one of his pals.

Suddenly Nicky dropped off the bike and made for the seat with Katie and the lasses. They were all holding onto the safety bar for dear life and their skirts were flaring. Nicky leaned over Katie and kissed her mouth. She pulled back. Then he slid his right hand up between her legs. He leered at the crowd as he groped and pretended to wank with his left hand. Katie screamed as the ride got faster and the music louder. Nicky leapt off the ride and did a lap of 'honour' on a motorbike, chin and crutch jutted, daring any local lad to react. Nobody did. The ride slowed down and Katie walked off in tears. I wanted to smash the dirty greasy bastard's face in. I did precisely nowt.

My parents were over the moon with my exam success and I was paraded around the family on 10 August, my sixteenth birthday, taking modest-ish bows as I went. As usual, Uncle Jack gave me a ten-bob note. I took it reluctantly, noticing the lost look in his eyes. The doctors were no nearer finding out the cause of his illness. A good sign was that, though he could not work, his speech and movement were not impaired – yet. Auntie Bab gave me two pound notes – then demanded that I shovel half a ton of coal in off the street for her. On a trip to Alnwick my Uncle Sam gave me ten bob and he and my dad took me to the Crown pub near Alnwick marketplace. The landlord, Jimmy Jeffrey, was a good pal of my dad's, and on hearing of my latest academic triumph poured me a pint of lemonade shandy and slipped me a half-crown.

To top all this, my dad's pal Billy Mann, who owned a corner shop in Lynemouth and had a small painting and decorating business, gave me two weeks' work. He had taken on a job at nearby Hagg Farm and my task was to strip wallpaper and apply undercoat to woodwork. Billy had a great baritone voice and on the job kept bursting into 'Charmaine' and the like. One day I let forth with some loud tone-deaf Bill Haley.

'Sidney,' said Billy, hands over his ears, 'If you don't shut yer gob, I'm sacking you. You cannit sing – stick to running and them books.'

I got the message and ten welcome pounds, which I tipped up to Martha. My present from my parents was a trip to the Co-op in Ashington. Mam had her passbook and I had big rooty-toot-toot plans. I persuaded her that a snazzy semi-drape jacket in Donegal tweed – the colour of Ovaltine sprinkled with iron filings – was much better than a

Harris tweed hacking jacket. The jacket was for best and for dances, but it was 'wide boy' gear that was really on my mind. I knew she would explode if I suggested basketball boots, so I settled for navy-blue bumpers, with thick white rubber soles. I looked longingly at narrow-leg jeans but caught her horrified expression. The purchases were ticked onto Mam's account.

I was now more or less equipped to make my grand reappearance at Docherty's billiard hall after nearly one month's absence. I had an old brown suede windcheater, bought from a 'club' in the *News of the World*, my baggy jeans and the bumpers, but no suitable shirt. My running T-shirts would expose my puny arms. Then, under a heap of Dad's old pit clothes, I found a pale-blue long-sleeved vest like rowers and gymnasts wore. I snuck it into Mum's next wash and bingo - I was ready to rock into Docherty's dive.

It was a sweltering summer Saturday afternoon, so hot that the greasy windows were opened – a rare occurrence. Still, the air was anything but fresh; fag smoke curled lazily in the sunrays. Bubbles, taking the piss as ever, was wearing shades and looking more like a Chicago street hoodlum than ever. He bent to play a long red, flipped his cig under the table towards the intended pocket, bounded round to his next position and scooped up the still-rolling cig. He curled his lip and greeted me.

'Well, if it isn't Sid the Swot.' His eyes took in my gear. 'Can you get a GCE in jumble-sale studies?'

The laughs gurgled out quite gently. I bought a round of ginger beer and Oxo crisps.

There were two new faces in the gang. Stan the Scrapper was playing Bubbles and, as I learned from Joe Morris, he was one of the hardest blokes in Ashington. He had high cheekbones and very powerful long arms. He was 18 and worked as a filler at the pit. 'Even Killer Ramshaw counts Stan as a marra,' whispered Joe. This was the ultimate accolade. Jimmy 'Killer' Ramshaw was a legend; the hardest man in Ashington, probably in all of East Northumberland. He had once been beaten up by five older men when stupid drunk, then had gone to their houses one by one, dragged them out and battered them senseless in front of family and neighbours.

The other new guy was a short stocky lad who looked as though he ought to be at a point-to-point over Ponteland way. He wore cavalry-twill trousers, thick wool shirt and suede shoes. He was also 18 and his name was Cliff Howe. Joe told me Cliff was plodding along as a clerk in an office but was hoping to become a paratrooper.

Jimmy the Screw was chatting to Tom Cowan who had bad acne but otherwise was good-looking. He had a quiff at the front and a DA at the back. He'd been at the Duke's School in Alnwick till a couple of years earlier but was now at Ashington Mining College. This meant 16 weeks of being shown all the jobs in the pit like filling or putting and doing some easy tasks like fastening tubs together. Lads with 'O' Levels, like Tom Cowan, could go to the Ashington Mining College and become skilled at mining trades like electrician. They could go on to get pit management qualifications. And there were exams whereby the lads who started on the 'ordinary' scheme could transfer to the college.

The subject under discussion in the billiard hall that night was a sortie the following Saturday to High Pit Social club near Whitley Bay. There was to be a live rock band and 'loads of tash', according to Bubbles.

'We're all bound to score,' said Bubbles. 'Sidney can hold our pants while we're boning it.'

That was what passed for an invite and it was as good as an extra GCE pass; I was accepted as one of the gang. Tom Cowan had a battered old car and the team would be Screw, Bubbles, Tom and me. The rest would not be out on the pull; they already had girlfriends in Ashington.

'If you pass a rag-and-bone man, Sid, exchange the windcheater for some pegs or a goldfish,' said Tom. 'With yee looking like a tramp, the High Pit birds will run a mile.'

'Fuck off,' I said.

'Language!' laughed Joe.

Halfway through the hop at High Pit the joint was certainly not jumping. The dance end of the social club was packed but the live group was a disappointment. They were four lads from Gateshead doing Bill Haley covers. With a slack drummer, thick Tyneside vocals and no driving saxophone, all the jumping around in tartan tuxedos and goosing each other with guitars got only polite applause and a sigh of relief when half-time came. Then pow-bam-sock! 'See You Later, Alligator', the real throbbing thing, whammed through the speakers. Bubbles came alive. He strutted over to a busty blonde in leather jacket and flouncy red skirt. She appeared to recognise him from somewhere because she accepted his kiss on the lips. The pair began to jive expertly, Bubbles's crepe soles banging out the beat and the lass spinning like a top. Other couples started dancing but stayed on the periphery, letting the glitterball sprinkle the stars. Then there was a movement near the bar and the crowd parted.

'Holy fuck!' said Screw. 'The bastard has landed us right in it now. I bet that's the tart he shagged at Butlins in Filey the other week. Her bloke passed oot with the beer and Bubbles gave it one. The mad fucker.'

Cowan tightened his tie and smoothed the lapels on his maroon blazer. I rolled up the sleeves of my canary-yellow jumper. My mouth and throat went dry. Now all the other dancers had stopped and only Bubbles and the bird were dancing. Four big lads in jeans and leather jackets stood round the two, like seconds at a boxing match. Which is what the hop became…

The biggest lad, all dark lank hair and tattoos, pushed the lass roughly in the bosom. She kept dancing. The lad kicked at Bubbles, who jumped over his leg and socked him on the cheek. Then Bubbles sprinted towards us.

'We don't know this twat,' yelled Jim.

It was no use. The four were on us like tigers. I was punched in the belly. I fell on all fours.

'Get up, you pansy,' the lad shouted.

I did, swung a punch and missed. Tom and Jimmy were kicking at the lads and backing away towards a toilet. There was no sign of Bubbles.

'In the toilet,' shouted Tom. 'Window!'

We ran into the toilet and Tom barred the door with his back. We looked round; there was no sign of Bubbles. There was a small window about a foot square above the urinals. It was open. The spawny sod had managed to squirm his skinny body through. We ran out kicking and pushing tables at the throng. Beer glasses, tin ashtrays and chairs flew at us. Then I was pulled to the floor by the left sleeve of my jumper. A lad tore at it while trying to punch my face. He hit me hard under the eye. Half the sleeve of the jumper tore away. I got up and scrambled out the main door with my pals and across the car park. Tom gunned the engine and we heard a voice.

'Wait for me, lads or they'll fucking kill me,' Bubbles whined from under the car. He got up and banged on the window, but was left to face the music.

'If they don't, I'll fucking kill you mesell next time I see you,' shouted Tom as we screeched off.

As we approached Ashington I filled up with dread. The left sleeve of my precious jumper was hanging half off and I felt my right eye and cheek throbbing. There would have to be some serious lies told at 102. Once back I rushed upstairs and slung the jumper at the back of a drawer full of *Razzle* and other dirty mags. I chucked two encyclopaedias on top of it. Then, rubbing my cheek, I brazenly entered the parlour where my parents were watching telly.

'You'll never guess what my marra Bubbles did at the billiard hall – he swung the rest round after a fancy shot and smacked me eye.'

Mum shot off to get a raw piece of steak for me to use as a poultice while Bob looked me hard in the eye.

'I hope these billiard hall wallahs aren't hooligans.'

'Just high-spirited, dad, that's all.'

Back on the school bus a few weeks later I persuaded a young high school lass called Annette Crosby to sew the sleeve back on my jumper.

My parents obviously loved each other very much and had few rows, and when they had one it inevitably ended in good humour. One weekend in early October 1956 Mam was pleading with Bob to take her to the Sunday dance at the social club. He sat behind the *News of the World* as she ranted. 'We never dee nowt or gan anywhere. You're only 50 but yee act like an auld gadgie. If I didn't have me bairns and me Woodbines I'd gan doon Cresswell and hoy mesell in the sea.'

My brother and I gulped in the echoing silence.

'Hoy yersell in the sea?' my father said calmly.

'Aye!' she yelled.

'Well, lassie, I'd wait a couple of hoors if aah was yee – cos the tide's oot.'

My mother picked up the poker and slashed the newspaper he was reading to shreds.

Shortly after this she started bending his ear after he had had a rare three pints of Federation Special ale at the club before his Sunday dinner. She had been on at him for weeks to give her more kitchen space by getting rid of the pantry wall.

'If yee'll not get somebody to knock it doon, I'll ask Billy Perfect to dee it next time he calls. Or Freddie Gray...'

The mention of our neighbour Freddie, who was definitely daft enough to take the job on, lit the blue touch paper. Bob flung off his jacket and ran into the yard. He got a mell hammer from the shed and began smacking the pantry wall. The door frame splintered and plaster flew all round. Dust sprayed into the pans of sprouts and potatoes bubbling up for dinner. Mam, Derrick and I went into kinks of laughter, but as his face reddened and he began to wheeze, Martha and I both thought 'angina' at the same time. It would be great to have Bob avoid dropping boulders, buckled girders, gas explosions, coal cutters, runaway tubs and flash flooding down Betty only to have as his epitaph: 'Passed away while attacking a pantry wall.'

The three of us wrestled the hammer from him and persuaded him to have a half-hour kip before his Sunday dinner.

We still had a jagged half pantry wall a week later on 11 October when Derrick had his eighth birthday party. It was my idea to make the party fancy dress. The previous Christmas Derrick had brought the house down at the school pantomime. He had been the leader of a band of Scots, all wearing kilts and tammies, and I had added a really daft touch to his gear. He came on stage wearing a toilet roll as a sporran. As the play went on, his henchmen kept grabbing their bums, tearing paper off Derrick's sporran and racing offstage as if taken short – then returning with enormous sighs of relief. The audience rocked with laughter.

So 102 Dalton played host to seven pirates, three Robin Hoods, two coal miners with lamps and three cavemen. The latter were Terry Brown, toting two enormous bones courtesy of Billy Smail the butcher, Ronnie Redshaw, complete with a teddy bear with cardboard dinosaur fittings, and Derrick in a smock and leggings I had sewn up from Mam's old black fur coat. I had also painted him with woad in the form of Reckitt's Blue.

The party was bedlam. The lads ate loads of Spam and meat-paste sandwiches, scones and Martha's jam sandwich cakes. When they played Pass the Parcel they got so excited that the parcel flew in the fire and I had to chase the lads all out into the yard while Bob chucked water on the blaze. I awarded Ronnie Redshaw the box of Black Magic choco-lates for best fancy dress, which started an argument between Terry and Derrick, both claiming they should have won. I calmed them down by saying I would design even more elaborate cavemen costumes for the 1957 Children's Gala for the pair of them.

As usual, gaiety was followed by harsh reality in our street. One week later, on the morning of 18 October, little Ronnie Redshaw's uncle Archie, who was just 26, was crushed by a massive stone at Lynemouth Colliery. The 'stone', in fact a boulder 18 feet long and five feet thick, did terrible damage. Archie's body was wrecked. His spine was broken and there were fractures to the ribs, collarbone and the base of the skull. There was damage to his bowels and kidneys. After two days of inten-sive activity by staff at Newcastle Royal Victoria Infirmary, and two occasions on which the staff thought they had lost him, Archie was still alive but told that he would be completely paralysed for the rest of his life. Archie proved them all wrong. Eleven months later he managed to walk one single step with crutches.

I remember seeing Archie 'shuffling' on his crutches round the backyard at number two Dalton Avenue. He would tell anybody who passed the same thing. 'Aah telt that doctor aah would waaalk, you see.'

It was as if his every smidgeon of recovery, every painful inch, was because he had given his solemn word.

What happened to Archie Redshaw haunted me for weeks. The savage environment that the men of Lynemouth entered every working day took a toll one way or another. Bob was 50 years of age but had been doing heavy bone-wearying labour since he was 16. The sleeps after his Sunday pint and big roast dinner became longer. Sometimes he would go upstairs to bed and chuck his pyjamas over his long johns, but most often he would curl up in a foetal position on the settee in the parlour. He would lay one heavily muscled arm under his head and his skinny white legs would show between his pants and socks. I would drape the old Otterburn rug gently over him.

I had a recurrent nightmare at this time. I dreamed I was 'spoaching', Mam's word for rummaging, through our sideboard drawers. I tunnelled under old ration books, cotton reels, tape measures and thimbles, just lazily curious. Then I opened the side door and there were silver platters of my dad's innards. Piles of yellowy orange intestines were bundled up like sausages in Billy Smail's window.

CHAPTER FOURTEEN

Waddell of the Wizard

I loved every minute of life in the lower sixth form, though I was not a very diligent prefect. When I was supervising fifth formers in private study I did not check whether they were studying Biology or Physics or reading the latest raunchy thriller by Hank Jansen. Nor did I smell their clothes or breath when they came back from toilet visits to see if they'd been at the Park Drive or Woodbines. I was assigned to form 4B, traditionally a bunch of wastrels who were fooling around till they could go out into the world or into Ashington Mining College at 16. My main duty was to watch them during assembly and make sure they did not go to the Joiners' Arms or the billiard hall during the dinner hour. This was a bit tricky because the wastrels knew that I regularly took a sherbet at the Joiners' myself.

Rugby was still one of my passions. When the school field was cut in late August and the pollen swirled round Dalton, I had a bit of sneezing and wheezing but nothing debilitating. I had spent hours at Lynemouth Welfare in the summer holiday punting a rugby ball high and racing to catch it.

On the last Saturday of October 1956 a team arrived at Top Field from Stockton, a bunch we knew could be very physical. I tackled my opposite number down cleanly three or four times. Next time my opponent stopped dead and lifted his knee into my face as I dived at his legs.

I did a full backward somersault off the bloke's knee. My head was full of fog and my mouth full of blood. My jaw ached like hell. The referee and my dad, who had raced on from the touchline, lifted me up and carried me off the pitch. They tried to stand me upright but I collapsed. My jaw ached when I opened my mouth and prodded around with tongue and fingers. Two back teeth were loose and my tongue found two fissures in either side of the lower jawbone, wet canyons pumping my blood. Dad and Mr Danskin made a fireman's lift with their arms and carried me off. I could hear my team-mates screaming 'Dirty twat!' at my assailant.

Mr Stokoe, our other sports master, took me and dad in his car to a dentist in Morpeth's main street. The dentist began to tut-tut and shake his head when I opened wide – in extreme agony. He said that at least three back teeth had been loosened and would have to come out. But the main priority was my jaw; the impact had not only broken the lower bone in two places but the whole bone had been dislocated from its sockets. He offered to take out the three loose teeth there and then, but dad insisted we get to the Royal Victoria Infirmary, 12 miles away in Newcastle, as quickly as possible. Mr Stokoe drove like a maniac and we did the journey in about 40 minutes, and with every minute the agony increased.

When the X-rays came back the damage was confirmed: there were two deep fractures to the right and left of the lower jaw. Three back teeth would have to be removed immediately, then they would fix the bones. The doctors told me they could sort me out in two different ways. Even though I was in agony and concussed I was expected to make a choice. They could wire my upper and lower jaws together with wires. I would be on a liquid diet but there were already gaps in my teeth where the straws could go. The alternative was a plastic device that held the jaws apart, with a hole in it for feeding. Either way I would be out of action for at least seven weeks.

'Wiresh,' I mumbled, groggily.

At 5.30 that night I was in the operating theatre and an anaesthetic mask was put on me by a bloke in green scrubs who was holding the football paper in his other hand. Only in Newcastle.

I came to about three the next morning. I tried to yawn and was convulsed with pain. It was as if somebody was stabbing my gums with hot needles. I reached past my lips and hit hard metal thorns; my teeth were laced together by strands of wire. I ran my swollen tongue around my back teeth and found three new raggy craters. I felt at the joints of my jaws and found bandages. I followed them up to a bow on top of my head, like an Easter egg. I felt in the cupboard near the bed for tissues to blow my nose. I found some and a lady's small vanity mirror. I looked at myself and was shocked. My right eye was purple, rising black, my face was like a diseased yellow balloon and when I opened my mouth I looked like a great white shark with metal teeth extensions.

I slept deeply through the Sunday till about six. Outside my window the rain beat down in the dusky Tyneside night. I felt at an all-time low. I ran my tongue around my foisty mouth, tasting bits of my liquid cocoa and porridge breakfast. I sat up and found radio headphones. I pushed back my bandages and put them on. On came the latest Johnny Ray hit 'Just Walking in the Rain'.

When Johnny started whistling the woebegone middle eight, I let fall a tear or two myself. Then I slept again.

'You'll never play that bliddy stupid rugby again,' was the banshee scream I heard as Martha ran down the ward.

I shot upright from sleep, wiping dried blood trickles from my chops. I looked like something from a horror movie. The mummy bandages had been purely to support my jaw after the operation, and the bow on top was a jokey flourish done by two young nurses to cheer me up – or so I had been told by the old nurse who fed me warm milk like a baby in the night. Martha did not get the jolly wheeze; she held my head and kissed the bandages. I tried to greet her, but couldn't.

She began to keen.

There were three other visitors: Bob and John Wilson, my rugby captain, and John Coslett, his number two. I flashed my wired mug at them and all three dutifully smiled. At the sight of my full-metal mouth Martha hit a pitch a concert violinist could not match. Other patients looked miffed. Dad took Mam off for a cuppa.

I mumbled to the lads that I would be out for seven, maybe ten, weeks, and they told me not to worry. My place was rock-solid and they would miss me. Wilson said we had won the match even with 14 men. I smiled and the wires gave me hell. Then Coslett leaned near. 'You'll be glad to know we got the bastard who kneed you. He was touching down behind his own line and Nigel swung his head into one of the goal posts. He's in Ashington Hospital now.'

That really made me stretch my wires. It hurt but I was doubly happy; Ashington Hospital was then a notorious boneyard and they would probably amputate the kid's head just to be sure there was no lingering infection.

Martha might have thrown a complete wobbler at the hospital, but over the next seven weeks she played a pure belter.

The hospital people gave me a list of 'food' that they recommended I slurp every day for seven weeks if I wanted to be really fit when my wires came off. Two tins of any flavour soup, one pint of Guinness, six pints of milk. The latter did not seem to be a big problem; I had always hated tea because of the leaves in it and coffee was unknown in our house. So normally I drank milk with all my meals. I had soup and milk for breakfast. At school they warmed tins of chicken, mushroom and kidney (my favourite) soup for lunch and I even sucked up semolina awash with even more milk. At five, with the family, I had soup, Bovril or Mam's broth. I was determined to down the six pints of milk every day. The rugby might be out of the window, but there was still the England School's 100 yards. So as evening approached and I had not managed the lot, Mam would rack her brains to make it more palatable. She would make thin blancmange and custard so I could drink it and she would add it to my soup. At bedtime I would force down cocoa. The only time I suffered was once when I followed a mug of Horlicks with Guinness and I began to vomit into the fire. I felt like a human volcano with a stopper on top. I gagged but, thanks to all my missing back teeth, I managed to honk a creamy spray all over Ranunculus, the red metal knight who held our pokers and hearth brushes.

My mam's ministrations did not stop at nutrition. In the long vigils between shots of hot Bovril, warm milk and Guinness she would massage my legs with wintergreen oil. I would lie on the floor in my underpants and the strong hands that kneaded dough and scrubbed clothes would work the stinking gunk into my hamstrings and calves. I reckon my dad put her up to this. My accident had been a godsend to his plans for my sprinting; no rugby for nearly three months meant the leg muscles would get no jolts and jars. Bob also encouraged me to go to the Welfare sports ground within two weeks of my accident. In track-suit and sandshoes I would lap the cricket pitch on the shale path, jogging and breaking into sudden all-out sprints. Breathing through a slit between my teeth was difficult at first, but after a session or two I found my lungs were working harder. Packing in oxygen and umpteen pure calories a day was making me just like Wilson of *The Wizard*, a running, jumping robot.

The final piece in my rehabilitation regime was dancing. Mam would pour herself a neat gin and wind up the gramophone. Soon 'Begin the Beguine' would be slushing out and we would swirl round a prone Derrick, goggling the box, and Bob slouched in his favourite armchair. It did not end there. One Sunday night Mam fixed for Nellie Foster to mind my brother while she and Bob took me to the social club for the dance. Dad was in his finest, Mam dolled up in an emerald-green dress and I got suited and booted. Nobody minded that I was not 18 – nor was I going to be supping much with a wired-up jaw. I danced the first couple of dances with Mam, feeling very self-conscious in the packed Big End. But then a real dancer took over. Billy Chatt, hair neatly parted and white hankie spilling from his suit pocket, bowed to Martha, asked permission from Bob and off they spun. They were like professionals. Mam arched her back and held her head like a duchess, face like a porcelain figure on Granny's mantel-piece. She was back at the Northumberland Hall, forgetting Clayport Close, working all hours at the bakery and being Mary-Jane's skivvy. Bob sipped a half of Fed and winked at me; seeing Wor Martha happy made him happy.

The dancing did not stop there. Every Monday and Saturday night I would put on my charcoal suit and red paisley tie and hit the Arcade dance. One Monday I was at the Arcade early doors having a lemonade with Screw and Joe Morris. As usual lasses sat on the right of the dance floor and lads on the left. This night, just after eight, there were about 50 per side. Most of the lasses were dressed in blouses and full skirts, made fuller by stiff petticoats. But one bunch were rebels. Screw called them 'Chinese Guards', and in fact they had a uniform: jet black hair, black tight skirts, black T-shirts, black pumps, and, for all we knew, black chewing gum. Their dead eyes dared any lad to ask for a dance.

The Arcadians started up 'The Dark Town Strutters' Ball' in an attempt to get folk up and trotting.

'Bet you half a dollar, Sidney, you cannit get one of the guards to dee this with yer,' said Screw with a smirk.

I nodded and flashed my wires.

I strode across the floor and approached the toughest-looking 'guard'. She was stocky and had fleshy arms. Her scent smelled like Dettol. Her mates looked at me as though I was dirt on her shoe. I kept my mouth shut and pointed at the dancers. She bounced her gum from cheek to cheek and nodded. She stalked to the far end of the hall nearest the band. She turned and put up her arms. I engaged and stiff as two planks we quickstepped backwards in an absolutely plumb straight line. All around us couples swirled and did curves and turns. Not us – Mam had not taught me to turn in the quickstep; nor had hers. At the end of the hall, we bunny-hopped through 90 degrees, then one-two-hitched on right round the four corners. Jim and Screw nearly wet their pants laughing. The rest of her black platoon's faces cracked. The band could hardly play for laughing. As the vocalist merrily segued into 'Chattanooga Choo-choo' we both called it a draw. I grinned widely and her eyes nearly popped out when she saw my wires. Her pumps hardly touched the polished boards as she sloped off.

Soon after this debacle I actually became a dancing instructor. I was sitting in private study in the school library four weeks after the accident, minding my own business. Then two of the upper-sixth lads began acting very strangely. They had a copy of a magazine called *John Bull* and one lad was calling out instructions while the other tried to implement them. 'Black right foot forward, white left foot backward, black left foot forward,' read out one.

The other stood as though he was holding a dancing partner and strutted forward awkwardly, eyes locked on his feet. I went over and looked at the magazine. The article was a visual guide to ballroom dancing by the great bandleader Victor Sylvester, men's steps in black and ladies' in white. It looked like rocket science illustrated this way.

'It's a piece of piss if you do it with a partner.'

I was now speaking quite clearly despite my wires.

'Who says?' They were both dubious.

I assumed the man's position for the start of the Modern Waltz. I shot off doing spins and corners with an imaginary lady partner. They were both impressed. But that was nothing to what happened when I assumed the lady's position and called one of them into my arms. Off I went doing the 'white' steps and calling on my partner to keep his head up and his back arched. I had both lads waltzing and then quickstepping in no time. They were delighted. It was three weeks to the School Dance and nobody wanted to be a wallflower. The word got round that I could teach dancing and before long I had eight pupils. I did not do this for the good of my fellow students. My fees were two shillings cash or eight bars of McDonald's Highland Toffee, with a hairy cow on the wrapper. It would be a while before I could eat any of those, so Derrick got them and, for a while, became the most popular lad in school as he doled them out piece by piece.

Yes – it is me! Mam got the ritzy jacket and tie from the Co-op on tick in 1957. I signed autographs for lasses as 'James Dean'.

In mid-December came the fateful day when I reported to the Royal Victoria Infirmary to have my wires removed. I was very worried because the enamel of my teeth had grown as the wires sank into my gums. A doctor had a quick look and then handed the clippers to a medical student not much older than me. The lad looked terrified as he snipped delicately at the ends of the wires near my jaw joints. But he lost the plot in trying to loosen the wires interlaced with my teeth. Eventually he picked up an instrument like pliers and ripped the wires lengthwise, snapping enamel and tearing gum tissue. The pain was awful and there was blood everywhere. Hearing my grunts and screams, the doctor ran back into the cubicle.

'You should have snipped the wire round every individual tooth, you idiot!' he yelled.

When the blood was mopped away, the doctor had a good look inside. The bone had healed fine but my jaw was still misaligned to the left a bit. I asked the big question. When could I start playing rugby? He gave me a solemn look.

'For the foreseeable future you should not risk any impact to either side of your jaw. These were very bad breaks.'

So Bob had got his way: the sprinting would be it.

I was looking forward to the School Dance. I was going to wear my Donegal jacket and purple socks and I'd had a James Dean upswept quiff hairstyle coaxed into shape by Wilson Cochrane, Lynemouth's barber and king of the 'pudding basin' cut. I aired my ritzy outfit at the Playhouse cinema in Alnwick one Saturday and got much more than I bargained for. Her name was Rosie. She had white-blond short hair and she was a bundle of alluring promise. I had seen her at the cinema before, flashing her knickers from the back seats of the balcony to Duke School lads. I propositioned her halfway down the cinema steps at the end of the first house.

'Do you fancy a walk to the Pastures?' I chirped.

The azure eyes took in my flashy hair and jacket and she nodded. We did not get as far as the Pastures. Once away from the main street lights, she dragged me into a dark doorway, unbelted her cream camel coat, unclipped her bra and began French kissing. I put my clumsy trembling hands up her jumper and massaged her lower ribs. She reached to my crutch but found only limp disappointment.

'Are you some kind of puff?' was all she said as she fastened up and went off looking for a real man.

The doorway of frustrated desire was only 50 yards from the convent where Mother Theresa had imbued me weekly with strict moral holiness.

A few days later I got all dressed up in my speckled jacket and purple socks and headed for the Joiners' Arms prior to making a James Dean-style entrance to the School Dance. Billy Mitchell was there already in a dark suit and a perfect Teddy Boy haircut, a pompadour at the front and a Duck's Arse at the back. He was not alone; a slinky brunette with a full figure and a maroon shiny dress was wrapped round him. The lass looked all of 25 and Billy introduced her as one of the nurses who 'looked after him' during his long stay in hospital. This remark was accompanied by eye-rolling and throaty dirty snorts from the lady. After two pints of scrumpy and a couple of stories of their congress in loos and cupboards at the hospital, we made our way up the street to school.

On the stage in front of the glory board was a Jimmy Shand-type accordion band of fairly senior citizens and I was glad to see several of my dance trainees lolloping round more or less in time with the music. Bill and the nurse began dancing quite expertly and I mooched around the hall looking at the available talent. I asked a high-school girl I knew vaguely to dance the waltz with me and she agreed. But as soon as we got going the band began playing rock and roll and I began to jive, legs going like two India rubber bands. My partner scowled at me and left the floor. It got worse. I was foxtrotting with another girl and telling her all about my broken jaw trials in detail when she suddenly said she had to go to the toilet. I stood like a lemon till she came back but she ignored me completely and sat down with her pals.

Then my luck changed. A girl with pale gold wavy hair, pretty face, bright blue flared skirt above acres of petticoat gave me the eye. At first I thought it was the scrumpy kicking in, but as I walked towards her she made it clear that I was indeed her target. At first I did not recognise this girl, since I'd only ever seen her without make-up and wearing a green bobble hat. But then I twigged that it was Jean Sanderson, grand-daughter of Morpeth's most famous citizen – Alderman W.S. Sanderson, farming tycoon, sometime mayor and a bloke notorious for walking round in a cream ten-gallon stetson.

'Would you like to dance?' I asked, intoning as if my mouth was full of marbles.

The smile and nod I got made my heart leap into my throat. We floated round the floor like Fred and Ginger. As turns became more flamboyant I held her closer and she did not seem to mind. My 'pupils' and my pal Mitch were impressed. When the music stopped, Jean kept hold of my hand. She led me out of the hall and through the main oak door onto the steps. It was freezing but she shook her golden hair, stood on tiptoes and kissed me hard. I was about to launch into the saga of my broken jaw when bells rang. Don't be boring, or she'll bugger off, I told myself.

'Do you want to go to the pictures tomorrow night? I'll meet you outside the Colly...'

She shook her head. 'Ashington is easier for you,' she said. 'I'll get a bus over there.'

It seemed to be too good to be true: the glad eye, the eager kiss, now she apparently knew where I lived and she was willing to travel miles for our first date. The next couple of weeks were a fairy tale. Jean and I held hands in the back row of the movies, snogged and did what the Kinsey Report euphemistically described as 'petting' – and the billiard hall mob described as 'You tickle mine and I'll tickle yours.' I was completely smitten. When I did get round to my jaw and my plans for the England Schools 100 yards, she was all ears. She even offered to pay her turn at the pictures, which I of course declined. Then came an invitation that completely bowled me over. 'My parents are having a pre-Christmas party at Espley Hall – our house – and you're invited. You can bring a couple of friends. There will be some boys there who play rugby.'

Stately home; lads to impress; I could take any amount of that.

I did not tell Bob and Martha a quarter of the story. If I had said I was mixing with the nobs, Bob would have said I was selling out the working classes. If Martha knew 'petting' was now on my agenda, she would have locked my equipment up in chastity underpants. All I said was that I was going to a party at Morpeth and would be staying the night with a school pal. As it was, Dad ducked back behind the racing pages and Mam sniffed disapproval and tossed her hair. Jimmy the Screw had given me an ancient condom in a wrinkled silver packet with the advice, 'Don't get too excited and fumbly when you try to put it on, or you might get it inside out. Then you won't know if you're coming or going.'

I kept it deep in the change section of my imitation leather wallet.

At about seven on the appointed night John Whalley, Colin Slaughter and I got off a bus at the end of the drive of Espley Hall, a few miles north of Morpeth. Beyond a pair of weathered sandstone columns was an elegant Georgian mansion with a portico and big square bay windows. All three of us wore suits and Whalley and I had on fancy waistcoats – mine maroon with silver buttons, his yellow tartan. We crunched up the gravel path and knocked on the door. It was opened by a woman of about 50 with the same blond wavy hair as Jean. It had to be her mother and she was dressed like a marchioness; jewels, hair up, everything bar a tiara.

'You must be Sidney, Jean's friend,' she purred like a BBC newsreader. She clocked the three of us and I thought I detected a slight frown.

'This is Colin and this is John. We go to Morpeth Grammar.'

I realised I was abubble with nerves. Mrs Sanderson turned and led us through a fancy vestibule into a room that looked like a scene from one of Noël Coward's plays. Grand piano, nibbles, expensive rugs, high posh voices and bow ties, dinner jackets, tulle and silk ball gowns. And here we were like three trainee Hoover salesmen ready in our glad rags for the firm's piss-up. I declined a bottle of beer and accepted a half-tumbler of whisky. The warm slug calmed me down a bit.

The night ended with Jean and me petting very heavily indeed on the billiard table in the games room. I kept thinking about Screw's tatty scrunched-up old condom, but this was not the night. But it was patently obvious from the look in her eyes and the husk in her voice that it wasn't far off.

There were very good vibes at 102 Dalton Avenue as New Year's Eve 1956/7 approached. My mother had had us all worried sick over lumps in her breasts, but Dr Pearson sent her for tests at Ashington Hospital and she was told they were only cysts. And, after years of putting crosses on a Littlewood's football pools, Bob got six draws on the coupon. But it was a good job we did not open the Pomagne prematurely. The angina had got no worse and Dad was still working overtime on Saturday mornings, and putting on the table just over 11 pounds a week. He expected the pools company to send him at least 100 pounds, but when the registered letter arrived it was very skinny. We clustered round as he pulled out the loot: two white flimsy five-pound notes the size of a hankie, the first we'd ever seen, and a couple of shillings. Martha started the laughter, and we all followed. There had been dozens of draws. 'I thought it would be gold in gawpins, but it'll buy more spirits for Hogmanay,' said Mam.

It was a good job we laid in more booze. Our little cottage was full of folk as twelve o'clock approached. We now had a Dansette record player and all the old favourites were belting out, 'The Runaway Train', 'Kathleen' and 'Galway Bay'. Derrick was acting as barman and dolloping out large rums and whiskies. My granny Mary-Jane had a fire going that would have pleased a blacksmith and she was giving her bloomers a good toasting. The only worry was my uncle Sam who was sitting on a buffet looking pale and sipping shandy. He kept coughing and spitting into the fire. Granny put her arm round him and I noticed she was on the verge of tears. Sam pushed her away saying,

'Divvent ye worry, mother, I beat them bloody Japs, I'll beat this effer.'

I wondered what 'this' could be.

At twelve o'clock Derrick and I went outside with whisky and coal in our pockets and did the first-footing. As the buzzers of Betty and the other pits blew, we all joined hands and sang 'Auld Lang Syne' and then attacked Mam's finger buffet; corned beef pie, cheese pie, stand pie, sausage rolls, pickles, pease pudding, the lot. Then a loud tuneless voice echoed out near our leek trench singing, 'I'll get wrong when I get home but I don't care.'

We opened the door and in staggered Uncle Tom Chester, three sheets to the wind. 'Elsie will kill him,' said Martha with a grin.

Auntie Elsie was no socialite and she kept Ches on a very tight leash. Next came Cousin Robert, in full evening dress, half of it on and half of it off, like he had come via a wind tunnel. He began dancing with Martha.

'Where's me dad?' asked Derrick.

Martha stopped dancing and her eyes narrowed but still exuded a gin-inspired glow. 'That bloody man. Gets the party started and then mizzles off up the dancers to bed. Bob! What do you think you're playing at?'

Off she stomped up the stairs and began yelling at him. Five minutes later he slunk into the room like a chastised lurcher. He made himself a cup of tea and sat on the settee like a visiting alien.

'She might have got him oot of his scratcher,' said my brother. 'But she hasn't made the old bugger presentable.'

I looked over and saw Bob's pyjamas sticking out from the top of his jumper and the bottom of his pants. I raised my glass of rum and Pepsi to him and he wagged his fore finger. He stood up, got down on his marks like a runner and wagged his finger again. Even at our annual Hogmanay bash my coach was bang on my case.

Over the next few months I put my heart and soul into my dream of getting an England running vest. Jean Sanderson was taking a clutch of 'O' levels and her parents curtailed her social life severely. We saw each other in the coffee bar after school and still went to weekend dances and movies and when the weather got better we petted and snogged in the woods above the Wansbeck river. I never returned to her stately home and she never ever visited our cottage in Lynemouth.

At school I was extra diligent at my studies but I did not always toe the line. In those days the England football team were often on telly on Wednesday afternoons, with vivid commentary from Kenneth Wolstenholme, and I just happened to get my asthma and other illnesses on Wednesdays. This was not just bunking off; after raw eggs and a drop of sherry – but no horse manure – for breakfast I would go out for a two-mile run. After one of these I was just dropping to a jog at the west end of Dalton at about ten o'clock when a familiar figure sneaked out of a ginnel. It was my cousin Little Sid, apple of my uncle Geordie's eye. Like Derrick, Sid was a comedian and never far from mischief. He was ten, always scruffy and, like me, should have been at school.

'You shouldn't be here,' said Little Sid. 'Yee should be at that granny school, hitting yon books.' His tone left me in no doubt that he himself had nothing but contempt for 'yon books'. His eyes flicked up looking for the school-board man.

'Er – er – I'm in training for some very special races,' I managed weakly.

'Special races my arse,' he sneered. 'I'll bet you're playing the wag like me cos today's the day for spellings. Am I right?'

I nodded in sage agreement. He gave me a gappy-gobbed grin and sloped off towards the wilds of the dene.

On Pancake Tuesday I took yet another 'sabbatical' from school. On that day every year a crazy football match took place in the Pastures in the shadow of Alnwick Castle. A bagpiper led the ball and a procession of 200 men and boys over the Lion Bridge and into the lush meadow. The two teams represented the two parishes in the town; St Paul's was the Protestants, and I was in St Michael's with the Catholics. The pitch was over a quarter of a mile long and nowhere near flat. At each end was a leafy arch that acted as the goal and the game was over when one side scored two goals. There were no referees and anything short of punching was allowed.

Clad in tracksuit and rugby boots I hurled myself into the fray. I scored a goal after half an hour and the winner after another 40 minutes. I was presented with 30 shillings for each goal and carried off the pitch on the shoulders of my teammates. I gave an interview about my family and local roots in the *Northumberland Gazette* and they took my photo.

Back at King Street Mary-Jane cooked Uncle Sam and me a great mixed-grill tea and I took Sam to the Oddfellows' Arms, one of his favourite watering holes. I was ordering two pints of Vaux bitter when Sam put his arm across mine.

'Sidney. Divvent get me a pint. A Mackeson will do.'

He was subdued, morose even. Mackeson? An old woman's tipple? I was about to make a crack. When we sat down with the drinks, I saw he was on the verge of tears.

'I'm not that clever, son.' He was staring fixedly at the blind stocking hanging from a candlestick on the mantelpiece. 'Me doctor thinks I've got TB. I've got to go for tests in Gateshead.'

He wet his lips in the froth of his stout. I glugged clumsily at my pint. Uncle Sam's life had been very hard; his father died when he was only three; poverty-stricken childhood sustained largely on charity and the good heart of nuns; put up with over four years in the 'Japsands' and now flattened by odd severe bouts of malaria plus lung disease. I felt ashamed for taking for granted the many blessings in my own pampered existence.

'Does me mam know about this?'

The reply was a fiery splinter of the spirit that defied the nasty Japs. 'No. And she's not ganning to, is she?'

I put the arm of my mud-stained tracksuit round his neck and hugged him and chewed more Vaux ale to stifle the dry sobs in my throat.

On the Friday of that week I paid the price of my lies and vanity. The *Northumberland Gazette* was a popular paper in Morpeth as well as Alnwick, and several masters saw my write-up and photos. I was hauled in front of the Beak who called me totally irresponsible and threatened to sack me as a prefect if I stepped out of line again. I said nothing; I just looked at the wall and stuck my pet lip out.

Over the next few weeks my dad brought me to a peak with the sprinting. I worked on the weights at the Institute in moderation. With no rugby jolts and stresses for nearly six months, my legs were going like clockwork. Bob even forbade visits to Ashington baths because swimming worked the muscles the wrong way.

My dad would only put the watch on me every two weeks, arguing that time trials brought the risk of strains. But he did let me go flat-out against high-class opposition. I raced against – and beat – Malcolm Musgrove, who was 24 and had been playing for West Ham for four years. His reaction was to put his arm around Bob and tell him he had a champion on his hands. You would have thought from Dad's beam of pride that this time he really had hit bingo on the pools.

But as usual in our small vulnerable world the sky did not stay blue for long. My Uncle Sam was confirmed as having TB and in the last week of May was taken into a sanatorium in Gateshead. We were told he would be in for months, so Mam and Granny prepared to trek there and back on three buses every weekend.

But there was worse news; yet another Sidney Waddell died. My cousin Little Sid would never be pushed around or bullied; he was brought up to stand his corner in a row. On 4 June 1957 he was playing cricket on a patch of grass with two of the Adamson boys. The younger Adamson, aged nine, was batting and Sid was bowling. The ball hit Adamson's legs and Sid claimed he was out. The boy threw down the bat, there was a row and the elder Adamson, aged 13, picked up the bat and hit Sid on the back of the head. He died in the ambulance on the way to Ashington hospital.

I entered our house from school at just before five to find Bob, Martha and Derrick all crying, in a wretched helpless clump. My first reaction was pure anger; the elder Adamson had a reputation as a kid with a wild temper. I wanted to run the few yards to the Adamson house and smash him to a pulp. But, seeing how distraught my parents and my brother were, I didn't let my anger get the better of me. Instead I grieved with my family.

My uncle Geordie and his other sons were devastated. Mary Ross, Geordie's feckless wife, had left them for good months before and gone to live in Yorkshire. Little Sid had been the kernel of their home life. My uncle was too shocked to go to Ashington to identify the body, so Bob, the pillar of the Waddells, had to do it. He came home that night a grey-faced wreck.

Next morning I awoke at about seven and heard throaty sobs coming from the parlour downstairs. We did not have dressing gowns, so I put on my old gabardine mac. I walked down the stairs and opened the parlour door. My wild wanton uncle Bill lifted his head from his hands and his jaw dropped as though he had seen a ghost. He hurled himself across the room and hugged me, shouting, 'God help me, I thought it was yee was deed.'

My parents both shook their heads in pain and confusion. Bill had heard in Ashington that Sid Waddell had been killed playing cricket and assumed that the dead Sid was me. He had jumped on a bus, come in the door and cried his heart out for the previous ten minutes, too upset to talk.

The funeral was traumatic, with half the village turning out in pelting rain as the hearse with the small white coffin, swamped with flowers, set off from Dalton on the two-mile drive to Cresswell church. Despite the downpour my uncle George and his three other sons walked as a guard of honour, wearing no overcoats, rain sluicing their ashen faces and flushing their cheeks and drenching their suits. They marched for well over a mile before my dad persuaded them to get into the cars as we passed our old bungalow on Cresswell Road.

Desolation hung over the little churchyard where all the Waddells lay buried. The early loss of this untidy motherless little laddie had scourged the souls of all of us. Some, like Martha, took faith in God as a comforter and saw some divine logic in the grim tableau unfolding. But in the main the Waddells were an atheistic bunch and now I was one of that group. Our faces showed only raw pain and in my heart was only anger. Around the open grave were strewn wreaths and bunches of flowers. I saw a woman bend down and read the card on some lilies. 'Mary bloody Ross,' she hissed. The word got round and a couple of men 'accidentally' stamped the flowers. If Little Sid's mother had shown up she would have been battered.

When the first soil was shovelled into the grave and pattered onto the coffin wood with an echo of awful finality, Uncle Geordie got up from his knees and tried to throw himself into the grave, shouting, 'Me bairn. Me bairn.'

His three red-eyed lads dragged him back, his legs and shoes smeared with wet mud, his face a helpless snarl of agony.

A very happy day for my uncle Geordie's lads. They are scrubbed up for Robert's wedding. Left to right: Thomas, known as Hot Shovel, Robert, Billy and Little Sid.

A few weeks later a post-mortem report declared that Little Sid had had a weak spot at the base of the skull where the blow landed. No action was taken against the Adamson boy. For a long time after he was shunned by other kids, and sometimes called a killer. My uncle Geordie never got over the death of his bairn. Till his dying day he carried the misty stare of a man looking down at a small white coffin.

CHAPTER FIFTEEN

Lady in Red

By the end of July 1957 I reckoned I had all the juggling balls of my life in the air, spinning in controlled synchronisation.

On the academic front, I passed my 'mock' Advanced and Scholarship GCEs. It was suggested to Bob and Martha on a parents' evening that in December I sit an Open Scholarship exam in History at Pembroke College, Oxford. They were told that it was the only way I would get into Oxbridge; Morpeth Grammar School had no guaranteed quota of places. It was a gamble; most lads would be sitting the exam in their third year of the sixth form and would be coached in extensions to the GCE syllabus. I would only have done half the syllabus. In fact, Mr Parry made it clear to me a few days later that I almost certainly would not get a place but it would stand me in good stead for the following year after I had sat my 'A' levels, I neglected to tell my parents this, however.

The experience would be costly. There would be a £30 fee just to sit the exam and then there would be expenses for travel to Oxford and food. There would not be much change out of £50, nearly five times Dad's weekly wage. But my parents did not hesitate; if the masters said I was in with a chance, then it was all part of my path away from Auld Betty. After the sale of the bungalow there had been a profit of a few hundred pounds but it had gone on improvements to 102 Dalton and the steady drip of supporting two children.

My romance with Jean Sanderson, though still cemented by solemn vows and limited passion, was on the back burner.

On trips to the billiard hall the lads still greeted me as 'Big Heed', but like much Geordie insult there was affection underneath the cruel words. And Jimmy the Screw was determined that I should not go to the dreaming spires a virgin. He described various wiles to get Jean to dissolve into a shivering jelly of lust.

'It's the pressure points you've got to aim at,' he said. 'Stick yer tongue in her lugs gently like, then blow in them. Or stroke the back of her neck, there's one there. And the most sensitive ones are the back of the knee and the inside crook of the arm. But you've got to be gentle, like brushing the nap on a billiard table.'

Tom Cowan did not look impressed. 'Listen to Dr Screw, Sidney … and you'll get fucking nowhere. He's been trying them tricks on a 13-year-old who's hardly old enough to bleed, never mind butcher – and he's never even got a wrist job, never mind a dip of the wick.'

Tom's words brought a blush to Screw's pale freckly chops, It was clear that he had yet to press the right buttons with Dirty Carole. I shuddered to think what Martha would do if she could hear a word of this catechism of filth.

The Under-17 All-England 100 yards was coming up; I had three weeks to get the pure white vest with the scarlet rose. Bob stood beaming by the finish line as I won the county 100-yards title on a cinder track in 10.4 seconds. His professional watch had me at 10.3. He knew I would be faster on grass at Southampton in the All-England Schools meeting. We could not afford for him to take time off from the pit to travel south, but I had moral support. Nigel Savage was also in the Northumberland team.

On the first day the sun was out and the grass was a bit long. I slipped at the start of my heat but lunged at the end to win by two yards. I cruised the next two stages before the final. Savage said he had never seen me run better. But the competition was hot. A stocky kid from Liverpool had been just over 10.2 in the semis on a rain-affected surface.

Because of the rain they had to move the start several times and when I got on the blocks it was a quagmire. I was so worried at the possibility of slipping that I froze. I normally 'jumped' the gun, but now I was grasping to get into stride as the Liverpool kid and a scrawny six-footer led. I hit form at 50 yards and went into a late lunge. From the stands I heard Nigel yelling 'You did it, Sid!' All six runners finished within one foot; it was a complete blanket. It took five minutes to work out the first three – and I was fourth. They gave me a medal for running 10.3 in the heats and Nigel pounded my back. But the hard truth was that only first and second would run for England.

A few days after the Southampton meeting I ran for the county against Durham and Scotland at Houghton-le-Spring. The sprints were held on a green sward of short grass that had been baked by sun for a week or two. I tried it out before the race and it felt like a trampoline; I glided down it. I got ready for the 100 yards near the Scottish number two. He was telling us we were wasting our time turning up because their number one had clocked 10.2 at the weekend. I looked over at the lad in question. He was my height, red-haired, pale-skinned and had thighs like a rhinoceros. I envied his midnight-blue vest with the red lion rampant.

I was determined not to freeze on the blocks this time. The gun went and I blazed into full stride early. I felt the Jock on my shoulder at halfway. Then all the milk-given strength in my thighs kicked in and I hit the tape over three yards clear. There was no call for my famous dip. The top Scot was the first to shake my hand. 'I kenned ye had me with that start, it was brilliant.'

He must have wondered why I took his acclaim with my eyes fixed between his nipples on his prancing red lion.

When I got home to Lynemouth I got massive praise from my dad. I felt fulfilled and went for a walk along the dene banks to my special place, the bower under a large hawthorn bush. I stood outside and sucked in the salty wind off the North Sea.

Elsewhere word of my running exploits had got round. Dad and I were having a sort of debriefing in the last week of August when a couple of men in suits and trilby hats joined us. They looked like bookies and certainly money was on their minds. They invited us up into the pavilion where some professional runners were being massaged before training. I knew the masseur. He was Jimmy Blake, alias 'Sex', after Sexton Blake, a radio detective hero. One of the suits nodded at Sex and he invited me to lie down and have a rub. Sex had a terrible stammer as he went on about the local football team whom he helped coach. I wasn't even trying to listen to him because it was clear the two wide boys were saying things that were upsetting Bob. He was pointing over at me and going red in the face. I caught the words 'amateur' and 'England'. Suddenly he walked away from the men and beckoned me to leave.

As we walked quickly along the shale path round the cricket pitch he let rip. 'Bliddy money, that's all some buggers think aboot. Them two has a school of runners and they slip them a few bob, stake them while they're training, and bet on them. I was in a school like that when I met your mother, but we did it to get a bit extra cash for the family, not to get fat. They say they could make me hundreds if you ran professionally at the handicaps like the Powderhall. And when I said it was an England vest we were after, not lowy, the buggers laughed.'

It was then that I fully comprehended what Bob dreamed about all those hours in a black tunnel under the North Sea, enduring what one writer has called 'a daily wager with death'. It was of seeing his son in the red rose or three lions livery of sport, a triumph that would prove that the spawn of a mucky Geordie pitman was as good as any bugger in England.

As the day approached to start back at school I got some disturbing news about Jean Sanderson. Apparently a friend of a friend said that her family disapproved of her going out with a pitman's son. I didn't know if this was true but she had been sent on a long visit to Scotland. It had been over seven weeks since I had talked to her and early in the first week of term an opportunity arose. Jean was taking science in the lower sixth and had to come to our school for chemistry. I saw her outside the laboratory talking to a lad called Neil Marley, a kid with pouty lips, and tried to make conversation. She would not even look at me but stormed off into the lab. Marley shrugged. When they came out after the lesson he had his arm around her. I don't know which annoyed me most: being considered not good enough for her or the ribbing I got from my pals at a younger lad invading my turf.

But then on a warm late September Saturday night my emotional life took a twist that would rock 102 Dalton Avenue to its very core.

I will call her Anne.

She was a year older than me and she had left the high school after 'O' Levels to work in a Morpeth chemist's shop. She was slim, more striking than pretty and had long ash-blond hair. She had the deep narrow eyes of a lady fox. Her voice had a throaty edge to it, a rasp of gentle sensuality. On the night in question she was wearing a flame-red duster coat. It matched her lipstick. She looked sensual but at the same time vulnerable.

The first house had just come out of the Coliseum in Morpeth marketplace. I had been in the Joiners' with pals and was about to get on a bus to Ashington to go to the Arcade dance. Then I saw her looking at the stills of the next movie. I recalled a lad at the pictures weeks earlier pointing her out and saying she was hot stuff. A friend of his had gone out with her and she had insisted that he buy a sex manual all about douches, pessaries and creams after their first date because he was so ignorant. The story was surely embroidered but something stirred inside me, something adult, something dangerous.

I don't remember my first words to her. But she agreed to go for a walk along the riverbanks. It was getting dark and the famous Morpeth ducks were having their last squawk of the night. She did not fasten the coat and I could see her shapely legs under her tight skirt. She offered chewing gum but I turned it down. She took one piece and chewed like a dormouse. 'I have to be careful, my two front teeth are false. They are on a plate.'

'Do you have any bother kissing?'

The words just came out. We both started to laugh. She took out the wad of gum and held it to one side as she pulled me to her and gave me a long, deep kiss. We went higher up the banks and sat down on a wooden bench. An orange gaslight filtered through the trees and its light made her pale face and slightly hooked chin look predatory. She kissed me again and pulled my left hand to her breast. My right hand slid to her stocking tops and inside her knickers. Her legs opened wider and her hands went to my crutch. I froze, secretly terrified of where this might be going.

She sensed my qualms. She pushed my arms away roughly. She smoothed her skirt and fastened the coat. She put her hands on her knees and stared at the gaslight. 'You've got to get this straight. I don't believe in halfways.'

The brutal honesty of the words, combined with the wantonness implied in them, shocked me. I had only met this lass half an hour before and she was ready to go all the way. Martha and Mary-Jane had warned me of fast lassies but even they had no idea I would meet an express train like this. In truth I felt inadequate, as though I had been offered a virility test and failed it.

I walked her back to the bus station where I thought she would get her bus and I'd get mine and that would be it. I was not prepared for her sudden shift of mood. She told me quietly that she lived in a farming village a few miles north. She was the main breadwinner for her mother and two younger sisters. Her father was a handsome wastrel who had walked out on them a couple of years earlier. Her mother made a few pounds here and there by knitting jumpers to order.

As the bus engine throbbed she kissed me deeply again and said she would meet me outside the Colly next Saturday at six. I was dumbfounded. This girl ,with her false teeth and writhing body, was stretching my experience. I was hooked good and proper.

In the autumn of 1957 my Uncle Sonny went into a sudden decline. He had no appetite and his agonising cries for 'Mammy' were merely throaty gasps. The doctors were all for putting him in a home but

Mary-Jane would not hear of it. My granny's anger at her lot in life bubbled over on our visits to King Street. If Sonny's noises meant he needed the toilet, Bob or Martha or I would dash to lift him. But Granny would set her face and shove us out of the way and clutch him to her breast, making shushing noises and sighing, 'My bit laddie, my bit laddie.' She would drag him out to the yard like a sack of potatoes. It made my mother weep and me want to get on the first bus out of Alnwick.

A few days later we got a letter from Granny saying that Sonny had gone into a coma and been taken to hospital. My mother dashed off by bus and next day she phoned our friend Jimmy Morrison at the Post Office. He came to tell us that Uncle Sonny had died peacefully in his sleep.

The funeral happened in teeming rain. A gathering of 20 people stood at the graveside as the priest said a prayer. The coffin was laid on wooden boards above the grave, which was completely water-logged. Granny and Martha huddled weeping and there were tears too from Uncle Sam and a gang of red-nosed topers from the Bird and Bush.

I stood holding Derrick's hand, hoping some men would come and put the coffin in the grave. It did not seem right just to leave my uncle, who'd had a dreadful life, alone on some muddy planks at its end. But nobody came and we dispersed, most people back for tea and sand-wiches at King Street and Sam's gang back to the pub.

I will never forget my granny sitting looking at a photo of bright-eyed Sonny before his accident, or her last words before the grief swamped her. 'They are always your bairns.' And I cursed the times I had condemned my stricken uncle as a nuisance.

At home there was more bad news. My mam came back from Alnwick with the 'rations' one Saturday evening and she was in tears. Uncle Sam had been rushed back into hospital, coughing phlegm and blood. He was going to have to move back into the TB sanatorium at Gateshead, 40 miles from Alnwick, for a more prolonged stay. I saw the

A very sad sight in the summer of 1956. My uncle Sonny, crippled at the age of 15, has been lifted onto a chair to get a bit of sun and fresh air.

look of panic on Dad's face as he tried to console her. It meant that not only would he lose his wife to the 'Alnwick gadgies' every Saturday, but now Sundays would mean she was off on three buses with her mother to minister to Sam again. And I was about to make a sacrifice as well.

I had won a prize through *The Adventure* boys' comic book – a shiny chrome sports watch with glow-in-the-dark numbers. One Saturday afternoon, just after Mary-Jane had arrived at our house prior to a Sunday visit to the sanatorium, Martha got the watch out of the drawer. Granny looked at it with bright eyes and murmured, 'Just what my laddie needs.'

My heart sank. Mam put her arm around me. 'He has no watch, your poor uncle Sam,' she wheedled.

He wouldn't be poor if he stayed out of the bloody Bird and Bush, I thought.

'It would make him so very happy if you would lend him your special watch. It would make the long lonely hours pass quicker.'

They both gave me the Bambi eyes. I sighed and agreed.

One month later I politely asked them to bring the watch back. Granny's lantern jaw dropped. She scowled at me. 'We cannot dee that, Sidney. Think of all them germs in his bit lungs and the other diseases that Jap camp put into him. The watch would spread them on to you!' Martha nodded her concerned but total agreement. There was no point arguing or reporting the matter to Bob; he'd throw a wobbler, harsh home truths would be swapped and Granny would go home in a self-righteous huff.

My relationship with Anne was blossoming. We had developed a regular routine. After school two or three nights a week I would either go to Top Field and practise my kicking or huddle in the school library over a list of books that Mr Parry had recommended for the Oxford Scholarship exams. Then at half past five I would meet Anne outside the chemist's after work. We would go to the pictures and snog, or we might sit in a coffee bar for an hour or two talking about movies or pop music. Her big favourite was Elvis Presley, which worried me a little as I certainly was nothing like him. Anne had seen *Love Me Tender*, in which Elvis played a moody guitar-picking farmhand, four times.

And it didn't help that Anne's last boyfriend turned out to have been an Elvis lookalike named Winston. One night she very animatedly told me about how, after a date with Winston, she went home on the bus with her bra in her handbag. I became silent, jealous that someone else had been that close to my girl. Catching my coolness, she rapidly assured me that fondling and feeling was as far as it had got. I nodded but I was not totally convinced.

In a strange way my doubts about Anne's 'past' deepened my obsession for her. Her line on our first date about 'halfways' being no good to her excited and appalled me at the same time. I grew to love the pride she had in her appearance and the way she made male heads turn. I liked the way she gently mocked me my eagerness for academic and sporting glory. I also admired her as the breadwinner for a family. I saw her in a rosy glow as a cross between my mother and sexy film star Rita Hayworth, a mixture of female earth mother and dangerous siren.

I started going to her house, a large rickety farmhouse owned by her grandfather, at the weekends. Her mother was a small neat woman with a thin smile and dark suspicious eyes; no doubt assuming from her own sad experience that I had the same wastrel tendencies as her wayward husband. Anne's younger sisters were friendly and Sunday tea was always plentiful with home-made cakes and scones.

In my arrogance and misguided self-belief I assumed that my presence added a much-needed happy atmosphere to the family. But I was soon brought down to reality. One Saturday night after the pictures Anne sadly asked me not to come to tea next day. I thought it meant she was giving me the push. Seeing my stunned look, she hugged me. She told me her mother simply could not afford the extra food, so had suggested I only visit occasionally. I said I would bring some of Martha's cakes but she said her mam would be insulted; she would see it as charity.

Nor was it all sweetness and light when Anne swanned into 102 Dalton Avenue for the first time, all Tweed perfume, pink lipstick and swishing duster coat.

My dad was in his shy way the perfect host. He shook her hand, hung up her coat behind the bathroom door above the dog's basket and offered her a cup of tea. Derrick told her a couple of jokes, asked if she was dressed up for a garden party and shot out to play. Martha was very cagey. I had been to Anne's for tea half a dozen times and had once referred to Anne as 'Wor Lass', a term usually applied to a wife, and Mam had jumped on it. She was obviously worried that my courtship was becoming serious and thus a threat to my future and her high hopes. Anne sensed this and praised the furnishings and comfort of our parlour as well as the jammy sponge cake offered for Sunday tea. I thought I had cracked it when I heard Anne telling Mam the various fry-ups she lashed together at dinnertimes at work. I would never go hungry if I hooked up with her.

But Martha's hackles really bristled when I suggested that she and Dad get gussied up and go to the social club dance. She knew fine well I did not want the personal space to show Anne my stamp collection. Bob, however, though no party animal, got my drift. 'It'll dee you good to get oot, Martha. You can have a dance with Chatty while I have a game of dobs,' he said, reaching purposefully for the Brylcreem.

Mam was not best pleased, but she got ready and off they went.

That left baby brother to be taken care of. I slipped him half a crown and told him to get lost till at least half past nine. He rolled his eyes and wagged his finger. He clashed the front door.

As Anne sat gazing into our roaring coal fire I locked Whisky into the bathroom, hoping she would not slaver or get hair on Anne's best coat. I pulled the parlour curtains shut. But Anne seemed reluctant to kiss me. When I touched her leg she brushed my hand away.

She got up and walked to our bookcase where two books Mr Parry had recommended sat next to the *Children's Encyclopaedia*. The books were H.A.L. Fisher's *History of Europe* and Bertrand Russell's *History of Western Philosophy*. She held one up thoughtfully. 'If you get a scholarship to Oxford or Cambridge, what will happen to us?'

'I've got to try for Oxbridge. My parents have sacrificed a load. The masters at school say I'm good enough...'

'But you could just as easy go to Newcastle or Durham.'

I said nothing. I began to cuddle her on our old saggy, uncut moquette settee and soon we were writhing on the home-made proggy mat. Soon we were undressed and Anne lay naked before me except for her stockings. Suddenly she stopped kissing me and looked me icily in the eyes, beads of sweat on the tops of her breasts. She seemed to be daring me to go all the way.

Then, breaking the moment, Derrick's high-pitched laugh rang out from halfway down the garden path. 'Wait there,' I heard him shout.

I re-trousered and sack-raced to the front door as he started to bang the knocker. He pushed open the letter box and I saw his laughing eyes. 'Kaney wants his Yankee comic back,' he explained.

I flung another half dollar out at him.

'Oh, overtime is it? Keep yer timber in, marra.'

His words made me laugh despite the farcical situation. But Anne's expression wiped the smile from my chops. She was fastening her bra with a face like thunder. She told me that she would go to the bus stop by herself.

I let her go. The evening that had promised so much had dribbled away in broad comedy. And part of me felt relieved. I was becoming mesmerised by Anne, but, in the long term, I knew that my future was going to be away from here.

I put Anne out of my mind in the run-up to the Oxford Scholarship. I had no contact at all with her for about three weeks. In that time I tried to broaden my knowledge by dipping into Russell, Fisher, Kant and, above all, the lush prose of G. M. Trevelyan. By the time I got the train to Oxford in the first week of December I could imitate the long convoluted flowery sentences of the last of these masters.

My mother had made a trip to my auntie Bab's and borrowed the money to cover the fee and expenses for my trip. When she came home with the money she told me she had seen my cousin Robert and his wife Gladys and told them about Oxford. I knew she would not have mentioned Auntie Bab's part in the campaign.

The subject came up a few days later when I bumped into Robert and Gladys at Lynemouth Co-op. 'When are you off to Oxford?' asked Gladys.

'At the weekend. But it's only a dry run for the year after next,' I replied cockily.

They both frowned. Gladys looked particularly concerned. 'That's not what your mam said. She's all for you being at Oxford next year.'

'Well, Mam and Dad might have misunderstood but I'm sure Mr Parry explained it to them,' I replied defensively, but I knew he hadn't. I had not enlightened them either. They were not impressed. They looked at each other as if deciding who would draw the short straw. Robert spoke softly but firmly. 'Sid, hev yee any idea what Martha and Bob have done for you? They both work their pluck oot for yee and Derrick. Bob's not weel. Without them two ye'd be nowt.'

'Spending their money on dry runs is a hell of a thing to dee. I hope you appreciate it.' Gladys's solemn tone hinted that she didn't think I did.

I tried a last shot. 'It isn't my idea. It's the school's.'

'Well, them bloody school teachers don't live in the same world as us. They're just seeing yee as a feather in their caps. You should tell the buggers that.'

I nodded but was sure I wouldn't.

They went on their way with no smiles. It was a severe shot across the bows, and in my heart I knew I deserved it. Gladys had come from a poor mining family in Ashington and Robert and his father and brothers had had a struggle. Nobody had treated them like gilded stock. And added to that was my realisation that in my generation in the Waddell family, I was the only one that went to grammar school, the only one who had a chance at going on to higher education. My male cousins went down the pit at the end of secondary school and the girls went into shops or offices. In a very real sense I had not only my immediate family's expectations riding on my getting into Oxbridge, I had my aunts', uncles' and cousins' as well.

When I got home I half-grasped the nettle.

'You know there's not much chance of me getting in at Oxford,' I said to my parents. 'But it'll do me good for a shot next year.'

They looked at each other. Bob spoke quietly, 'Give it all you've got, son. You never know your luck. If yee have to go back again it's fine with us.'

It felt good to have come clean. And I wished that Robert and Gladys had been able to hear what Bob said. Even they did not understand the lengths my parents were prepared to go to give me the best chances in life.

Pembroke College, where the great Dr Samuel Johnson had been a student, did not seem to have changed much since his day. It was small and pokey, and a rainy misty winter night did it no favours. I got there too late for dinner the first night, so I went to a pub and had two pints of bitter and two cold steak pies. I was billeted in a bleak garret student's room with no bathroom or toilet. At three in the morning I got up to pee and trolled a dark corridor in search of a toilet. I had no luck, so I peed copiously in two empty beer bottles I found in the pantry.

At breakfast next morning, in the small but ornate dining hall, I joined a group of fellow hopefuls. They were all from public schools, had posh voices and were all nearly two years older than me. Even when I tried speaking in the stretched-out Geordie voice which I thought was classy they had difficulty understanding me. They had been coached for months in what the questions would be on the written papers and they were talking about authors like Braudel, Popper and Butterfield that Mr Parry had failed to introduce me to. Worst of all, when I mentioned Fisher, Russell and my hero Trevelyan they openly scoffed. You would think I had done my swotting in the *Beano* and the *Dandy*.

That day I wrestled and waffled through the exam papers. In the general essay I lobbed in gobbets of a book called *The Common Weal*, a sort of bible for the United Nations and its high moral ethos. That night I gave dinner a miss and had three pints and two pies at the pub for my supper. I did not want to get more depressed by listening to the superfluent flannel of the kids from the posh schools.

But if the written exams were a disaster, the interview was pure farce. From the kick-off I did not like the look of three of the dons on the panel. The ancient chairman looked benign, but the other three looked like brainy vultures sitting on a branch fancying a slice of a dumb dying wren. But the posh lads' scoffing had primed my lamp and I was determined to go down in a blaze of anti-intellectual sarcasm.

The old man flipped through some papers as he welcomed me formally. It slid over my head because it was obvious that one of the vultures was hot for blood.

'You do not seem too clear about the role of the British navy in the seventeeth and eighteenth centuries.'

I knew he meant that I knew fuck all about the British navy.

'I'm only halfway through the syllabus. I'm not sitting the Advanced Level till July.'

It was a reason, not an excuse.

No quarter was given. He looked airily at his pals, and waved piano player's fingers. 'From the very start of the period we were defending a world trading empire, were we not?'

'There are other things in life,' I shot back with damp powder.

Over the next five minutes it got worse. They mocked my plagiarised scribblings from Fisher and Russell as well as the large gaps in my knowledge. I felt like walking out. The old chairman sensed this and tried to be kind. 'What do you know of your local hero Admiral Lord Collingwood, who lived in Morpeth?'

Stumped yet again, this time by a question from my own backyard, I gave an answer that even Derrick might have baulked at. 'I reckon he was better than that Nelson.'

I stood up to go, inwardly cursing Mr Parry for sending me into this nest of snipers. The chairman flapped his hands, indicating that I should sit down. I did and did not believe my ears. 'Mr Waddell, would you consider accepting a place at this college in October 1959?'

I addressed my reply to the vulture who had fried me on the British navy.

'No, thanks. If I don't get a scholarship to Cambridge next year, I'm off to the London School of Economics.'

That was telling them.

When I got back to Geordieland I made Mr Parry laugh with my story of the Oxford Inquisition and he admitted that handling highbrow smart arses had been part of his plan. At Docherty's billiard hall the lads laughed as well and even Joe Morris, who was a good scholar, scoffed at me for wanting to go to university at all. Joe was aiming at a good office job after the sixth form at St Cuthbert's.

The weekend I got back I was sitting in Joe's parents' colliery cottage in Maple Street in Ashington on Saturday afternoon listening to Buddy Holly. The street name was a misnomer; there were no leaves or flowers around, just long straight rows stretching like an army barracks. Dalton Avenue was Park Lane compared to most Ashington houses, with their wooden stable-style kitchens and netties over the road. And the house was the least of Joe's worries. His dad was a hard-working miner through the week, but at the weekend he drank heavily and took it out on his family. There was no violence, but Joe's mam looked haggard and much older than her age. I reckoned that Joe wanted a job sooner rather than later so that he could have a life of his own.

By chance I mentioned Anne, and Joe, ever open-faced and honest, coloured up. He began peering down at his records. I smelled something off. 'Have you seen Anne in the past week or two?' I could not keep the tremor from my voice. He would not look me in the eye.

'Me, Screw and a couple of lads went to Morpeth last Market Day on the night-time. And we seen Anne in the Red Bull with a sailor, with curly hair. No kissing or cuddling or owt, but definitely together.'

My heart sank.

It did not take me long to find out. Our rugby team had a pre-Christmas booze-up at the Joiners' Arms a few nights later. I was on my fourth pint of scrumpy in the snug when Joe the landlord called me through to the main bar. He pointed to the door and I saw a flash of poppy red through the ribbed glass. Sober, I'd have re-entered the piss-up, but I was mellow, heading towards well fresh.

She had her little-girl-from-a-broken-home look on and there were fairy lights in the trees opposite the castle keep.

'How did you get on at Oxford?' she asked, trying to kiss me.

I dodged the kiss. 'Failed! How did you get on with the sailor?'

The booze as usual had made me lead with my tongue. I expected tears and some sort of confession. But no, she was just plain angry.

'I've known Ronnie Dodds for ages. He was a pal of Winston's. All I did was have a drink with him. He used to go out with my friend Margaret.'

It struck me that she might well be telling the truth. I had been neglecting her. We kissed properly. I told her about the mess I had made on the Oxford papers and my skirmish with the snotty dons. She laughed more than she should, happy that I was still in her emotional orbit. We agreed that she should come to Lynemouth and stay on New Year's Eve. I went home on the bus feeling like an idiot for doubting her.

New Year's Eve was a terrible night. It had snowed for several days and that night the temperature dropped quickly. I met Anne in Morpeth at seven and we skated round drifts of packed snow to the posh pubs. She was in a wan, brittle mood and downed several Babychams very fast. I chewed McEwan's Exports, my heart filling with dread. Perhaps her errant father had shown up and upset her. Perhaps Winston the greaser was back on the scene. Perhaps she had gone well past halfways with the sailor. On the bus ride to Lynemouth social club she stared dully at the snowflakes bombarding the bus window. Her grip on my hand was like a cold vice.

The Big End at the club was rocking like the last days of the Roman Empire. There was a band and a crooner, and red-faced folks were drinking in the New Year like crazy. Bob and Martha called us over to a table where they'd kept two seats for us. My uncle Jack, still pale and stary-eyed from his illness, shook Anne's hand. She looked straight through him and dodged his attempted peck on the cheek. Martha noticed and glared at me. I got Mam up to dance and Anne looked daggers at me. After the dance I returned to the table to find Anne drinking gin and tonics, fast. Uncle Jack asked her to dance, getting up and tugging at her arm. Surely she would oblige a bloke who had risen from his sick bed specially to join the family celebrations.

'I don't like dancing,' Anne shouted at him harshly, batting his arm away.

Folks at other tables noticed. Jack stood with arms still up, pleading. Anne stuck her nose back in the gin. Martha bristled. Even Bob showed his feelings.

'You could just dander round the floor with him, pet. It's New Year.'

Anne stiffened, clenched her teeth and retired to the ladies'. Neither of my parents met my eyes. I wanted to say that the lass could not dance very well, that she was shy. But the time had gone for excuses.

Back at 102 Dalton, Anne and I avoided the jollity in the parlour. At midnight we had joined the ring for 'Auld Lang Syne' and Anne dutifully kissed and was kissed for good luck. After that we sat in the kitchen getting ever more drunk, she still on gin and me on 100 per cent Alnwick Brewery rum laced with blackcurrant. She was now slurry and had still given me no clue to her black mood. To avoid more fall-outs with my folks I took Anne out first-footing. I put a half-bottle of whisky into my pocket and led her out of the back door into the yard. The snow had stopped but there were drifts everywhere. I tried to lead her up Dalton towards my relatives' cottages but she dragged me to the dene banks. We staggered through drifts and ended up at my 'special place', the hawthorn bush where I came to think.

Kids must have used it as a den, because inside its drooping branches it was like a wigwam with old potato pokes on the floor. Anne pulled me to the ground and the mood changed. She opened the poppy red coat and began kissing me wildly. She sobbed, groped at me, pressed my hands to her breasts and said over and over again, 'I love you.'

I began to respond, but suddenly she pushed my eager hands away and began a flat, slurring monologue. It sounded rehearsed, as if she knew that she needed to tell me this, and had to practise for it. 'I want to tell you why I am not a virgin. And you know what people say about people when they are drunk – they speak the truth. I swear this is the honest truth. It happened one night last summer when the funfair was in Morpeth. I went with my friend Margaret and another lass. We stood on the side of the Speedway, dancing a bit, just having a laugh. Then we went on and this lad who worked there wouldn't let us pay. '

I was tensing up like a coiled spring. My mouth was going dry. The bloke on the Speedway surely could not be the evil-faced greaser who groped a lass when I was there in the summer.

'Later I walked around the back of the penny slot machines with him and I let him kiss me. I swear that was all. Then we went back and I had missed my last bus. So I let him drive me home. He parked up a cattle track and again I let him kiss me. But he persisted and … I didn't want to. I swear I didn't want to.'

She was now uttering a slurred scream in between sobs. 'I swear, Sid, that it was rape. I am drunk now and this is the truth. I missed my period and I thought I was pregnant.'

'What was his name?'

'Nicky.'

As she spoke she tried to kiss me. But my head was reeling and inside my drunken body my lovesick heart shrivelled to the size of a dried-up grape.

All the following week I tried to make sense of it all. Was she telling the truth about this and the rest of her sexual experiences? But the whole thing came down to this: if she had been a victim of this man, then I had to be man enough to extract retribution. I had to face him and fight him.

Happy New Year, I thought.

CHAPTER SIXTEEN

Payback Time

My hangover from New Year's Eve lasted the next eighteen months.

I was used to waking in the middle of the night sweating with worry about my dad dying down the pit. Now I had sleepless nights about Anne's confession. On our first date she had wanted to go all the way, saying that she did not believe in 'halfways'. Was this just talk to impress me, or was this the real Anne? Had the episode in the car with the funfair guy been her choice?

One fact kept beating in my tortured brain. A few days after the weepy monologue she told me that she had returned to the funfair a couple of nights later. One of Nicky's mates had dragged her down a lane and tried the same thing. She had kicked him in the bollocks and run away. But it seemed strange that she would go back so soon after.

Whatever I did in the way of sport or academic grind in those months, the scene in the moonlit old Cresta came back like my asthma, tightening my chest and making my breath rasp.

Early in the New Year I met Anne after work and we got a bus to her village. She went pale, fixed her eyes on the steamed-up window and clutched agitatedly at her handbag. I racked my brains to think of something I might have said.

I laid my hand over hers and steadied myself to speak. Suddenly a hunched figure with curly greying hair got up from a seat in the front of the bus and made to leave. Anne leaned towards me. 'It's my father,' she whispered. 'I saw him as soon as we got on.'

The man nodded at Anne as he passed us. Anne studiously and theatrically ignored him.

'Thank God,' she said, 'I thought he was on his way to our house. You wouldn't want to be there when he's rowing with my mam. We all end up crying, apart from him, the bastard.'

On her visits to Lynemouth Anne tried very hard to get Martha on her side. When the family set-to to decorate the two upstairs bedrooms, she brought along one of her overalls from work and began stripping paper feverishly. After an hour's hard graft she stood back and shouted, 'Shit, that was my best one.'

I looked over to see her pulling off the remains of a long painted fingernail and laughed.

Martha wasn't amused. 'That lassie says she's here to help but aal she's worried aboot are her bloody fingernails,' she muttered.

It was obvious that Martha was never going to change her mind about Anne, no matter what she did.

Then our Bedlington terrier, Whisky, was the subject of a mighty row. She technically belonged to Derrick, but neither he nor anybody else ever groomed the dog. So the dog walked round like a bedraggled lamb, curly coat all knots and eyes gummed. One night Bob had a go at trimming the dog with the kitchen scissors and Whisky went wild. We all laughed – except Anne. Her family dog was a sleek well-kept Labrador, and she let rip. 'Why do you have a dog if you can't look after it?' she fumed.

She had a point. Bob bit his lip and went out into the yard for more coal. Martha was on the verge of exploding but reined herself in and merely muttered something about people watching their mouths in other folk's houses.

All in all it was a blessing when Easter came and I had to buckle down to try and get a State Scholarship. Some weekends I did not see Anne at all, and for several months she did not visit 102 Dalton.

I was doing well at school. We had a new young English teacher called Frank McCombie, a Newcastle lad. He worked hard with me on the set books and also tweaked my crude cramming method of revision. He said it was fine to sit in the bathroom and learn parrot-style but that I must call a halt at set times.

'Go for a walk or a run, or get some chips or a pint even. Stop in mid-sentence if you have to, but get off the clock totally at key points. Then you can go back fresh.' Meanwhile, Mr Parry gently took the piss out of my flowery prose style and scoffed at my dodgy punctuation right up to the mock exams.

Sadly, my jinx as first team rugby captain showed up again to disgrace Mr Parry and tarnish my own reputation. My last act as captain should have been the climax of several glorious years. Our school old boys, Morpeth Old Edwardians rugby club, asked our school first team to represent their junior section in the Northumberland Under-18 Cup. We battled through the preliminary rounds and faced Gosforth in the final at the County Ground in Newcastle. In front of a crowd of about 800 we swept to victory, thanks to two great tries from 'Tanky' Scott, a burly farmer's son. In the dressing room some of the old boys filled the cup with cider and Pomagne and promised more to follow at the Joiners'.

Mr Parry had organised a win-or-lose dinner for the team after the match at the Newcastle House Hotel in Morpeth. I sat under a chande-lier supping McEwan's Export, feeling like one of my sporting heroes at black-tie dinners that I had goggled at in my annuals. All round my lads supped beer and wine and Mr Parry smiled obliviously. Feeling no pain after some very good claret, at nine o'clock he told me he thought I would get a Cambridge Scholarship and that the Barnard Castle debacle was water under the bridge. So it was with a joyous heart that I paraded the silver cup into the Joiners' Arms across the square. Boisterous old boys filled it with round after round of exotic fizz, cloudy scrumpy and creamy Guinness.

At ten o'clock closing time the well-oiled old boys escorted me and the team to the bus station. The cup, still brimful with booze, was being passed from hand to unsteady hand. Then Ronnie Wood, pompous fixture secretary when sober but a nutter when jarred up, began running with the cup as a 'ball'. Other old boys formed a three-quarter line, all calling 'To me!' Two passes were caught but the third went under the front wheels of the 10.15 bus to Rothbury. My cup had been runneth over. When I picked it up it looked more like a frying pan than a sports trophy. The next day I took the cup to a friend of my cousin Robert who was a panel beater and he did his best but it still looked like it had been made by a clumsy child out of crushed silver paper.

Mr Parry tut-tutted when he saw the damage and an official presentation to me on-stage in assembly was cancelled. He tried to hint that the old boys were totally to blame, but I could see 'Not suitable to handle authority' in the back of his mind. So I clutched the dented trophy in a Co-op carrier bag while the details of our triumph were spelled out by the Beak. A wag behind me sang 'Any Old Iron'.

In June 1958 it became clear to me, Mam and Derrick that my dad's health was failing. His short naps after a shift were becoming longer. Often we had to wake him to eat his dinner. Normally in fine warm weather he would be out in the garden tending his beloved leeks, but now he moped in his armchair. When he did go out, the slightest bit of digging made him breathless. I almost wept to see his furtive looks at the house when he slid his hand inside his shirt to massage his pectoral muscles as he wheezed and sucked for breath. At last Martha prevailed on him to go to Dr Pearson and the result was drastic. The doctor said that Bob's angina had got worse and that he should take lighter work at the pit immediately.

Dad went to the colliery management and asked to be put on salvage drawing. This meant there would not be the heavy tugging and heaving at chains and girders of work at the face, nor so much chance of a fall of stone. For days Mam and Dad were muttering to each other and sometimes voices were raised. Bob would go off in a sulk and then Martha would flounce out of the house. For a while I was put off my swotting, and even Derrick was affected by the atmosphere. Finally they sat me and Derrick down to tell us the score.

'You know I'm taking a lighter job down the pit,' said Bob. 'Well, it means that I won't be getting the money I was before.'

Martha interrupted, 'He'll only be getting nine pounds now and he was getting over 11 pounds before. But I don't want you to worry, either of you. We'll be all right.'

Bob was shifting around in his chair. He was not enjoying this conversation at all.

'Because,' continued Martha, 'I've gone and got a cleaning job with Jean at Lynemouth Social Club. I'll be getting about two pounds 10 shillings a week, so we'll be just as well off as before.'

Jean Bone was Mam's best mate and she looked almost excited at the prospect of working alongside her.

'I'll talk mesell donnered each morning. I'll have no puff left to fill your lugs.'

'Some chance,' said Derrick. Mam clipped his ear playfully.

My dad looked to me for my reaction. I could not hide the look of dismay on my face. 'Don't worry, son, we'll have the money for you to take that exam,' he said.

I walked out along Dalton and down the ginnel to the dene banks. I stood at my special place by the hawthorn bush. I thought back as usual to Anne's drunken confession. With a father in poor health but still grafting his guts out down Auld Betty and a mother on her knees daily scrubbing up tab ends and stale beer, I had better get my priorities straight. I vowed to hit the books like never before.

Two weeks before the start of my exams I went to the pictures with Anne and told her my plan: I would not see her for nearly three weeks. I was working madly and needed no distractions. All I wanted was to get a few papers under my belt, then I would take a Saturday night off to be with her. She was not best pleased. 'Do what you have to,' was all she said. It sounded like a threat.

Soon after, her name came up in an odd context. Mam and Dad came back from a parents' evening and proudly told me how confident all my masters were about my exam prospects. Then Mam's face fell. 'But one of them, a fat bloke with glasses…'

'Monty Williams. Big bruiser,' I said.

The bloke was a science master, so what did he have to do with me?

Martha frowned. 'He said you would do well to stop hanging around the streets of Morpeth with a red-coated *trollop*!'

The word hit me like an uppercut. Monty came to town on the same bus as Anne. To him thick make-up, tight skirt and a bright red coat could only mean 'tart'.

'I want you both to sign a letter to bloody Monty saying we as a family resent that slur.'

They both shook their heads.

'He might know something that we don't,' said Martha darkly.

On the Sunday before the exams started I was confident enough. I had sat in the empty bath till midnight cramming in the facts and by noon I remembered Mr McCombie's advice about packing in and letting my heated brain cool off. So, after Sunday lunch, I set off by bus for a surprise visit to Anne's village. Her mam came to the door and her face showed shock.

'Oh, I thought Anne was seeing you in Morpeth. She went out all dolled up!'

She asked me in for a cup of tea but I said no.

I mooched up the village and sat down in the wooden bus shelter on the main road, my stomach a tight lump. It was very sunny and lots of cars were heading south after a day up in the Cheviot Hills. It was in my mind that Anne might be out with girlfriends enjoying the weather. I hoped she would get off a bus and hurl herself into my arms. Then a cream Morris Minor went past and in the back I saw a familiar blond head, resting on the shoulder of an Ashington lad.

I went home on the bus and wrote a 'Dear Anne' letter. I addressed it to her, care of the chemist shop she worked at. I told Bob and Martha, who didn't seem surprised. Martha did not actually say 'Good riddance to bad rubbish' but I could see those sentiments in her eyes.

In the two weeks the exams lasted I heard nothing back from Anne. I was desperately hoping for a simple innocent explanation.

I really let my hair down after the last paper had been handed in. As an early birthday present, Mam took me to the Co-op in Ashington and got me an Italian suit, all the rage at the time, on her credit account. It was lovat green, had narrow lapels, four buttons and almost drainpipe pants and in truth I suspected it was a prize for kicking Anne into touch.

It caused a sensation in the back bar of the Portland pub in Ashington when I joined Screw, Joe and the lads round the jukebox on a hot early-August Saturday night. 'Fuck me,' said Tom Cowan, 'he's turned into a spiv.'

I accepted the ribbing and got stuck into several quick pints of beer.

Jimmy the Screw asked me if I was still courting and I said no and told him the story of seeing Anne in the car with another fella. Jim confirmed my worst fears. He said the guy in question was the biggest tomcat in Ashington.

'Lisley fucks every lass he gans out with,' said Jim with the air of an expert. 'If she's in the back of the car with him, she'll have dropped them.'

This hurt badly; I had bottled up my feelings for Anne and now they flooded back.

Results day was burning hot with no wind and I went to Morpeth in my Sloppy Joe and blue jeans. I walked up the drive of the school as slowly as a monk going to matins. Then a lad walking down the hill called Geordie Dodds, a curly-haired smiley lad who did science, grabbed me by the shoulders. 'Well done, Sid, you've won a State Scholarship.'

I walked slowly in a turmoil of conflicting emotions. I knew Bob and Martha would be ecstatic at my success, but the love of my life had failed me.

On my way home I indulged in some sombre nostalgia by walking a couple of the paths we had trodden by the Wansbeck river. I passed the front of the Coliseum, opposite where the Speedway had spun. If bloody Nicky had bumped into me then, I would have shown the world that I was no yellow belly.

When I got back home Mam was still in her the old pinny she cleaned the social club in. Her pal Jean Bone was having a cuppa and a Woodbine with her. My news went down a storm. Martha began to cry, and after showering me with kisses she got the medicine bottle full of holy water and 'baptised me', much to Jean's amusement.

At quarter to four I ran like the clappers to the pit yard at Betty and waited for Bob coming out of the cage. He walked slowly towards me in boots, knee-pads and battered black helmet. Through the coal dust on his cheeks I could see exhaustion. He carried the loaf-sized battery of his lamp as though it weighed a ton. His face split in pride when he saw my beaming face.

'State Scholarship,' I said. 'Four distinctions.'

He hugged me and I smelled the acrid tarry tang of the coalface on him and his old pit clothes. I looked up at the NCB flag flying from the headgear. It meant that once again Auld Betty's lads had hit their production target, putting them on track for 800,000 tons of coal a year once again. If Bob had not worked his guts out down the pit proudly, stoically and regularly, I would have got no further in life than the end of Dalton Avenue. I could not keep it in, I bubbled like a bairn.

Not long after I got my results Joe Morris came tapping on our door in Dalton. He had done moderately in his 'A' levels and was looking round for office work, but meanwhile he had been told of two vacancies for welders' mates going at the new colliery workshops in Ashington.

'I'm told we could get 15 quid a week,' said Joe with relish. My parents heard this with more than interest. Between them they were bringing in 11 pounds. Wouldn't it be lovely if Wor Sid could get his hands dirty and win a bit of honest bread for a few weeks before he went for the Cambridge exams?

Joe and I got the bus to Ashington and made our way to the new workshop site just west of the mighty smoking pit heaps. We found the big shed where the welders, from a Doncaster firm of heating engineers, were based. A tall young lad in overalls with goggles round his neck was supping tea by the door. We said we were after work and he said, 'You'd better see Fordy.' He said the words with a note of mild warning.

He pointed to a corner of the shed that had been partitioned. Inside doing paper work was 'Fordy', Bill Ford, the chief ramrod. Joe tapped on the wall and Fordy looked up, eyes welling with fag smoke. He had thick curly hair, piggy little eyes and a permanent sneer. He was the most sour-faced man I had ever clapped eyes on. He popped a Rennies tablet into his mouth – later I would learn his sourness was down to stomach ulcers – and spoke in a nasal South Yorkshire whine. 'What can I doo for you gentlemen?' He oozed sarcasm and insincerity.

Joe told him we had both finished exams and needed work. He did not say that I was going back to school in September. Fordy asked us to hold out our hands. We did and he stood up and felt them. 'You're not used to hard graft, are you?'

Joe and I looked at each other and nodded agreement. I thought we were about to be sent packing.

'Well, you're in luck. My lads will tell you I'm a hard bastard. Your pansy mitts will be covered in blisters this time next week. Be here at eight sharp on Monday. Bring snap and billycans. Now piss off.'

He hit the Rennies once again and Joe and I obeyed his instruction, fighting to hold in our delight and mirth.

At about three o'clock on the Sunday before I began my career as a welder's mate, there was a light knock at the front door of our cottage. Derrick went to see who it was and crept back into the parlour as if he'd seen a ghost.

'Sid, it's that Anne and she's asking for you.'

Dad put down his *News of the World* and frowned deeply. Martha was upstairs, thank God. She would have got the yard brush and chased Anne down the garden path. I put down the *Ashington Post* and went out the door.

Anne was wearing her red duster coat. My first thought was that she must be very hot on this dusty baking summer afternoon. Her head was bowed and her face was white. She was wearing no make-up and looked as though she had not slept for a month. She was holding a large green Fenwick's carrier bag. She whispered, 'Can I please talk to you?'

Fearing a Martha onslaught any minute, I nodded and hustled her past Dad's leeks. She did not speak another word till we were down the ginnel and by my special spot, the hawthorn bush. She did not look at me when at last she started to speak. 'You can be a very cruel person, Sidney Waddell.'

She said those words in the same leaden tone as the story of the night at the funfair. It echoed the same pitiful sadness, the lament of a victim. 'Your letter said that I'm easy. Well, let me tell you how I ended up in the back of that car that you saw. And it wasn't what you thought.'

I started having deep qualms about what I was all too ready to believe.

'I was bored sitting in the house while you swotted for your exams. So I got dressed up and me and Margaret Monaghan went to Rothbury on the bus. We went round Cragside and down the main street. We started talking to these lads from Ashington, who knew you. They said they played billiards at the same place. They referred to you as "the star runner". I felt proud. They offered us a lift down to Morpeth. I wasn't keen, but Margaret fancied the lad whose car it was. So I sat in the back and, yes, that lad Lisle did put his arm round me. But that's all that happened.'

'Why didn't you write back and explain?' was my weak reaction.

She dipped into the carrier bag. 'I wasn't sure I wanted to keep seeing a lad who thought I was a tart.' She spat out the words. She held up a sky-blue jumper with raglan sleeves, beautifully knitted. 'But as I worked on this I realised how much I loved you.'

I took the gift with my head down and my face flushing up. Not knowing what else to do, I pulled the jumper on over my shirt. It fitted brilliantly and I loved the colour – Cambridge blue.

There was a gentle long kiss and a hug.

'Sorry. What a fool I've been,' I said.

Then she reached into her handbag for make-up. She was not going to face Martha ungirded and penitent.

In the house I told my parents that there had been a misunderstanding; that Anne and the lad had just been fooling about. Bob bought the explanation but I could see that Martha was not convinced.

Despite my mother's misgivings, I really cared for Anne and wanted to make her happy. It must have been hard for her to come to my house and explain herself to me. My rekindled romance with Anne also fired within me a stronger resolution to smash the funfair guy to bits.

Bill Ford had only been joking; our delicate pen-pushing hands were perfectly adequate for work on the site. All we had to do for our fifteen quid – thirteen and a bit after tax – a week, was to climb gantries carrying the welders' tool bags. When they had the torch lit we rolled loose pipes towards them as they welded on flanges. They even let us both have a bash with the torch after a couple of days. We also had to alternate as the tea boy. Joe did the tea job on day one and I did it on day two. Just before ten I went to the shed where about 16 billycans were lined up, most with tea leaves and sugar already in. I added two heaped spoons of tea to the empty ones. I hated the leaves swirling round in tea, so I was a milk and cocoa drinker only. I had never even made so much as a cup, never mind a can-full. I asked a bloke where the hot water was and he pointed to a big shed a hundred yards away. I walked to the shed, which acted as a kind of canteen, and borrowed two big metal jugs. I filled them with hot water and began my trip back to our shed. A Lynemouth bloke called Bonner Graham, a famous mushroom collector, stopped me for a chat. Ten minutes later I dolloped the water into the billy cans, stirred them with a spoon and then went to the door and hollered, 'Tea up!'

The gang jogged into the cabin and nearly all added milk. I saw a couple feel at the cans with funny looks.

'Who made this fucking jollop?' Fordy screamed as he spat out the unmashed luke-warm gunk. 'Is some bugger trying to poison us?'

The rest were spitting out my precious tea and getting very angry.

'What did you do?' Joe muttered.

I told him loudly about getting the jugs full of hot water and bringing it to the shed and the gang did not believe their ears.

Fordy collected the cans and gave them to Joe.

'So State sodding Scholarship boy doesn't know that to make tea you have to take the bloody cans to the boiling bloody water. Does he know what a fucking P45 is?'

I was sacked forthwith from the tea roster but not from the site.

One day a little buck-toothed ugly guy, a steel fixer from Byker, came to the shed asking for me. He said his mate, a 25-year-old, was training for Powderhall and could murder me over 120 yards. He added that he had a tenner to prove it. Fordy, a compulsive betting man, heard this and immediately accepted the challenge on my behalf. He'd put up a tenner and was sure his gang would swell this to fifty. The steel fixer accepted the stakes.

On the day of the race, I was terrified. Joe had lobbed in a fiver and persuaded me to put in two pounds. I was told the stakes were over sixty quid a side, winner takes all, The idea was we would race in stockinged feet over 120 yards on some boggy turf along the side of the pit heap. I was trembling as we got down in a crouch for the start. My opponent was stocky, heavily muscled but looked more worried than me. His mates looked the kind who would duff him up if he lost their money. We started on a hand-clap and I got the drop on my opponent by jumping the clap slightly. I flew over the tussocky turf and won by five yards.

Fordy collected the stake money on our gang's behalf, then held up his hand. 'If you Byker lads want a chance to win your cash back, you can have it. Our Sidney goes faster than that in wellies! Same stakes?'

They immediately agreed. Then somebody pointed out that wellies on grass might be dangerous, so we shifted the race to a muddy lorry track with foot-deep pools. Having no suitable working boots, I had been wearing wellies every day on the site. But my opponent had to be found some, an old pair with turned-over tops. It was not a fair match; Bob had taken me training on Cresswell dunes in pit boots and it had really built up my thighs. I splashed my way to another easy win. So I had won the welding gang a bundle. Fordy was so chuffed that he gave me two quid out of his winnings, meaning the next Friday night I put £19.8s down on the kitchen table on the Friday night. Bob handed Martha £10 because he had done a bit of overtime – and we sent Derrick out for a giant fish supper.

As we ate the feast, swilling it down with Tizer, Mam waxed lyrical about her job at the social club. She loved the crack with Jean and the steward's staff. She was also enjoying daily glasses of shandy with the 'Black Pint Men'. These were workers down Auld Betty, just yards from the club, who came off shift in their muck at 8 a.m. Some preferred to wash at home but needed their thirst attending to first. So the licensing laws were bent and the lads clomped into their tiny cottages happy as Larry.

Martha also told me that she had danced with my boss Bill Ford at the last club dance. 'He's a lovely dancer and he speaks well of you,' she said.

I had a black thought. 'Don't tell Fordy I'm going back to school soon.'

She laughed and stabbed a chip. 'Oh, he knows. Your pal Joe let it slip. Bill says you can come back on the site in the holidays.'

'Tell the tight Yorkshire gett he'll have to pay me more if I'm ganna be his own personal whippet.'

Derrick laughed but wagged his finger at me for using the very naughty word.

CHAPTER SEVENTEEN

Fun at the Fair

In September 1958 I went back to the grammar school for my third year in the sixth form. This meant that I was, literally, in a class of my own. I sat in an attic in the west wing and devoured a list of books prepared for me by Mr Parry. He set me various essays and I wrote them out carefully.

I was destined for St John's College at Cambridge. One of the most eminent medieval historians in Britain, Dr Edwin Miller, was a Fellow of the college and a former pupil of King Edward VI Grammar School, Morpeth. 'Eddie', as he was known to the Beak and other masters, would be one of my key examiners. I knew that he would do me no favours, but at least he would give me the benefit of the doubt if I waxed too Geordie in my interview.

With the the State Scholarship, I was relaxed in my preparation. I did no cramming at all; I knew all the facts on the set periods. What would get me noticed was breadth of knowledge. I read Arnold Toynbee on the history of civilisation, the hated and derided Winston Churchill's *History of the English-Speaking Peoples* – very flowery but with first-class insights – and the way-out theories of an American called Pitirim A. Sorokin. He had devised a methodology that gave marks out of ten to famous figures for their influence on historical development. For example: Genghis Khan 8/10; Jesus Christ 9/10 and Napoleon 10/10. I had to laugh; this was making an art form out of sweeping generalisation. I made copious notes.

A pattern had emerged in my relationship with Anne. I would stay reading in my little room at school until five o'clock, then I would mooch down to the coffee bar by the clock tower. After work she would meet me and we would go for a drink or two or a walk.

One night, two weeks before the Cambridge exam, I was sitting alone sipping coffee and listening to the jukebox. Then a denim-clad figure hurried in the door. There was no mistaking the side-burns, jutting cheekbones and mouth pulled into a sneer; it was Nicky, the greaser who raped my girl. He was buying cigarettes from the counter near the door. I was sitting ten feet away, bristling with hate. He turned and caught my stare; did he know who I was? He must have sensed my emotions because he looked at me long and hard and shrugged. I stuck out my chin and glared. He laughed, tapped his brow to signify that he thought me a nutter and ran out.

My mind was on fire with visions of him in the car that night.

'Are you all right?' Anne smiled through recently applied make-up. She sat down and took my hand. It was shaking and she looked worried sick. 'You look as though you've seen a ghost.'

In a way, she was dead right. His face haunted me. I knew I should bluff out a story of not feeling so good. But I could not keep the jealous bile pent up.

'That bloke from the funfair was just in here.'

I would not use his name. Her face dropped. I could not stop myself.

'Why didn't you tell your mother that he'd raped you? She could have gone to the police. And why did you go back to the fair the next night?'

She had come in expecting the warmth of a lover, but was getting only a bitter inquisition. She stood up as if to go. 'If you don't let what happened that night drop it will be the end of us.'

She spoke the words with sorrow but also with icy finality. I stood up and tried to put my arm around her. She shrugged me off and started to walk. I followed her down the street. I knew she was right; my obsession was becoming totally destructive. When I drew level she began to gabble.

'My mother would have had a blue fit if I'd said a dicky bird. Getting in cars with lads is asking for trouble. I went back to the fair the next night because I promised Margaret I would. Another funfair bloke approached me, tried to drag me into his car. I kicked him.'

She was now shouting and in tears. I stopped her and hugged her. She was right. I had to stop interrogating her. I was going to fight the funfair bastard and that was that.

We walked up to the woods where we'd had our first date. I wanted to redeem myself. We began kissing passionately. She said she loved me and I said the same. The petting got very heavy. Desperate to make up for my savage words, I went further than ever before. I entered her for one tentative moment and then withdrew. To my horror, I thought I had felt a slight emission. Anne rearranged her clothes.

'I'm sorry,' I mumbled 'I've got so much on my plate, I'm dead nervous.'

I saw her off on her bus. As I waited for mine I looked over the bus station to where the Speedway stood when the fair came. In my mind I heard the rock music and the screams of the girls.

Ten days later I set off to sit the Cambridge Scholarship exams. Mam and Dad had bought me a new winter coat, a tan duffel with toggles. I wore it over my lovat-green Italian suit. I was very relaxed because this time I was not going to stay in some musty college room with dodgy facilities. Instead I was to be the weekend guest of my Auntie Jean and her husband, Uncle Charlie. The couple lived on an estate up Cherry Hinton Road in Cambridge. I got to the house at about three in the afternoon on a Thursday and Jean gave me a slap-up cooked tea. I knew I would be having dinner at the college later that evening, but I thought it would be rude to turn down Jean's Geordie hospitality. We talked about the family and then Charlie came in. He looked like Sid James, chain-smoked and talked like a Cockney bookie. He had a job as a catering manager and sometime major-domo for a catering firm that supplied the colleges. At about six he drove me down to St John's in a shiny second-hand Armstrong Siddeley Sapphire. When I got out of the car, the two porters on the gate looked at me as though I was royalty.

As Charlie drove off into the misty night, I looked up at the ornate gates. Above the stout oak doors was a turreted riot of fancy red brick-work inlaid with gilded heraldic shields. It made the facade of poky little Pembroke in Oxford look like a chip shop, I noted with satisfaction. I walked across a quadrangle with the massive chapel, a mini-Nôtre Dame, to my right and kept on going over the famous Bridge of Sighs over the Cam. I was now in the 'Wedding Cake' court, all pale Victorian stone spires and academic solemnity. As instructed on my letter, I found the rooms of Dr Edwin Miller up an ancient staircase.

Eddie was a small stocky man with thick glasses and a friendly smile. 'Welcome to St John's, Sidney. How are things at MGS?'

I chatted about some masters he might remember as I looked around the book-lined room with sheer awe. Some books were open on tables, flagged with strips of paper. A gas fire guttered and mullioned widows sparkled. In a voice that was frilled with posh Geordie, Eddie told me of the exam format. There would be two days of written papers, then a short one-to-one interview. I sighed with relief; no snotty inquisition here, thank God. He told me that I was expected to take dinner in Hall on the next three nights. And he told me how to get there.

Already with my hopes and self-confidence pushed sky-high, the dining hall put the tin hat on my mood. It was lined in dark oak and the roof had high-arched ornamental beams. I was early and it was empty. I walked the length of the historic room gawping at the portraits of famous Johnians. The one I liked best was of William Wordsworth, smiling a smile of proper pride. As people started wandering in, I went looking for a toilet. Even there I was impressed; most of the graffiti was in Latin.

Back in Hall I mooched about looking for a place. My Italian suit and winkle pickers got some funny looks from the callow youths from public schools in their Harris tweed jackets and school blazers. Then a lad in a gown pushed past me and walked over one of the long tables and sat down. I did exactly the same and sat next to some chinless wonders from Manchester Grammar. This time I did not let the chat about fancy books faze me. After telling them all about my feats at rugby and running, I finished my apple crumble and said, 'Best of luck tomorrow, lads. I'm off for a few pints with my uncle Charlie.'

I walked over the table again, dodging the plates and bowls with dexterity.

In fact, I had only a couple of bottles of beer back at Auntie Jean's and went to bed early. For the next two days I sat in the famous Senate House, just along from King's College, and poured out my knowledge in a controlled yet imaginative stream. In one essay on historiography I even chucked in a bit of nutty Sorokin and his league tables of relative influence. I had Sunday free till five when I had to go back to St John's to see Dr Miller again.

Now, my uncle Charlie did not seem to twig why I was in the Fens at all. I think he thought I was sitting a City and Guilds exam, maybe with a view to being a plumber. At one o'clock on Sunday he took me in his fancy car to a boozer called The Rock. I played darts with his cronies and drank four pints of Greene King Abbot Ale, the local rocket fuel. We had a roast dinner at three. I had a kip and, slightly bleary eyed, I presented myself at Dr Miller's door at five, sucking on an extra-strong mint.

Eddie offered me sherry, which I had the sense to decline. He said he'd had a quick look at my papers, and I jumped to attention. He smiled as he said I seemed to have done well. I read the smile as a positive. We talked generally about History and he said he had more lads to see. As I left, he called out, 'Oh, Sidney. I would cut Sorokin off your reading list.' I laughed, feeling more good vibes.

I walked across the main court, hoping against hope I would be seeing more of these ancient stones.

Back home in Lynemouth I told my parents that I had done well and that Dr Miller seemed impressed. At school I told the same tale to Mr Parry and my other teachers. They said I would know the result within a week; if I had got an award I would get a telegram, if not there would be a letter later. As usual my nerves kicked in and when I met Anne my first night back I was a wreck. I was so preoccupied it took a while for me to see that she was very pale. She would not look at me. We walked in silence to the bar of the Queen's Head hotel. I had a pint and she had a Babycham. She had her eyes fixed on the floor.

'What's the matter?' I asked.

'My period is over two weeks late. And I'm never over by more than a day or so.'

I slugged at the beer. It tasted like old socks. I knew I had to say the right thing but I cursed myself for 'dipping my wick', as Screw would put it, for one miserable moment.

'I love you,' I managed, holding her hand tightly.

Her face loosened and she tried a smile. 'You'd better,' she said softly. It sounded a bit like a threat.

I did not sleep a wink that night. I tossed and turned and kept waking Derrick up. Next morning at eight I went to our local post office, run by my pal Jimmy Morrison. I asked if he needed any helpers on the Christmas post. He said he already had a few students doing the rounds but the volume of mail had increased and I could start there and then. The mechanical drudgery of pounding the streets of Lynemouth stuffing cards and letters through slots took my mind off Anne's news. But family members kept asking about Cambridge, serving only to increase my angst. Then, on the Friday morning after I had returned from Cambridge, I walked into Jimmy's post office at eight sharp. He grinned at me from behind a grille.

'Telegram for Mr Sidney Waddell.' I almost jumped the counter. The ticker-tape writing blared out at me: 'CONGRATULATIONS. AWARDED OPEN MINOR SCHOLARSHIP. BURSAR ST JOHN'S CAMBRIDGE.'

My dad could have heard my whoop as he crossed Betty's yard a full mile away.

Lynemouth letters had never been delivered so fast. I ran up garden paths and jumped hedges stuffing half the contents of my mailbag in the wrong doors. I calmed down enough to deliver two parcels that were obviously presents and both housewives gave me a two-bob tip. My normal break was eleven o'clock but I was back home at 102 by half past nine. Martha was washing the dishes in the kitchen sink when I hurled open the back door.

'I've got in, Mam, into St John's!' I stuck the telegram under her nose.

Martha's face opened in a proud smile. Then her eyes narrowed and she pointed at one word. 'Minor, Sidney? I thought yee'd get a major scholarship.'

I knew that mine was a great achievement; there were only about 80 open awards dished out every year. But Mam's reaction epitomised the standards that had been expected of me since I was 11.

Then my racing happiness was damned into a deep pool of depression. What if Anne was pregnant? It would be just my luck to have botched my young life just at the moment a new one was beckoning. As Martha hugged me I was on the verge of tears. Imagine walking in that door and telling my parents that a baby was on the way. On the pretext of telling my auntie Bab the good news, I dived out into the back lane. One miserable thrust, I kept saying to myself.

I got a bus to Morpeth late that afternoon to see Anne. I was early, so I went to the Joiners' Arms for a pint of scrumpy. I told Joe the landlord about my Cambridge success and he pulled me another pint on the house. Around me happy factory lads in overalls and farmers with cow shit on their boots were starting their weekend with beer and laughter. If I had to marry Anne I would be in here too, trying to forget my boring office job and the routine of nappy changing. I felt like ordering up whisky chasers and getting completely arseholed. Instead, at six o'clock I presented myself opposite the chemist's where she worked.

She must have read my gloomy expression to mean failure at Cambridge, because she began to smile as she crossed the street. I noticed the wan face had some colour in it. She pecked me on the cheek, opened her handbag and showed me a pack of Tampax. 'My period started yesterday. Floods...' It was as far as she got.

I began kissing her wildly, but she did not respond. My transparent joy clashed with what must have been a hope to her.

'I got the Cambridge scholarship,' I yelled to half of Morpeth.

Her sharp chin jutted and her face set. 'I'll bet your mam and dad are pleased,' she said icily.

She did not need to add that she was not. After we spent a miserable silent hour in a pub, she said she had a headache and she went home. I ended my own little spree at the Portland in Ashington, where I had several more pints of cider with the lads and had to be helped onto the last bus to Lynemouth.

The following morning I did the rounds to tell the family of my Cambridge success. At the Chester's smallholding my uncle Jack, now very ill, with his skull very close to his skin and his body withered, hugged me and gave me a pound note. Auntie Bab was delighted and pooh-poohed all the loans she had delivered over the years when I thanked her for all the help she had been to me. Everywhere I went in Ellington and Lynemouth people congratulated me. The next weekend I got dressed up and went with Bob to the social club. We met a party of his mates from the pit, and one of them, Buzz Ogilvy, gave me five shillings. All the four men were pit veterans and Betty had demanded a harsh price of Bob and Buzz. At the water tower we had to stop so the 'Angina Brigade' could get their breath. They both laughed as they bashed their chests. It was announced on the stage before the bingo that Sid Waddell had got into Cambridge and I had to take a bow.

After years of being supported by Mam and Dad, it was now time for me to start helping the family coffers. In the middle of January 1959 I presented myself at the headquarters of the United Bus Company in the shadow of St James' Park in Newcastle to commence training as a bus conductor. I was not a very good pupil in the month I had there. The chief instructor was an ex-sergeant major and I drove him to distraction. He could not fathom how a bloke heading for Cambridge University could not take the pains to issue accurate tickets or work out how to get rid of copper coins and end up with only silver. If you did not do this methodically, your change bag weighed a ton by mid-shift. Still, he passed me and I went to Ashington depot and began the job proper.

Every Saturday, half of Ashington went by double-decker to Newcastle for the football match and many of my mates were amongst them. One day I had Screw, Joe and four others all riding for free in the front seats on the top deck. Then at Wide Open, about six miles from town, I spied an inspector waiting at the next stop. In panic I raced upstairs and, red-faced, rapped off six tickets, to the consternation of the other passengers. I got back to my platform just as the inspector waved us by. I could not lose face by demanding the money from my pals, so I balanced the books by a bit of short-changing of short-sighted pensioners.

Apart from taking home about nine pounds a week, just a bit less than Bob, one big handy bonus came out of my months on the buses. I had started going to Anne's village at weekends and the bus trip involved a change at Morpeth. The only trouble was that my bus was timed to arrive as the Rothbury bus left, and there was an hour to wait for the next one. So I persuaded the drivers to speed the last two miles or so from the village of Pegswood and get in early. Often we left a trail of fist-waving would-be passengers in our wake.

My relationship with Anne was as strong as ever, but with the passion and the petting never bubbling over. When she came for tea or a stopover at Dalton Avenue there was always tension between her and Martha.

I treasured the beautiful jumper she had so carefully knitted for me. I wore it only occasionally and thought that in it I looked like a preppy version of James Dean in *Rebel Without a Cause*. Then one sunny Sunday when Anne was expected I looked at the back of my drawer for it and could not find it. I asked my mother if she had seen it and she would not look me in the eye. I twigged where my jumper had gone.

'It's with Sam, isn't it? You and Granny have taken it to the sanatorium.'

She nodded. 'He needs summat warm when he's sitting out in the grounds letting fresh air get to his lungs.'

I was not buying the sob story. 'But it was a present from Anne. She worked on it for hours. What's she ganna say?'

Martha tossed her head and sneered. 'Pity aboot her. But if she gave you a present, then it's yours to dee what yee like with it.'

'Mam. You didn't even ask. Just like my Adventure watch. I want it back.'

'Yee cannit have it back. It's got germs on it.'

I was so angry I went out and waited at the bus stop for Anne. I told her the whole story and she took it calmly. 'My mam wouldn't do that,' she said, 'She thinks about other people's feelings. Anyway, don't worry, I'll knit you another.'

Anne, to do her justice, never raised the subject again, that day or any other. She maintained a mannered politeness with Martha and I managed to get my own back.

I was tipping up all my wages from the buses to Mam, so I felt no qualms about using her Co-op credit account to buy Anne a birthday present. I went to the Co-op ladies' department in Lynemouth and sought out a girl assistant who knew me. I got her to show me some soft white leather Aladdin slippers with sequins and curly toes that cost nearly three pounds. I explained I had left our 'tick' book at home and she said it didn't matter. She knew my mam's account number and she simply noted the purchase.

I happened to be with Martha on settling-up day. She looked down the list of purchases and shouted out,

'Slippers! Two pound nineteen for slippers! I've never bought nee slippers.'

I whispered in her ear. 'Anne didn't like you making free with the jumper, so I kind of set things to rights. My sweater was worth more than any three measly pound.'

She fussed and fretted but took the point.

The plan to avenge Anne's honour and prove to myself and the world that I was not a coward took shape in Docherty's billiard hall on a warm Friday night at the end of May. Screw and the lads were playing snooker and they were all wearing T-shirts. Screw and Joe were as puny in the arms as I was, but Bubbles, Cowan, Cliff and Stan had big arms and rippling chests. I was determined to beat Nicky into a pulp in August when the fair returned to Morpeth. I would take two of my hard pool-hall friends as back-up, but before then I would have to pack some muscle into my wiry frame. In the magazine *Reveille* I had seen an advert for a muscle-building course called Body Bulk, very similar to the Charles Atlas course for wimps who got sand kicked in their faces at the beach. I had sent off the coupon and the postal order and was itching to start.

When the parcel was delivered I mumbled something to my parents about bopping up my muscle tone for the athletics, then secreted it into our bedroom. That evening after tea, while Derrick was out playing, I opened up the Body Bulk pack. I was disappointed that there were no pulleys or other gadgets, just a thick booklet with diagrams. I found out that my body type was 'thoracic'. I was long in the belly and chest rather than short, so my 'dynamic tension' had to be more whippy than it would have been had I been stocky. The whole idea was to use body weight to create tension and thus build up muscles. So I set out diligently doing press-ups, squats and abdominal crunches for an hour, twice a day. Derrick stuck his head round the door once as I was twisted up in a red-faced knot, and had hysterics.

'Wor Sid a muscle man? I've seen it all now – I've seen bigger bee stings.'

I did not just work on my physique. Uncle Sam, in his cups, had occasionally taught me some army hand-to-hand dirty fighting, like using your elbow to break somebody's nose. I practised this and head-butting on an old caser football and the bolster that lay between me and my brother. I sometimes went down to tea in the parlour and had to explain away livid red marks on my brow as eczema. I even diced with the crazy idea of picking a fight with a drunk at the Arcade dance and rehearsing my moves. But having seen how accurately violent even the pissed-up lads at the dance were, I sacked the idea.

After about six weeks of Body Bulking I learned just how well the course had worked. Often Bob would take off all his clothes except his long johns before bed and have a daft wrestling match with me or Derrick. This night he sat astride me, pinned me to the floor by my shoulders and claimed a 'fall'. I reacted by gripping my thighs round his ribs and squeezing as hard as I could. He strained to break my grip and his face went red. I squeezed harder, shouting,

'Do you give in?' He nodded and I gave him a squeeze for good luck.

Bob got no sleep that night. The next morning the doctor sent him to hospital and they found two cracked ribs. He had to be strapped up and take a month off work. As penance I did masses of overtime on the buses.

In the last week of August, a few days before the funfair was due in Morpeth, I chose my battledress. I put on my baggy denim jeans, base-ball boots – which I had bought myself though my mother still didn't approve – and new white Sloppy Joe with blue trim. I wondered if Screw and the lads would notice my pumped-up biceps and forearms. At Docherty's I called the lads round a far table and described my plan to avenge Anne's honour. There were frowns and sarcastic grins – and nobody mentioned my new muscles.

'Three summers ago my lass Anne was raped in the back of a car by a twat off the funfair at Morpeth. I know that some of you think I'm a coward but I'll show you different. Can two of you come with me and back me up if the bloke's marras join in?'

Jimmy the Screw started the laughter, Stan joined in and then Bubbles. Cliff merely shook his head sadly. Joe Morris summarised the gang's viewpoint. 'You are fucking crackers. Them show lads are hard sods. You're as soft as shite and you'll get murdered. I'd stop at home and read me books if I was yee.'

Bubbles was equally cruel. 'I've had lasses tell me they've been raped before. Most times it's the opposite. They've got the taste for a bit of Charlie but they don't want you to think badly of them. I'll bet yon Anne's had more hot cock than hot dinners.'

There were nods and grunts of agreement. Joe put his arm around me. 'I knaa I called you a coward at the Portland, so if you're trying to prove summat to us lot, forget it. You're our marra.'

They were right. I did not need to prove myself to these lot, Anne, or the world at large. I needed to prove something to me.

'Who'll come with me?'

Jim, Joe and Bubbles shook their heads. But Stan, hard-looking and mad-eyed, combed back his quiff and agreed to come along. So did little Cliff. He said, 'Some bugger's got to pick up the pieces and parcel them up for Cambridge.'

On the Monday night the fair was due to open I sat in the Joiners' with a pint. My pal Alan Pearson, back from university, went along to the fair as my spy. Twenty minutes later he was back to report that Anne was on the side of the Speedway with another lass and Nicky the greaser was doing his act of standing on the motorbikes. My guts knotted; the attraction that had got her in the car that night was still there. I no longer knew what to think or what the real truth was. I went home and tried to sleep.

The next night at seven I got off the bus opposite the Coliseum with Stan and Cliff. It was a very warm humid evening and I had the sweat on that I usually worked up before getting down on the starting blocks. Stan and Cliff wandered off and began rolling pennies. I walked towards the Speedway, feeling the throb of generators, smelling oil and hot dogs and with Eddie Cochran growling 'C'mon Everybody' to a blood-thumping beat. Over to my left I saw two policemen ambling past the Colly to the river.

I slouched up the trembling steps of the Speedway and leaned on the side rail. Nicky was in the glass booth in the middle of the ride. Three other men were taking the fares. One was stocky, blond and wore overalls. I thought this bloke's family owned the ride, because he was often in the booth counting the cash. I beckoned Nicky over with a sneer. He stood up, waved the blond guy to the booth to take over and stopped the ride. Then Nicky walked to the last motorbike on the edge near me. He beckoned me on.

'You once raped my friend Anne,' I said, in what passed for a menacing voice.

He rolled his eyes. 'Rape? If it's the girl I'm thinking of – blond hair, red coat – it was nowt like rape. She took a bit of working up but when she got going she bucked like a bunny. In fact, she was here last night. We had a chat.'

While he was speaking, the Speedway had started up slowly and I had stepped inside the motorbike. 'Fucking liar,' I yelled.

I let fly with my right fist and caught him on the side of the face. The blond guy in the booth cranked up the ride to top speed. As Nicky kicked out at me, I fell back against the motorbike. Two sets of arms pinned me to the safety rail.

The blond bloke jumped on me, bashing my face and neck with a fist full of chunky rings.

'Fucking hard man, are you? I'll teach you to start bother here.'

I swung a punch and missed. Fingernails gouged my neck. Blood poured down my Sloppy Joe. Girls screamed and Eddie wailed.

Somehow I wrenched myself free of the arms pinning me down. The thigh muscles, primed by Body Bulk, thrust me down the steps and my face ground into oil-smeared gravel chippings. I sprinted towards the Wansbeck Woods as police whistles rang out. I hid in some bushes for a while, then ran along the river to the Ashington bus stop. People stared as I leaned my bloody face against the bus window. Then a familiar female voice said, 'What the hell have you been up to?'

It was Nancy, a conductress from the Ashington bus depot canteen. She wiped blood from my face with her headscarf and said I should go straight to Ashington Hospital.

I did not take her advice. I sneaked into our cottage and went upstairs on tiptoes. I went into my parents' bedroom and looked at myself in the mirror on Mam's dressing table. There was blood all over my clothes and bruises coming up all over my face and neck. There was a noise behind me and I turned to find Derrick.

He started to cry and ran downstairs, shouting, 'Dad! Dad! It's Wor Sid, he's aal blood.'

Bob and Martha ran upstairs and into the room. Martha was screaming. 'Who did it to you, son? I'll swing for the bastards.'

Bob touched my cheeks where the rings had gouged. 'Hev yee been in a fight, Sid?'

I nodded.

We went downstairs and I took off my Sloppy Joe and jeans. Martha bathed my face with warm water. I blabbed out a highly edited version of the fracas. There had been an argument on a darts-at-cards stall with me claiming I had won a box of chocolates. Some funfair lads had set around me and duffed me up. My mates had got me out of it. No mention of me starting the bother and no mention of Anne. Mam was all for rounding up a Waddell posse and wreaking instant vengeance. Bob said it was bad news battling with the show folk because they were a rum lot. Derrick looked the most suspicious, maybe thinking about the significance of the Body Bulk regimen.

Next morning I looked in Mam's mirror again. Both eyes were turning black and my nose and cheeks had dents where the rings had hit. My neck was torn by deep red weals and scratches. I stayed in my bedroom for two more days. I got a letter from Alan Pearson saying that the police had come to the fair after the fight and there was a strong possibility that they would lose their licence. He added that so far nobody had mentioned my name.

Four days after the event I ventured into the billiard hall. I cut a sorry sight in my canary jumper and school flannels. My eyes and nose were so bruised that I looked like I had gone ten rounds with Freddie Mills. The lads gave me a sarcastic round of applause. Screw shouted, 'Let's hear it for Fighting Sidney.'

Stan and Cliff shook their heads. Joe touched the scabs on my neck. 'Why did you do it? You knew you'd get plashed.'

I tried to defend myself. 'I did hit the greasy bastard in the denim.'

'One powder puff punch and a pansy swing that missed. Then you got filled in,' sighed Stan.

Cliff patted my shoulder. 'But I'll give you one thing, Sidney, you're a fucking trier.'

'Where did you two get to? You were supposed to be my back-up.' I bleated.

Stan looked at me as though I was mad. 'We never thought you'd start owt with two coppers snooping around. By the time we got to the steps of the ride you were doing the fucking 100-yards dash!'

'Which is what you should stick to in future,' added Cliff.

I had to admit he had a point. I said no more. I ate my Oxo crisps and drank my ginger beer and suffered open looks of pity for my sheer wanton stupidity.

I had a visitor on the Sunday afternoon. There was a knock at the front door as I lay on the bed. There was a murmur of voices, then a light step on the stair. Anne came in the door wearing her red duster coat, in full make-up and carrying a bag of grapes. She did not come near me. She stood at the foot of the bed staring at my wounds.

'Why?' was all she said.

I said nothing about the rape. I said nothing about my irrational need to prove I was not a coward.

'You couldn't stay away from the bloody shows, could you?' was all I could come up with.

She began to cry and turned to go. I heard her running down the stairs and then the front door banged.

Three weeks later, at the end of September, I had a farewell party for my billiard-hall mates. We'd had a party with girls at Joe Morris's house in Ashington a week earlier, so it was decided that Sid's should be lads only. Martha stocked the house with food and drink as if it was New Year's

Eve and we all started the night at Lynemouth Social club. By 11 o'clock 102 Dalton was jumping. Derrick was having the time of his life with older lads and he was showing them abstract drawings you have to put a name to. He drew a circle with sticks coming off it, which I knew was meant to be a spider wearing a sun-hat.

'What is it?' asked Derrick.

'It's a fanny' said Screw beerily. The lads laughed.

Derrick proceeded to draw a passable sketch of a vagina and said, 'Now, that's more like a fanny.'

Not bad for an 11-year-old. His crack got louder laughs than Screw's.

The only ladies at my 'do' were Martha and my cousin Robert's wife, Gladys. They were passing round hot sausage rolls when there was a bang at the front door. Gladys went to open it and she came back with a big frown on her face. Four people followed her in, two local lads, Andrew and Jim, a dark-haired lass in a flimsy red dress, and Anne in diaphanous green. Jim had a tin leg after a motorbike accident when his leg was amputated, and he limped in with his arm around Anne.

Martha looked daggers; she had a good idea that my funfair fight had something to do with Anne and was hoping she would never have to set eyes on her again. But there was no question of turning the newcomers away; that wasn't the Geordie way. Andrew apologised when he realised it was blokes only, but I told him to just dig in.

I was in the yard on my way to the toilet when Anne stopped me. 'Why are you being so mean to me?' she asked, drunkenly, and then she tried to kiss me. I pushed her away.

About one o'clock Anne and Jim disappeared. Cliff came racing up to me. 'Come with me,' he said.

We went out the back door past Gladys, who was washing dishes. In the corner of the yard nearest the door Anne and Jim were having it off up against the wall. His trousers were around his ankles and his tin leg was clanking with every stroke. Anne's green dress was up round her hips.

*Christmas 1958 in the back room of the Joiners' Arms. I am celebrating
my Cambridge Scholarship with a pint of scrumpy. My pals are
already at various universities.*

I turned as somebody came out of the door. It was Martha. She saw
what was going on and she hissed in my ear, 'Trollop.'

I went back into the house. Jim and Anne did not reappear. I felt
almost euphoric. The sight of Anne up against the wall in the yard had
been exactly what I needed to see. I could now leave with a clear
conscience.

My last days before leaving for Cambridge were spent in a flurry of
shopping. Cost was not a problem: the State Scholarship, Open
Scholarship and a Coal Industry Social Welfare Award meant I would
have about £420 a year for clothes, sports equipment, travel, books and
beer. All my food and academic fees would be covered.

Martha and I went to Doggart's department store in Ashington,
which smelled of mothballs and where customers' change whizzed
about on overhead wires in little copper pots. We bought shirts, trousers
and underwear, especially woolly vests, because I had to be wrapped up
to guard my poorly chest against the dampness of the Fens. Then Mam
pulled out the letter of essential requirements that the college had sent.

High on the list was 'a warm dressing gown'. In Lynemouth on cold winter nights we went to the outside netty in a donkey coat with 'NCB' stencilled on the back or an old raincoat. I tried on several tartan dressing gowns before settling for a real Noël Coward job, with Cambridge blue brocade on lapels and wrist cuffs.

On the great day, my cousin Robert drove me and my parents to Newcastle Central Station. My tin trunk of gear had been sent on ahead by road and I had only a small suitcase with me, half full of Martha's sausage rolls and pease pudding sandwiches. It was grey and rainy as I kissed my folks goodbye. Martha snuffled a bit and Bob looked very solemn.

'If it gets too much for yee, son, divvent forget your hyem. We'll be here for you. Stick in and dee yer best.'

He kissed me on the cheek and I hugged his broad bowed shoulders. I vowed I would never let them down.

Four hours later I was a bag of miserable nerves. The train was pulling into Ely, and the Fens looked cold and hostile in the rain and gloom. I was wearing a garment I had recently acquired, a long Crombie overcoat that had been my uncle Jack's. He had died in the summer and had asked Bob to make sure to pass the coat on to me. It was very warm in the carriage and I took the coat off. A figure came down the carriage like a character from a John Buchan adventure. He was a fat bloke with a red face and he was smoking a bent pipe. Round his neck was a stripy college scarf and he was dragging a wooden trunk behind him.

'Mind if I sit here?' the voice was pure cut glass.

'Smashin', I managed.

He sat down and regaled me with tales of the long vacation which he had spent as a travel courier in Europe. He was at Caius college and was delighted to find I was going to St John's, just along the street.

'You'll have to pop along for tea or maybe a sherbet at the Blue Pig.'

I agreed warmly and felt instantly better. Maybe there would be more matey lads like this at Cambridge, even if their voices could pierce armour.

My new friend produced bottled beer from his luggage and we shared it. I offered him Martha's home-made fare and he loved it. Then

I had a problem. I wanted to go to the buffet for more beer, but didn't know if I had enough cash. I was planning to go to the bank next day. Then I remembered Uncle Jack's coat. I was sure I had put some coins in the pockets. I held the coat up and began feeling at the pockets. Suddenly I felt a lump at the bottom of the lining. I pushed a finger through the stitching and waggled a small hole. I pulled out five pound notes, wrapped with an elastic band.

It was the ever-thoughtful Uncle Jack's rainy-day kitty, for times when sure things ran like donkeys at Redcar or Hexham. Once again the Waddells were looking out for one of their own, even from the grave.

'Same again, old chap?' I asked with a plum in my mouth.

I managed to lose my precious virginity in my first year at Cambridge. Thanks to dire warnings from Mam and Granny about 'fast lasses', reinforced by dogmatic convent training, I had avoided carnality with a vengeance. So you can imagine my surprise when my son Daniel, having researched our family's history in 2007, found some fascinating facts in the marriage records. These show that both Martha and Mary-Jane were four months pregnant when they got married.

Being conceived out of wedlock was not something that worried me unduly but I wonder if my early life would have been quite as monastic if my saintly granny and my moralising mother had levelled with me about the facts of their lives.

Pithead Revisited

Bob and Martha Waddell achieved their life's ambition; I never went to work down Auld Betty or any other coal mine. Neither did my brother Derrick. But, after three years at Cambridge, where I got a 2:1 degree in Modern History, I did not quite know what to do next. And so in the summer of 1962, I returned to my Lynemouth nest and applied for a clerking job at the NCB colliery offices in Ashington at £7 a week. I was told I was too well qualified.

I then got a job as research assistant to the professor of Economics at Durham University and toyed with the idea of a life in academia. But in 1965 I went into the television industry and worked my way up from researcher to producer in current affairs programmes. I became BBC TV's first darts commentator in 1977 and switched to Sky Sports in 1994.

I would have been nowhere without the sacrifice and dedication of my parents. I look back to my life before Cambridge and I am astounded about just how much I took for granted, how selfish I was many a time. Inspired by the gung-ho lads' comics like *The Wizard* and *The Hotspur,* with their larger-than-life sporting heroes, I lived in a fantasy world. My parents gave me the material and moral support to live my sporting dreams and realise my academic potential. But I like to think that I paid them back a little over the years and I know they and the wider Waddell clan were extremely proud of my achievements.

My parents visited a big darts event at Middlesbrough in 1985. Though I got them the Gold Star suite, Martha took chicken legs, pork pies and packets of salt from her bag and laid their feast out on the posh duvet.

My father ended up his days at the pit working on light surface work until he was made redundant in March 1968. He was given a lump sum of £660 for 48 years continuous work at the same colliery. Typically, he waved the cheque at Mam and me and said, 'We're all bloody Tories now.'

He also got £1.30 a week pension.

On 16 August 1984, six months into the Miners' Strike, I made a nostalgic visit to the village of Lynemouth from my home in Leeds.

At that time I was working as a director of children's television programmes at the BBC in Manchester. Watching the coverage on TV and reading the papers' accounts of the strike, which started in early March, I had been appalled by the bias shown against the strikers and the demonisation of their leader Arthur Scargill. When Ian MacGregor, the NCB chairman, was accidentally pushed to the ground by a noisy group of miners on a visit to Auld Betty, a TV reporter turned on the men and accused them of trying to harm an old man.

I started my visit with what I hoped would be a quiet beer in the buffet bar on the train as it passed through Northallerton, when a fat businessman came up and ordered a large gin and tonic. The bloke was wearing a blue-and-white striped shirt with a plain white collar, blue silk tie and pinstripe suit. It was not his first gin of the day and as he poured down the drink and ordered another his chops flushed deeper.

'I hear that the coppers are doing rounders' practice on the heads of those pickets.'

The two buffet attendants, lads I knew from using the train regularly, blenched and looked away. Not me. I grabbed the loudmouth by the tie and shouted, 'If you say another fucking word I'll smack your teeth in.'

He snorted, put his drink down and prepared to throw a punch. The attendants rushed round and separated us. I withdrew, thanking God that my McEwan's Export was the first of the day. If I'd had half what the windbag had drunk, things would have got very nasty indeed.

Two hours later I was on a bus from Ashington when it stopped to drop people at the stop near Lynemouth colliery. The driver got out and went to talk to the pickets who manned a 'bunker' by the roadside. This was my first live sighting of the people whom Mrs Thatcher, the prime minister, had called 'the enemy within' a few days earlier. They looked like a dozen grizzled sun-scorched Apaches as they swarmed around their stockade with its sign that read 'The Alamo'. This had started as a tent but was now reinforced with beer crates, orange boxes and sandbags – these to keep the tent up rather than the coppers out. Amongst the lads in long vests with shaggy manes of hair I recognised Jimmy Sweet, a lad with the face of an angel but a devil when riled, and one of my brother Derrick's best friends. Jimmy waved at me and pointed to a 'Coal Not Dole' sticker on his vest.

Looking out of the bus window I noticed that there were no longer any wooden fences lining the fields where the pit ponies used to graze. When I got to 102 Dalton, I asked Bob about his health. He told me that he was taking pills for the angina and that he had been told by the doctor not to do heavy tasks like shovelling coal into the coal house from the back lane. He said that Cousin Robert came and did the job for him. I asked him what had happened to the NCB's fences and his face lit up.

'It's Wor Robert, Tommy Chester and the pickets. The bloody coal board stopped retired miners' concessionary free coal cos they said we were giving some of it to the strikers. So the lads have chopped doon every NCB fence round the pony fields, the slag heaps and the pit yard and given it to us auld folks to use as fuel.'

And the people of 102 Dalton had responded in kind. My dad had used half his precious leek trench to grow lettuces, and had donated potatoes and cabbages from the rest of his garden to soup kitchens for strikers and their families who were trying to survive on strike pay of one pound a day, and that only if you went picketing.

'I thought I'd seen the last of little bairns lining up at soup kitchens in 1926,' said Bob with a low husk in his voice.

My mother was in her element. She was making sandwich cakes and bread for the soup kitchens and one of her famous rum-laced Christmas cakes for a raffle for the strike fund. She let her powerful flair for invective loose on the prime minister, whose name she would never lay her tongue to.

'That bloody woman with her drunken toff of a husband has strangled the lifeblood oot of this village. She hates us mining people and I hope to almighty God that she rots in hell.'

Before Mrs Thatcher famously said, 'There is no society ... there is no such thing,' she should have spent a few days with the folk of Lynemouth.

I walked with my brother Derrick past more fence stumps on the way to Lynemouth Social Club. He pointed out where there had been an NCB plantation of fir trees that the pickets had demolished for fuel. Derrick had been on the dole for several years. He had tried various jobs but just could not settle into civilian life after 18 years in the RAF. He too was helping the strikers. Each day when the tide was right he took his fishing tackle to the rocks at the village of Cresswell and caught mackerel, flatties and the occasional cod, which he handed over to the soup kitchens. His view of the much-maligned Arthur Scargill was typical of people in our village.

'He might have been a Commie and I think he should have had a proper ballot of the whole membership before he called the lads out. But he's no dictator. They always use the phrase "holding the country to ransom". But he is deed right about the Tories wanting to butcher the coal mines. Seventy pits doon is only the start. That woman will close a lot more before she's finished.'

There were about ten people in the bar at the club. My cousin Billy who had gone from Lynemouth years back to work in the pits of Nottinghamshire was there. He was on strike and proudly wore a badge declaring, 'We're NOT all scabs in NOTTS.' Nottinghamshire had formed its own breakaway union, the Union of Democratic Miners, and was against the national strike. The government had told them that their pits were safe. He told Derrick and me about the antics of our uncle Tommy Chester, a union stalwart, on the Betty picket line.

'So Ches sees this lorry coming along and he is convinced it's transporting coal. He flags the man down and tells the driver to take the tarpaulin off his load. The man refuses, so Ches jumps up and lifts the tarpaulin himself only to find the load is actually pigs' intestines. And Ches vomits all over the place.'

Derrick and I began chatting to a young couple who had two kids. Jimmy, the husband was on strike, but was too proud to make use of the soup kitchens themselves.

'Me and wor lass tek the two bairns to fill their bellies. We smoke tabs while they eat and the smoking stops your hunger.'

They went off to take their bairns to the soup kitchen near Lynemouth Co-op. I offered them ten pounds and they would not take it. The Tories might be axing their jobs and life prospects but they could not axe their pride.

*Ellington Colliery, alias 'Auld Betty', where the Waddell menfolk sweated cobs
and risked their lives so their families could have canny lives.*

The miners went back to work with lodge banners held high after one year
on strike. The closure of the pits accelerated, even in Nottinghamshire
where the non-striking miners had hoped for special treatment. When the
industry was privatised in December 1994 there were only 15 working pits
and a workforce of 18,000.

On 26 January 2005 UK Coal announced that, due to flooding, Auld
Betty, the last deep coal mine in the North East, was closing down. All
340 miners were made redundant. A few days later the men marched
from the colliery for the last time carrying the Ellington branch of the
union's banner proudly. It was the last act in 800 years of mining in the
north-east region.

How very different from the glory day in 1983, just one year before
the 'enemy within' remark, when Betty's workers posed for an NCB
photograph captioned 'Million-Tonne Marvels'. By the sweat of their
brows they had mined that amount of coal in a record 29 weeks, making
them the most productive pitmen in Britain. Their faces shine with
simple pride, as if the future was bright ahead.

There are now no pits and no coal miners left in Northumberland, but there is still a union and in 2007 there was a ceremony for the blessing of a brand new NUM banner. On the front is a mighty miner hurling a javelin at the greedy dragon of capitalism. On the back happy workers watch children dance merrily round a maypole. It hangs in the Woodhorn Mining Museum, three miles over the fields from where Auld Betty once stood. It flies high in processions at working-class rallies like the Durham Miners' Gala, still held annually despite there being no pits left in County Durham.

I think my parents Bob and Martha Waddell would have appreciated, and been wryly amused by, the flying of brightly coloured banners in villages with no work and no hope. They commemorate a special way of life that has died, some would say has been butchered, but whose human values live on.

In the parlour at 102 Dalton a joyous group meets for Derrick's wedding. Back row: Bob, Derrick, Martha and Mary Jane. Front row: David Price, Derrick's pal, and Sid. Note: Martha has polished everything – even the Lyncrusta.

GLOSSARY OF GEORDIE AND
PITMATIC WORDS

Aal	All
Baccy	Tobacco
Bairn	Child
Blether	To talk non-stop
Bonny	Pretty, good-looking. Satirically: drunk
Bray	To give a good hiding
Bubble	To weep
Caad	Cold
Canny	Pleasant
Ched	Mischievous child
Chow	Chew
Cossie	Swimming costume
Claggy	Sticky, muddy
Crit	Witch, monster, deformed person
Crowdy	Cooked food scraps for pigs
Dancers	Stairs
Deek	Look
Deed	Dead
Doon	Down
Donnered	Stupid, dozy
Dottle	Sheep shit, also hard pipe ash.
Ettled	Determined
Gadgie	Man, bloke
Gan	Go
Gawpins	Handfuls
Geet	Great
Guddies	Sweets

Guffie	Pig
Gully	Bread knife
Hacky	Very dirty
Hammers	Blows
Hissel	Himself
Hoy	Throw
Howway	Come on
Hyem	Home
Kidda	Mate, pal
Ladge	As in 'Oh, for ladge', 'For God's sake'
Lonnen	Lane
Marra	Friend, workmate
Mazer	Wondrous person, phenomenon
Mesell	Myself
Mizzle	Misty rain, also verb 'to disappear'
Morn	As in 'the morn' – tomorrow
Muckle	Large
Nee	No
Neet	Night
Netty	Outside toilet
Nitty comb	Comb for head lice
Oot	Out
Pant	Horse trough
Peevy	Boozy, drunk
Pittle	Pee
Poke	Sack, also wallet
Plodging	Wading
Pluck	Heart
Pop	Beer
Radge	Crazy
Scraffling	Searching
Scranchins	dry scraps of fish batter
Shite	Shit
Skelp	Smack
Sleck	Coal-soaked river mud
Snaffle	Steal

Stookie	Hay rick
Stot	Bounce
Stythe	Pit gas
Tab	Cigarette
Tappy-lappy	Pell-mell
Tetties	Potatoes
Warking	Starving with hunger
Winnit	Will not
Wor	Our
Workie	Workhouse
Yacker	Pit worker
Yarking	To thrash heavily
Yee	You

ENGAGED TO

In a fit of temper and humiliation after
the cavalier way he had treated her,
Brooke Faulkner published a notice of
her 'engagement' to the tycoon Jarrod
Stone—and had plenty of time to rue
her hasty action when he insisted that,
to suit his personal convenience, they
make the engagement a real one. And
only after she had fallen in love with
him did Brooke realise that 'personal
convenience' meant concealing his
affair with someone else's wife . . .

ENGAGED TO JARROD STONE

BY

CAROLE MORTIMER

MILLS & BOON LIMITED
15–16 BROOK'S MEWS
LONDON W1A 1DR

First published 1980
Australian copyright 1980
Philippine copyright 1980
This edition 1980

© Carole Mortimer 1980

ISBN 0 263 73403 X

Set in Linotype Baskerville 10 on 10½ pt.

Made and printed in Great Britain by
Richard Clay (The Chaucer Press), Ltd., Bungay, Suffolk

CHAPTER ONE

BROOKE sat down at the reception desk, turning to face the girl who sat behind her. 'Has he arrived yet?'

Jean gave her an innocent look. 'Has who arrived?'

Brooke gave her an impatient glance. 'You know very well who. Don't tease this morning, Jean.'

Her friend quirked one eyebrow. 'Had one of those nights, did you?'

'Morning, actually. *Has* he arrived?'

'I gather you mean Mr Stone? Then yes, he arrived about ten minutes ago.'

'Oh damn!' Brooke frowned her displeasure.

'Why? Did you want to see him?'

'Not really.' She pursed her lips. 'I'm—— He—— What did he look like?' She watched the other girl closely.

Jean gave her a strange look, dealing hurriedly with a call that came through on her switchboard. They weren't due to open until nine o'clock, and yet invariably there were calls coming through before then. 'How do you think he looked?' she said finally. 'How does he always look—gorgeous. Just as tall, dark, and handsome as usual.'

'He didn't look—well, different?'

Jean gave a firm shake of her head. 'He always looks the same, he always acts the same. He walks in here, gives me an arrogant nod of his head, and then walks straight into his private lift. He does the same thing in the evenings, only in reverse. The man's as impersonal to his employees as the machines he produces. Three years I've worked here now, and he still wouldn't recognise me if he saw me out in the street.'

Their conversation was broken off as the office

5

workers started to crowd into the building in preparation for starting work at nine. As the receptionist Brooke found the next half an hour very busy, directing people up to the various offices and dealing with the tannoy system.

The morning rush over, she relaxed in her chair for a few minutes. Jean was kept busy with her switchboard, which gave Brooke time to think. She was a fool, a prize idiot. She was likely to lose her job for what she had done, and it was a good job, paying very high wages.

She must have been temporarily insane, must have had a brainstorm. When she had seen the announcement in the newspapers this morning she had felt sick, physically sick. And yet no one else had seen it— at least, no one had commented on it. Someone had to see it soon, it was so noticeable. It had seemed larger than life to her.

It had been there in the newspaper for all to see, an intended marriage between Brooke Faulkner and Jarrod Stone. Her own engagement to the owner of this prosperous computer firm! And to make matters worse, he knew nothing about it!

She picked up the internal telephone on her desk as it began to ring. 'Brooke Faulkner speaking,' she said automatically.

'Get up here!' snapped a deep male voice.

She almost dropped the telephone in her panic. Jarrod Stone, it had to be! She cleared her throat. 'I—I beg your pardon?'

'You'll do more than that when I've finished with you,' he growled. 'I'll expect you in my office in precisely five minutes.' The receiver was slammed down at the other end.

She didn't need to be told that he knew about the announcement in the newspapers, the anger in his voice had been enough. Besides, he had hardly ever spoken to her before, and there could be only one reason he wanted to see her.

'Everything all right?' asked Jean, noting her pale face.

Brooke realised with a start that she was still holding the receiver in her hand. She put it hurriedly back on its cradle. 'I—I have to go up to one of the offices. Would you—would you look after the desk for me for a while?'

'Sure,' Jean agreed readily.

Brooke didn't quite know how she got into the private lift for the tenth floor, but somehow she seemed to have managed it. She had only ever used this lift once before in the six months she had worked for Stone Computers, and that had been two weeks ago when she had been induced to seek this terrible revenge on him.

It had all started when the model had arrived to take the advertising photographs. No one else had been available to take her up to Jarrod Stone's office and so she had offered to take her up herself. It had been a good excuse to see him. As Jean had so rightly said, he walked in in the mornings and out again at night, taking no notice of them in reception at all.

As it had turned out Jarrod Stone's secretary had gone to lunch that day and her assistant was off sick. Brooke had hardly been able to believe her luck when she had stepped out into the outer office. The place had been deserted, which meant she would actually get to speak to Jarrod Stone herself. Since the day she had begun work here, and he had walked into the building to begin his day's work, she had fallen for him, hard.

He was so fantastic-looking, like a film star or something. He was tall, well over six feet, with a lithe athletic body that suggested he did not spend all of his time in an office, his skin tanned from much time spent in the sun. His dark over-long hair was styled away from his face, his deep grey eyes narrowed and enigmatic.

But if she had been instantly attracted to him he

hadn't reacted at all; those grey eyes looked right through her. She knew she wasn't beautiful or anything, but she wasn't that plain either. Dark brown hair with deep red tints swung easily about her shoulders in gleaming waves, her deep blue eyes surrounded by long thick lashes, her small uptilted nose, curving mouth that was never far from a smile, and slight slender figure all added up to an attractive young girl. And yet to Jarrod Stone she might not even have been feminine.

But she knew he wasn't always that reticent about noticing a woman's charms; he was reputed to have had many beautiful women in his life at one time or another. And his completely self-assured arrogance pointed to them not all being platonic relationships. No, here was a man who had shared his bed with many women—and he had known how to satisfy every one of them.

In a way it had been his confirmation of these conquests that had sparked off her desire to hit out at him. Leaving the model in the outer office, she had passed through to the reception room. In here she could hear the faint murmur of masculine voices, and had realised Jarrod Stone wasn't alone.

She soon knew the reason she could hear their voices too; the office door was slightly ajar. She was just about to knock on the door when she was arrested in the action by the words being murmured in her boss's deep throaty voice, his amusement obvious.

'I'm afraid I only find women good for one thing,' he scoffed lightly. 'And I don't mean housework,' he added with a laugh.

Brooke had stepped back with a gasp. What a cheek! What a nerve! The meaning behind his words had been obvious and she had waited open-mouthed for his companion's answer. She knew she should really knock on the door, make them aware of her presence before they said anything else, but she was held mesmerised by the arrogance of the words she had just overheard.

'Come on now, Jarrod,' the other man replied, this voice sounding younger. He had called the first speaker Jarrod, confirming her belief that Jarrod Stone had made that insulting remark about the female sex. 'You like women as much as I do,' he continued.

'I *enjoy* them,' Jarrod Stone had corrected. 'I don't know that I've ever actually liked them. But I've desired them, yes. But I find them preferable as bed-companions than as anything else.'

'If one of them could hear the way you're talking . . .'

But one can, Brooke wanted to shout. She had never felt so disgusted and degraded. How a man as success-ful and good-looking as Jarrod Stone could judge all women by the type he had obviously been associating with for years was beyond her. To her he appeared the handsomest man she had ever seen, and to think he had that low opinion of women just didn't seem fair. His looks and charm had obviously done him no good whatsoever, making him cynical about women.

'Why should they care?' he replied carelessly. 'They're usually well compensated for their—charms, for want of a better word,' he added with a sneer, 'with jewellery and clothing. No woman will ever trap me into marriage while there are women like that about, but they can never accuse me of being mean.'

'I'm sure,' laughed the other man.

Brooke had decided she had just about heard enough of this distasteful conversation, knocking firmly on the door and entering when bade to do so.

'Yes?' Jarrod Stone raised one dark eyebrow, his eyes broodingly grey in his deeply tanned face.

Brooke stopped in her tracks, the anger that had been the momentum behind her being able to walk into the room slowly fading. Her breath caught in her throat at the lazy smile he directed at her, leaving her momentarily speechless. When she finally did manage to speak it was in a voice that sounded strange, even to her own ears. 'I—er—I—I've brought up the model for the advertising photographs. She's waiting outside.'

'Thank you.' He smiled at her again, his eyes crinkling at the corners. 'Would you like to show her in? My secretary's at lunch, I'm afraid.'

'Certainly,' she answered breathlessly.

He looked every inch the arrogant businessman sitting behind his imposing desk, and Brooke turned in confusion to leave the room. She hesitated outside the door as she heard him give a throaty chuckle.

'You see what I mean,' he said with amusement.

'What?' The other man was obviously puzzled, a younger man that Brooke had recognised as being Philip Baylis, a business associate of the owner of Stone Computers.

'A smile and a few softly spoken words and any woman will do exactly what you ask them to, even that little mouse. She knows very well it isn't her job to bring people up to the offices, and yet she did it anyway.'

'So?'

'So that's a perfect example of what we were just discussing. No, Philip, while there are still girls like her about no woman will ever catch me in the matrimonial trap. I don't see that it's necessary when what you really want can be obtained without feeling as if you're in a cage.'

Little mouse indeed! She still felt angered at his condescension. His looks might be fantastic, but his nature wasn't so impressive, at least, not the part she had seen. But even if his words had angered her she shouldn't have played this stupid trick on him. It had been the confident way he had escorted the model out to lunch that had fired her anger anew, and given her the crazy idea of announcing her own engagement to him.

And now she had to face him. She hoped she looked more self-confident than she felt. He was likely to rip her to shreds with his tongue when he had her in his office, and it was no more than she deserved.

Today the outer office wasn't deserted. Catherine Farraday, Jarrod Stone's personal secretary, and her young assistant both busily working as Brooke entered the room.

Catherine gave her a cool look. 'Yes?'

'Mr Stone is expecting me. My name is Brooke Faulkner.'

Catherine gave her a disbelieving look but buzzed through to the inner office anyway. 'A Miss Faulkner to see you, Mr Stone.'

'Send her straight in,' he snapped, letting Brooke know that his temper hadn't cooled at all since his telephone call down to her.

The cool beautiful girl stood up with a slight raising of her delicately shaped eyebrows, as if she were mentally trying to work out the reason for her boss to be seeing a mere receptionist.

'I know the way,' Brooke told her hurriedly, unwilling to let this girl witness her humiliation if Jarrod Stone should be unable to contain his anger and lash out at her with his icy tongue as soon as she entered his office.

'Very well.' Catherine subsided back into her chair, resuming her work with a coolly detached air.

Brooke moved through into the small reception room, hesitant about actually confronting Jarrod Stone. But if she didn't go in there soon he would come out here looking for her, and she had no intention of letting him find her cowering nervously outside his office.

He bade her curtly to enter as she knocked on the door, which she reluctantly did. This time there was no charming smile for her, only a furious look on his face and an angry glitter to his eyes.

He stood up, coming round his desk to walk slowly

around her as she stood in front of his desk. He came back to rest on the front of his desk, his arms folded in front of his powerful chest.

Even in her embarrassment Brooke could appreciate how attractive he looked, the navy blue pin-striped suit he wore fitting him as if it were tailored on him, his linen immaculate.

'So you're Brooke Faulkner,' he said softly.

'Yes.' Did he have to be so taunting? She was perfectly well aware that her navy pinafore dress and light blue fitted blouse in no way matched up to the expensive clothing some of the women he escorted out of the building wore. But did he have to look at her quite like that?

'The girl I'm engaged to,' he continued even more softly.

She moved with a start. 'I—I can explain that.'

He gave a smile, but it owed nothing to humour. 'Can you now?' he mused. 'You can explain how I come to be engaged to be married to a complete stranger, can you?' His light eyes snapped angrily. 'It had better be a damned good explanation!'

Brooke moved uncomfortably. 'I wouldn't say that, but it is an explanation. The only trouble is I don't think you're going to like it.'

He made an impatient movement to sit behind his desk. 'I don't *like* being engaged to a girl I've never met before either!'

Brooke gasped. 'Oh, that isn't true. I work here, I've seen you hundreds of times.'

'Seeing isn't the same as meeting. I've seen hundreds of people many times over, but that doesn't mean I know them.'

'But we have actually met,' she corrected him. 'I brought a model up to your office a couple of weeks ago.'

Jarrod Stone studied her for a moment. 'So you did.'

'And that's why I told the newspapers what I did.'

'Because you brought a model up to my office?' he sounded astounded.

'Don't be ridiculous!' She had had enough of his taunts. She realised he was angry about what she had done, of course he was, but he didn't have to take this attitude with her. 'I did it because I overheard your conversation that day, overheard what you had to say about women.'

'Did you indeed?' His grey eyes narrowed. 'And that prompted you to announce your own engagement to me? After hearing what I had to say about your own fair sex?'

'Yes, it did!' Her blue eyes deepened almost to violet. 'I wanted to make you eat your words, to show you you could be caught in the trap of matrimony as easily as any other man. But I—it didn't work out the way I intended it to. As soon as I saw it in print I knew it was wrong. But at the time I wanted only to hit out at you, to get back at you for what you think of women.'

'Oh, you got back at me all right. This morning, not half an hour ago in fact, I had a telephone call from Philip Baylis congratulating me. I didn't know what the hell he was talking about,' he said forcefully. 'I felt a damned fool. But I managed to bluff my way out of it. Can you imagine what it felt like to be told by a third party that I'm supposed to be getting married? I didn't even know who Brooke Faulkner was, but I did know the name sounded familiar. Then I realised I saw it every morning when I entered the building.'

'You called me a mouse that day I came up here,' she reminded him resentfully.

'And for that you landed us in this mess?'

Brooke flicked back her hair. 'It will be all right. We can just announce in the next issue that it was a mistake.'

He stood up again, his height making her feel very

tiny, and he was so big and masculine with it, so very male. 'You think it's as easy as that, do you? What a ridiculous child you are! Don't you realise that by accepting Philip's congratulations this morning I as much as admitted the engagement was a real one? He's also invited the two of us to a party this evening.'

'You—you didn't accept?' She frowned her nervousness.

'Of course I did. What else could I do?—they all want to get a look at you. And I didn't have time to think of a good excuse not to take you along.'

'You could have—could have told him we wanted to be alone this evening—to celebrate,' she said desperately.

'We don't all have your devious mind.'

'But you—you can't mean this engagement to stand?' Her voice was becoming shrill now.

'Oh, but I do. I'm in business, I can't be seen to become engaged one day and renounce it the next. That wouldn't do much for my reputation as a reliable businessman. Oh no, Brooke, you started this and you can damn well see it through to the bitter end.'

'The bitter end?' she echoed hollowly.

Jarrod Stone shrugged. 'Just a figure of speech.'

Brooke wasn't so sure; there was an inflexibility about him that pointed to him not liking to be thwarted. A pity she hadn't noticed that sooner, like two weeks ago.

'But I don't want to be engaged to you,' she told him crossly.

'A pity you didn't think of that before. I'm sure you realise that I feel exactly the same way.'

'Yes,' she admitted guiltily, knowing that this was all her own fault.

'Mm,' he said thoughtfully. 'Well, now that it seems to be public knowledge you can start acting the part. We'll meet for lunch at twelve-thirty.'

'I couldn't—I couldn't go out to lunch with you.

What would everyone think?' Besides, she was hardly dressed to go out with him.

'They can think what they damn well please,' he muttered grimly.

'I think you've taken this far enough,' Brooke snapped, suddenly angry. 'I admit that what I did was wrong, and I'll leave your employ straight away if that will please you.' Although how she would support herself until she found another job she had no idea! 'But I'm not going to let you make a fool of me——'

'I think you've managed that quite successfully without any help from me,' he interrupted dryly.

'You have no right——'

'I have every right! Think of how much more of a fool you would have looked if I'd denied all knowledge of you. Think of the adverse reaction you would have got from the press if I'd done that. They would have hounded you to death.'

She knew he was right. The trouble with her was that she hadn't thought of the consequences when she had made that stupid move, and now Jarrod Stone was going to make her pay for it. But what else had she expected? He was a well-known personality, he couldn't afford the publicity of a broken engagement. And neither could she!

She could just imagine the unpleasantness it would cause. But she couldn't stay engaged to him either. Just to look at him terrified the life out of her. How she had ever thought herself in love with him she would never know. She must have been mad. Yes, that must be it; at twenty years of age she was definitely past the stage of infatuation.

'Brooke?' he cut into her thoughts.

'Don't call me that!' she snapped her resentment.

'What would you have me call you—dearest, darling, my love?' he taunted.

She looked away. 'Of course not!'

Jarrod Stone shrugged. 'Then I'll call you Brooke.

It is your name—and you are my fiancée,' he added mockingly.

'I am not!'

'Oh yes, you are—until I say otherwise.'

Her blue eyes widened. 'And how long do you think that will be?'

'Oh, four, maybe five months,' he told her carelessly.

'What!' She walked forward to rest her knuckles on the front of the desk. 'Now I know you're joking!'

'I rarely joke about anything this serious.'

'You're—you're telling me I have to be engaged to you for *four months*?'

'At a minimum,' he nodded.

'But won't that cramp your style a bit?'

'A little, but I can take it if you can. I gather there's no boy-friend—no, of course there isn't. He wouldn't exactly welcome the announcement.' He straightened some papers on his desk, giving an impatient look as the telephone rang and he picked it up. 'Yes, Catherine? No—and I don't want any more calls put through to me until Miss Faulkner has left.' He put the receiver down, looking up at her. 'Now, is there anyone I should talk to about our engagement?'

'Why on earth should you——'

'Consent, Brooke. It's usually considered polite to consult parents when contemplating marrying their daughter.'

Brooke paled even more. It all sounded so—so real when he put it like that. 'My parents are dead. I was brought up by a maiden aunt.'

'So do I speak to her?'

'She died last year,' Brooke told him. 'But I hadn't had a lot to do with her—for the past four years anyway, not since she made it perfectly clear to me that she disapproved of my father marrying her sister.'

'And four years ago you were——?'

'Sixteen,' she admitted quietly, remembering all too well the terrible things her aunt had said to her about her father.

'That makes you twenty now. God, I'll be thought a cradle-snatcher!' Jarrod Stone muttered in disgust. 'I'm thirty-seven,' he added by way of explanation.

'And you've never married?' It seemed strange in this day and age to think of a man of his age not marrying.

For the first time since she had entered the room he smiled, and she felt some of the tension start to leave her body. He sat back in the chair. 'I thought about it once, when I was a couple of years older than you are at this moment. She turned me down, thank God.'

'Oh.'

'Right—well, I think you've taken up enough of my time for one morning,' he said, rising. 'I'll see you downstairs at twelve-thirty. And arrange to have a two-hour lunch break.'

'I can't do that,' she protested. 'I have a job to do.'

'And I'm your employer. Get whoever it is that usually covers for you when you're off sick to take over. And I won't expect an over-show of emotion in front of other people, but I will expect you to be a little bit more relaxed with me than you are at this moment.'

'Relaxed? How can I possibly feel relaxed? I've never even spoken to you until today!'

'Too bad,' he said callously. 'Now I'll see you out to the lift.'

Brooke stiffened. 'That won't be necessary.'

He opened the door for her. 'But I insist. I must show a natural consideration for my brand new fiancée,' he taunted.

Her eyes were beseeching. 'Please, Mr Stone, don't——'

'Jarrod,' he corrected curtly. 'Call me Jarrod.'

She couldn't do that! 'Please don't make me go through with this. I've apologised, I don't see what else I can do to make amends.'

'An apology isn't enough,' he said cruelly. 'I've already explained my reasons. I could make things very unpleasant for you if you prove difficult.'

'I could leave.' Brooke hung back defiantly, not willing to leave his office until she had this thing settled. 'You're far from being the only well-paying firm in the country.'

'Oh, I know that. But with no references from here you could find things rather difficult.'

'You—you can't do that! I've been a good employee.'

'You call what you've just done being a good employee?' he demanded. 'Are you aware that you could land up in court for that deliberate lie you chose to tell the newspapers? I could sue you. You're quoted, so it's pretty obvious who gave them the story.'

She went first pale and then red. 'You—you wouldn't?'

'No, I wouldn't. But I do expect a little co-operation from you. This is your fault, after all.'

'All right, all right. I'm sorry, I'm sorry, *I'm sorry*!'

Jarrod Stone looked unmoved. 'Like I said, it isn't enough.' He opened the door further. 'I have an important appointment in five minutes.'

'Okay, I—— But what do I tell everyone?' she cried.

'Oh, tell them I've fallen madly in love with you and rushed you off your feet.'

'Don't tease—*please*!' Her head was downbent.

He wrenched her chin up roughly between thumb and forefinger. 'I don't know what the hell else you expect me to do. I can assure you that if I did what I really want to do to you you wouldn't like that either.'

Brooke was mesmerised by his glittering grey eyes, aware of the darkness of his skin and the tangy aftershave he wore. 'What do you want to do?' she asked breathlessly.

His hand fell away and he turned her firmly out of the room. 'Put you over my knee and give your backside a good thrashing. Just what you hoped to achieve I have no idea. But still, it might prove interesting.'

He silenced her as they entered his secretary's office, pausing at the door to look down at her with dark brooding eyes. Again he raised her chin, uncaring of the two curious pairs of eyes watching them. 'I'll see you later, darling,' he said, huskily soft, but loud enough for the other two girls to hear. 'We'll have lunch at the usual place.'

Before Brooke could answer him his dark head swooped low and his lips fleetingly touched hers. She felt herself tremble in his arms, her eyes wide with surprise. She looked self-consciously at the girls in the room, but they were apparently busily working. She doubted they had been so engrossed a couple of seconds earlier!

Her mouth tightened. 'Did you have to do that?' she muttered angrily, her almost violet eyes glaring her dislike of him.

Jarrod laughed throatily. 'You say the nicest things, Brooke.'

He was obviously still playing to his audience, and she decided to play him at his own game, reaching up to wind her arms about his neck, her lips raised invitingly. 'Just to last me until lunch-time, darling,' she coaxed, revelling in the anger displayed in his deep grey eyes. 'Darling?' she questioned innocently.

His grip on her arms was quite painful and it took great effort not to cry out. 'Later, Brooke. Later.' His words sounded romantic enough, but she knew his words promised something completely different from what they were implying.

She pouted up at him. 'Oh, Jarrod!'

'If you don't behave yourself I'm like to give you that good hiding I promised you,' he warned her quietly.

'Oh, Jarrod, how sweet of you to say so,' she smiled

up at him, uncaring of the dangerous look in his eyes. 'Until later, darling.'

By the time she stepped out of the lift into the reception area the two bright wings of colour in her cheeks seemed to be a permanent fixture. How she was going to get through the next few months she had no idea.

Jean was looking rather harassed by this time, having difficulty managing her switchboard and also dealing with people at the desk. Brooke hadn't realised she would be so long or she wouldn't have left her alone. She had expected to be only a few minutes, just long enough to be sacked.

'What gives?' Jean asked once the rush had died down and they had a couple of minutes to themselves again. 'First of all you receive a telephone call that makes you look like death and then you calmly step into the boss's private lift and disappear for an hour.'

'I'm sorry I was gone so long, Jean. I didn't mean to leave you in the lurch like that.' She shuffled the papers about on her desk, not anxious to answer the real question in Jean's words.

'So what's happened? Is someone you know ill or something?'

'Er—no.' She didn't quite know how to explain what had just happened to her. She certainly couldn't tell Jean the whole truth, it would be too humiliating. 'I—er—I seem to have got myself engaged.'

Jean's eyes brightened with excitement. 'You do? Who to?' She frowned. 'You haven't mentioned seeing anyone special.'

'No—well, it seems to have happened all of a sudden. I've hardly had time to think.' Which was true; she certainly hadn't had time to realise exactly what this bogus engagement was going to mean to her. She did know that she had felt a strange floating sensation at the touch of Jarrod Stone's lips on her own. And also, to her shame, she had responded! Only momentarily, but it had been a definite response. But she blamed that solely on the suddenness of it, nothing else. She didn't even like the man now, let alone imagine herself in love with him.

Jean still looked puzzled. 'But what does it have to do with Jarrod Stone?'

'Everything,' she said with feeling.

'Everything?' Jean's frown cleared, to be replaced with a look of amazement. 'But surely you don't mean——'

'Yes. I'm engaged to Jarrod Stone.'

'Goodness! But you—you can't be! I didn't even realise you were seeing him.' Jean's face showed her disbelief.

'It has been rather sudden. I——'

'Excuse me,' interrupted a husky female voice. 'I'm looking for Mr Stone's office.'

Brooke turned to look at the woman, her nostrils twitching sensitively with the deep heavy perfume she wore. This woman was beautiful, absolutely beautiful. She was very tall, her blonde hair shoulder-length and waving provocatively about her face, her eyes a glowing green, her tiny nose uptilted, her pouting mouth painted an inviting scarlet. To Brooke she looked exquisite and she wondered who she could be. Obviously one of Jarrod Stone's women, of that she felt sure. She looked the type he would go for, about thirtyish and very sophisticated.

'Mr Stone's office is on the tenth floor,' she answered politely. 'If you would like to take the private lift up I'll telephone them of your arrival.'

The woman nodded coolly. 'Thank you, Miss— Brooke Faulkner!' Her green eyes narrowed as they looked at the gold lettering on the nameplate. '*You're* Brooke Faulkner?'

Brooke frowned. 'Yes.'

'Well, well, well.' The woman seemed to have regained her composure. 'Clever old Jarrod,' she murmured to herself.

'I beg your pardon?'

The woman gave her a dazzling smile. 'It isn't important. So nice to have met you, Brooke, you have helped to explain a lot.'

'But I didn't do anything.' She needn't have bothered to speak; the woman had already walked away from the desk to enter the lift. How rude of her! 'Who was that?' she asked Jean.

Her friend's eyes widened. 'You mean you don't know?'

'I didn't get the chance to ask her,' she said ruefully.

'You shouldn't have needed to. That was Selina Howard.'

Brooke gasped, looking after the woman. 'The wife of the multi-millionaire?'

Jean nodded. 'The same.'

'Oh.' What on earth could a woman like her want with Jarrod Stone? There seemed only one explanation, and yet that didn't seem at all likely. Charles Howard was even better known than Jarrod Stone, and one of the richest men in the world. He was also a very good-looking man, although being in his late fifties he was much older than his thirty-year-old wife.

Brooke looked up sharply as the woman came back down again half an hour later. She must have been Jarrod Stone's important appointment, a very beautiful appointment, and it certainly wasn't a business appointment, of that she was sure. Selina Howard gave her a cool smile before leaving the building.

But the time Jarrod Stone came down in the lift at twelve-thirty Brooke had managed to stir herself up into a very nervous state. But perhaps he just intended for them to look as if they were leaving to go to lunch together, perhaps they would part when they got outside. She hoped so.

She grabbed her leather jacket and handbag from the cloakroom before he came over, smiling nervously at the girl who was taking over for her during her lunch break. Jarrod's eyes narrowed as she reached his side, but he said nothing about her flushed cheeks and too-bright eyes, merely taking hold of her elbow to guide her out of the door opened for them by the door-man.

Once outside the building his hand dropped away and he turned left towards the shopping centre, leaving Brooke to run to keep up with him, his long strides taking him along much faster than her own.

'Could you slow down a little?' she asked breath-lessly.

Jarrod turned to look at her as if suddenly becoming aware of her, his pace slackening slightly but still much too fast for her.

'Where are we going?' She looked up at him.

His mouth turned back in a sneer. 'I would have thought it was obvious.'

'But I—I thought we were going to lunch. It's mainly shops in this part of town.'

He sighed. 'One shop in particular.'

'What shop is that?'

'A jewellers. There's a very good one not far from here.'

Again Brooke felt panic rising within her. 'A jewellers? Whatever for?'

'My dear girl, if we're going to be engaged you're going to need a ring. That's where we're going now, to buy you an engagement ring.'

CHAPTER TWO

BROOKE stopped in her tracks, unconcerned when he turned to scowl his impatience. 'I don't want an engagement ring,' she declared.

Jarrod walked back the short distance between them, grasping her arm roughly and pulling her to one side of the pavement. 'Don't shout like that in the street!' he snapped.

She shook off his hand. 'What else did you expect me to do? You were miles away from me.'

'Only because you deliberately hung back, behaving hysterically. What on earth is the matter with you? Surely you realise we can't be engaged without a ring? People will be looking for that, especially this evening.'

'I don't want a ring and I don't want to go out with you this evening. I don't mind keeping up this pretence at work, but I will not put on a show for all your high-class friends to laugh at!'

His well-shaped mouth tightened angrily. 'You say the most ridiculous things, *do* the most ridiculous things. You act far too impetuously, but I put that down to your youth. And my friends will not laugh at you, but they will think it odd if you aren't wearing my ring. This isn't something I care to discuss. I've already telephoned the jewellers and requested him to get together a selection of rings for you to look at.' He looked at his wrist-watch. 'He's expecting us about now.'

'I'm sure he'll wait for the valued customer that you undoubtedly are. I suppose it's the place you buy all the jewellery for your women,' she said bitchily, for the moment not bothered by her outspokenness. She had already far overstepped the line as far as this arrogant

24

man was concerned and nothing she said or did now could make matters any worse for her.

'And if I do? What does that have to do with you?'

The fight went out of her at his coolness. 'Nothing, I suppose.'

'You suppose correct. Now, let's go.'

'Please!' Brooke held on to his arm, liking the feel of the expensive material of his suit beneath her fingers. 'Don't make me do this.'

Jarrod's dark head was held at a haughty angle, his grey eyes unyielding. There was no doubt that he was a hard man when crossed. He must terrify his business opponents into retreat; he certainly terrified her. 'Must I keep reminding you that you started this?' he drawled.

'But do you have to take advantage of it?' Her eyes pleaded with him.

'Yes. Now that's the last time we discuss this. From now on you'll just do as you're told. And there will be no repeat of your behaviour this morning,' he added warningly.

They were walking along side by side now, Jarrod at last seeming to realise she had shorter legs than he did. She looked up at him innocently. 'Did I do something wrong?' she asked, knowing very well to what he referred.

'The way you drooled over me was completely unnecessary. I told you I wanted no over show of emotion.'

'Ooh, I didn't *drool*!' she exclaimed.

'You gave a very good impression of it.' His eyes remained fixed ahead.

'You kissed me first,' she accused.

'I admit that, but it was nothing like the provocative act you were putting on.' He stopped outside an expensive-looking jewellers. 'I don't want anything like that in here, just a little natural affection for a new fiancée.'

'I hate you, Jarrod Stone!' she said furiously.

He looked down at her with enigmatic eyes, making her aware of just how attractive he was—so tall and commanding, really majestically male, and very, very, handsome. She felt the old familiar flutterings in her stomach. It seemed she wasn't over her infatuation after all!

'Let's just keep it that way, shall we?' he said softly. 'I must admit to feeling slightly curious about your motivation for announcing our engagement this morning. At first I imagined it to be a not very subtle form of blackmail, then after reading your file, your age and so forth, I wondered if it might not be infatuation.'

'Not for this girl,' Brooke answered quickly. It *had* been infatuation, but that infatuation had quickly turned to dislike. His contemptuous words had turned her supposed love into a desire for revenge on his mercenary attitude towards women. He was the sort of man women fell for in their hundreds, and he walked away from them all untouched. Well, she had just made sure he hadn't got away so easily this time!

'Why so vehement?' he asked. 'It wouldn't be the first time a young girl has imagined herself in love with an older man. Some of these girls have been known to take the initiative when they don't think they're achieving their aim fast enough.'

'Like I said, not this girl,' she assured him.

'No, your move was made from pure revenge, wasn't it, little mouse?'

Brooke knew he was deliberately baiting her and she obstinately refused to let him ruffle her. 'Can we get this over with? I have to be back in forty minutes.'

His eyes snapped with anger. 'I thought I told you to get an extended lunch break.'

Brooke pretended an interest in the jewellery window. 'You did,' she confirmed disinterestedly.

'Then why the hell didn't you?'

She flung back her head, her hair gleaming auburn-brown in the sunlight. 'I didn't because I'm not the owner of the firm. I can't just take two-hour lunch-breaks when I feel in the mood.'

'You're engaged to the owner, that amounts to the same thing.'

'I would have thought that was all the more reason for me not to take advantage of the situation. By the way, there's a little man bobbing about inside the jewellers. I think he's looking at us.'

'No doubt. Well, if you only have forty minutes left I suppose we'd better get inside.'

The jeweller had obviously seen Jarrod Stone numerous times before and Brooke wondered if she had been right in her assumption about this place. That he was a valued customer there could be no doubt, it was there in the exaggerated respect he was receiving.

'So nice to see you again,' the jeweller gushed. 'And to meet your fiancée.' He smiled at Brooke. 'I'm so glad you chose our establishment to buy your ring, Miss Faulkner.'

Jarrod gave what Brooke considered to be his first natural smile of the day, at least, in her company. 'You know you're the best in town, Green.'

'So kind of you to say so, sir. And may I say I agree with your decision not to include sapphires in your choice. Miss Faulkner's eyes *are* more violet than blue.'

'Could we see the rings?' Jarrod requested tersely. 'We don't have a lot of time.' This last comment was obviously meant for Brooke.

She waited until the jeweller had left them alone before making a comment. 'I didn't realise you'd even noticed the colour of my eyes.'

'I didn't,' he replied curtly. 'It was in your file.'

'Didn't your secretary think it odd for you to want to read my file?'

'I don't pay her to think about my personal life.'

Brooke frowned. 'I'm sure it didn't say anywhere in my file that my eyes were violet.'

'Maybe not. But they are, so let's not argue about it.' He straightened as the tray of rings were presented for their inspection.

They were beautiful rings—diamond clusters, solitaires, emeralds and rubies surrounded by sparkling diamonds. And all of them looking as if they would cost a fortune! She felt sure they all would. This was one of those exclusive expensive jewellers that only the very rich frequented. And Jarrod Stone was very rich.

Her eyes glowed as she picked up first one ring and then another, almost afraid to touch them but tempted by their beauty. As she had very long slender hands some of the smaller stones just didn't look right on her finger, but she chose these rings to try on because she knew they would be the least expensive. Finally she looked up at Jarrod for help. 'Which one do you like?' she asked helplessly.

Without hesitation he chose a large diamond set on a thin gold band, sliding it on to her finger before she had time to protest. 'That's the one,' he nodded his approval.

She could tell by the satisfied smile on the jeweller's face that Jarrod had chosen the most expensive ring on the tray. She tried to pull it off her finger, but Jarrod's strong brown hand came out to stop her movements.

'You may as well leave it on,' he told her. 'It fits perfectly.'

'Oh, but I——'

Mr Green had already picked up the tray containing the other rings and was in the process of locking them away again.

'No arguments in here, please, Brooke,' Jarrod warned her out of earshot of the other man.

'But this ring is much too expensive,' she protested.

'Leave that to me. That's the ring I want you to wear.'

'But I'll be frightened of losing it.' She looked down

at it wide-eyed.

'It will be insured,' he said uncaringly.

'Yes, but——'

'Leave it, Brooke,' he ordered as Mr Green came back.

Brooke felt a natural curiosity to know just how much this rock on her finger was going to cost, but she knew it wasn't expected of her to stay and listen to the money side of the sale, so she wandered over to look in some of the other cabinets, looking at the glittering necklaces inside.

Once outside Jarrod handed her a large square box, ignoring her questioning look. 'Open it,' he ordered.

She did so with trembling fingers, crying out her surprise as she saw the contents. Nestling in blue velvet was a large teardrop diamond set on the most delicately fine gold chain she had ever seen, and lying within its circle were a pair of matching earrings. They were really lovely.

She thrust them back at him. 'I don't want these.' She remembered too well what he had said about giving his women jewellery. 'The ring I'll wear until I can be free of you, but I don't have to accept anything else from you.'

'They're for you to wear tonight.' He ignored the proffered box. 'I want you to look the part.'

'And a little receptionist like myself isn't likely to have this sort of jewellery hidden away,' she sneered.

'Exactly,' he agreed cruelly.

'You're an arrogant swine, Jarrod Stone. But I'll wear your diamonds for you—as long as I can return them to you as soon as we've left the party.'

'Don't be so childish!'

'Then I won't wear them. You can't force me to,' she declared obstinately.

'What an obstructive little girl you are! All right, I'll keep them locked up for you. Now let's go on to a shop where we can buy you a dress.'

Brooke stiffened. 'I have my own clothes, thank you.'

'I'm sure you have, but I want you to have something new.'

'I have my own clothes,' she repeated through gritted teeth. As it happened she had exactly the right dress to wear to go out with this sophisticated man, a gown that had been bought for a special occasion that had never taken place. It was an expensive one, bought to impress a boy-friend that she had finished with before the promised evening out. At the time he simply hadn't measured up to her rather romantic impression of Jarrod Stone. How ironic that she should now wear the dress to go out with Jarrod Stone himself!

'Do you have to argue about everything?' he snapped.

'If it means I hold on to my identity against you— yes!' she answered defiantly.

'God, you're impossible!' He hailed a passing taxi, bundling her inside before sitting beside her. 'Before you start a full-scale argument in the street,' he explained.

'You're too dominant, that's your trouble!' she snapped.

He began to smile, and finally the smile turned into a genuine laugh. It changed his whole face, not making him appear quite so grim and also making him look younger. Brooke felt her senses stir at the real humour in his deep grey eyes.

'*I'm* dominant?' he chuckled. 'You seem to be the one organising my life for me at the moment.' He got out and opened the door for her as they reached the building he owned. 'I'll pick you up at eight-thirty this evening.'

'But you don't know where I——Oh yes, my file.'

'Mm, it has your address in it. Not much else, but it does have that. I'll see you later.' He got back into the taxi.

Too late Brooke realised she still had the necklace

and earrings in her hand. She would have to keep them with her now, something she hadn't wanted to do. Her handbag seemed the best place to stow them away, and putting the case at the bottom of what she jokingly called her 'shoulder suitcase' she went back to her desk.

She was so conscious of the huge diamond on her finger that for the first half an hour after her return she kept her left hand hidden. Jean soon noticed it, though, exclaiming enthusiastically over its beauty.

'You still haven't told me how you come to be in love and engaged to him. Why, only this morning I was insulting him to you, doubting his ability to be passionate if he tried. Now you must know first hand that I was wrong.'

Brooke didn't know first hand at all, but Jarrod's lower full sensuous lip didn't point to him being the cold impassionate machine Jean had implied this morning. And he hadn't kissed like an amateur, that brief caress evoking a response within her in spite of herself.

'You were wrong,' she confirmed, sure that this was so.

Jean smiled dreamily. 'It's all like a fairytale, isn't it? Engaged to be married to the unattainable Jarrod Stone. Lucky old you!'

Yes, lucky old her. She wasn't thinking that way later that evening as she nervously got herself ready to go to Philip Baylis's party. If Selina Howard was an example of Jarrod Stone's friends then there would be some really sophisticated people at this party tonight.

Her dress was a russet coloured silk, bringing out the red lights in her dark brown hair. It clung in soft folds over her breasts and hips, the high roll-neck adding fragility to her swan-like neck, the long sleeves finishing in a point at the wrist. It was a dress that emphasised her slenderness and suited her like no other she had ever possessed.

She had washed her hair and brushed it dry until it

gleamed reddish-brown, crackling with health and cleanliness. She had applied a light eye make-up, brushing a soft peach lip gloss over her lips. The earrings and necklace glittered in glowing beauty against the dark material of her gown and she knew she was looking her best.

Jarrod Stone's dark grey eyes gleamed his approval of her as she let him in to her tiny flat. He was looking particularly attractive tonight, wearing black trousers, a white silk shirt, and a grey velvet jacket that matched the steely grey of his eyes. He carried a large white box under one arm, and Brooke had to admit to feeling curious about its contents.

He stood back to survey her. 'Very nice,' he said finally, placing that intriguing box on the table.

Brooke blushed prettily. 'Thank you. Tonight, you —you won't leave me on my own too much? I—I don't know any of the people who are likely to be at this party.'

'You'll know Philip.'

She gave a throaty chuckle. 'I don't *know* Philip Baylis, I've only seen him a couple of times when he's come to see you. I know about him, as I know about you, but I don't actually know him.'

'You soon will,' he said dryly. 'I have no doubt that Philip will waste little time introducing himself to you. But don't ever forget that you're supposed to be engaged to me,' he added warningly.

'I can hardly forget it with this huge rock weighing my finger down,' she retorted hotly, resenting his implication that she was stupid enough to flirt with his friends. 'You didn't even bother to ask me if I wanted this ring. I may not have liked it,' she said petulantly.

Jarrod shrugged. 'It isn't important.'

'Only that it looks expensive enough to be worn by the fiancée of the great Jarrod Stone,' she scorned. 'You're enjoying this, Mr Stone. Enjoying the fact that I stupidly got myself engaged to you.'

'I'm not enjoying it at all, Brooke,' he contradicted grimly. 'But I have little choice about it. So I mean to make the best of it, and you would do well to do the same. After all, isn't that partly the reason you did it? You denied infatuation, so it must have been partly blackmail.'

'It was pure revenge,' she denied hotly.

'If you like to think so. Nevertheless, the jewellery you now have in your possession will bring you a sizeable sum when you decide to sell it. That should make it all the easier for you to bear being engaged to a man you say you hate. For some reason women seem to find jewellery a great comfort.'

'This jewellery isn't mine to sell,' Brooke told him fiercely. 'The earrings and necklace I'll return at the end of the evening, the ring when you decide you've punished me enough for my impetuosity. Whether you believe me or not, blackmail didn't enter into my thoughts at all. I once believed myself——'

'Yes?' he prompted at her hesitation.

She shook her head. Why should she give him the satisfaction of knowing she had once thought herself in love with him? He would probably laugh in her face at such an admission. 'It isn't important. Shouldn't we be leaving now? It's getting late.'

'I suppose so.' Jarrod picked up the box he had carried in, handing it to her. 'I realise this should be mink or ermine, but I don't happen to believe in killing animals to provide a woman with something beautiful to wear.'

She gave him a puzzled look, ripping off the lid to the box to stare at its contents. Lying amongst the tissue paper was a snowy white velvet cape. She picked it up, smoothing its softness lovingly. 'It's beautiful!' she said breathlessly.

'Good.' He took it out of her hand and draped it casually about her shoulders. 'We'd better be going now.'

His car was fast and sleek, moving with a speed that was completely effortless. It was a dark green Ferrari, and he drove it with a skill that was purely habitual. It seemed incredible to Brooke that she was actually sitting here at his side on her way out with him for the evening.

Philip Baylis's house was about ten miles out of the centre of London, a house set back off the road and reached by the long gravel driveway leading right up to the oak front door. Cars adorned the driveway and the whole house was bathed in light. Soft music sounded from inside, and Brooke followed Jarrod Stone up to the front door with some trepidation.

They were admitted by a manservant, and Brooke left her cape in his capable hands. Jarrod turned to look at her. 'I suppose you want to powder your nose or whatever it is that women do when they disappear for hours on end?'

'Yes, please.' Her hair could definitely do with a tidy up.

'It's through there,' he pointed to a door on the left. 'I'll be inside having a drink.'

'Oh, but——'

'Don't be such a baby,' he said impatiently. 'I won't be far away.'

She set her mouth determinedly and entered the powder-room. There were several other women in here and she moved through them awkwardly to the large mirror along one wall, brushing her hair self-consciously.

'I notice Jarrod hasn't arrived yet,' remarked a tall blonde girl to another girl standing a few feet away.

'He'll be here. Philip said he invited him,' the other girl replied.

'I can hardly wait!' The blonde applied her lipstick.

Brooke had remained rooted to the spot at the first mention of Jarrod's name, curious to find out what was going to be said next. Both these girls were beautiful, perhaps they had been some of the girls Jarrod was reputed to have escorted in the last few years.

'Have you seen his girl?' the second girl asked.

'Never. No one seems to have heard of her until today. He really kept quiet about this one.'

'Selina won't be very happy about it,' the other girl laughed bitchily. 'She really thought she had him where she wanted him.'

The blonde arched one thinly plucked eyebrow. 'I'm sure she's had him *there*, several times.'

'You think it actually went that far?'

'Charles is such a simpleton where Selina is concerned. He has no control over her at all. And she wanted Jarrod, we all know that.'

'But I wouldn't have thought Jarrod——'

'He's a man, Sonia, and Selina *is* very beautiful.' The blonde frowned. 'This engagement of Jarrod's is all a bit sudden, a bit too convenient if you ask me.'

The girl called Sonia looked puzzled. 'What do you mean?'

'Well, it could all be a ruse, couldn't it? Jarrod could have persuaded some poor creature into believing herself in love with him and that he feels the same way about her. Charles would never suspect anything between Selina and Jarrod with him a newly engaged man.'

'I suppose so. There was quite a lot of gossip going about. I'm sure Charles must have heard some of it.'

'You see what I mean? I bet this girl of Jarrod's is a real little mouse.'

The use of that name for her was enough to snap Brooke out of her stunned silence, but before she could actually say anything someone else came into the room and the other two girls wandered back outside to the party, still gossiping.

So that was Jarrod's little game! Furious colour flooded her cheeks. Jarrod Stone was using her to cover up his own affair with a married woman. How dared he! Of all the despicable things to do! All the time he had been making out he was the wronged person in all this, when really it suited him to be an engaged man right now.

No wonder Selina Howard had rushed over to see him this morning! But she had soon been reassured when she had seen Brooke, knowing she had absolutely no competition in her. And Jarrod must have reassured her even more when she was up in his office with him.

How dared he! How dared he use her in this way! He was disgusting, covering up his own behaviour by taking advantage of this situation. He was having an affair with Selina Howard and using her to shield it from the woman's husband.

But what could she do about it? There was no way she could get herself out of this engagement, not without causing embarrassment to both of them. Besides, Jarrod had made it perfectly clear he had no intention of releasing her. His obstinacy now became transparently clear.

But she wouldn't let him think he had got away with fooling her. Oh no, she would make sure she let him know his sordid little affair was known to her. And she wouldn't feel guilty any more. Why should she?

It didn't take her long to find Jarrod among the crowd, his height and distinguished appearance making him conspicuous. She moved swiftly through the people to be at his side.

Jarrod turned to look down at her flushed face and gleaming eyes, raising one eyebrow questioningly. 'I thought you'd got lost.'

She took the glass of bubbly liquid he held out to her, flicking back her head haughtily and ignoring the curious stares of the other people. 'You don't seem to be particularly bothered even if I had,' she replied coolly, sipping the chilled champagne.

He frowned. 'What's the matter with you?'

Brooke looked up at him challengingly. 'Why should there be anything wrong with me? I've merely been tidying my hair.'

'For fifteen minutes?'

She shrugged. 'I have a lot of hair.'

'Now look, Brooke——'

His angry words were cut off by the appearance of their host at his side. 'She's turned up, then, Jarrod,' Philip Baylis grinned good naturedly, putting his hand out to Brooke politely. 'I'm very pleased to meet you.'

She smiled shyly, meeting his gesture. 'Thank you.'

He looked at the grim face of his friend. 'She's lovely, Jarrod. You'll have to keep your eye on her amongst this pack of wolves.' He smiled at Brooke again. 'You should be safe with Jarrod by your side.'

'That's providing he remains there.' She gave her 'fiancée' a sly look.

Jarrod's fingers dug painfully into her soft flesh as he put his arm about her shoulders. 'Where else would I go?' he teased, but his eyes told a different story, warning her to behave.

'I have no idea,' she returned softly.

'This isn't a line,' laughed Philip, seemingly unaware of the tension between them. 'But haven't I seen you somewhere before?'

'Possibly. I work for Jarrod.' That grip on her shoulders tightened even more and she winced with the pain of it.

Philip looked astounded. 'You do?'

'Mm,' she nodded, taking no notice of the looks she was receiving from Jarrod. 'I'm the receptionist.'

'So you are!' His amazement was obvious. 'You sly devil, Jarrod!' he slapped the other man on the shoulder. 'Keeping her hidden away like that!'

'Jarrod likes to keep secrets,' Brooke put in softly.

He gave her a sharp look. 'Not from you, darling,' he drawled.

She gave him a cold angry look. 'Even from me.'

Philip laughed. 'I'm sure not. He's a reformed person, engaged to be married and all that. It was the shock of my life this morning when I saw your engagement in the newspaper.'

'No more of a shock than it was to Jarrod,' she smiled tightly.

'Mm, he seemed rather bowled over when I spoke to him this morning.'

'No doubt he was,' she agreed.

'Only because it wasn't supposed to be announced just yet,' Jarrod put in calmly. 'But you know how the press get hold of these things.'

Philip grimaced. 'Oh, I know the press all right.' His attention was caught and held by a woman on the other side of the room and he excused himself before going over to her.

Brooke sipped her champagne, pointedly ignoring the man at her side as she looked about her disinterestedly.

'What the hell is the matter with you?' Jarrod demanded tautly.

She gave him a chilling look. 'I'm perfectly all right, thank you.'

'I wasn't asking you if you were all right, I asked you what was the matter with you! You're—you're different, more——'

'More self-confident, you mean. But then why shouldn't I be? You're not such a great person after all, are you? I think you're disgusting!' she spat the words at him, glaring her dislike. 'And I actually felt guilty about playing this trick on you. You deserve all that you get—and more!'

Jarrod's mouth tightened and he retained his temper with effort. 'What the hell are you talking about?'

'You know very well what I'm talking about, so don't try to act the innocent with me. I never would have believed you could stoop so low. To——'

'Jarrod!'

Brooke didn't need to turn to know who that voice belonged to. Selina Howard! And she was smiling in an intimate way at Jarrod, her arm through his. But of course, they didn't need to worry about gossip now, not now that Jarrod was engaged to her! Oh, it was so humiliating to be used in this way.

She watched the two of them, watched the way Selina Howard made Jarrod bend his head so that she could whisper in his ear, the way he laughed throatily at whatever it was she had said to him.

It was several minutes before either of them seemed to become aware of her still standing there. Finally it was Selina Howard who turned to include her in the conversation.

'We meet again, Brooke,' she said softly, her green eyes assessing as they took in Brooke's figure-hugging dress. 'I'm sure you didn't expect it to be so soon.'

'I didn't expect it at all, Mrs Howard,' Brooke replied shortly.

The small beautiful woman gave a tinkling laugh, but the humour didn't reach her hard pebble-green eyes. 'Please call me Selina,' she invited graciously. 'Being Jarrod's fiancée you're sure to see a lot of me in future.'

Brooke raised one eyebrow. 'Really?'

'Oh yes. Jarrod and I are great friends,' Selina Howard informed her triumphantly.

'And your husband.' She smiled sweetly at them. 'We mustn't forget your husband. Where is he, by the way?'

'Charles is in Europe at the moment.'

'How convenient for you!'

'I beg your pardon?' Those green eyes narrowed dangerously.

'I said how miserable for you,' Brooke replied.

'Yes, isn't it?' Selina glowed up at Jarrod. 'But friends always help to ease the loneliness. Jarrod has been so good to me during Charles' absence.'

'I'm sure he has. But he could be rather preoccupied in future, arranging the wedding, things like that.' Brooke smiled glowingly at Jarrod, uncaring of the scowl on his face. 'There's always such a lot to organise. You must realise that, being married yourself.'

A faint flush coloured the other woman's pale cheeks. 'When is the wedding to be?'

'We——'

'Oh, quite soon,' Brooke interrupted Jarrod. 'We have no reason to wait. Jarrod's very anxious that the wedding should take place soon, aren't you, darling?'

He looked thunderous, and she knew that once they were alone he would let her feel the full force of his anger. But she didn't care about that now. He wasn't going to get away with making a fool out of her!

Selina Howard looked less sure of herself now, look-ing uncertainly from Jarrod to Brooke. 'I didn't realise you'd already set a date. You've only just become engaged.'

Brooke looked deliberately shy. 'The engagement is only a formality as far as Jarrod and I are concerned. The marriage will take place next month.'

Jarrod looked visibly startled, his expression be-coming grimmer as she calmly met his furious gaze. 'I thought we'd agreed not to disclose that,' he said tautly.

She smiled at him. 'As Mrs Howard is such a friend of yours it can't possibly matter if we tell her. Besides, we'll be sending out the invitations quite soon, and we wouldn't want Mrs Howard to be too shocked when she receives hers, now would we?'

Selina Howard's head flicked back haughtily. 'I'll call you tomorrow, Jarrod. Goodbye, Brooke.'

'Oh, surely not goodbye,' she returned sweetly. 'As you said, we'll be seeing a lot of each other.'

Another cool look was directed at her before Selina Howard swept away from them, leaving behind a cloud of perfume. That perfume seemed to belong exclusively to her, and Brooke wouldn't be at all surprised if that wasn't the case. Charles Howard was rich enough to buy a hundred perfumes exclusively for the use of his wife if he wanted to.

Brooke looked innocently up at Jarrod, sipping her champagne with cool deliberation. 'She's very beautiful.'

Jarrod grasped her arm, his fingers pressing painfully into her flesh. 'Selina Howard's looks don't seem important right at this moment,' he muttered between gritted teeth.

'Really? They seemed very important to you this morning.'

He frowned darkly. 'This morning?'

'Your important appointment.'

'Oh—oh, yes. Forget that for a moment,' he dismissed. 'Why did you tell her we were getting married next month? What game are you playing now.'

'No game, Mr Stone. I just don't like being used.'

He shook his head dazedly. '*You're* being used? I thought that was my fate.'

'So did I. I even felt sorry for you—but not any more. You disgust me.'

'That's the second time you've said that,' he said curiously. 'You were like this when you came back from the powder-room. What happened in there?'

'How clever of you to guess,' she smiled at him brightly. 'Just a couple of your so-called friends having a cosy little chat about you. Quite enlightening really.'

'Let's leave,' Jarrod said abruptly. 'We can talk about this better alone. Wait here while I make our excuses.'

'I would prefer to wait outside.'

'I said wait here.'

'I'll be outside,' she declared stubbornly, moving away before he could stop her. She could imagine what construction his friends would put on their early departure. Let them think what they liked! She didn't care as long as she knew in her own mind that it wasn't true.

At least she had got him back for using her, stirring

things up a little between him and his mistress. Not that she thought he would have much difficulty explaining his way out of that, but no doubt Selina Howard would give him a difficult time for a while. Good, she thought spitefully.

'Why are you always so damned stubborn?' Jarrod demanded on the way home.

'I'm not stubborn. I just don't like to be bullied.'

'What did these so-called friends of mine have to say? I take it that's the reason for your attitude?'

'Oh, they just told me of your sordid little affair with Mrs Howard. Well, I wouldn't exactly say they *told* me. They were discussing it between them, I just happened to be there at the time.' She made a determined effort not to look at him.

'My *affair* with Selina?' he repeated softly.

'Yes.'

'And that's why you told her we were getting married next month?'

'Yes. She looked quite worried when I told her that,' she said with satisfaction.

'So did I,' he admitted grimly. 'I've never met anyone as impetuous as you are. I'm only surprised you haven't got yourself into more trouble than you have. Do you realise that by the end of this evening the fact that our wedding is to be next month will be all over London?'

Now she did look at him, her mouth dropping open. 'Surely Mrs Howard wouldn't——'

'No, she wouldn't. But you said it loud enough for several other people to hear. Believe me, by tomorrow everyone will be expecting their invitation to our wedding!'

CHAPTER THREE

BROOKE'S hand flew up to her pale cheek. 'Oh no!'

'Oh yes,' he nodded curtly.

'Surely they wouldn't——'

'I tell you they will.'

'Oh God!' Now what had she done! Things seemed to go from bad to worse as far as she and Jarrod Stone were concerned. And it was all her own doing!

Jarrod sighed. 'I thought an engagement was bad enough, but this is something else completely. Marriages aren't so easy to get out of.'

'I'm not marrying you!'

'You may damn well have to,' he told her shortly.

Brooke wrenched the ring from her finger and threw it on to the dashboard of the car. 'I won't do anything I don't want to! You were using me to cover up your affair with Selina Howard, but I won't be a party to that any more. No doubt she'll soon get over her anger with you at my saying we were getting married and you can carry on as you have been doing.'

'So you've already decided that what you heard was the truth?'

'Oh yes. She was your important appointment, remember? I suppose you told her then about our phoney engagement. It really gave her a shock when I said we were getting married. So you can keep your ring and explain to your mistress that it was all a mistake, that I was just being bitchy.'

Jarrod sat forward and picked up the ring, watching as it glittered and shone. He thrust it at her. 'Put it back on. The engagement still stands. Nothing has changed since this morning.'

'It has as far as I'm concerned,' she said shrilly. 'I've

43

found out about your mistress and I won't help you to fool Charles Howard!'

'You will do as you're told. My threat about your future employment still stands. Put the ring on,' he ordered.

'I don't want to. You still haven't asked me if I like it,' she added resentfully, pushing it back on her finger when he seemed adamant that she should.

'Do you?'

'Well, yes, but I—— That isn't the point! You didn't bother to ask me earlier.'

'I've asked you now. Be satisfied with that.'

'Mr Stone, I——'

'For God's sake call me Jarrod!'

'Do you have to be so angry all the time?' Brooke quavered. 'It isn't easy to suddenly be thrust into this intimacy with you when for the last six months I've thought of you as nothing but my boss. It doesn't seem right for me to be calling you Jarrod.'

'Do you know, Brooke, until this morning I believed myself to be quite a patient man. Since meeting you all that's changed. Everything about you angers me, your stubbornness, your impetuosity, just about everything. But until a few minutes ago I thought I was handling this situation with moderate calm.' He ignored her snort of disbelief. 'That was until your tongue ran away with you just once too often, as it did just now. I hope you have more forbearance over the weekend.'

Brooke's eyes widened. 'Over the weekend?'

'Mm, something else I'm sure you hadn't thought of.' He gave a wry smile. 'My mother and father have invited us down to their country place for the weekend.'

Her heart sank. 'I didn't know you had any family.'

'Oh yes, besides my mother and father I have a brother of twenty-two and a sister of eighteen. I need hardly say that they're all anxious to meet you.'

His taunting voice angered her. 'Did you have to tell them? Surely we didn't have to involve your family in all this?'

Jarrod stopped the car outside the building that contained her flat, turning to face her in the confines of the car. 'I didn't tell them—you did.'

'I didn't——'

'They found out the same way I did, Brooke. The only difference being that they were pleased about it.'

She suddenly felt breathless by his closeness. He might be arrogant and cynical, but he was still the handsomest man she had ever seen. Tonight at the party he had easily stood out as the most attractive man there, a certain aloofness about him making him a challenge to any woman.

Brooke felt her old stirrings of attraction towards him, the longings she had had to be in his arms and be loved by him. But he had never even noticed her until this morning when he could do little else, and she hadn't been brought to his attention in a way that would endear her to him.

But then he was never likely to be attracted to her anyway, not with someone as beautiful as Selina Howard in his life. No, she knew her own limitations; she might be moderately attractive, but she could never be called beautiful. She would have to leave Jarrod Stone to women like the lovely Selina Howard, women who understood the sophisticated games he engaged in.

But that didn't stop her feeling attracted to him now, didn't stop her being completely aware of him. She should have remained adamant when she had handed him back his ring and not been browbeaten into putting it back on. But she wouldn't marry him, no matter how she had committed herself in the hearing of all those people. She wouldn't be strong enough to hold out against him, and she had no intention of being his wife while he had the other woman as his mistress.

She looked away from the warmth in his grey eyes. 'Your family want you to get married?'

'My brother and sister consider me quite ancient not to have settled down, as they put it, with a family of my own. I'm sure you think the same way, you're about their age,' he said almost thoughtfully..

'You could hardly marry when the woman in your life is already married,' she put in bitchily, still reeling under his potent attraction—and resenting every moment of it.

'That's true,' he agreed mildly. 'I think my family are going to like you. You have my mother's way of thinking, black is black and white is white and grey is just a lighter shade of black.'

'I wouldn't consider you grey, Mr Stone. You're definitely black.'

'As the devil, hmm?' he mocked.

'Himself,' she nodded agreement.

'My mother is going to love you,' he smiled. 'She considers my behaviour reprehensible.'

'I think I'm going to like your mother too.'

Jarrod watched her closely, that smile still on his lips. 'You're not at all as I imagined you to be.'

'As you—as you *imagined* me to be?' She sounded her surprise. 'I didn't think you even knew I existed.' This conversation was proving interesting.

'Oh yes.' He settled back more comfortably in his seat, stretching his long legs out before him. 'Can you see me missing a beautiful woman?' he taunted. 'You always looked a cool little thing, sitting there behind that huge desk, always neat, always tidy.'

'I'm not little,' she said crossly. 'You keep calling me that.'

'You seem little to me, you must be at least a foot shorter than me.'

'I should think so, you're at least six foot two.'

'Six four actually.'

'Well then. At five foot two I consider myself medium height for a woman.'

'You see what I mean, your appearance is deceptive.

You're a fiery little thing, quite surprising really.'

'I have a temper like anyone else, but I'm not fiery,' Brooke denied.

'Oh yes, you are. I never would have thought it with those pansy blue eyes of yours.' He sat up suddenly, his look cool again. 'Isn't it time you disappeared like Cinderella?'

Brooke stiffened. 'I don't consider myself to be in the least like Cinderella. But I mustn't keep you from your—your friends. It's only eleven-thirty, I'm sure you have no intention of going to bed yet—at least, not your own.'

'You see, another surprise.' He didn't appear to be angered by her words, more amused. 'I wouldn't have thought the sweet little thing I considered you to be capable of such terrible thoughts. Charles Howard may be away from home, but I have no intention of sharing his wife's bed in his absence.'

Brooke turned to open the car door. 'Then maybe it will be your own bed you occupy, but not alone.'

'I never sleep alone,' he told her softly. 'I have a rather large cat called Rupert who insists on sleeping at the foot of my bed.' He laughed openly at her indignation. 'You shouldn't jump to conclusions, little girl.'

'Will you stop calling me that!'

Jarrod shook his head slowly. 'I think perhaps I should keep reminding myself that's what you are. You can be quite attractive when you're angry. But I don't play with little girls,' he added hardly.

She thrust the door open far enough for her to get out. 'Goodnight, Mr Stone!'

'Brooke!' He stopped her just as she was about to slam the door shut behind her.

'Yes?' she asked tautly, deliberately averting her head.

'I'll pick you up at two-thirty tomorrow, that way we'll arrive in time for tea,' he informed her.

'How nice,' she retorted sarcastically. 'Are you sure that when it comes to dinner I'll know which knives and forks to use?'

With a slam of his own car door he came quickly round to her side, wrenching her startled face round to meet his look. 'You can dislike me all you want, Brooke, but leave my family out of this vendetta you have against me. I won't have you being sarcastic about any member of my family. Don't you think it's time you snapped out of this persecution complex of yours, stop thinking everyone is putting you down all the time?'

'Why, you——' Her hand flew up, but it never made contact with his arrogant face, his fingers passing round her wrist and squeezing so tightly she felt sure he had cut off her circulation. 'You bast——'

'Don't say it, Brooke,' he threatened. 'That's the foulest word in the English language.'

Her eyes were purple with feeling. 'Then it suits you perfectly!'

'You little hellcat!' he said fiercely. 'If you have to hate me I might as well give you a damn good reason for it!'

He pulled her roughly against him, bending his head to loom over her for several long seconds. Brooke watched him as if in a dream, watching as he slowly lowered his head, his lips claiming hers in a kiss that was totally savage. He forced her lips apart, his arms like steel bands as she struggled to be free.

He persisted in that kiss until all the fight went out of her, her whole body feeling bruised. Against her will she found herself responding, her mouth moving beneath his as the kiss became gentler, Jarrod's mouth caressing now rather than demanding.

Her arms moved up about his neck, his hands moving searchingly across her back. This was incredible! Jarrod Stone was kissing her, and she liked it, loved it even. His mouth and body had taken possession of her in a way that was totally masterful.

He put her away from him as quickly as he had pulled her into his arms. 'Get inside!' he ordered harshly. 'I'll see you tomorrow.'

Brooke made her way slowly up to her flat, still dazed from his unexpected kiss. That he was a master of the art she had no doubt, and her burning anger soon turned to something completely different. Instead of making her hate him he had just confirmed that she was in love with him!

Brooke had been very nervous about meeting Jarrod again, but she needn't have bothered; he was acting as if nothing had happened between them. If anything he was acting cooler than ever towards her, not having spoken more than a few sentences to her since she had got in the car.

He was looking vitally attractive in cream trousers and a black fitted shirt, turned back at the cuffs to expose a tanned length of arm, the hair here lighter than the raven sheen of his head. His clothing was more casual than anything else she had ever seen him wear, and it made her all the more aware of him.

Not that she needed to be made any more aware of him; her senses were already heightened to the ripcord muscle beneath his shirt, the strong column of his throat and that strong handsome face that made her heart flutter just to look at him.

But his eyes could be so chillingly cutting, so disdainful, and she hadn't forgotten what his own temper could lead them to. Not that she had minded that part of his anger.

'What are you thinking about?' he asked abruptly.

'I was just thinking about your family,' she lied. 'Do your brother and sister work?'

He gave her a hard look as if doubting this had been her thoughts at all. 'My sister is at college—art,' he added in disgust. 'Dave's at medical school.'

'What's your sister's name?' Anything was better than their former silence.

'Angie,' he supplied shortly.

'And is Angie good at art?' she continued, trying to draw him out.

He gave a slight smile. 'She says she is.'

'And is she?'

'Not bad, I suppose. Don't worry, you'll have plenty of opportunity to judge for yourself. I have no doubt she'll show you round her studio. Dave will probably want to know your medical history. Don't tell him,' he warned. 'By the time he's finished with you you'll wonder how many days you have left. Angie and Dave are an incorrigible pair. But you'll soon find that out for yourself.'

'They sound—frightening.' And they did to someone who had been an only child brought up by a maiden aunt. Brooke had always been a little shy with people her own age, never having mixed with a lot of other children out of school hours.

Jarrod gave a throaty chuckle. 'That's the one thing they aren't. A highly spirited pair perhaps, but not frightening.'

'What have you done with your cat this weekend?' she asked.

'I have a housekeeper.'

'Oh, of course,' she blushed. 'I should have guessed.'

'I'm a lousy cook,' he offered by way of explanation. 'Egg and bacon is about my limit. Besides, it beats having a wife.'

'One of your own anyway,' she put in softly.

His mouth tightened. 'I don't want any of those comments in front of my parents,' he told her angrily. 'They wouldn't understand your reason for doing it.'

'As long as you do.'

'I know why you *think* you're doing it. But none of this in front of my family, agreed?' he quirked an eyebrow at her.

'I suppose so. I don't want to make the weekend any more difficult by having your family dislike me. That I can do without.'

'Mm, it could prove difficult if we let it.' he agreed. 'A little bit of acting on your part and it could all pass off quite smoothly. I told them we'd stay until after lunch tomorrow.'

Brooke felt a sense of apprehension. 'When you say acting, you mean ...?'

His look was cruel. 'I mean a little of that show you put on for my secretary yesterday morning. My family would appreciate it more than she did,' he said dryly.

She shook her head. 'I couldn't—I couldn't do that. Yesterday I did it because—well, because——'

'Because you wanted to get back at me,' Jarrod finished for her.

'Yes,' she agreed unhesitantly.

He swung the car down a long gravel driveway, a huge red-brick building standing in the midst of sweeping green lawns and neat flower beds. The front door of the house stood open in the heat of the day, and a young girl ran out to greet them as Jarrod parked the car in the driveway.

'Jarrod!' she squealed. 'It's so lovely to see you!' She launched herself into his arms.

Brooke supposed this must be Angie. She was quite lovely to look at, her hair as raven black as her brother's and brushed in glowing waves down to her shoulders. She also had the same grey eyes as Jarrod, but whereas his were often cold and chilling hers were full of warmth and an underlying sense of mischief.

Angie was dressed much more informally than herself, in denims and a checked shirt. Very tall and slim, she carried herself with a self-confidence that was inborn in her, turning from greeting her brother to appraise Brooke with curious eyes.

It wasn't a disapproving stare, but nevertheless Brooke felt relieved that she was at least smartly dressed. She had gone out this morning and bought herself a new casual day dress, packing an evening dress in case the Stones dressed for dinner. The day dress she had bought was a lemon and black flower print, fitted at her slim waist and finishing just below her knee.

She felt quite good in it and she met the younger girl's gaze unflinchingly, almost sighing her relief as Angie's face broke into a welcoming smile.

She came forward, her hand outstretched. 'Hi, I'm Angie.' She gave Jarrod a rueful look. 'For once this brother of mine seems speechless.' She grinned at him teasingly. 'You must be in love!'

He had a relaxed smile on his face. 'It isn't a case of being in love, you just haven't stopped talking since you came out of the house.'

Angie grimaced. 'I hope he doesn't bully you like this.'

Brooke laughed at her expression. 'All the time, but I'm getting used to it.'

'Surely not all the time? He seems to have taken time out to ask you to marry him.' Angie put a friendly hand through the crook of Brooke's arm. 'Can I see your ring?' she asked excitedly.

Brooke held out her hand for inspection, avoiding Jarrod's mocking gaze in her direction as his sister admired the ring. The two girls left him to bring in the small amount of luggage they had brought with them, Angie taking her in to the lounge where the rest of the Stone family were waiting.

Brooke hung back in the doorway. Angie had proved to be just as nice as Jarrod had said she would, but that didn't mean the rest of his family would be as welcoming. After all, Jarrod was an important man, and his family would be expecting something a little bit special in his intended wife. The fact that it would never come to that wasn't important; they didn't know that.

'Little coward!' Jarrod muttered in her ear as he

entered the room ahead of her, his firm grip on her wrist impelling her forward.

His taunt was enough to give her courage and she stood silently by his side as he greeted his family, making the introductions with practised ease. First of all his mother, a small neat woman towered over by the rest of her family.

'At least I won't get a crick in my neck talking to you,' her grey eyes twinkled. 'It's like living in the land of the giants,' she explained.

She wasn't half as daunting as Brooke had expected her to be and she found herself smiling naturally, being made to feel as if she already belonged to this family. But she mustn't forget this was only a temporary arrangement, she mustn't become too involved. Never having had a family of her own she could find that all too easy.

Jarrod's father came next and it was obvious where his son got his looks from. His eyes might be the deep grey of his mother, but the rest of him was all Clifford Stone. Tall and lean like his son, the black hair winged with grey at the temples, Clifford Stone was still a very attractive man, although Brooke guessed he must be well into his sixties.

'Pleased to meet you, my dear.' He bent to kiss her cheek warmly. 'I'm glad to see that Jarrod has chosen wisely.' He shook his son's hand.

'You're not at all what I expected,' said the fourth and last member of the family. 'The type of girl Jarrod usually goes about with—I expected you to be completely different.'

'David!' his father reprimanded sternly.

'How different?' Brooke queried softly.

'Oh, you know—heavy perfume, so beautiful you almost don't look real, and so sophisticated it just isn't true,' he grimaced.

Brooke looked at Jarrod, her eyes mocking him. 'His taste must have changed.'

'Definitely for the better,' Dave said approvingly. 'You've picked a real winner, Jarrod.' He slapped his brother on the back. 'Not that I'm sure you deserve her.'

Jarrod grinned goodnaturedly. 'Oh, I'm sure Brooke thinks I deserve her.'

'Definitely,' she agreed firmly, his family not aware of their double-edged conversation.

'Would you like to take Brooke upstairs and show her her room?' his mother suggested. 'I've put her in the one next to yours,' she informed him.

'Fine. Ready, darling?' He quirked one dark eyebrow at her.

'Yes,' she replied huskily, the endearment embarrassing her.

Once upstairs in the room prepared for her Jarrod threw her case on to the bed before sitting down in the bedroom chair. It was a lovely room, beautifully furnished without losing any of its character, the gold and brown decor warm in appearance.

Brooke cleared her throat nervously, ever conscious of Jarrod watching her through enigmatic eyes. 'You have a nice family.'

'And that surprised you.' It was a statement, not a question.

'A little,' she admitted.

'They liked you too, but then I knew they would. I have only one complaint.'

'C-complaint?'

'Mm.' He looked thoughtfully at his wrist-watch. 'Your attitude towards me will have to improve. You jumped like a scared rabbit when I called you darling, and you studiously avoid calling me Jarrod.'

'I've already explained why that is.'

'Yes, but you can't just not call me anything.'

'I find it easier that way,' she said obstinately.

He stood up to leave. 'Practise it to yourself while I freshen up. I'll just be next door when you're ready to go down to tea.'

Brooke unpacked her evening gown and denims so that the creases should fall out before she next wore them. She washed her face and freshened her make-up, feeling infinitely tidier when she had finished.

She hesitated about knocking on Jarrod's bedroom door, finally doing so with determination. She entered the room at his command to do so. That this had been his room since childhood was obvious from the pictures on the walls and the model aeroplanes suspended by string from the ceiling.

It was a nice room, with a couple of pictures of Jarrod as a child on display on the dressing-table. One of them had been taken when he was about twelve or thirteen, and already at that age he had the promise of the good looks that were now so destructive to a woman's peace of mind.

Brooke turned almost guiltily as she heard a movement behind her, her eyes widening with shock as she took in Jarrod's bare chest and the way his trousers rested low down on his lean hips. It was impossible to look away from him as his muscles rippled as he dried himself with a thick fluffy towel. He must have just taken a shower, and Brooke felt her cheeks colour with embarrassment.

She dragged her eyes away from him with effort. 'I'm sorry, I didn't realise you were——' she bit her lip nervously.

'I'm perfectly decent, Brooke,' he taunted at her hesitation. 'Much more so than if I'd just been swimming.'

She moved awkwardly. 'Yes, but this isn't a beach, and we—we're alone up here.'

Jarrod threw the towel down on to the bed, shrugging his powerful shoulders into a black silk shirt and buttoning it with unhurried fingers. 'You only have to make the slightest noise of protest and my mother and father would be up here like a shot.' He tucked

his shirt back into the waistband of his trousers.
'They're the best chaperones you could ever wish to
have.'

'I'm sorry. It's just that——'

'You're a prude,' he finished dryly. 'It was only a
bare chest, Brooke, nothing more. I was more than
adequately dressed.'

'It's just that I don't know you. You took me by
surprise.' She was making verbal excuses for her purely
physical reaction to him. Her pulse had began to
beat erratically at the sight of him, her breathing con-
stricted.

'I'll have to remember not to do it again until you
know me better,' he said sarcastically.

'There's no need to mock!' she retorted crossly.

'Then don't be so damned stupid! You couldn't
have been more shocked if I'd been completely naked.
You're twenty years of age, surely your life hasn't been
that sheltered that a man with his shirt off can throw
you into confusion? You must have had boy-friends in
the past.'

'A few,' she admitted. 'But none of them ever acted
the way you do.'

'All of them gentlemen, hmm?'

'Yes.'

'Something we've already agreed I'm not.'

'Yes,' she said sharply. 'If you're ready to go down,
Mr Stone, I——'

He grasped her wrist as she turned to leave the
room. 'Jarrod!' he snapped savagely. 'I thought I told
you to call me Jarrod. If you can't manage a simple
thing like that you're going to make complete fools
out of both of us. Now say it! And manage to put a
bit of feeling into it. Go on, say it!'

'Jarrod,' it came out as a strangulated cry, his fingers
painful on her wrist.

'Again,' he ordered. 'And say it properly this time.'

'I—I can't. You're hurting me,' she cried.

'Brooke!' he warned.

'All right, all right. But let go of my arm first.' She sighed as he released her, rubbing the reddened skin. 'You're a bully,' she accused.

'You do seem to bring out those feelings in me,' he agreed.

She pouted sulkily. 'Jarrod,' she said obediently, softly, with feeling. How well his name rolled off the tongue, and how nice it sounded.

He grinned down at her. 'Just try to keep it like that and they'll all believe you're in love with me.'

'Jarrod,' she repeated, looking up at him below lowered lashes, feeling more than usually shy with him alone in the intimacy of his bedroom.

To the girl entering the room at that moment they looked like a couple very much in love with each other, with Brooke gazing up into Jarrod's eyes and he grinning down at her, his expression softened.

'Am I intruding?' Angie asked mischievously.

Her brother turned to look at her. 'Would it stop you if you were?'

She grinned. 'No. I came to look for Brooke, and when she wasn't in her room I knew she must be in here with you——' she blushed as she realised what she had said. 'What I mean is——'

Jarrod laughed at her embarrassment. 'I think we know what you mean, Angie. Why were you looking for Brooke, as if I couldn't guess?' he grimaced.

She made a face at him. 'I came to ask her if she would like to see my studio, away from you oldies for a while.'

'Minx!' He made a threatening step towards her, relenting as she looked set for flight. 'What did Mum say about your little idea?'

'She told me to wait until after tea.'

'I agree with her.'

Angie looked appealingly at Brooke. 'Wouldn't you rather——'

'Tea first,' Jarrod said firmly. 'We've had quite a long drive here and we both need a drink and something to eat. No,' he silenced her as she made to speak, 'it can wait until later. Brooke?' he held out his hand to her.

She put her own hand into it, feeling the firm strength of his grasp. Amongst his family he was a different person, laughing and teasing, not at all the severe businessman she was used to seeing, and much less frightening.

They were a closely knit family, and made Brooke feel like one of them. By the time tea was over she found herself feeling very much as if she had come home, and she felt guilty about these feelings. She was deceiving these kindly people, living a lie. She could only feel relieved when Angie renewed her suggestion that she might like to look at her studio.

'Of course, Jarrod is right,' Angie said as she led the way up the stairs. 'I'm not that good, but I do enjoy it, and I think I could make a career for myself in advertising.'

'I'm sure Jarrod didn't——'

Angie laughed. 'Oh yes, he did. My brother is nothing if not honest.' She threw open the door to her studio.

There were numerous sketches and paintings on the walls, all very good likenesses of her family. There was a half finished portrait on the easel next to the window, but it was already clearly recognisable as Clifford Stone.

Brooke turned to look at the younger girl. 'This is very good.'

'Thank you, although it isn't very easy to get Daddy to sit still. He may be retired, but he's still very active. I have some sketches of Jarrod if you'd like to see them?'

These sketches were in a separate portfolio, a few firm lines on paper showing Jarrod's strong face perfectly. 'These are even better,' Brooke said softly.

Angie grinned. 'Jarrod refuses to sit still for five seconds, but he has such an arresting face that I just had to try and get him on paper. Handsome devil, isn't he?'

'Very,' Brooke agreed unhesitantly.

'He's kept you a big secret, you know. Mummy and Daddy were very surprised when they saw yesterday's newspapers. They called Jarrod immediately and he confirmed that it was him. Where did you meet?'

She ought to have realised that Jarrod's sister would ask personal questions, but she hadn't, and now she wasn't ready for them. 'We met at work,' she answered evasively.

'And have you known him long?'

'About six months,' she said truthfully.

Angie raised a surprised eyebrow. 'I always knew Jarrod was clam-like about his friends, but we've heard absolutely nothing about you. I suppose that proves just how serious he was about you.'

Or more likely that he hadn't even known of her existence, which happened to be the truth. She quickly changed the subject, channelling it into something much less personal to herself.

Dinner proved much less traumatic than she had imagined too. Seated next to Dave she was suitably entertained with the antics of his medical training. Despite all the hard work that went into the training Dave appeared to be having a lot of fun.

Brooke enjoyed his company, finding him much more approachable than Jarrod. He was younger for one thing, much less cynical and worldly. He looked like Jarrod in some ways, with his dark hair and powerful physique, but he had the laughing blue eyes of his father.

Jarrod came to sit beside her on the sofa as they drank their coffee in the lounge after dinner. 'Stop flirting with my little brother,' he warned her softly, a smile on his face for the other people in the room but a dangerous glitter in his eyes for her.

'Not so little,' she muttered resentfully.

'Keep your sharp little claws out of him. You've managed to trick me into a phoney engagement, don't try to get him into a real one. I wouldn't let him marry you, you know.'

Her eyes glittered deeply violet. 'A little premature, aren't you? We only met today.'

'*We* only met yesterday—and we're engaged now.'

'Only temporarily,' she said crossly.

'Right. So don't get any ideas about Dave. He has his life pretty well mapped out for the next few years, and it doesn't include a wife.'

Her eyes spat her dislike at him. 'I don't intend marrying you or your brother.'

'You may have to,' he pointed out. 'If our supposed wedding date is spread about too much.'

'That doesn't mean I have to marry you. Playing your fiancée is something I don't mind doing, especially as I was the one who started all this, but marriage is a different matter.' Brooke put her empty coffee cup down on the table. 'I think I'd like to go to my room now, would your family mind?'

'It doesn't matter if I do?' he drawled.

'No.'

'Then go ahead,' he told her grimly.

She stood up, excusing herself before leaving the room, closely followed by Jarrod. 'Where are you going?' she demanded angrily. 'To make sure I don't run away?'

He looked bored. 'The idea never crossed my mind. I'm trying to look the part of the loving fiancé. Coming to your room for a long and passionate goodnight seemed to be called for.'

Brooke gave him a scathing look before going determinedly up the stairs to her room. She hesitated at her bedroom door. 'There's no need for you to come any further.'

Jarrod's look was taunting. 'Frightened I might

give you a repeat of last night?'

She blushed a fiery red. She had hoped he had forgotten last night, deliberately keeping off any subject herself that could bring that embarrassing interlude into the conversation. But it seemed Jarrod wasn't going to forget so easily. 'Certainly not!' she replied indignantly.

He watched her through narrowed eyes. 'That was a punishment, you know.'

She glared her dislike at him. 'I never presumed it to be anything else,' she snapped, going into the room and slamming the door behind her.

She leant back against the door, her mouth set in a firm straight line. How dared he treat her like an impressionable child who had fallen in love with him! How dared he! Her shoulders slumped; he dared because until a few weeks ago that was exactly what she had been.

And now she found herself falling into that trap again. Jarrod was everything she had ever dreamt him to be and more. If only he weren't having an affair with a married woman!

CHAPTER FOUR

IT was happening again, that terrible nightmare that she couldn't escape from, that came to haunt her when she least expected it. She tossed restlessly about in the bed, anxious to free herself from the nightmare before it reached its terrifying climax, but knowing it would be impossible.

Tears streamed down her face as she witnessed once again with startling clarity the way her mother and father were laughing together, the sun shining down on them brightly as the three of them drove down to the coast for the day.

Her father hadn't seen the man driving at them on the wrong side of the road until it was too late. The screech of brakes were amplified now in her dream, her mother's scream echoing time and time again in her brain. The car rolled over and over again until blackness took over and she woke up screaming.

Instantly the room was flooded with light, and a tousled-haired, pyjama-clad Jarrod rushed into the room. His face creased into a concerned frown as he saw Brooke's pale cheeks, the tears still flowing freely. He came swiftly to her side. 'What's the matter? What happened?'

Brooke buried her face into his chest. 'Oh, Jarrod, it was awful, awful!' she sobbed brokenly.

'What was?' he demanded, holding her against him.

'The dream. I had the dream again.' The sobs were easing now. 'It's so long since it last happened I'd almost forgotten about it.'

His grey eyes were still darkened with concern as he held her at arm's length, searching her deathly white face for several long seconds. 'What dream,

Brooke?' he asked gently. 'Tell me about it.'

'I—I can't. I've never spoken to anyone about it.'

'Tell me,' he said persuasively. 'After all, I was the one you cried out for.'

Her eyes widened with disbelief. 'You were?'

'Yes,' he confirmed. 'You called out my name several times before I got in here.'

This surprised Brooke, as she usually called her father's name. She looked worried. 'Do you think I woke the rest of your family?'

'Well, no one has turned up yet, so I would say no. I only heard you because I was next door and I hadn't fallen asleep yet. Look,' he stood up, 'if I pick you up and take you back to my room will you question my intentions?'

'No.' She was shaking so much she just wanted to be back in his arms, held safe from that horrifying nightmare. She didn't want to stay in this room where the memory of that nightmare was so vivid.

Jarrod carried her to his room without another word, placing her gently between the sheets before getting in next to her, holding her against him with his arm about her shoulders, her head resting on his chest. 'Now tell me about your dream, Brooke,' he coaxed.

She shivered at the memory of it. 'It was the accident—the accident that killed my parents. I saw it again—the crash, the way the car rolled over and over. I was unconscious before the car stopped turning.'

'How old were you?' he asked.

'Five.'

'And that's when you went to live with your aunt?'

'Yes. You see, I was only kept in hospital for forty-eight hours and apparently the medical staff thought it better for my aunt to tell me of my parents' death in the comfort of her home, away from the clinical atmosphere. But she—my aunt didn't care, she didn't care for my father, or the fact that he had married my mother. She—she woke me up the night I came out of hospital to tell me they were both dead.'

Jarrod looked grim. 'She woke you up to tell you that?'

Brooke snuggled closer to him, repressing a shiver. 'Yes,' she admitted huskily. 'Ever since then I've had these nightmares periodically. But the time between each one is getting longer and longer, this is the first one I've had for about a year.'

His arms tightened about her. 'That woman had no right to have the care of a young child given to her!'

'She was kind enough in her own way, maybe hurting me was her way of showing her grief.'

He reached out his hand and switched off the light, instantly putting the room into darkness. 'Go to sleep now, Brooke. You're quite safe, I'm here with you.'

'But I—I can't stay here,' she protested.

His warm breath ruffled the hair at her temple. 'You aren't going back into that room on your own. You're obviously still upset. You'll stay here with me. Go to sleep now, I'll stay awake until I know you're asleep.'

'Thank you.'

She felt his lips at her temple and her feelings changed to something quite different from fear. She was here in Jarrod Stone's bed being held in his arms. It was still frightening, but fear of another kind.

'Go to sleep, Brooke,' he ordered abruptly. 'And stop letting your imagination run riot. I think you've had enough of an upset for one night, so let me assure you I have no intention of doing anything to upset you any more. We can talk again in the morning.'

Brooke didn't think she could possibly sleep held in his arms like this, but the even rise and fall of his chest soon lulled her into a false sense of security, and within minutes she was asleep.

She woke slowly the next morning, wondering where she could possibly be. Then she remembered. As she looked down at the dark head resting on her breasts, Jarrod Stone was still very much asleep. His arm rested about her waist, his body moulded to her side.

She could just see the angle of his face, softened now in sleep. He looked younger, but just as handsome. And she had slept in his bed with him all night! She was sure that none of his friends would believe that they had spent the last few hours together in this bed and he hadn't made one single pass at her. She wasn't sure she believed it herself. With his reputation she would have expected something quite different; maybe she was even a little disappointed.

But she didn't have time to puzzle over that, because at that moment someone came unannounced into the bedroom. Brooke felt her heart sink as she recognised Angie, an Angie who hadn't seen her yet because she was preoccupied with fastening her wristwatch to her arm.

'Come on, Jarrod! It's——' her voice trailed off as she saw Brooke cradled in her brother's arms, her cheeks colouring a fiery red. 'Oh dear, what have I done now?' she groaned. 'I didn't mean to——'

'You haven't,' Brooke said firmly, gently shaking Jarrod to wake him up. 'I—— We——'

'Hey, come on, Jarrod! You can't——' Dave too stood transfixed in the doorway. He took Angie's arms, pulling her out of the door. 'Excuse us, Brooke. We didn't realise.' With a cheeky grin he closed the door behind them.

Brooke shook Jarrod more forcefully. 'Wake up, will you?' she demanded. 'Jarrod! Wake up!'

He lay on his back, stretching his arms above his head. 'Mm,' he groaned. 'What time is it?' He looked at her with sleepy eyes.

'Never mind the time,' she retorted crossly. 'We've just had visitors.'

'Really?' he asked disinterestedly, turning on his side to look at the clock on the side table. 'Angie or Dave?'

'Both. But how did you know?' she frowned.

He shrugged, pushing back the bedclothes to get out of bed. He stretched again. 'It's a bit cramped in there for two people.'

'How did you know it was either your sister or your brother?' she repeated to cover her embarrassment.

'Because it's after seven-thirty and when I'm home we always go for a ride at seven-fifteen. Obviously they thought I'd slept in and they'd come to wake me.'

'Oh, obviously,' she said dryly. 'Don't you care that they saw us together in this bed—and drew their own conclusions?'

Jarrod raised his eyebrows. 'What's the point of worrying about it? I'm sure that by now Angie has rushed in and told my mother too.'

'Oh no!' She paled. 'I couldn't bear it! And I certainly couldn't face your mother and father again if they've been told.'

He pulled a clean shirt out of the wardrobe. 'Why not? They probably think we sleep together anyway. A lot of engaged couples do nowadays.'

'I wouldn't, and especially not with you. You're the sort that would take advantage of the engagement and forget about the marriage.'

'With you I may not be allowed to. My mother and father won't simply accept the end of our engagement in a couple of months' time, not after this morning. We may just have to get married to satisfy them.'

Brooke gave him a puzzled look. 'You're very calm about it.'

He stripped off his pyjama jacket, his torso rippling with muscle. 'What else do you expect me to be?'

Brooke sat up in the bed, uncaring of the inadequacy of her cotton nightdress. 'I expect you to be angry at perhaps having to marry someone you don't love.'

'But you do see it may be a possibility?'

Remembering the looks she had received from Angie and Dave and the kindness Mr and Mrs Stone had shown her she knew that it could happen. They were Jarrod's family, and no matter how he might behave away from home, here he behaved like any normal son would to his parents, with respect and love. Besides, she couldn't bear for them to think badly of her.

'Yes,' she acknowledged softly.

'I'm no happier about it than you are,' he snapped, picking up the sound of finality in her voice.

'Then why don't you get angry, shout a little?'

He walked to the bathroom door, his fresh clothing in his hand, clothed only in the silk pyjama trousers that rested low down on his narrow hips, showing clearly the strength and power of his body. 'Being married to you may not be so bad, you felt quite good in my arms last night, and when I kissed you on Friday I wouldn't say we disliked each other.'

'You mean——' she paused for breath. 'You mean you would expect—expect a normal marriage?'

He gave a mocking smile. 'You've been reading too many romantic novels. Marriages of convenience don't happen nowadays, or if they do they certainly have a physical side. I wouldn't marry any woman just to look at her,' he scorned.

'But it *would* be very convenient for you, wouldn't it?' she queried softly.

Grey eyes narrowed to steely slits. 'Would it?'

'Oh yes,' she scorned. 'A newly married man would hardly be suspected of having an affair with another man's wife.'

'And who would that be?' he asked tauntingly.

'You know very well who I mean,' she said tartly.

'The beautiful Selina,' Jarrod replied unhesitantly.

'Exactly.'

'Mm, you could be right,' he said thoughtfully.

'I wouldn't stand for that if I were your wife. I

couldn't condone you having an affair with that woman. I didn't even like her.'

'Oh, I see, if you had liked her it would have been a different matter.'

'Don't be ridiculous! And I certainly wouldn't be your real wife. I may have been reading too many romantic novels, but I think I prefer the way they turn out.'

'You do?' He looked surprised. 'But they usually end up with the hero and the heroine in each other's arms, don't they?'

'Well, yes, but—we won't! And that's why you aren't ever going to make love to me. I happen to believe that sort of thing should only happen between people who love each other.'

'And you don't think you could ever love me?'

'Never!' She couldn't meet his probing eyes in case he should see her lie. He was much too astute to miss the love shining in her eyes for him.

'Then that's too bad, because I have no intention of having a wife just to put her in a glass case. Women are for loving and——'

'And you love them,' she finished bitchily.

'Yes.'

'God, you're such a——'

'I warned you once before about calling me names.' His eyes glittered dangerously.

'If the cap fits ...' Brooke said pointedly.

He laughed softly. 'I'll see you at breakfast. I'm going for that ride now—if I were you I'd try to get a little more sleep, it may improve your temper.'

His laughter still echoed in the room long after he had left it. Brooke threw one of the pillows at the closed bathroom door. Damn the man! Damn the arrogance of him.

She went back to her own room; how could she be expected to sleep in his bed after what had happened to her this morning? She still blushed at the thought of Angie coming into the room and finding her in Jarrod's arms. Whatever must she have thought? What a stupid question, it must be obvious what she had thought, what the whole family would think when they knew.

And she had to face them all, probably at breakfast. Not that she was hungry, but she knew the dreaded moment had to be faced some time, and she would rather it was sooner than later. Besides, she knew Jarrod wouldn't let her cower in her room all day.

If only he weren't so calm about the whole thing! It didn't seem to bother him that his young sister had walked into his bedroom and found them in a compromising situation. And then he also had the nerve to say they would have to get married and that he would expect the marriage to be a real one.

He had already called the tune far too many times in a situation that she herself had created, and she wasn't going to let any man make love to her simply because he considered it his right to do so. Oh no, Mr Jarrod Stone had pushed her about far too much already, she wasn't going to marry him too!

Only his mother was in the dining-room when she came down to breakfast at eight-thirty, the others obviously not back from their ride yet. Brooke accepted the cup of coffee Sarah Stone had poured out for her, sipping the scalding liquid in an effort not to look at the other woman, her embarrassment too acute.

'Have the two of you discussed a wedding date?' Jarrod's mother asked softly.

Brooke's cheeks flamed. No preliminaries, but straight to the point! 'Not really. Look, Mrs Stone, I——'

'Call me Sarah, please,' she invited graciously. 'And I hope that when you know me better you'll call me Mother like my other children do.'

Everything this woman said made her feel more and more guilty for her deceit. Her last words made her feel choked with emotion, never having had anyone she could call mother. And Sarah Stone was exactly the type of mother she would have liked herself, loving and concerned for her children but not interfering.

'Thank you,' she accepted huskily. 'But I want you to know that what Angie saw this morning was not as it seemed. Jarrod and I hadn't—well, we hadn't——'

Sarah smiled gently and patted Brooke's hand reassuringly. 'I know that, my dear. Jarrod has already explained to me what happened and I think he did the right thing. It wouldn't have been right to leave you on your own after such a horrible experience. Jarrod did the only thing possible.'

'Jarrod told you?' Brooke repeated huskily.

'My son is a very forthright person, if he'd been making love to you he would have told me that too.'

'Oh.'

'You mustn't mind us, Brooke. We aren't a family that likes to have secrets, although my eldest son rather surprised us with this engagement.'

'It was all rather sudden,' Brooke excused.

'So he explained, and the press do have a way of finding out these things when you don't want them to. Jarrod explained that the engagement wasn't to be officially announced until your birthday on Tuesday, but as the press had already announced it to the world you decided to go ahead with it now. These newspaper men can be so annoying at times,' Sarah tutted.

Her birthday on Tuesday! How on earth had Jarrod known about that? Of course, her file. And he had used that knowledge to his advantage. But then that was probably how he had got to be the successful businessman he was today, by remembering things and using them when the opportunity arose. Well, he was certainly using her to his greatest advantage, hiding his affair with this phoney engagement.

'Yes,' she agreed quietly, helping herself to a slice of toast.

'I want you to know that Clifford and I would like to arrange for the wedding to take place from here,' Sarah told her. 'I hope you'll allow us that pleasure.'

Brooke blushed once more. 'I—well, I—We haven't really——'

Jarrod came in at that moment, tall, lithe and attractive in a black polo-necked jumper and fitted cream trousers. He bent to kiss his mother's cheek. 'Good morning, Mother.' He grinned down mockingly at Brooke before kissing her too, on the lips. 'Good morning again, my love,' he drawled, sitting down next to her.

'Good morning,' she mumbled.

His mother beamed at the two of them, unaware of the tension between them. 'I was just explaining to Brooke that your father and I would like the wedding to take place from here, to arrange it all for you both.'

Jarrod raised one dark eyebrow. 'You've been discussing the wedding?'

'No, I——'

'Not Brooke, no,' his mother laughed. 'Just me. I'm so excited about having a wedding in the family at last that I can't seem to stop talking about it. I wondered if you'd decided on a definite date yet.'

'Not really,' he sipped his coffee. 'Next month has been mentioned, but we——'

'Next month!' his mother gasped. 'But that's much too soon. I couldn't possibly get everything arranged in so short a time, and Brooke will have so much shopping to do. And you can't possibly live in that apartment of yours, you'll have to look for a suitable house.'

'Calm down,' Jarrod laughed. 'I only said next month had been mentioned, not that it had been decided upon.'

Brooke's mouth tightened at the mockery in his eyes for her. Next month had been mentioned, by her to Selina Howard, and he wouldn't let her forget it.

Sarah Stone sighed her relief. 'Stop teasing me, Jarrod. So you haven't decided when the wedding is to be?'

'Not really.' He sat back in his chair. 'We've only just got engaged, Mum, I think that's enough commitment for the time being. Besides, Brooke needs time to adjust to having a family, time to adjust to me.'

His mother stood up to leave the table. 'I'll just go and talk to Cook about dinner.' She stopped next to Brooke's chair. 'I hope you don't feel that I'm trying to rush you into anything. Jarrod's right, you need time. I'm sorry.'

Brook gave a shy smile. 'You have nothing to apologise for.'

'Thank you.'

She turned on Jarrod once they were alone. 'Did you have to do that, embarrass your mother in that way?'

He looked at her calmly. 'What would you have had me do, agree to everything she suggested? I thought you said you didn't want to marry me.'

'I don't. I wouldn't marry you under any circumstances.'

'My, my, my,' murmured Dave from behind them. 'You've only been engaged two days, I think you ought to give Jarrod a little longer than that!'

Brooke paled even more, the strain she had been living under the last two days coming to the fore. She stood up with a scraping of the chair. 'Excuse me,' she muttered before dashing out of the room.

She didn't care where she went, all she knew was that she had to get away from Jarrod and the way he kept taunting her. Was he going to punish her for ever?

She rushed out of the house, answering Angie's greeting as she came in, her smile vague, before running off in the direction of the woods to the right of the house.

Finally she stopped running and dropped down into the undergrowth in utter exhaustion. What would Dave think of her statement? What could he think? She had made an absolute fool of herself. But Jarrod would keep goading her, taunting her until she had to retaliate.

But at other times he could be quite thoughtful, helping her out of a situation when it became too complicated for her to handle. But he hadn't helped her this time, he had just made things worse.

She wasn't really surprised when she heard someone else moving about in the denseness of the wood; obviously Jarrod's family would pressurise him into coming to look for her. She made no attempt to move, not even looking up when she knew he was standing directly in front of her, his firm muscled thighs clearly outlined in the cream trousers.

He sank down in the grass beside her. 'That was a bit stupid, wasn't it?' he said softly.

Brooke was clutching at the long grass as if for support, unnerved by his closeness. Her cheeks were still wet with tears. 'I couldn't—couldn't think what to do. What did—did you tell Dave?'

Jarrod lay back in the grass, his arms behind his head as he gazed up at the blue sky through the tree tops. 'I just told him that you were still embarrassed about this morning, that you were so upset about it you refused to marry me.'

'And did he believe you?'

He turned to look at her. 'Why shouldn't he, you *were* embarrassed about it.'

'But that wasn't the reason I said I wouldn't marry you.'

'No,' he agreed, sitting up to gently touch her

cheek. 'You did that because once again I pushed you too far. I'm sorry.'

Her eyes widened, her senses reeling at the touch of his hand on her cheek. 'You're—you're sorry?'

His eyes deepened in colour as his gaze rested on her parted lips. 'Yes. Brooke ...' he murmured throatily, bending his head to claim her lips. 'Brooke!' he gasped, gently lowering her back into the undergrowth, his body pressed urgently to her side.

She hadn't been expecting this onslaught, and responded without thought. His mouth was sure and experienced, reducing her to a quivering mass in his arms, his body firm and demanding on hers.

His mouth left hers to travel down the column of her throat to the hollow between her breasts, her nipples clearly visible through the lime green vest-top she had chosen to wear with matching trousers. His lips evoked a response wherever they touched, soft and caressing and totally in control.

Brooke's fingers were entwined in the darkness of his hair, inciting him to further caresses. It was peaceful here, the only noises ones of the birds and the soft rustle of the leaves in the trees. They were in a world apart, a world without time or meaning. And Jarrod was kissing her as if he really enjoyed doing it, drawing a response from her but not demanding one.

As his lips burnt across her throat she kissed the strong angle of his jawbone, aware of the tangy smell of his aftershave and the slight roughness of his skin. His hands moved with certainty across her waist to trail a path of fire up to her shoulders, smoothing the hollows of her throat with impatient fingers.

Brooke was aflame with longing, longing for Jarrod's possession of her. She had never felt this way in any other man's arms, never responded so totally to the senses. If he chose to take her now she wouldn't raise a single objection, would give herself up to just being made his.

He drew back his head, his eyes a deep aroused grey, his own breathing as laboured as her own. 'I want you—you know that, don't you?' His voice was husky, his tone one of passionate intensity.

'Yes.' She was mesmerised by the look in his eyes.

'Do you mind?'

'Do you?'

He shook his head in the negative. 'At the moment I don't mind a thing, except perhaps that this isn't exactly the ideal place for this sort of thing.'

Brooke gave him a dreamy smile, caressing his furrowed brow with great daring. 'I think it's just perfect.'

Jarrod gave a husky chuckle. 'Someone may come along,' he pointed out reasonably.

Her hands were slowly pulling his head back down to her. 'They won't,' she murmured against his lips. 'They wouldn't dare.'

With a groan he took possession of her mouth once again, less gentle now and more demanding. Their hearts beat as one, the rest of their bodies crying out for the same thing. They both knew what they wanted and there was no holding back, on either side.

Brooke's hands caressed and touched his muscled back beneath his sweater, his skin firm and smooth, all of him totally male. His lips played with hers until she rose up to meet him, lying on top of him now, she the one doing the kissing.

Jarrod's hands moved across her back to the waistband of her trousers, pulling her vest-top free so that he could touch the heated skin beneath. She shivered at his hands upon her body, lifting her head to look at him.

Even lying beneath her like this he was still the master, arousing her with just the look in his eyes. 'What's wrong?' he asked softly. 'Changed your mind?'

She shook her head wordlessly, knowing that she was irrevocably in love with this man. She had known it last night when she had woken up to scream his name. Always in the past she had called for her father, sobbing for him until she had almost made herself ill, but last night she had cried out for Jarrod, for the man who now meant everything to her.

'Then come back here,' he demanded throatily, once again bending over her to press upon her those soul-destroying kisses that made a mockery of will-power.

She responded passionately, as she knew she always would in this man's arms. One of his hands moved to cup her breast and she felt him shudder against her.

'God, you're naked underneath this top!' he groaned against her lips.

'I know,' she answered happily.

'Oh God, Brooke, how do you expect me to have any control with you dressed like this? I can't——'

'Ssh!' she silenced him swiftly. 'Someone's coming through the woods towards us.' She could hear the snapping of twigs as whoever it was came closer and closer to them.

Jarrod swung away from her. 'Oh, hell!' he swore angrily, his expression grim. 'It just has to be Angie or Dave, it just has to be! Only they would dare.' He was proved correct when a few seconds later Dave emerged out of the trees. 'What was that you were saying about they wouldn't dare?' Jarrod muttered, standing up to brush the leaves off his trousers. He turned to pull her to her feet. 'My family dare anything, you'll learn that in time.'

The scowl he gave Dave was evidence of his displeasure, and Dave wasn't insensitive to his mood. 'Did I arrive at the wrong time again?' he asked innocently.

'Completely the wrong time.' Jarrod brushed past him on his way back to the house, anger in every line of his rigidly held body.

Dave shrugged helplessly at Brooke as his brother marched off. 'I'm sorry.'

She brushed the grass from her trousers to cover her embarrassment. 'That's all right.' She made to follow Jarrod, but Dave's hand on her arm stopped her.

'I really mean it, Brooke. I didn't mean to interrupt.' He looked as embarrassed as she did.

'You didn't interrupt anything.' On top of her embarrassment she had the hurt that Jarrod could walk away and leave her like this.

Dave followed her gaze as she watched Jarrod's fast disappearing figure. 'I shouldn't worry about Jarrod, if he hadn't left when he did he would probably have hit me. I've seen him mad in the past, but never that mad,' he whistled between his teeth.

Brooke tried her hardest to regain her composure. 'You'll have to blame me for that. I had rather a silly argument with him.'

He nodded. 'And I came along and interrupted you making-up your argument.'

'Not really, you just came along at the wrong time and said the wrong thing.' She gave a light laugh. 'I suppose I'm just feeling particularly sensitive at the moment.'

'They tell me it isn't easy being engaged.'

'After two days?' she teased.

'Well, Jarrod's a pretty arrogant man and very overpowering. Considering the way he rushed to protect your name with my mother this morning I would say you aren't sleeping together yet. That can make things rather tense.'

Brooke's eyes widened at his forthright attitude. 'I——'

'I'm too honest for you, hmm?' Dave guessed the reason for her hesitation.

'Blunt, I would say,' she agreed huskily.

'But right,' he grinned. 'Jarrod's really strung up about you.'

'I don't think——'

'Oh, but he is.' Dave fell into step beside her as she

began to make her way across the grounds. 'I guess you're the type of girl men marry, and Jarrod isn't used to waiting. Besides, he isn't getting any younger.'

She burst out laughing. 'I don't think he would thank you for saying that!'

'Neither do I,' he chuckled. 'But Mum's over the moon about the wedding. She'd just about given up on Jarrod, we all had. He never seemed to have the same girl-friend longer than a few weeks, and he never brought any of them home.'

'Perhaps they weren't the sort of girl he could bring home.'

'You could be right, in fact you probably are. Are you coming into the house now? I promise not to say anything too outrageous for the rest of the day.'

Brooke couldn't help smiling at the 'little boy look' on his face. 'I think I'll go for a walk, get myself an appetite for lunch.'

'Okay.' He gave a friendly salute before leaving her.

Brooke wandered around the well-kept grounds for well over an hour. It was a beautiful estate, really well cared for. It must take an army of gardeners to care for a place this size, and even more staff to run the house itself.

It made her all the more aware of the difference in background between Jarrod and herself. He had been brought up in the lap of luxury, surrounded by his family who loved him, whereas she had been brought up by an aunt who hated her, and who begrudged every penny she had to spend on her.

She would never fit into this sort of background, so perhaps it was as well that their engagement wasn't a real one. She could cope with a weekend, but anything else would be out of the question. But there never would be anything else; this engagement would end as soon as she could make it possible.

Lunch was a pleasant family affair, but Brooke fell in readily with Jarrod's suggestion that they leave mid-afternoon. His family protested strongly, but he was adamant, managing their departure with consummate ease.

'You'd had enough, hadn't you?' he remarked as they drove out of the driveway.

She sighed. 'Was it that obvious?'

'Only to me.' His narrowed eyes remained on the road.

'You didn't have to leave because of me,' she said stiffly. 'I was fine.'

'You were getting jumpy. You could have said something that would have landed us in a lot of trouble.'

'I see. I'm sorry,' she said shortly, angry with him and herself, angry with him because he was right and angry with herself for letting him get under her skin in this way. But she couldn't forget what had happened between them this morning, most of all, she didn't want to forget.

Jarrod had been very cool towards her when they had met again, treating her to a strained politeness solely for the benefit of his family. But his attitude had only made her more tense. He was right, of course, if they hadn't left when they had she would have exploded, with repercussions on both of them.

'No need to apologise,' he told her abruptly. 'I realise I'm to blame for your tension. But God damn it!' he swore savagely. 'You didn't resist me, you invited me even.'

Brooke was taken aback by this attack on her. 'There's nothing wrong with letting a man kiss you,' she answered hotly. 'You may consider me young, but I'm not that inexperienced.'

'I think you already proved that,' he said dryly.

'What do you mean?' she frowned.

He gave a harsh laugh. 'You know all the right moves, don't you, all the little tricks to turn a man on.'

She gasped, angered and hurt by what he was saying to her. She might have made all the right moves, but only with Jarrod had she ever come sensually alive, liking him to touch her and to touch him in return. But he was making it sound something it wasn't, making *her* sound something she wasn't and never could be.

'It would appear so,' she said chillingly. 'If I could manage to turn *you* on. With all your experience with women that can't be too easy.'

'Right,' he agreed grimly, obviously not liking what she said.

'If you can't take it don't dish it out,' she returned swiftly.

'Oh, I can take it, but from you I don't intend to take anything, not your body or your sarcasm.'

'The first you won't get a chance at and the second you shouldn't evoke.'

'I'll try to remember that,' he said coldly. 'You would do well to do the same.'

'Oh, go to hell!'

The silence during the rest of the journey was very oppressive and Brooke for one was glad when he stopped the car outside her flat. She hesitated. 'Would you—would you like to come in for coffee?' she invited, more out of politeness than a genuine wish for his company.

'No, thanks,' he replied curtly, getting her case out of the back of the car before opening her car door for her to get out.

'It's early yet.'

'Goodnight, Brooke,' he said firmly. 'I'll call you tomorrow.' His grey eyes raked over her with chilling intensity. 'I have a dinner appointment this evening,' he added coldly.

Brooke's eyes sharpened. 'With Selina Howard?'

His smile was cruel. 'Who else?'

CHAPTER FIVE

'You're very quiet today,' Jean said softly.

Brooke forced herself to take an interest in what Jean was saying. 'Sorry?'

'I said you're very quiet. You've been like this all day, and yesterday too. Is there anything wrong?'

Anything wrong! She hadn't heard from Jarrod since their parting on Sunday evening—that was what was wrong. He had said he would call her, but she knew for a fact that he had flown to Paris for the day yesterday. But he had no excuse for today. And he was definitely upstairs in his office.

'Brooke?' Jean prompted.

She gave a vague smile. 'Sorry. No, there's nothing wrong.'

'Sure?'

'Yes.'

'I didn't know if perhaps something had happened over the weekend. It must have been quite nerve-racking to meet Mr Stone's family. I would have been terrified myself.'

'They were all very nice,' Brooke said dully. Why hadn't Jarrod called her? It was her birthday today and he hadn't even remembered. He could remember it for the benefit of his family, but he hadn't even had the courtesy to send her a card.

'You don't sound very enthusiastic.'

'They really were,' Brooke insisted. 'Although as you say, I was a bit nervous. But they did make me very welcome.'

Jean sighed as her telephone exchange began to buzz again, but it left Brooke to sink into the misery of her thoughts. In just two days Jarrod had worked

his way into her heart, become the most important
person in her life. And she felt lost without any contact
from him, with no word from him at all.

He had already been up in his office when she had
arrived at a quarter to nine this morning and he
hadn't yet come down for lunch. She was hesitating
about going to lunch herself in the hope that she might
see him.

By the time two-thirty came round she had come to
the conclusion that he wasn't leaving for lunch and
by this time she really had no enthusiasm for eating
herself. It was as if Jarrod was deliberately avoiding
her. But that couldn't be so, he didn't consider her
important enough to go to that extreme.

She wandered home alone at five-thirty, still unable
to find any appetite when she saw the makings of the
chicken salad she had left in the refrigerator for her
dinner. It was miserable having to spend her birthday
alone, although she knew it didn't have to be that
way, one of her friends would have come out with
her. But tonight she wasn't fit company for anyone.
Oh, damn Jarrod, damn and blast him!

She moped about the flat for half an hour or more,
picking things up before putting them down disinterestedly again. Her twenty-first birthday, and she
was spending it alone. Not even her friends at work
had remembered.

Finally, through boredom, she washed and curled
her hair. That wasted at least an hour for her. Oh,
she was so bored! Only seven-thirty and already she
had no way left to fill her evening.

The ringing of the doorbell seemed a welcome
interruption to her loneliness and she rushed to answer
the door before whoever it was went away again. But
apparently they had no such intention: the doorbell
rang again as she reached for the door-handle.

She wrenched it open, staring open-mouthed at
Jarrod as he stood on her doorstep. 'Jarrod!' she mur-

mured wonderingly, completely overwhelmed by how handsome he looked.

He looked devastatingly attractive, the wine-coloured velvet jacket fitting smoothly across his shoulders, the black trousers moulded to his firm muscular thighs, and the velvet bow-tie matched the colour of his jacket perfectly and emphasised the snowy whiteness of the silk shirt he wore.

Brooke's breath had caught and held in her throat at the sight of him, and even though she felt slightly ridiculous standing there unable to say anything she just couldn't force a word past her lips. It was the complete unexpectedness of his appearance here that had unnerved her the most.

Jarrod quirked a mocking eyebrow. 'Are you going to keep me standing here all evening, or do you think I might possibly come inside?'

'Oh—oh, sorry,' she blushingly opened the door. 'Come in, by all means.'

He strolled into her cheaply furnished but clean lounge and Brooke followed him, feeling much too casually dressed in her denims and vest-top against his sophisticated elegance. She watched as he sat down on the sofa, placing a huge white box down next to him. The box looked familiar and she remembered he had given her one like it before.

She twisted her hands together nervously. 'Why are you here?' she asked bluntly, curiosity getting the better of good manners.

'I am your fiancé,' he pointed out.

'That hasn't seemed to bother you for the last two days,' she said bitchily.

'Are you angry about something?' He watched her through narrowed eyes.

'Angry?' Brooke repeated sharply. 'What do I have to be angry about? What *right* do I have to be angry about anything?'

'You tell me,' he said mildly—too mildly.

'You said you would call me,' she reminded accusingly.

'And now I'm here instead.'

'Two days later.'

His mouth tightened. 'I was out of the country yesterday.'

'I know that.'

'Then you also know the reason I didn't call you. Use your common sense, Brooke—I was away on business, I didn't have time to make personal calls.'

'Not to me anyway,' she muttered. 'I'm sure some of your other—acquaintances didn't merit the same casualness.' She didn't need to mention Selina Howard's name, he would know very well who she meant.

Jarrod looked impatient. 'What's the matter with you?' he demanded. 'I'm sure the fact that I haven't called you hasn't been enough to put you in this mood. You couldn't give a damn about me and you know it.'

'I care about the fact that I look pretty stupid when I can't even say when I'm seeing you again. You're the owner of Stone Computers, and as you can imagine we gained quite a lot of attention by getting engaged. I'm asked questions about you all day and I simply have no answers.'

'It's none of their damned business anyway,' he declared arrogantly. 'I don't care to have my personal affairs discussed with them.'

Brooke gave a harsh laugh. 'Then maybe you shouldn't cause so much gossip.'

His eyes snapped angrily, icily grey in colour. 'May I remind you that you started this charade, not I, and consequently caused the gossip!'

'But I didn't start the rumours about you and Mrs Howard, your so-called friends did that.' She allowed her hurt and disappointment to come out, hurt and disappointment that no one had remembered her birthday. But then that wasn't Jarrod's fault, he had no reason to remember it.

'I didn't come here to argue with you,' he said reasonably. 'But I think you would be well advised not to listen to rumours. They so often turn out to have no foundation.'

She gave him a scathing look. 'Are you trying to say your friends were wrong?'

'I'm sure the two women you heard talking weren't friends of mine.'

'But they would like to be,' she scorned.

Jarrod stood up forcefully. 'For God's sake what's the matter with you? I came over here to——'

'Yes?' she cut in rudely. 'Just why did you come here? Dressed like that I would assume you're going on somewhere.'

He nodded. 'You would assume correct.'

Brooke turned away. 'Don't let me keep you,' she said stiffly.

'Oh hell!' He ran an agitated hand through his thick dark hair. 'You *are* keeping me—I came here to take you out.'

'Why?' she asked suspiciously.

'Does there have to be a reason?'

'Oh yes, there has to be a reason. Who do you want to parade me in front of this time?'

He sighed heavily, picking up the box he had brought with him and handing it to her. 'Put this on and I'll show you.'

Brooke looked down at the box as if he had physically struck her with it, knowing it had to be some form of clothing in a box of that name. 'What is it?'

He pushed it towards her. 'Open it and see,' he encouraged.

Like most people Brooke had a natural curiosity and she reluctantly took the box, ripping off the lid to sort through the tissue-paper inside. Nestling amongst the paper was a silky gown, dazzlingly white in colour. She pulled it out with shaking hands and held it against her.

It was a beautiful gown, Grecian in style, and Brooke loved it on sight. She looked at Jarrod over its silky folds. 'For me?' she breathed softly.

He gave a soft throaty chuckle. 'Well, it isn't for me.'

She blushed. 'I know that, but I—— *Why* is it for me?' She was still hoping he had remembered her birthday.

'Just put it on and then we'll go out.'

'But I——'

'Brooke!' he said warningly. 'Go and change.'

She hurried quickly to her room, anxious to do as he said. She rushed into the bathroom, washing quickly before applying a light make-up. Thank goodness she had washed her hair earlier and the red lights were very pronounced.

The dress fitted her perfectly and she could only wonder at Jarrod's correct assessment of her size. That certainly hadn't been in her file! The gown had a plunging neckline, making it impossible for her to wear a bra, and she felt slightly self-conscious as she saw how her breasts were emphasised under the thin material.

She felt even more so a few minutes later as Jarrod's grey eyes roamed freely over her body, lingering slightly on her firm uptilted breasts. She looked back at him below lowered lashes, longing for his approval.

'Do you like the dress?' He watched her closely.

She smiled shyly. 'Do you?'

His eyes darkened. 'You look beautiful in it.'

'Thank you. You have excellent taste. I would never have bought a dress in this style for myself.'

'That's a shame, because you have the perfect figure for it.' He looked at his wrist-watch. 'We have to go now, Brooke.'

She collected the velvet wrap he had given her the last time they had gone out for the evening. 'I——'

she hesitated. 'I don't like you to keep buying me things.'

'If you look good in them what does it matter who bought them?' He took the familiar flat jewellery case out of his pocket. 'I want you to wear these too.' He held out the necklace and earrings she had insisted he keep.

Brooke attached the earrings, bending forward as Jarrod fixed the clasp of her necklace. She liked the feel of his firm sure fingers against her skin and the memory of the way he kissed her on Sunday came all too vividly into her mind.

She moved away from him jerkily. 'We must be going somewhere important if you want me to wear all this finery. I would look decidedly out of place in a restaurant or somewhere equally casual.'

'We're going to a party,' he told her shortly. 'And we're already late.'

'I suppose it will go on for hours yet—most parties do.'

'Possibly,' he nodded distantly. 'Ready?'

'Yes,' she agreed huskily.

They drove to one of the largest hotels in town and Brooke looked at Jarrod interestedly. 'The party is here?'

He turned to look at her. 'Yes, in one of the smaller reception rooms.'

Once outside the car she hung back, nervous about meeting Jarrod's friends for a second time. But his possessive hold on her arm impelled her forward. He opened the door for her and ushered her inside. They found themselves in a small cloakroom area where her wrap was taken by the young man obviously there for just such a purpose, the room behind the double doors surprisingly quiet for a party.

'Are we the only ones here?' she whispered to Jarrod.

He grinned at her and moved forward to throw open the double doors. Instantly the feeling of quiet disappeared, people shouting 'Surprise!' from every corner of the room. And they were talking to her!

Jarrod bent his head to kiss her fleetingly on the lips. 'Happy birthday, Brooke.'

She looked from him to his family, all the girls she knew at work, and a few other people who were probably his own personal friends, and tears gathered in her violet-blue eyes. 'You hadn't forgotten,' she choked. 'I thought everyone had forgotten.'

'They'd all been sworn to secrecy,' he corrected. 'It took quite a lot of organising to get everyone here at such short notice.' He lowered his voice. 'It can be quite difficult to do when you've only known for four days about the birthday.'

She looked up at him mischievously. 'You've only known *me* four days.'

'True,' he chuckled.

Without hesitating Brooke threw her arms about his neck, kissing him enthusiastically before her attention was taken by the guests he had invited for her. She received all the presents and cards that had been sadly lacking this morning, loving them all, but the present she liked most came from Jarrod's sister Angie. It was a portrait of Jarrod, a very good portrait that Brooke would treasure as long as she lived. A portrait of the man she loved.

Jarrod grimaced as she put it in place of honour amongst her other gifts. 'Angie!' he guessed with feeling. 'She could have thought of something a little more original than that.'

Brooke looked at it admiringly, a slight curve to her soft pink lips. 'I think it's just perfect.'

'Hardly perfect,' he denied. 'I'm sure I don't have quite that physique. She's made me out to be some sort of Adonis.'

'It's beautiful,' Brooke insisted.

'God, now I'm really insulted!'

'Surely Brooke isn't insulting you, darling,' drawled a familiar husky voice. 'Sorry we're late, Jarrod, but

Charles' flight was delayed.'

Brooke quickly masked her displeasure at Selina Howard being invited here to her party, turning to smile at the other woman politely. But Selina Howard wasn't looking at her; her eyes were for Jarrod alone, slanting green eyes that devoured him at a glance.

Brooke found that look frankly disgusting, especially as the man at her side was instantly recognisable as Charles Howard, her husband. He was a tall distinguished man with a handsomeness that was almost as breathtaking as Jarrod's. Selina Howard must indeed be greedy to possess a husband and lover with such virility.

Charles Howard put out his hand. 'Nice to see you again, Jarrod,' he smiled. 'As Selina has already said, my flight was delayed, hence our lateness.'

'I'm pleased you could come at all, you must be tired after your flight.' Jarrod moved to put a possessive arm about Brooke's shoulders. 'My fiancée, Brooke Faulkner.'

'Happy birthday, my dear,' Charles said smoothly. 'You don't know how much pleasure it gives me to see Jarrod joining us other poor downtrodden devils.'

She laughed, noting his twinkling blue eyes. 'He hasn't yet, an engagement isn't necessarily a marriage.'

'But you did say the marriage was to be next month,' Selina Howard spoke to her for the first time. 'All of Jarrod's friends are waiting in anticipation of their invitation. Have you decided on the actual date yet?'

So Jarrod hadn't yet told her it was a lie! Brooke wondered why that was. No doubt he had his reasons, he had one for everything he did, unless of course Selina did know it was a lie and they were continuing with this pretence to cover up their affair. That seemed the most likely explanation.

'We're still discussing it with my mother,' Jarrod put in smoothly. 'She insists it can't be arranged in a few weeks.'

'I've never met your mother.' Selina put her hand

through the crook of his arm. 'Introduce me.'

'Excuse us,' Jarrod said politely, leading the beautiful blonde woman over to where his mother was chatting quite easily with some of Jarrod's employees.

Brooke looked at Charles Howard nervously, returning his smile. 'I believe you've been away on business,' she said conversationally, feeling extraordinarily shy in the company of this well-known man.

He nodded. 'For over a week now. I returned at seven o'clock this evening.'

'Then I'm very honoured that you've come straight to my birthday party.'

'I had to see the girl who's managed to capture the elusive Jarrod. I thought he was a confirmed bachelor. I can see why he changed his mind.'

She blushed at his intended compliment, looking up sharply as she heard Selina Howard's throaty chuckle. The two of them had left Jarrod's mother now and were standing to one side of the room deep in conversation.

Charles followed her gaze, frowning as he saw his wife's hand on Jarrod's arm. He looked back at Brooke. 'You'll have to forgive Selina,' he said gently. 'She's never been able to accept the fact that she's a married woman.'

'Sorry?' She pretended ignorance, all the time aware of just how close Jarrod and this man's wife were standing.

Charles sighed. 'My wife likes to flirt. But she doesn't mean anything by it,' he added hastily. 'At least, not usually,' he muttered, watching his wife through narrowed eyes.

For such a successful businessman Charles Howard certainly didn't understand his wife as he should, although he obviously had suspicions about her relationship with Jarrod. That wasn't surprising in the circumstances. Brooke felt as if everyone could see that possessive hand on *her* fiancé's arm.

She felt relieved when the small band at one end of the room began to play, moving into Charles Howard's arms at his request that they dance together. He was an amusing companion, very attractive, but nevertheless she still knew the exact moment when Jarrod stepped on to the dance floor with the beautiful Selina. And she resented the way the woman's arms were clasped about his neck, her body moulded to him as she moved to the music. They made no attempt to dance in the conventional way and she knew Charles Howard had noticed them too.

Jarrod's father claimed her for the next dance, and she felt the tension start to leave her body. If Jarrod had hoped to cover his affair with the other woman by keeping up this phoney engagement he needn't have bothered. Charles Howard was very very suspicious of his wife's friendship with him now and it would take drastic measures to allay those suspicions.

And the fact that Jarrod had now danced with the woman three times in succession would not help the situation. Brooke was keeping her eye on Charles Howard and knew that he was aware of his wife's every move.

'Jarrod really surprised you this evening, didn't he,' Clifford Stone remarked with a grin. 'Springing this party on you.'

She smiled up at him as they danced. 'He certainly did,' she agreed.

'Has he given you his present yet?'

'He gave me this dress. And I would like to thank you once again for the lovely pearl necklace you gave me. It's very beautiful.' And something she had told Jarrod she couldn't accept. He had cuttingly told her she would do as she was told. Perhaps for the moment she would, but later she would see it returned.

'We're just glad you like it. Sarah assured me that the modern setting of the necklace was perfectly suitable. And although it's a charming dress I'm sure I can tell you without spoiling any of Jarrod's fun that it isn't your birthday gift from him. That's something very special.'

Like any other woman when told something like this Brooke now felt a burning curiosity to know what the gift could be. Unless Jarrod had just told his parents this so that they should think a lot of thought had gone into his present to her. Not that she wanted anything else from him; he had given her far too much already, including this huge ring glittering on her finger like a brand of possession.

Dave claimed her for a dance next, looking very handsome in black trousers and a white evening jacket. He wasted no time in coming straight to what was on his mind. 'What's big brother doing with the blonde bombshell?'

Brooke was startled by his straightforwardness, but she should have expected it after Sunday. Dave wasn't one to mince his words. She arched one eyebrow. 'Do you mean Mrs Howard?' she asked innocently.

'So that's who she is! Yes, what's Jarrod doing with the lovely Selina?'

She looked over his shoulder at the other couple. 'Dancing, I would say.'

His hold tightened as he pulled her closer into his arms. 'I know that,' he said in disgust. 'But she's a bit—well, she clings a bit. And she's monopolising Jarrod's attention, she has been for the last half hour or so.'

'It could be the other way round, you know.'

He frowned. 'What do you mean?'

'I mean Jarrod could be monopolising her,' she pointed out wryly.

Dave looked down at her. 'When he's just got engaged to you? I don't believe it.'

Brooke gave a hollow laugh. 'Being engaged to someone doesn't mean you suddenly stop noticing how attractive other people are.'

'Does that mean you could come to like me?' he asked softly against her earlobe.

'Dave!' she looked shocked. 'I'm engaged to your brother.'

'Do you love him?'

'Very much,' she nodded.

He sighed. 'Lucky Jarrod! I wonder if you would have fallen for me if we'd met first. I'd like to think so.'

She had known that he liked her by his attitude towards her over the weekend, but she hadn't imagined it had been this much. 'I would too,' she said gently. 'But I'm afraid that as soon as I saw Jarrod I knew he was the one for me. It was just something I instinctively knew.'

'Well, I instinctively think we should break up his little scene with the lovely Mrs Howard. That woman means trouble if you don't watch her.'

If only he knew! Selina Howard had been the cause of all her trouble of late. 'So how do you expect me to get Jarrod away from her?'

He took hold of her hand and began to make his way through the other dancers. 'Just leave it to me,' he turned round to murmur. 'I'll get her off your back.'

Once he reached the other couple he tapped his brother on the shoulder, grinning in the face of Jarrod's obvious displeasure. He smiled at Selina Howard. 'I'm Jarrod's brother, Mrs Howard,' he introduced himself. 'And I've been longing to meet you all evening. Would you give me this dance?'

She couldn't do much else in the circumstances, and Brooke tried to pretend she hadn't seen the wink Dave gave her over the other woman's shoulder as he whisked her away. She looked uncertainly at Jarrod as he towered over her.

'Did Dave think that up on his own or did you put

him up to it?' he rasped.

'I don't know what you mean,' she evaded.

'I'm pretty damn sure my little brother had no intention of going near Selina before he had that last dance with you.' His look was grim. 'You must have given him the idea.'

Her eyes snapped, deeply violet in colour. 'It wouldn't occur to you that people have begun to gossip about the time you're spending with your mistress, that your own brother wanted to know exactly what was going on. Oh no, you wouldn't think about that, would you? Because that's just what happened, so don't blame me for the fool you're making of yourself.'

Jarrod pulled her roughly into his arms, moving angrily to the slow melodious music. 'Okay, point taken. But don't talk to me like that again.'

'Someone has to tell you,' she said heatedly, stiff and unrelaxed in his arms. 'And I think I should also tell you that we might as well forget about this phoney engagement. You aren't fooling anyone, especially Charles Howard. He knows exactly what's going on between you and his wife.'

Jarrod's grey eyes narrowed. 'Did he tell you that?' he demanded.

'He's been watching you all evening, and there's been plenty to see. If you can't keep your hands off her then you shouldn't have invited her here.'

'I have a better idea.' He pulled her so close to him she could feel the taut outline of his body. 'If we're seen to be so much in love that we seem inseparable people will forget I was ever with Selina tonight.'

'I wouldn't count on her husband forgetting.'

Jarrod put her arms about his shoulders. 'He will if you give a good performance.'

'A good performance?'

'Act as if you love me,' he explained roughly.

But she did! 'Why should I do that? That would

prove nothing, except that I'm in love with a man who loves another woman. I'm not going to make myself appear any more ridiculous than I do already.'

His grey eyes bore down into hers. 'You'll do this, Brooke, or you'll learn just what humiliation really is,' he told her grimly.

She flinched at the look in his eyes. 'Meaning?'

'Meaning that if you found my talking to Selina embarrassing you'll find I can do much worse things than that. I could make things so bad for you you'll feel like dying of shame. Especially as my family already consider us to be lovers,' he added cruelly.

Brooke gasped. 'They don't! Your mother said——'

'My mother believed me about the weekend, I said nothing about us not sleeping together at other times. I'm thirty-seven, Brooke, I haven't lived that long without a certain amount of physical relationships. I admit it, I'm not ashamed of the fact. So as you're my fiancée they would naturally expect us to be—— Well, I'm sure you can draw your own conclusions.'

'Oh God!' She danced against him automatically, uncaring that they were moving slowly to music that required much faster movements. They looked like a couple so much in love that they wanted only to be close to each other, everything else irrelevant to both of them.

If only that were the case, but she wasn't even aware of the music or the other people in the room. She hadn't thought of people assuming they had that sort of relationship, and she now found it so embarrassing she couldn't look anywhere but at him.

'That's terrible!' she groaned.

Jarrod laughed, a deep throaty sound that mocked. 'Don't be such an innocent, Brooke, engaged couples often do, you know.'

'So you keep saying. But it isn't my idea of an engagement,' she said resentfully.

'You're nothing but a little prude!'

'At least I have some morals,' she burst out angrily. 'Unlike some people. Doesn't it bother you that Charles Howard is a friend of yours, that people openly know of your affair with his wife?'

He had that cold angry look on his face now. 'Would you believe me if I said it did?'

'No.'

'That's what I thought, that's why I've made no effort to deny your accusations. You've already made up your mind about me and I wouldn't like to ruin any of your illusions.'

'I doubt you could ever do that,' she scorned. 'Everyone warned me when I came to work for you, everyone knew your reputation with women. But I still thought you——'

'Yes?' he prompted.

She hesitated about continuing, realising she had been about to admit to her attraction to him. 'You're very attractive,' she finished abruptly. 'I'm sure I'm not the first female to tell you that. I thought you quite romantic, very sophisticated. But then I found I didn't like the games sophisticated people play, that I didn't like you very much. I like you even less now.'

He looked down at her as her bright head rested on his shoulder. 'No one would believe it to look at you,' he taunted.

Instantly she moved away from him, but he stilled her movements, making her gasp at the force of his body on hers. 'Let me go!' she ordered. 'Stop making an exhibition out of us!'

He forced her to remain still. 'You're doing that,' he growled angrily. 'People expect to see us gazing into each other's eyes, so do it!'

She obstinately continued to look away from him. 'I don't like your eyes,' she declared childishly. 'They're cruel and unkind.' And incredibly sexy, she could have added. Grey eyes that could be coolly calculating could also be dark with sleepy passion,

passion she had aroused only once but assuredly knew existed.

'They probably are at this moment,' Jarrod agreed carelessly.

'They are most of the time,' she added bitchily.

He laughed at her anger. 'Okay, off you go and act the gracious hostess.' He pushed her away from him. 'Your acting is lousy, I'll have to give you some private lessons.'

Her face aflame, she rushed away from the taunting mockery of his face, well aware of what sort of lessons he had in mind. And she had no defence against the brand of seduction he practised.

She found herself standing with Jean, her boy-friend Nathaniel off dancing with one of the other girls from the Stone office building. 'Everything all right?' she asked her friend.

Jean gave her a glowing smile. 'Lovely. Mr Stone's family are all very nice. I've had a chat with all of them and they aren't in the least snobbish. His father is a real charmer.'

'Yes. Thank you for the perfume, Jean. It's my favourite brand.'

'That's what I thought. This actually seems real now, your engagement and everything. It seemed unbelievable at first, but now I've seen the two of you together I can understand how you feel. I was so excited yesterday when Mr Stone invited Nathaniel and me to your party.'

'I knew absolutely nothing about it,' Brooke smiled. 'Jarrod's very good at keeping secrets.' He was also a better actor than she was if Jean genuinely believed him to be in love with her.

'Mm, I could see how disappointed you were today when everyone seemed to have forgotten your birthday. As if we would!'

'Jarrod explained how you were sworn to secrecy.' Brooke was once again aware that Jarrod was talking to Selina Howard.

She chatted to Jean and her other friends for the next hour or more and never once did Jarrod leave his mistress's side. Brooke found this very humiliating and she knew Charles Howard was displeased by it too.

She felt quite relieved when the party eventually broke up and Jarrod drove her home. She had more or less decided to give him back his ring by the time they reached her home. She could put up with this deceit, but she wouldn't be humiliated in this way.

She got out of the car as he held the door open for her. 'Thank you for my party,' she said formally. 'It was very thoughtful of you.'

He quirked an eyebrow. 'It was all I could do on your twenty-first birthday. It would have looked very strange if I hadn't given you a party.'

Brooke bridled angrily. 'I didn't think you'd made the gesture out of kindness.'

'I'm sure you know me better than to think that,' he taunted.

'I'm getting to know you very well,' she snapped. 'And what I'm learning I don't like!' She turned on her heel to enter the building.

'Aren't you going to invite me in for coffee?' he called after her softly.

She turned round fiercely to look at him, subconsciously noticing how handsome he looked as he leant back against the sleek car they had driven up in only seconds earlier. 'Do you want to come in for coffee?' she asked breathlessly.

'Would I be asking if I didn't? Besides, someone has to carry in your presents.'

She shrugged. 'Okay then, you'd better come in.' She went in without bothering to wait and see if he followed her.

Once inside she put her jacket and handbag in the bedroom before walking over to the kitchen to prepare the requested coffee. She was only halfway across the lounge when a hand shot out and pulled her hard against an unyielding body.

She looked up at Jarrod with defiant eyes. 'What do you want now? Haven't I already made recompense enough for one evening?'

Grey eyes glittered down at her before the dark head swooped down and firm punishing lips descended on hers, forcing her soft lips apart with ruthless brutality. For long seconds the world seemed to spin dizzily as she clung to him for support. And then she was free, rubbing her hand across her bruised mouth as he moved away from her

Her eyes were pools of deep violet hurt as she gazed up at him reproachfully. 'What did you do that for?' she asked accusingly.

Jarrod looked unperturbed, a devilish glint in his grey eyes. 'You've been asking for that all evening.'

'I have not! I——'

'Oh yes, you have,' he told her calmly, unmoved by her anger. 'You've been giving me filthy looks all night and——'

'Only because of the time you spent with that woman! Everyone noticed it and——'

'And launching into a string of accusations every time we've spoken,' he continued as if she hadn't interrupted him. 'You've just received your punishment, remember it for future reference. I have my own method of revenge. And just for the record, I couldn't give a damn about what other people think. Now,' he flexed his shoulder muscles, 'perhaps you wouldn't mind driving me home? Forget the coffee, that was just a way of getting in here.'

Brooke frowned. 'Drive you home? Don't you feel well?'

'I feel fine.' He handed her the car keys. 'But as it's your car I thought perhaps you might like to garage it downstairs. Besides, I'd like to be with you the first time you drive it, an Aston Martin is slightly different from a Mini,' he added mockingly.

She paled. 'That car—the Aston Martin—— It's *mine*?' She looked down at the car keys in disbelief.

He nodded. 'Your birthday present from me. Of course if you would rather have something else, a Porsche, or a Ferrari, then I don't mind changing it.'

She gave a choked laugh. Jarrod had given her an Aston Martin for her birthday and said she could change it if she preferred another car. Change it! It was a dream of a car—and Jarrod had *given* it to her!

CHAPTER SIX

BROOKE shook her head. 'You can't mean it,' she said huskily.

Jarrod shrugged. 'Of course I mean it. It should be quite easy to change the make of car, and the colour too if you would prefer something different.'

She gave a breathless laugh. 'That wasn't what I meant. I meant that you can't really want to give me a car like that for my birthday. I don't expect anything from you.'

He frowned darkly, all humour leaving his face. 'I didn't get you it because it was expected of me,' he rasped coldly. 'Every girl should have something special for her twenty-first birthday.'

'But a car like that!' she pointed out desperately.

'I'm glad you like it.'

'I love it, but I couldn't possibly——'

'My wife will be expected to have a style of car fitting for her position in life.'

Brooke gasped. 'Your wife? But I'm not going to be your wife. This is all an act, a ruse.'

He nodded agreement and sat down in one of her armchairs. 'You might as well sit down too, I think we have some talking to do.'

She dropped into the chair rather than sat down. 'We—we do?'

'Yes.' He watched her through narrowed thoughtful grey eyes. 'Now don't start to panic when you hear what I'm going to say. All right?'

'All right,' she agreed apprehensively.

'Okay then,' he sighed. 'I think we should get married.'

'What!' Brooke sprang out of the chair to glare

down at him as he watched her so calmly. He had no right to look so composed when she had been reduced to a quivering mass of nerves! 'What did you say?' she asked shakily.

'You said you wouldn't panic,' he reminded her impatiently. 'And if that isn't panic you're showing it's a very good impression of it.'

Brooke gave him a disgusted look. 'Of course it's panic. When I said I wouldn't I had no idea you were going to say something so outrageous.'

'It wasn't outrageous, I merely suggested that we do what everyone is expecting of us and get married. What's so outrageous about that?'

She almost choked in her effort to give him all the reasons in one go, finally saying the one that seemed to matter the most. 'We aren't in love with each other.'

Jarrod raised one dark eyebrow. 'Does that matter?'

'I would have thought so if we intended getting married.'

'It's not necessary. We have something else equally volatile.'

Her eyes widened. 'We do?'

Instantly his eyes darkened almost to black and he stood up in one slow fluid movement. Brooke stood mesmerised as he came towards her, her head back to look up at him as his arms passed around her waist to pull her close against the lean length of his body.

'Wh—what do we have?' She fought for sanity, aware of the weakness of her lower limbs at his closeness, of the even rise and fall of his chest just inches in front of her fixed gaze.

'Don't you know?' he murmured, his dark head bending so he could nuzzle his mouth against her arched throat.

Slow drugging kisses to her skin had her breathless within seconds, her arms clinging about his neck, her pulse sounding so loud it seemed like a bass drum to her ears.

She cleared her throat. 'No, I—I don't know.'

His strong firm hands ran experimentally over her body, lingering on her taut breasts. 'Oh, you know, Brooke,' he groaned throatily. 'Your body knows it too.'

His mouth claimed hers, and her lips blossomed beneath the cajoling seduction he chose to exert, knowing with all his experience that he could arouse her to the heights so easily. She gave up all pretence of appearing unmoved, knowing that she gave herself away at a touch of those sure tanned hands.

Her breath was coming in short gasps when his lips finally released hers, her eyes glazed with feeling. She shivered as his mouth travelled across her cheek to her earlobe, his hands moulding the contours of her body to the hardness of his.

'Jarrod?' she queried tremulously.

He didn't raise his head. 'Can't you feel it too, the attraction between us?'

She knew she was attracted to him, she couldn't deny it when she melted in his arms like this, but how did he feel about her? He wasn't a man to show his feelings for any woman, except the beautiful Mrs Howard, and Brooke knew she was no competition for her.

She moved against his probing mouth, cherishing these few moments in his arms. These kisses were nothing like his earlier punishing onslaught, and she was loving every moment of being this close to him.

'Don't you feel it?' he persisted, straightening slightly to look down at her, his eyes black with desire.

'Yes, I—I suppose I do.' She was embarrassed by the look in his eyes. 'But what difference does that make? You're in love with Selina Howard.'

He scowled. 'Forget Selina, for God's sake! I'm only interested in you and me at this moment in time.'

'Forget her!' Brooke scoffed. 'How can I forget the woman you're openly having an affair with?'

His hands tightened painfully on her arms. 'You're

going to accuse me of that just once too often,' he ground out viciously. 'But I want you, Brooke, and I don't think you'll let me have you any other way but through marriage.'

'You're right.'

'Okay, so so we get married.'

Her head was thrown back defiantly. 'I may only be a little nobody, but I wouldn't marry a man knowing he was in love with someone else.'

'You'll marry me,' he promised. 'I'll see to that.'

His head lowered and his kiss was totally savage, a deliberate onslaught on the senses, and in her already heightened state she had no way of denying him her full response. She shivered in sensuous delight as he slipped her dress off one shoulder to caress her skin with his rousing lips.

Jarrod swung her effortlessly up into his arms, his lips still firmly in control of her as she made to protest at his progress towards her bedroom. But those lips just kept on kissing her until she felt drugged by her own emotion, making not a murmur of protest as he lowered her down on to the bed before joining her with such rapidity his lips never left hers.

Her dress was no barrier to his searching hands and her breasts flowered under his touch as he slipped the dress completely off her shoulders and down her body. He discarded his jacket, removing his bow-tie, and leaving it to her to do the rest.

Brooke needed no second bidding, completely un-buttoning the silky shirt to slip it off his shoulders. It wasn't the first time she had seen his naked torso, and yet the heat of his body against her own bare skin was enough to launch her into ecstatic delight.

'Do you want me now?' he asked as his lips teased the tip of one taut breast.

'I——' she gasped with the pleasure of feeling he was evoking. 'Oh God, Jarrod! Please stop now, I can't stand any more.'

'Do you want me?' he repeated harshly.

She flung her head from side to side in an effort to escape those pleasure-giving but drugging lips. 'Don't make me say it, Jarrod,' she begged. 'Don't make me answer.'

He pinned her to the bed by her wrists, his legs also helping to hold her immovable. 'Tell me you want me, Brooke. Tell me!'

'I want you, I want you!' she cried, her eyes wild.

'And you'll marry me?' His hold on her wrists tightened, forcing her to answer him.

'No, I——'

His lips descended before she had time to even think of evasive action. The kisses he devoured her with over the next few minutes were just as destructive as his earlier caresses, and Brooke's hands were buried deep in the dark thickness of his hair long before he raised his head again.

His breathing was ragged and his heartbeat sounded just as loud as her own. 'If you're very wise, Brooke, you'll agree to marry me. It could just be the one thing that will stop me taking you here and now.'

She knew he meant what he said and she also knew she wouldn't be able to resist him; he had aroused her too easily for her to be able to do that. At least he was offering her marriage, even while knowing it wasn't necessary. He was a man of experience, he would undoubtedly know he could take her any time he chose, without the least opposition from her.

But still she fought against the fate of having to marry a man in love with another woman and feeling only desire for the woman he offered marriage to. He might think that second best was better than nothing, but she had other ideas. 'I can't do it, it wouldn't be right.'

'Right!' he scorned. 'What's *right* about desire? It's a gnawing ache inside you that has to be assuaged. I want you and I'm not prepared to see my brother walk off with the prize.'

She struggled against him in the darkness, but all her efforts were futile against his superior strength. 'What does Dave have to do with us?' she demanded, admitting her defeat by slumping back against the pillows.

Jarrod gave a harsh laugh. 'My little brother is already half in love with you—and don't deny it, because you know it's true. And he would offer you marriage. But I don't aim to let him have you. You're already half mine, and I mean to possess all of you.'

'I am not yours!' she exploded angrily. 'I belong to whom I want to belong,' she added defiantly.

His eyes glittered down at her dangerously. 'And who else have you already belonged to?' His eyes slid insolently over her almost naked body. 'No doubt you've used the power of this delectable body to taunt the hell out of other men.'

This time she did wrench away from him and up off the bed altogether, tugging her dress back over her shoulders and pulling up the zip with agitated fingers. She turned to glare at him, resenting the easy way he sat up on the bed and began to pull on his hastily discarded shirt.

'What I have or haven't done in my lifetime is none of your affair,' she pushed back her tousled hair. 'Get out of here—right now!'

Jarrod stood up slowly, buttoning his shirt before tucking it back into the low waistband of his trousers. He watched her through amused eyes as she threw his tie at him.

'Get out of here, damn you!' she almost screamed the words.

He slipped on his jacket in unhurried movements, putting the bow-tie in his pocket. 'I'll bring you to your knees before I've finished with you,' he taunted softly. 'I'll have you begging me to marry you, you'll see.'

'Like hell you will!' she blazed.

'Oh, I will, Brooke. I'll twist you up in knots so tight you'll be glad to marry me just to find the release I can give you.'

'Physical gratification,' she said in disgust.

'Don't mock it,' he warned. 'You won't find it so disgusting in a couple of weeks either.' He smiled, a cruel taunting smile. 'I'll look forward to seeing you grovel.'

'Go to hell!'

'I'm going home,' he corrected mockingly. 'But I'll see you tomorrow evening.'

Brooke looked at him sharply. 'Tomorrow evening?'

'Mm,' he nodded. 'The start of the torture.'

She shook her head dazedly. 'I don't understand you. Why me?' she pleaded.

'Why not you? I want you, not just once or twice, but for all time. I could take you now, but if I did that you would never want to see me again. So I'm going to marry you.'

'But what about Selina Howard?'

He shrugged. 'I can't marry her, she already has a very possessive husband.'

'Oh, I see, you mean to marry me because you can't marry the woman you really want.'

Jarrod gave a throaty chuckle. 'You silly child,' he scolded almost gently. 'You felt my desire for you a moment ago, that was for you, no one else.' He bent his head to claim her lips in a brief kiss. 'Tomorrow I begin my pursuit in earnest. I hope you're ready for that.'

'Oh, go away!' she retorted, more shaken by his threat than she cared to admit.

She waited until she heard the door close behind him before breaking down, deep racking sobs shuddering through her body. He had no right to play on her desire in this way, no right to torment her as he had. And if he meant to do what he said it could only get worse.

*

'It was a fantastic party last night,' Jean enthused half-way through the morning, the first break the two of them had had in their daily routine.

'Thank you,' Brooke replied distantly, unwilling to enter into any conversation about last night. She was doing her best to forget the events of the latter part of the evening and hoped Jarrod had done the same.

'Everyone said what a great time they had.' Jean obviously hadn't noticed her reluctance concerning the subject.

Jarrod seems to be adept at arranging things like that.'

'Your Jarrod's dreamy!' Jean became starry-eyed. 'I never would have thought him capable of being that human. He always appeared haughty and slightly re-moved from the rest of us poor mortals.'

He was also devious and selfish and totally without morals. He used people—well, he used her—shame-lessly. And he was going to get even more demanding. Brooke had to admit that the thought of it both excited and frightened her. And she wasn't sure which feeling was going to be predominant next time she saw him.

'He's just a man.' She shrugged. 'Like any other, he needs a woman.' Often in the plural, she could have added. He would obviously still be seeing Mrs Howard even while determined to make Brooke want to marry him.

Jean raised a questioning eyebrow. 'You sound very —well, a bit fed up, actually. Aren't you really excited about marrying Mr Stone? I know I would be.'

She wouldn't be marrying him if she had her way— no matter how much she really wanted to. With his experience of women he would soon realise that she was in love with him, probably believing that she would be gullible enough to put up with his affairs. Well, she wouldn't marry him and give him that power over her, and she wouldn't become his wife to hide his affair with another woman either.

She smiled wanly. 'Sorry, Jean. Late nights don't agree with me.'

Jean grimaced. 'Me neither. But it was such a lovely surprise for you. Mr Stone was——'

She broke off, and turning in the direction of her gaze Brooke saw the reason why. Jarrod had just stepped out of his private lift and was walking with purposeful strides over to the reception desk.

Brooke blushed under the force of his unflinching stare, unconsciously noting how attractive he looked in his dark business suit. She fidgeted nervously as she waited for him to reach her desk, looking impatiently at the diamond ring he forced her to wear as proof of his possession.

As if he had seen that look he deliberately lifted up the hand containing his ring, his eyes glittering with barely suppressed humour as he watched her reaction. She steeled herself to make none and saw his amusement deepen. His manner gave her the feeling of a very small mouse being tormented by a cruel feline.

'Brooke darling,' he murmured softly, his hold on her hand not loosening, 'I'm going to be out the rest of the day.'

She wanted to ask what that had to do with her, but knew he wouldn't let her get away with that. 'Yes?' she queried huskily, all the time conscious of his thumb slowly caressing the palm of her hand.

'So I brought your car in today—as you were too tired to drive me home last night,' he added mockingly. 'And I'll be using it to go to my business appointment.' His mouth tightened as he saw the disbelieving look in her eyes that it was a business meeting and her hand was instantly set free. 'I just want to reassure you that I'll be around at eight-thirty and you can have your car back then.'

'Thank you.' She didn't want his wretched car! And she didn't want to see him tonight either, didn't want him to destroy her peace of mind any more than he already had.

He bent forward and kissed her lingeringly on her parted lips. It wasn't a caress he hurried over, and by the time he raised his head Brooke was breathless— with embarrassment *and* excitement.

She fumed up at him silently, her eyes deep violet pools of frustrated anger. How dared he! How dared he kiss her here in full view of anyone who cared to look! And plenty of people were doing just that!

'Just to keep me going until tonight, darling,' he murmured throatily, taunting her with the steely glint in his eyes. He straightened, turning to smile at the gaping Jean. 'Good morning,' he grinned at her. 'No ill effects from last night, I hope?'

Jean glowed. 'No, thank you, Mr Stone. I had a lovely time.'

'Good.' He nodded to them both. 'Goodbye for now, then, ladies. I'll see you later, Brooke,' he added with a warmth that almost made her cringe.

She didn't answer him, pretending an interest in the person making enquiries at her desk. The poor man had to repeat himself three times before she heard what he was trying to ask her. She finally sent him off quite happily to the fifth floor.

She hardly dared turn and look at Jean once they were restored to peace and quiet again, but she knew that inevitably she had to. She sighed. 'Okay, Jean, you're right, he *is* very attractive. But he—well, he unnerves me, especially here at work.'

Jean grinned. 'He would unnerve me too if he kissed me like that.'

Brooke blushed anew. 'Don't tease, Jean. I'm embarrassed enough already.'

This time her friend took the hint and changed the subject, talking about things that were much less personal to Brooke.

By eight-fifteen that evening she had worked herself up into a great state of nerves. His display in reception today had more than shown her that he meant to carry out his threat to make her want him enough to marry him.

But she already did! She wanted him now, he had no need to make her want him any more. How was she supposed to cope with the brand of sensual attraction he exuded with every pore of his body? She had the feeling she wasn't going to be able to—and he knew it.

Jarrod arrived at exactly eight-thirty, walking into her flat before holding out the car keys to her. 'Yours,' he said with a grin.

Brooke weighed the keys in her hand. 'I would rather not if you don't mind.'

He ignored her words and settled himself comfortably on the sofa. He was dressed more casually than she had ever seen him before, and this casualness gave their relationship an intimacy she had been determined to avoid. He wore tan leather boots, cream corduroy trousers that moulded to the firm length of his thighs, a cream silk shirt opened almost down to his waist, and a short brown leather jerkin. He looked very tall and very attractive, and her pulse raced just at the sight of him.

She looked down at her own clothes, realising that her deliberate donning of denims and checked shirt had all been in vain. And she had the feeling that Jarrod had known exactly what she had been going to do, hence his own attire.

'Have you had dinner?' he asked.

'Yes, thank you. I don't want it, Jarrod,' she said firmly, unconsciously using his first name.

'I've already eaten too.'

'Jarrod!' she glared at him. 'You're deliberately ignoring me.'

Grey eyes raked over her with slow appraisal and she was blushing profusely by the time his gaze settled back on her face. 'I'm not ignoring you, Brooke,' he denied huskily. 'The opposite, I would have thought.'

'You know what I mean,' she sighed. 'I don't want the car. It—it smacks too much like payment,' she said defiantly.

'Payment for what?' he asked softly.

'For—for—I don't know what for!' She gave him a furious look. 'Yes, I do! It looks like payment for services rendered.'

He gave a throaty chuckle, not angered as she had expected him to be, *hoped* he would be. If she angered him enough there was always the chance that he might walk out. But there didn't appear to be much anger about him as he smiled up at her, sitting forward to remove his jacket.

Jarrod turned back the cuffs of his shirt to just below his elbows. 'It's very hot tonight,' he offered by way of explanation. 'And I haven't noticed you providing much of a service,' he added tauntingly.

Brooke's cheeks flamed fiery red; the situation, as always, had backfired on her. 'Perhaps you like to pay in advance,' she returned bitchily.

'Not usually,' he replied thoughtfully. 'You could get let down that way. You know, a case of take the money and run.'

'Then take back your damned car!'

'It isn't mine. It was bought in your name and is registered to you.'

She turned away. 'You don't understand—or you don't want to. I'm an ordinary working girl—okay, I accept that for the moment I'm involved in your life, but when that's over I'm not even going to be able to afford the insurance on the car, let alone the weekly petrol.'

'It's never going to be over between us, Brooke. You're mine and before long you're going to admit it to me.'

'On bended knees,' she scorned.

He nodded. 'If necessary.'

'Never!'

Jarrod gave a knowing smile. 'Never is a long, long time, Brooke darling. And I can be quite determined when I make up my mind to do something. Ask any of my business colleagues.'

'Oh, I don't need to do that, I already know how domineering you can be.'

'Then why don't you sit down and relax?' he invited huskily, patting the sofa beside him.

Brooke moved away jerkily. 'Why don't you go and see Selina Howard? I'm sure she would be overjoyed to see you.'

'I doubt it,' he said dryly. 'She and Charles always spend their wedding anniversary together. I wouldn't like to interrupt.'

'Oh.'

He was openly laughing at her now. 'Sit down, Brooke,' he repeated. 'No, not over there,' he said as she went to sit in one of the armchairs. 'Over, here, next to me.'

'No, thank you,' she answered primly. 'What are you planning to do this evening?'

'Nothing, absolutely nothing.' Jarrod leant back against the sofa, legs splayed out in front of him. 'Why, what did you have in mind?'

'Nothing. But—but surely you don't intend just spending the evening here with me?'

'And the night too, if you would let me.'

'I won't!'

'I didn't think so. Put some music on, hmm?'

She moved to the record cabinet. 'What sort of music do you like?'

'Something romantic,' he murmured.

'R—romantic?'

'Mm,' he said throatily. 'Then you can come and sit next to me and I'll whisper sweet nothings in your shell-like ear.'

Brooke gave him a furious look for his mockery, deliberately choosing one of Leo Sayer's L.P.s that was anything but romantic. She sat down with a smile of satisfaction, enjoying the music but knowing it didn't meet Jarrod's approval.

When it moved on to the second number Jarrod stood up and turned the record off. 'Not that I don't like Leo Sayer, but those sort of songs don't exactly stir the senses.'

'They weren't meant to,' she said determinedly.

'That's what I thought.' He flicked through the extensive record collection, music of all kinds being Brooke's weakness. 'Barry Manilow or Johnny Mathis?'

'Johnny Mathis, please,' she answered instantly. 'Some of Barry Manilow's tend to be a little sad.'

Instead of going back to the sofa after putting on the requested record he came to sit on the arm of her chair. 'We have a lot of the same tastes in music,' he murmured softly.

Brooke obstinately looked away from him, although she could see his muscular thigh out of the corner of her eye. 'That's about all we do have in common,' she told him curtly, determined not to be moved by his closeness.

But how could she not be when just to look at him aroused her! He was so handsome, so dynamic. But she must remember that even though he expressed a wish to make love to her, would even go to the length of marrying her to get what he wanted, all the time he was having an affair with a married woman, an affair that wouldn't stop in the event of his own marriage.

These thoughts hardened her resolve not to be affected by his closeness, by the all male smell of him. It was so destructive just being near him like this!

His hand moved to touch one of her hot cheeks, the thumb moving caressingly over her soft creamy skin. 'I think we have more than that in common,' he said softly, his grey eyes never leaving her averted face. 'And we could have more if you would just let it happen. Have you always had these inhibitions?'

Her gaze swung angrily to his taunting face, only to look hurriedly away again at the warmth in his eyes. He was seducing her with a look and she couldn't stand it. Before he could stop her she had moved out of the chair and stood a few feet away watching him warily.

'I don't have inhibitions at all. You just—you just——'

'Yes?' He relaxed back in the chair she had so recently vacated.

'I don't want to have an affair!'

'Neither do I, not unless it's going to lead to marriage.' Jarrod sighed. 'Sit down again, Brooke. I promise to stay right here. We'll talk, nothing else.'

'What do we have to talk about?'

He shrugged. 'You can tell me more about your childhood. This aunt of yours—what was she like, besides her desire to hit out at a child?'

Off the subject of marriage, Brooke relaxed slightly, moving to the sofa to sit down. 'She was a lot older than my mother, there were fifteen years' difference in their ages.'

'And this aunt never married?'

'No, but then I could have been partly responsible for that. The prospect of a five-year-old child to look after would daunt a lot of men.'

Jarrod shook his head. 'Your aunt would already have been fortyish when she took you into her care, plenty of time to marry if she'd wanted to.'

'No—you see, she had to look after my mother for several years too.'

'Ah, I see.'

'Do you have to say it like that?' she asked resentfully.

He raised his eyebrows. 'Sorry. It just seemed to me——'

'I'm well aware of what it seemed to you. But Aunt Emma always said she didn't want to marry. '

'She didn't like men,' he stated dryly.

'Not my father, anyway.'

His eyes quickened with interest. 'Are you sure? How old was your father when he died?'

'He was ten years older than my mother, so that would make him thirty-five.' Her brow creased in puzzlement. 'What are you implying?'

'Only that the emotion your aunt felt towards your father might not have been dislike.'

'You're surely not trying to say that Aunt Emma *fancied* my father?' Brooke's horror was evident in her face.

'Is that so hard to believe?'

'It's disgusting!'

'What's so disgusting about a healthy woman feeling attracted to a handsome man?'

'But the man was my father, and he was married to Aunt Emma's *sister*!'

He shrugged. 'That doesn't mean she couldn't fall in love with him.'

Brooke stood up to pace the room. 'I can't believe it —She couldn't—But it——' He was right! She knew with startling clarity that he had guessed the reason for her aunt's hatred and jealousy of her sister's happiness. All these years she had wondered at her aunt's resentment of her, and within a few days of knowing her Jarrod had discovered that reason.

'I'm right, aren't I?' he asked gently.

'Yes,' she choked, 'I think you are.'

He moved quickly as he saw her distress, sitting down beside her on the sofa and pulling her into his arms. 'Hey,' he crooned softly into her hair. 'I didn't mean to upset you.'

'It was—was just such a shock,' she mumbled against his chest. 'I didn't mean to be emotional about it.'

'I shouldn't have surprised it on you like that.' He lifted her chin. 'I could be wrong, you know.'

'No, you aren't,' she sniffed inelegantly. 'I should

have realised before. It just never occurred to me.'

'You would have to have a devious mind like mine to think of it,' he murmured softly, his mouth only inches away from her own. 'Oh, Brooke, Brooke, kiss me . . .'

'Jarrod . . .' She kissed him like never before, clinging to him in complete abandonment. What did all the fighting and arguing matter when she could be in his arms like this?

He took her lips in slow drugging kisses that racked her body into sensuous pleasure, lowering her back against the length of the sofa before lying at her side.

Their caresses became fevered and she raised not one word of protest as he unbuttoned her shirt with sure quick movements, pushing aside the thin material to bury his face in her creamy skin.

'God, Brooke,' he groaned raggedly, 'don't you ever wear a bra?' His voice thickened with desire as he took the tip of one hardened nipple into his mouth, arousing her body to even greater heights.

Her sharp intake of breath precluded her answer for several long pleasurable seconds. 'I—er—I find them a cumbersome article of clothing,' she said finally.

Jarrod raised his dark head to look down at her partly naked body. 'Well, it's a sure fact you're lovely enough not to need one.' He caressed her with hands that seemed to burn where they touched. 'God, you're beautiful! So beautiful I'm almost afraid to touch you.'

Her arms moved up over his shoulders, her hands entwining in the dark thickness of his hair. 'Don't be afraid, Jarrod,' she invited. 'I like your touch.'

With a suddenness that took her completely by surprise he moved away from her to stand up, the passionate man of seconds earlier gone as if it had never been. Only the sight of her own nakedness remained to show her that it hadn't all been a dream. She fastened her shirt with shaking fingers.

'It's getting late,' he said abruptly. 'I have to leave. Don't bother to drive me home, I can get a taxi. I'll see you some time tomorrow evening. Goodnight.' He didn't look at her again but slammed out of the flat.

CHAPTER SEVEN

EVERY evening seemed to end the same way. They would talk for a while, listen to a few records, and then Brooke would somehow find herself in Jarrod's arms. Each night she promised herself that this time it would be different, that she wouldn't give in to the sensuous pressure of his mouth or the demand in his eyes, but each time she betrayed her resolve.

Jarrod controlled these interludes in a way that was totally infuriating. He knew exactly when she had almost lost control of her senses, knew when she would deny him nothing—and that was the time he always broke up their embrace.

Brooke knew that he purposefully used these frustrating tactics, that it was all part of his plan to bring her to her knees, and yet there was nothing she could do to stop it happening. As soon as he touched her she melted.

But tonight she knew things were going to be different as soon as she opened the door to him, knew it by the elegant dinner suit he wore. He hadn't said they were going out, so she didn't think she was included in his dinner engagement. She was right.

'Sorry I'm a little late.' He bent to kiss her fleetingly on the lips.

Brooke had become accustomed to these casual caresses by now, although they still excited her. 'Is there anything wrong?' She indicated the suit.

'I have to leave almost immediately,' he said with irritation. 'Something turned up unexpectedly.'

'Oh?' She gave him a knowing look.

Jarrod looked at her sharply. 'Don't you believe me?'

She shrugged. 'Why shouldn't I?'

'Because you don't,' he said with certainty. 'And I don't have the time to stay here and argue with you. An important business colleague arrived from the States this afternoon and I have to entertain him.'

'Oh, I see, a night out with the boys, hmm?'

'God, you can be so infuriating at times! But perhaps your attitude proves you can be jealous. A good sign,' Jarrod added with satisfaction.

'I wouldn't count on it being jealousy,' she told him coolly. Disappointment was a better word. Each evening she wondered if she would be strong enough to hold out against him, and yet now that he was leaving after only a few short minutes she was disappointed. 'Elation might be a better word,' she lied.

'Elation, is it!' he said grimly, pulling her effortlessly into his arms and forcing her lips apart with no sign of gentleness at all. He was bent on punishing her, and although she didn't want to respond there was nothing she could do to stop herself.

By the time he had finished the onslaught she lay limp in his arms, her lips swollen and aroused, her eyes slightly glassy.

Jarrod drew back to look at her, passion blazing as he saw the desire in her face. 'Damn Clive and his business dinner!' he groaned throatily. 'I'd much rather stay here with you.' His lips moved along her neck. 'Much rather,' he repeated with agonising intensity.

'But you can't.' It was almost a question.

'No, I can't.' His eyes half-closed as he continued to look at her. 'Oh God, I want you!'

Brooke wanted him too, but common sense was starting to return. He could just be trying to trick her into admitting defeat, as he had done in the past. And that was the one thing she wasn't going to do, not if it meant becoming the wife of a man in love with another woman.

She looked pointedly at her wrist-watch. 'It's getting

late, you'll be late for your dinner engagement.'

He too looked at the time. 'You're right, I have to leave now. How the hell I'm supposed to think and talk of business when all I have on my mind is you is going to be quite interesting. I'll probably babble about what a beautiful body you have in the middle of an important discussion,' he said self-disgustedly.

Brooke pouted. 'You don't consider my body important?'

His eyes darkened. 'At the moment I consider it the most important thing in the world,' he admitted thickly.

'But you'll get over it,' she taunted.

'You think so?' His mouth moved to caress her throat again. 'I'm not so sure.'

'You seem to get over it every other night, so why not tonight?'

He looked down at her, a mocking smile lighting his cynical features. 'That rankles, doesn't it?'

So she had fallen into his trap after all! She moved stiffly out of his restraining arms. 'Why should it?' she asked carelessly. 'I believe men get over these little disappointments much easier than women.'

Jarrod's snort of laughter showed his scorn for such a statement. 'You've just proved to me that you know little or nothing about the mechanism of men. We don't get over our disappointment at all. We may be able to dampen things down a little, but inevitably it flares up again. You don't hear of many rape cases being carried out by women.'

'But it does happen.'

'Oh, sure,' he grinned. 'But even so I don't believe it can be classed as rape. He may have been coerced into it in the beginning, but a man really has to be willing. I'm sure you know what I mean, you aren't that innocent.'

'I know what you mean,' she answered, her cheeks fiery red.

He laughed. 'I see you do.'

'Shouldn't you be leaving now?' she said hastily.

'Embarrassing you, am I?' he mocked.

'Not at all,' Brooke said sharply. 'But you did say you were in a hurry. I was just reminding you.'

'After being aroused so much I don't want to leave you at all,' he said derisively. 'God, you're torture to be with!'

'Then leave!' She turned away from him.

'I intend to—but I'll be back tomorrow. We'll go out to dinner and then on to a nightclub. Sunday we can spend the day together.'

'You seem to take it for granted that you can organise my free time for me,' she snapped resentfully.

He lifted her left hand, looking down at the ring he had put on her finger. '*This* gives me that right.'

Brooke snatched her hand away. 'I've told you before, it gives you no rights at all. Please go.' She pushed her hair back from her face. 'Please, Jarrod,' she implored him, before she broke down and begged him to stay.

'I'm going—but not because I want to.' He claimed one last kiss before moving swiftly to the door. 'I should get an early night, we could be out quite late tomorrow evening.'

'I'll go to bed when I damn well please!' She turned on him angrily.

'I thought you might.' He closed the door softly behind him.

Ooh, he was so infuriating, getting under her guard all the time! If only he weren't so attractive—and so expert when it came to lovemaking. But so he should be, he had had plenty of experience—too damned much!

Once again he had left leaving her quite unsatisfied, aroused her and then left her flat. Oh, this time he had expressed disappointment at their parting too, but it didn't ease the ache deep inside her or the restless feeling that would take hours to leave her.

When the doorbell rang again fifteen minutes later she thought Jarrod must have changed his mind and come back. Her face elated, she ran to the door. 'Oh, Jarrod, I——' She broke off as she saw who her visitor was. 'Dave,' she said weakly.

He looked a little hurt by her obvious disappointment at his identity. 'I'm afraid so,' he shrugged. 'Perhaps I called at an inconvenient time. You're obviously expecting Jarrod.' He turned away.

'Oh no, no, I'm not.' She put out a hand to delay him. 'Jarrod's already been and gone. He has a business engagement this evening. I just thought—well, I thought he might have forgotten something.' She could hardly say she had hoped he had come back to make love to her!

Dave looked slightly relieved. 'So you aren't expecting him back tonight?'

'No.' She opened the door further. 'Would you like to come in?'

'If you wouldn't mind.'

'No, I—I would be glad of the company. It's strange really, but even with so many people living in London it can still be the loneliest place in the world. I suppose it's because everyone has their own circle of friends and they rarely move out of that circle.' Brooke was aware that she was babbling nervously, but she didn't seem able to stop herself.

Dave looked about her sitting-room appreciatively. 'Nice flat you have here. You should see mine,' he grimaced. 'It's like a cupboard with a bed in.'

'Oh, but surely——'

'I know what you're going to say,' he interrupted. 'But I don't accept help from my family. Oh, they give me the usual boxes of food parents seem to think their children who have left home need, but that's all. I simply wouldn't fit in at the hospital if I were living in the lap of luxury while all my friends lived on the poverty line.'

'And is that important to you?'

'Fitting in?' He shrugged. 'I suppose so. Do you mind if I sit down?'

She blushed at her lack of manners. 'Please do. I'm sorry I didn't think of it earlier. The surprise of seeing you, I suppose,' she explained nervously. She sat down opposite him as he sat in one of the armchairs. 'I wasn't expecting anyone else tonight.'

'No, it is rather late.' He looked at his wrist-watch. 'Nine-fifteen. Did Jarrod leave very long ago?'

'He's been gone about half an hour, I should think.'

Dave grinned. 'It could have been rather embarrassing if he had been here. I know how suspicious my big brother can be,' he added by way of explanation. 'Lucky I picked a night when he had to be somewhere else.'

Brooke would have said fortunate, not lucky. Jarrod, in his possessive mood of late, would undoubtedly have suspected his brother's motives. She wasn't too sure of them herself, not after her birthday party when he had expressed such an interest in her himself. And she had to admit that he was very attractive.

'Yes,' was the only answer she gave to his statement.

Dave laughed. 'Hey, don't you start getting suspicious on me too! I've been meaning to come over and see you for weeks now. I would have been over earlier tonight, but I had to work late at the last minute. Perhaps it was as well I was later than I expected to be.'

'Because of Jarrod?'

'Mm. He's been very clamlike and possessive about his relationship with you. I've tried to talk to him several times about you, but he always changes the subject.'

'Probably because there's nothing to tell,' she evaded.

'Oh, come on, you're the interest of the year in his crowd. The girl to capture Jarrod Stone. That's no mean task, let me tell you.'

'I wouldn't exactly say I've captured him,' she denied

quickly. 'We're engaged, yes. But an engagement doesn't mean that much nowadays.'

Dave's interest quickened. 'Does that mean what I hope it means?'

Brooke's blue eyes never flickered once. 'What do you hope it means?'

'That you and Jarrod are breaking up.'

'I don't think that's the normal reaction of the brother of the engaged man. Or is it just that you don't approve of me for Jarrod?' She had sensed Dave's reluctance about them ever since she had first been introduced to him.

'For Jarrod, no—for me, yes.'

She gave an amazed laugh. 'Dave!' Humour wrestled with shock, and it was humour that finally won. 'How can you say such things?' she chuckled.

'It's the way I feel. The more I think about it the more I wish I'd met you first.'

'You're sure it's not just a case of wanting something that belongs to your brother?'

His candid blue eyes narrowed. 'And do you—belong to my brother, I mean?'

She blushed. 'We're engaged, so in a way I suppose I do.' According to Jarrod she belonged to him completely. Her mouth tightened at the thought of him.

Dave didn't miss that look. 'You don't exactly look ecstatic about that. And your engagement wasn't what I meant and you know it. I wondered if anything had changed since you were at the house together.'

The subject was embarrassing to Brooke and she wished he wouldn't pursue it. Things could have been very different for her and Jarrod by now if she had just verbally admitted how much she wanted and needed him instead of just physically capitulating. They could have been married by now and she wouldn't have these constant partings from him. The more she thought about it the more she wondered at herself for holding out against him. Pride, that's what it was, just pride.

And pride was a poor bedfellow.

'Well, we still haven't decided on our wedding date if that's what you mean,' she deliberately misunderstood him.

'You're being deliberately obtuse, you must have been taking lessons from Jarrod.'

She had been taking lessons from Jarrod, but not the sort Dave meant! 'I'm not being obtuse, Dave. There are just some things that are too private to talk about.'

'I see.' He chewed his bottom lip thoughtfully. 'And has Jarrod seen any more of the beautiful Mrs Howard?'

'How would I know?' she asked sharply. She had wondered the same thing herself, but as they had seen each other every night for the last two weeks she didn't think he could have had much opportunity. But where there was a will there was a way ...

'I really like you, Brooke,' Dave said gently. 'And I wouldn't like my big brother to hurt you in any way. If he's being faithful to you it will be the first time he's been faithful to any woman in his life.'

She gave a bitter smile. 'That's what I like, brotherly loyalty.'

Dave had the grace to flush a little. 'All's fair in love and war.'

'I don't think this could be called either of those things, not between the two of us anyway.'

'But with Jarrod it's different,' he said resignedly. 'If he feels that way about you why don't the two of you get married and stop putting temptation in my way? Or could it be that Jarrod is still holding out on actually getting married?'

Brooke shook her head. 'I'm sorry to disappoint you, Dave, but I'm the one holding out.'

'You are?' He didn't attempt to hide his surprise.

She nodded. 'Jarrod would get married tomorrow if I would agree to it. But marriage is the ultimate, and I want to be very sure before I make any definite agreement.'

'So you aren't sure?' Dave persisted eagerly.

She couldn't help laughing at his impetuosity, his complete lack of guile. She could imagine Jarrod had been very like Dave at this age, that once he had seen something he wanted he wouldn't rest until he got it. Maturity had given him a more subtle approach. And he used it shamelessly.

'I'm sure I love him, I'm just not sure a marriage between us would work.' She stood up, a tiny figure in her denims and checked shirt, her reddish-brown hair tumbling in disorder down her slender back. 'I'll make us some coffee.'

'Playing safe?' He quirked a mocking eyebrow.

'I am safe. Would you like some coffee? It's only instant, I'm afraid.'

'That will be fine. So you don't consider me a threat to Jarrod at all?' Dave looked disappointed, like a little boy denied a treat.

'I'm afraid not,' she told him gently. 'But I could do with a friend.'

He looked sulky. 'It wasn't what I had in mind.'

She chuckled. 'I'm sure it wasn't.' She went out into the kitchen.

She moved about the room with a familiarity that was habitual, preparing the tray with the coffee cups, humming to herself as she worked. She placed the tray on the coffee-table in front of Dave. 'Would you like something to eat? I don't suppose you've eaten if you came here straight from work.'

'I had something at about four-thirty, but I could eat a sandwich if it's not too much trouble.' He took the coffee cup she handed him.

'No trouble at all. Ham and tomato all right?'

'Fine. But drink your coffee first.'

'It won't take me two minutes. Are you sure you wouldn't prefer something a little more substantial? I have some steaks in the refrigerator. I could do you chips and peas with it,' she added temptingly.

He licked his lips at the sound of the appetising

meal, slowly shaking his head. 'You live well. I can't even afford mince, let alone steak.'

'I bought the steak because I thought Jarrod was staying to dinner,' she told him honestly. 'As a matter of fact I haven't had dinner myself yet.'

'In that case get cooking.' Dave smiled with relish. 'I shall enjoy eating the food intended for Jarrod.'

She grinned. 'I thought you might.'

She wasn't a good cook, but she could peel potatoes and get the chips cooking and open a packet of frozen peas with the best of them. The steaks were even simpler to cook and within twenty minutes she had the steaming hot meal on the table.

Dave's eyes lit up at the sight of the food and although he professed to be only moderately hungry he despatched the meal with consummate ease. Brooke opened a tin of cream to go with the apple pie she had and he ate this with similar gusto.

He sat back with a sigh of satisfaction. 'That was lovely. I could do with someone like you cooking for me full-time.'

'There wasn't much cooking involved. You could make yourself a meal like that if you wanted to. But I'm the same when I'm on my own, it just doesn't seem worth cooking for one. And I don't think, at this stage in your career, that a wife would be a good idea.' Brooke began to clear away the debris from the meal.

He raised one dark eyebrow. 'Who said anything about a wife?'

'But I thought—Oh, I see what you mean.' Her nose wrinkled up with disgust.

Dave chuckled at her expression. 'I thought you would. No wonder Jarrod finds you fascinating, your naïveté is charming. This is the age of the permissive society, or didn't you know that?'

'Does that mean we all have to forget our morals and jump into bed with anyone we care to?' she snapped, stung by his taunting tone. She marched out to the tiny kitchen and began to wash up noisily.

Dave had followed her out, shifting from one foot to the other as she continued to ignore him. 'Hey, I didn't mean to annoy you. It's just that most of the kids I know indulge in casual affairs.'

Brooke determinedly didn't look at him, handing him the cloth to dry the draining dishes. He had helped make them dirty so he could help with the work too. 'Including you?' she asked through stiff lips.

He was very red-faced. 'Well, I—I—— It's expected of a man!' he said defensively.

'Oh yes!' Brooke agreed scathingly. 'Don't say any more, I've heard it all before.'

'Hey, look—where do you come off preaching to me?' he asked nastily. 'You might look prim enough, but I actually saw you in bed with my brother. The whole family knew about it.'

She stopped what she was doing to glare at him. 'Jarrod explained to your mother exactly what had happened,' she said fiercely.

Dave looked equally angry. 'Oh yes, the nightmare you were supposed to have had. I doubt if it was true, you probably sleep with Jarrod all the time. It would be so easy to invent something like a nightmare to fool my parents.'

'Why, you——'

He threw the cloth down. 'You can't deny the evidence, Brooke. I saw you in my brother's arms, saw the possessive hold he had on you, as if you'd been together like that a lot.'

Her hand moved up as if in slow motion to slap him hard across the face. She was surprised at her action but not repentant. 'Don't judge everyone by your own rules,' she told him tautly.

Dave removed his hand from his stinging cheek, revealing the bright red weals on his face. His expression couldn't be called pleasant. 'There was no need for you to do that,' he said grimly. 'But I'll give you reason now,' and he took a threatening step towards her.

Brooke was becoming frightened now. This wasn't the Dave who had entered her flat, but a man with grim determination on his face. She backed away from him as far as she was able in the small confines of her kitchen. 'Don't be silly, Dave,' she trembled. 'You'll regret this.'

'I might do. But on the other hand it might be worth it. You have to possess something more than beauty to hold on to Jarrod.'

'I don't think your opinion of Jarrod is any more complimentary than the one you have of me!'

By this time he had her firmly pinned against the wall. 'I respect and love Jarrod more than anyone else I've ever known,' he contradicted. 'He's everything I ever want to be.' One of his hands moved to caress her suddenly pale cheeks.

'I see. I suppose it's all this love and respect you have for him that's making you make a pass at his fiancée,' she scorned, more frightened than she cared to admit. Dave was almost as well built and muscular as Jarrod, and he had an equal amount of determination.

'No,' he disagreed mildly. 'It's you that's making me do that, you with your coolness that makes me want to melt you until you're on fire for me.' His mouth tightened. 'As Jarrod has no doubt seen you any amount of times.'

She blushed. It was true, Jarrod had seen her like that, aroused and aflame with wanting him. 'You— you're mad! Jarrod will kill you for this.'

Dave shook his head, a slight smile on his lips. 'Jarrod will never know.'

'Oh yes, he will! I——'

'Won't tell him,' he finished for her. 'Because if you did I would have to tell him that you invited me over here this evening, encouraging me until it became impossible for me to refuse you.'

'He wouldn't believe you.' But there was a ring of uncertainty in her voice, a fact Dave was quick to notice.

'Would you like to risk it?' he murmured, lowering his head to caress her throat with his mouth.

She squirmed away from him. 'Please don't do this, Dave. Please,' she pleaded.

He didn't answer her, but pulled her fully into his arms and claimed possession of her lips. Brooke could have found the locality of this attack amusing if she wasn't quite so annoyed. Dave certainly hadn't chosen the most romantic of places to try and seduce her, surrounded by washing-up as they were.

As if sensing this, with a dexterity that surprised her, he had led her into the lounge, lying beside her on the sofa. Their closeness reminded her poignantly of Jarrod and other evenings when he had strained her to him with equal passion.

Dave was very like Jarrod to look at and it was easy to imagine that the lips demanding a response from her own were his, that he was right here with her and not out with a business colleague, if indeed that was who it was.

She was no longer fighting Dave, but she wasn't responding either, lying quietly in his arms as he further explored her creamy throat. That he was fully aroused she knew by the hardness of his thighs, and yet the knowledge didn't repulse her. It would be so easy to imagine him as Jarrod and give in to the longing that always enveloped her whenever she was in his arms.

'I want you, Brooke,' Dave murmured throatily.

'Unfortunately, so do I,' remarked a quietly controlled voice from above them. 'And I believe I have first claim to her.'

Dave shot up off the sofa at the first sound of his brother's voice. 'Jarrod! What are you doing here?'

Brooke could have asked him the same question, but on seeing the dangerous glitter in his eyes she was glad she hadn't. He hadn't looked at her yet, his anger was all centred on Dave at the moment. She sat up dazedly on the sofa, watching the two of them as if they were strangers to her.

Jarrod came further into the room, removing the black bow-tie he had been wearing, unbuttoning the top two buttons of his shirt before removing his jacket, a cold hard look on his face.

He looked at his younger brother. 'The same thing as you, I should imagine,' he answered curtly. 'But Brooke should remember when she has invited one lover to spend the night with her before inviting another. It could prove embarrassing—for her,' he added harshly.

She gasped at his words. 'But, Jarrod, I——'

'Weren't expecting me back just yet?' he finished for her, sitting down in one of the armchairs to look at the two of them interestedly, only the slate grey of his eyes showing just how furious he really was. 'I know that. I would say it was pretty obvious,' he added grimly.

Dave looked at Brooke, disgust written all over his face. 'Did you know Jarrod was coming back here to-night?' he demanded of her.

'Well, I——'

'Of course she did,' interrupted Jarrod. 'I stay here most nights now.' He smiled, but it couldn't be called a pleasant smile. 'I'm trying to pursuade Brooke that she would be a fool not to marry me.'

'If you ask me, you'd be the fool.' Dave turned on his heel and walked towards the door. 'She didn't put up much of a fight when I kissed her.'

'That isn't——'

Suddenly Jarrod was standing up, a menacing figure glowering down at them. '*You* kissed *her*, did you?' he asked, dangerously soft.

Dave realised his mistake too late, paling at the un-hidden danger in his brother's eyes. 'Well, I—I——' he blustered, reaching hurriedly for the door-handle. 'I may have done,' he continued defiantly. 'But she didn't fight me,' he repeated.

Brooke had heard enough. They were like two animals fighting over a mate. But she had to admit that the cool intensity of Jarrod's anger was quite frightening. And she would have to bear the brunt of it when Dave had left.

'Don't lie on top of everything else, Dave,' she said sharply. 'You threatened me.'

'With what?' Jarrod queried softly of his brother.

Dave looked even more unsure of himself and Brooke began to feel sorry for him. If they hadn't been interrupted the incident between them might have passed off quite easily, but Jarrod turning up in this way had made a big issue out of it.

'With what, Dave?' he repeated harshly.

Dave gave a nervous laugh. 'I didn't threaten her with anything,' he lied. 'Look, Brooke gave me dinner, does that sound as if I threatened her?'

Jarrod shrugged. 'You tell me.'

'Well, I didn't,' Dave maintained firmly. 'Now if you'll excuse me I have to be back on duty at seven in the morning. Thanks for the meal, Brooke.'

Brooke looked at Jarrod with pleading eyes once Dave had left. 'It wasn't like he made it sound,' she said desperately. 'I did give him a meal, yes, but I didn't encourage him to kiss me.'

He looked at her coldly. 'When you invite a man round for a meal you must expect to invite him round for something else too.'

'I didn't *invite* him here at all,' she declared vehemently. 'He just turned up.'

'Oh, really?'

'Yes, really.' His sarcasm hadn't gone unnoticed. 'Don't you believe me?'

'Why shouldn't I?' He flexed his shoulder muscles. 'The one night I have to leave you in two weeks and

Dave just turned up here unexpectedly. I quite understand that it was on the off chance that he turned up here.'

'But it was! Please believe me, Jarrod. We even laughed at the fact that Dave had just missed you. He said how lucky——' She broke off as she realised her frantic pleadings were just making things worse.

'How lucky that I'd already left,' he murmured softly. 'But I came back and ruined it all for you.'

'*Why* did you come back?'

He threw back his head and gave a harsh laugh. 'I'm not sure now.'

Brookes eyes were violet in her distress. She was going to lose Jarrod on the evening she had decided to marry him! She had decided that if he wanted her enough to marry her she wanted him enough to agree. 'But there must have been a reason for it. You said when you left earlier that you would see me tomorrow.'

He gave a deep sigh, impatiently watching the nervous movements of her hands. 'Oh, there was a reason for my coming back,' he agreed coldly. 'I came back for you.'

She looked at him sharply. 'For—for *me*?'

'Yes,' again that harsh laugh. 'How did you expect me to concentrate on talking business after the stormy scene we'd just shared? I made my excuses as soon as it was polite to do so and came straight back here,' his mouth hardened. 'Only to find you in my brother's arms.'

'It wasn't like it seemed. He——'

'If I'd realised my constantly arousing you but not giving you the satisfaction you craved would lead to you seeking that satisfaction with another man I would have taken you long ago. As it is,' he took a threatening step towards her, 'I don't think it's too late for that—yet.'

Brooke shrunk away from the desire now flaming in his eyes. 'You don't realise what you're doing, Jarrod. You're annoyed, I can understand that, but you're wrong about Dave and myself.'

'Forget about Dave!' he ordered fiercely. 'As long as you haven't gone any further with him than what I just witnessed I couldn't give a damn about him. Although it had better never be repeated.' He swung her effortlessly into his arms, throwing her roughly down on to the bed once he reached her bedroom. 'I told you I would have you begging for marriage, now I realise just how lenient I've been with you during the last few weeks, waiting for you to come to me willingly. Well, I'm not going to wait any more. I want you, you want me, and by God I'm going to take you!'

His hands on her body were not gentle and the wildness in his eyes told her that the tight control he always had over his desire for her had finally snapped. She had pushed him too far and would now have to pay the penalty.

He wasted no time in unbuttoning her shirt, ripping the material as he ruthlessly pulled it apart. Several of the buttons came off altogether, but Jarrod ignored them, once again devouring her flesh devoid of underwear.

She struggled against him. 'Please, Jarrod!' she cried. 'I know you're angry with me, but not like this. *Please!*'

'I'm not angry with you, Brooke. I'm bloody furious!' He continued to kiss and caress her.

She pushed at his body on her own, knowing only pain and humiliation in his arms this time. 'You have a right to be, I admit that. But I can't let you make love to me. When you wanted to marry me it was different, but now that's over I——'

That made him lift his head. 'Who said it was over? Oh no, Brooke, you aren't getting away that easily. For weeks now people have been asking me when our wedding is to be, mainly due to your bitchiness in broadcasting it at that party simply because you felt I was making a fool of you. Well, now I can tell them exactly when we're getting married. Three weeks tomorrow you're going to become my wife.'

CHAPTER EIGHT

'I—I am?' Brooke faltered.

'Yes, you damn well are!'

'But you—you can't still want me to marry you, not after——'

He gave a tight smile, some of the tense anger seeming to leave his body. 'I still want you, and I still have to convince Charles Howard that I'm much too interested in my own woman to want his. They were the reasons for the marriage in the first place and they haven't changed.' His grip tightened painfully on her arms. 'But if I ever find you in another man's arms once we're married I'll kill you—after I've dealt with him, of course.'

There was a dangerous edge to his voice that told Brooke he meant exactly what he said. 'Of course,' she said dryly.

Jarrod got up off the bed, turning to look at her with narrowed eyes. 'As long as you realise that.' He ran a hand through his already tousled black hair. 'Get something on, for God's sake!' he snapped abruptly, marching back out into the lounge.

She did so with jerky movements, removing the ruined shirt altogether and putting on a yellow tee-shirt. She came out of the bedroom smoothing the top down over her narrow hips. 'Might I remind you that it was you who ripped at my clothing like—like a——'

'An animal?' Jarrod queried softly, a stiff measure of whisky in his hand. Not normally a drinker herself, she had bought the bottle especially for Jarrod when she realised how much he appreciated it when he came here in the evenings.

'Yes!' Her eyes flashed. 'And then you have the nerve to talk to me as if I'm—— '

'A wanton?' he finished for her again.

'Yes!' she said vehemently.

'Then that makes us well matched. I see you've kept Angie's present to you,' he remarked suddenly.

'I'm sorry?' she evaded.

'The portrait in your bedroom.'

'Oh, that,' she dismissed casually. 'I had to keep it really, it would have been rude not to.'

'But did you have to put it in your bedroom?'

She gave a short laugh. 'The lounge didn't seem the ideal place. I didn't particularly want you looming down at all my guests.'

Jarrod threw the remainder of the whisky in his glass to the back of his throat, swallowing it without a wince. 'Then I'm surprised you chose your bedroom,' he said nastily.

'Why, you—— '

'Yes?' he asked softly. 'Can't you stand to hear the truth?'

'The truth as you see it?' She shook her head. 'No, I can't stand to listen to your biased opinion of me. Just because you've forced yourself into my bedroom a couple of times it doesn't mean other men have been in there.' She ripped off the ring that seemed to be more like a chain with every passing second. 'Take your ring and get out of here!'

'We're getting married,' he stated adamantly.

'I wouldn't marry you under any circumstances!' she lied. If he loved her she would marry him to-morrow, but his contempt she wouldn't put up with.

He moved towards her. 'Are you sure about that?' he asked, seductively soft.

'Very sure,' she answered firmly. 'And making love to me won't work this time,' she denied, forcing herself not to move as he stood a few inches away from her. 'You aren't that good a lover, Jarrod. Dave's just as good as you are, with much less practice, I would say.'

'You think so?' He jerked her chin up roughly. 'So things had gone further between you than I thought they had. How often does Dave come here?'

'Whenever he can.' Which was true; according to Dave this had been the first opportunity he had had to call on her.

Jarrod picked up his discarded jacket. 'You little bitch!' he stated calmly. 'Keep the ring, Dave will never be able to afford one like it.'

'Oh, we don't intend getting married.'

'You have discussed it, then?'

'We've talked of marriage, yes. But it isn't for us, not to each other anyway.' How could she talk so calmly when what she really wanted to do was launch herself into Jarrod's arms?

'So you would have married me while having an affair with my own brother?'

'Must I remind you that I have never at any time said I would marry you? But even if I had you have every intention of carrying on your affair with Mrs Howard.'

'That's——'

'Different?' she cut in. 'It may seem that way to you, but I wouldn't have liked it.'

'So you had an affair with my brother,' he repeated.

'Yes,' she answered because it seemed to be what he expected of her.

'I once said you were full of surprises,' he said bitterly. 'I just didn't realise how much.'

'Goodbye, Jarrod,' she said dully.

'Goodbye.' The door closed with a slam.

Well, she had done it now, alienated Jarrod beyond repair. But it had been the only course open to her when he could think such things of her. She couldn't marry a man who had such a contemptuous opinion of her. It would have been hell on earth, with her having to pay for every past indiscretion he believed her guilty of. No matter what Jarrod did himself he wouldn't want a wife who had had affairs with other men; his wife would have to be beyond reproach. And in his eyes she certainly wasn't that now!

The weekend now loomed before her like a black empty void. Jarrod might only have been in her life a matter of weeks, but during that time he had effectively cut off any of her other social life, making it impossible for her to meet any of her other friends.

She woke up Saturday morning with a feeling of dread for the weekend, especially tonight. No one stayed in on a Saturday night, and most of her friends would already have made plans for the evening.

But by mid-afternoon she had had enough of her tiny flat, and felt as if the walls were closing in around her. She had to get out, go *somewhere* this evening. She just had to!

A call to a couple of her friends confirmed that a crowd of them were going to a nightclub that evening and they were only too happy to invite her along. She had missed going out with the crowd, missed their camaraderie and good humour. She and four other girls had become good friends during the time she had stayed at a hostel and although they had all left to make their own homes they still kept in touch with each other.

Debbie and Lynette called for her in their taxi, none of them wanting to risk driving after an evening spent drinking. Both of her friends were agog with curiosity about what had happened to that 'tall hunk of a fiancé of hers'. Neither girl had ever met Jarrod Stone, but like most people they had seen photographs of him in the society columns.

The three girls left their wraps in the cloakroom and made their way over to the booked table next to the dance-floor, the band already providing music for half a dozen couples smooching around the floor.

Not having explained her suddenly free evening,

Brooke knew she would come in for a certain amount of questioning—and it wasn't long in coming. As they were the first of their party to arrive it gave the other two girls time to question her in private.

'So what happened to your engagement?' Debbie looked pointedly at her bare left hand, the ring that had adorned the third finger now locked away out of sight. 'Surely you didn't change your mind?'

Brooke sipped her dry Martini and lemonade. 'It was a mutual thing. We just decided we weren't suited.'

Lynette looked at her wide-eyed. 'Goodness, I would have made sure I suited a dreamboat like him. He's gorgeous!'

Brooke gave a distant smile. She had known there would be questions like this, even more so when she went to work on Monday, but it didn't make them hurt any less. No matter what she might have to tell other people about the end of her engagement, she loved Jarrod.

'He is very handsome, yes,' she agreed, pretending an interest in the band she didn't have, even though they were exceptionally good.

The place was beginning to fill up and in an hour or so's time what was now an almost empty dance-floor would be overflowing with people. Perhaps then she wouldn't be the focus of her friends' interest, although she couldn't really blame them for their curiosity; one minute she was engaged to Jarrod and the next he wasn't even speaking to her.

'Handsome!' scoffed Debbie. 'He's fantastic,' she corrected her. 'He has beautiful sexy smouldering grey eyes. I saw a picture of him in a magazine a few weeks ago. I couldn't believe how lucky you were when I saw you were engaged to him.'

'Thank you for your card, by the way.' Brooke sighed. 'But those smouldering sexy eyes can also be contemptuous and glacial as snow. Believe me,' she shuddered, 'I know.'

'Oh, but surely he wasn't like that with you?' Lynette gasped.

'Don't you believe it. No, Jarrod is a very handsome, exciting man, but he's also a ruthless one. I'm afraid I'm not up to being the perfect wife.' Far from it, in Jarrod's eyes!

'I think it's a shame. Still, as long as you aren't too brokenhearted about it.' Debbie looked at her sympathetically, obviously doubting the truth of that.

Brooke shrugged. 'I'm upset, naturally. No one likes to admit they made a mistake, but it was better to find out now than after we were married. I just realised I didn't fit in with his idea of a wife.' She had definitely never been the complacent sort and she wasn't going to become so in marriage, and Jarrod needed a wife who would accept his affairs with other women.

When the rest of their crowd arrived ten minutes later they were just as curious, but they were given the same vague excuses as Debbie and Lynette and had to be satisfied with that. There were two more girls as Sheila had brought along a friend of hers from work, and there were six boys. They were all known to Brooke and she soon found herself laughing and joking with them in the old way, thoughts of Jarrod pushed firmly to the back of her mind.

'You're really finished with this guy Stone?' asked Jerry, an American student over here studying English history.

Brooke turned to look at him, sobering slightly at the mention of Jarrod's name. 'I'm no longer engaged to him,' she confirmed.

'Temporarily or permanently?'

She frowned. 'I don't understand.'

Jerry grinned, a tall loose-limbed man with overlong blond hair and a winning smile. He and Brooke had dated a couple of times in the past, but nothing had come of it. 'What I mean is, are you finished for good or is this just a momentary disagreement—you know, a lovers' tiff?'

'Definitely the former.'

'Good,' he said with some satisfaction, giving a bash-ful grin at her shocked look. 'Sorry, honey, that was a purely selfish viewpoint.'

'Selfish?'

'Mm.' He took a large gulp of his whisky. 'We had dated a couple of times just before you got engaged to this guy and I was pretty surprised when you suddenly decided to marry him. I was quite interested in you myself, you know.'

'You were?'

'Yes, I was—I still am. I realise you're probably upset at the moment, but I could help you get over that a whole lot quicker.'

'You could?' Brooke asked with a smile, starting to relax a bit now. This was the sort of man she could handle, the sort of man she felt at ease with. It seemed that only with the Stone men did she feel that muscle-tightening feeling of fear and anticipation. She had been right to feel both emotions.

'Oh yes.' Jerry stood up, pulling her to her feet. 'We'll start by dancing together.'

Before she could protest he had pulled her on to the dance-floor, holding her closely against his body as they moved to the slow music. They laughed and talked as they danced and only returned to the table to drink thirstily. It was warm work trying to survive amongst that crowd, although it wasn't long before they went back again.

As it happened to be a fast-moving number they danced away from each other, and Brooke became lost in the music. She felt quite exhausted at the end of it and collapsed thankfully into Jerry's arms, laugh-ing happily up at him.

It was at just this moment, her head thrown back, her eyes violet with pleasure, her smile for Jerry alone, that she saw the couple just stepping on to the dance-

floor for the next dance. Jarrod and Selina Howard!
And Jarrod was looking at *her* with undisguised contempt.

She looked quickly away, all colour leaving her face.
'Would you mind if we sat down, Jerry?' she asked
breathlessly.

He put an arm about her shoulders. 'That last one
wore you out, did it?' he teased.

She gave a shaky smile. 'Yes.'

She deliberately swapped seats with Jerry, her back
now firmly turned to the couple she most wanted to
avoid. How dared Jarrod come here so blatantly with
that woman! She boiled inside, not hearing a word
Jerry said.

'Brooke?' He touched her hand.

'Yes?' she asked sharply. She smiled at him wanly.
'Sorry, Jerry. I think I have a headache coming on.'

'Would you like me to take you home?'

There was nothing she would like better, but it
would be too much like running away. No, she would
stay here and act as if nothing had happened. She
gave Jerry a dazzling smile. 'Another drink will soon
clear my head.'

'Sure it will.' He stopped a waiter and ordered the
required drinks. 'You haven't had enough to make
you feel relaxed yet.'

Until a few moments ago she had been completely
relaxed and enjoying herself immensely. Until she had
seen Jarrod, that was. Oh, damn Jarrod and the attraction she still felt towards him!

'Here you are.' Jerry handed her a cool drink. 'Get
that down you and you'll soon forget you ever had
a headache.'

As she hadn't had one to start with that was highly
likely. Nevertheless, after this she threw herself more
enthusiastically into the enjoyment of the evening,
electing to stay on with Jerry after the others decided
they had had enough. Debbie and Lynette were a

trifle reluctant about leaving her, but Jerry assured
them he would see her home safely.

'I thought they'd never leave!' Jerry pulled her
to her feet. 'Let's dance.'

And dance they did, for what seemed like hours—
and probably was. Occasionally Brooke looked about
the room for a sight of Jarrod, but could see him
nowhere. Perhaps he had already left; it was possible.

At twelve-thirty she excused herself. She was feeling
hot and sticky and wanted to brush her hair and
freshen up her make-up. Luckily she had chosen to
wear a cool flowing flower-print dress, sleeveless, with
a low neckline that revealed the dark shadow between
her breasts.

With her hair brushed back into some semblance of
glowing order and her lipstick re-applied, she left the
powder-room to return to their table. She didn't get
very far, a firm grip on her arm stopping her progress.
She looked up from that familiar-looking hand into
the grim face of Jarrod Stone. So he hadn't left after
all!

'What do you think you're playing at?' he snapped
harshly with no preliminaries.

Brooke blinked rapidly at this verbal attack on her.
'What do you mean?'

'Don't play games with me,' he said in a controlled
voice. 'Just what do you mean by coming here with
your boy-friend tonight?'

'Why shouldn't I?' She snatched her wrist out of
his grasp, causing extra pain to herself as he didn't
want to let go. 'You don't have a monopoly on this
place.'

'I don't have the monopoly on it, but I do part-own
it.'

'I should have guessed,' she said dryly. 'Does this
mean you're asking me to leave?'

'Not at all, it means I want to know who your
friend is.'

Her eyes sparkled with anger. 'It's none of your business—nothing I do is now.'

A cruel smile curved that firm mouth. 'I think it is,' he insisted determinedly. 'I haven't refuted our engagement yet and it could prove rather embarrassing for us both if you're spotted here with another man.'

She stood proud, her head thrown back. 'And who would I be spotted by? I'm not exactly a well-known face. Unless of course your companion sees me. But I can't really see that that would make any difference, she already knows our engagement was a sham.'

He frowned. 'My companion? And who might that be?'

'Now who's playing games?' she scorned. 'Let me go, Jarrod. Jerry will be wondering where I am.'

'So his name's Jerry,' he said softly. 'Have you known him long?'

'Long enough.'

'For what?'

'For whatever,' Brooke answered carelessly.

'I see,' his mouth tightened. 'Now perhaps you'll tell me what game *I'm* supposed to be playing?'

'I saw you with that woman, so don't try to deny it. I think you should be the one to worry if you're seen with *her*, not me.'

'By "that woman" I presume you mean Selina. Does it bother you that I'm here with her?'

At last he let go of her wrist and she glowered at him as she massaged the reddened skin. 'Why should I care? I've always known she came first in your life, so why should it bother me if you see her?'

'You tell me.'

'It *doesn't* bother me,' she said crossly. 'Excuse me, but I would like to rejoin my friend.' She turned on her heel and walked away, expecting at any moment to feel his hand on her arm. When it didn't happen she didn't know if she was relieved or disappointed.

Whatever her emotions were she became quite reck-
lessly enthusiastic about the evening, drinking heavily
between dances. Jerry was becoming quite friendly,
but in her state of rejection she didn't seem to mind
his attentions. Jarrod might no longer want her, but
she was still attractive to other men; Jerry made it
clear that he found her very attractive.

She swallowed the remainder of her drink, about
her seventh of the evening. 'Shall we dance again?'
she asked him gaily.

'Sure,' he agreed readily.

The music had slowed down a little with the pro-
gression of the evening and she snuggled against him
as they danced. It might not be the best reason for
her to be in his arms, but for now it was the only one
she had. He was quite good-looking and she badly
needed a salve to her dented ego at the moment.
Besides, he was fun to be with.

They danced close together, their bodies curved
together as they moved to the music. Jerry bent his
head to caress her throat with demanding lips. 'Can
we leave soon, honey?' he asked huskily.

'Soon,' she promised. 'But it's early yet.'

'It's after two in the morning,' he corrected. 'I
don't call that early.'

Brooke pouted up at him. 'Don't be a meanie. You
don't have to get up for college in the morning.'

'I wasn't thinking about the morning,' he murmured, his eyes admiring. 'When can I take you
home?'

She looked at him reproachfully. 'We have plenty
of time to go home. I'm enjoying myself.'

'So am I,' he brushed his lips across her mouth.
'But I can think of a way I would enjoy myself more.'

She giggled. 'That's naughty!'

'I know, but I——'

'Excuse me!' a harshly angry voice interrupted their
conversation.

Brooke turned with dazed eyes to see Jarrod standing at her side. She and Jerry had stopped dancing at the first sound of his voice, jerked out of their flirtatious mood by the coldness of his tone. Brooke felt sure he must have heard part of their bantering conversation and she knew what construction he would have put on it.

Jerry looked at the other man challengingly. 'Yeah? Can I do something for you?'

Jarrod gave him a glacial look. 'Not you, no. I would like to talk to Brooke.'

'She's with me.' Jerry had had as much to drink as she had and it had given him more courage than he might otherwise have had. 'So anything you have to say can be said in front of me.'

He received a look of arrogant disdain for his rude outburst. 'I don't think so,' Jarrod disagreed. 'What I have to say to Brooke is totally private.'

'We don't have any secrets from each other.'

Even Brooke looked sharply at Jerry for this statement. They might have dated a couple of times, but they had never been *that* close. Still, she couldn't altogether blame Jerry for his defiant attitude; Jarrod brought out those feelings in her too. It was all that arrogance that did it.

Jarrod gave a nasty smile. 'What I have to say to Brooke isn't exactly a secret, I should think everyone in the club has been thinking what I'm about to say.'

Brooke bristled angrily. 'What do you mean?'

'Could we go to your table and sit down?' Jarrod suggested. 'We're rather conspicuous standing here.'

For the first time she became aware of how they must look to other people, standing here in the middle of a crowded dance-floor having an obviously hostile conversation. She nodded distantly, her gaiety of a few minutes earlier gone completely.

'Now,' Jarrod leant forward in his chair, 'you're making an exhibition of yourself,' he told her coldly.

'I could almost say you're drunk.'

'Why, you——'

'And as for you,' he cut into Jerry's indignant outburst, 'if you don't stop pawing her I'm going to kill you!'

The words were spoken so softly and with such force that Brooke knew he meant it. Surely Jarrod couldn't be jealous? If only he were!

Jerry seemed to have got over his surprise at such a statement and now gave an assured smile. 'Perhaps the lady likes to be pawed,' he drawled.

'Maybe she does,' Jarrod acknowledged. 'But if anyone is going to paw her it's going to be me. Brooke is my fiancée.'

Jerry looked impressed. 'So you're Jarrod Stone!'

'That's right. So you can understand why I'm not too pleased at seeing her here with you.'

'Oh, I can understand it, but as Brooke claims to be no longer engaged to you I don't think it's any of your concern now.'

Brooke gasped. 'I don't *claim* anything. I'm not——'

'We've had a temporary setback, that's all,' Jarrod declared firmly. 'She's only here with you to hit back at me.'

Jerry grinned. 'She seems to have succeeded.'

Jarrod gave a wry smile. 'Doesn't she just! So in the circumstances I hope you will understand my wanting to take her home now,' he said smoothly.

'I don't want——'

'Neither do I, honey.' Jerry hadn't been fooled by the now charming manner of this man, remembering the threat he had made and the conviction behind the words. 'Brooke came with me,' he lied. 'And she's leaving with me.'

Grey eyes raked over him mercilessly. 'Are you sure about that?'

Jerry stood up, taking Brooke with him. 'Very sure. It's been—interesting meeting you, Mr Stone. No, don't bother to see us to the door, we know the way out.'

Brooke collected up her handbag, halted once again by Jarrod's grip on her arm. 'Let go of me!' she ordered.

'I want to talk to you, Brooke.'

'We've said all we had to say.' She held up her left hand. 'You see, I no longer wear your brand of possession.'

'Does Dave know about your new boy-friend?'

She shrugged, forgetting her earlier declaration that she was having an affair with his brother. 'Why should he? No one *owns* me.'

'Then perhaps it's time someone did,' he said softly. 'Goodnight.'

'Goodnight,' she answered, startled by his sudden turn-about of mood.

He looked at Jerry again. 'I take it you're not going to attempt to drive?'

'And if I were?' Jerry asked insolently.

Jarrod shrugged. 'I would simply make a telephone call to the police informing them of your inebriated state.'

'Thanks!' Jerry returned dryly. 'But as I don't possess a car that won't be necessary.' He put his arm about Brooke's shoulders. 'Goodnight, Mr Stone.'

Jarrod didn't answer but turned on his heel and walked away. Brooke was still shaking from the encounter when she returned to Jerry's side after collecting her wrap. They got into a waiting taxi, Jerry giving the driver Brooke's address.

He turned to her in the darkness of the car. 'A very determined man, your Mr Stone,' he remarked.

'He isn't my Mr Stone,' she answered crossly.

'He doesn't seem to be of the same opinion.'

'He just wanted to be nasty.'

Jerry shook his head. 'I don't think so. He was mad as hell to see you in my arms.'

'Not through jealousy, I can assure you!'

'Hey, come on, Brooke, there's no need to get aggressive with me. I'm only telling you that the guy didn't like you being with me. If we hadn't been in such a public place he would probably have hit me. And that was no idle threat he made about my touching you.'

She knew that, and instead of the elated feeling she had felt all evening she now felt thoroughly depressed, craving only her own company.

'I guess you would prefer me not to come in for coffee,' Jerry said as the taxi came to a halt outside her flat.

She was grateful for his understanding. 'Thanks, Jerry. Some other time, hmm? Call me.'

'Sure.' He leant forward and kissed her softly on the lips. 'Goodnight, honey.'

Brooke went straight into the bathroom when she got in, running the water for a shower before going into the bedroom to remove her clothes. The effects of the alcohol were beginning to wear off and her temples throbbed.

The warm water helped to ease her pain somewhat, but it couldn't alleviate her humiliation. Jarrod had made her evening with Jerry seem cheap, and reluctant as she was to admit it, he was right. She had made a fool of herself tonight, an absolute fool.

With her hair tied on top of her head with a black velvet ribbon and a towel secured about her body at her breasts she came back into the bedroom totally refreshed. The sight that met her eyes made her cheeks pale even more.

'Jarrod!' she gasped as she saw him sprawled full length on her bed. 'What are you doing here?'

He slowly sat up, his eyes appraising as he gazed boldly at her body. 'Waiting for you—what else would I be doing?'

CHAPTER NINE

'W—WAITING for me?' she repeated breathlessly.

He stood up now, and came towards her. 'Mm,' he murmured. 'Your eyes were promising things tonight I have no intention of letting any other man collect.'

'Promising things?' She clung to the towel that was in danger of falling off. 'You—you're mistaken!'

'I don't think so.' He touched her pale cheeks. 'You don't look well. Have you been ill?'

'No,' she answered huskily, unnerved by his closeness.

'Not sick or anything? You've been drinking steadily all evening.'

'I'm not drunk and I haven't been sick!' she snapped angrily, mainly as a defence against his blatant maleness than out of real anger. She hadn't expected to see him again tonight and she felt weakened by his presence in her bedroom.

'Then what's the matter with you, you look like death.'

'Thanks.' She moved jerkily away from his caressing hands. 'I happen to have a headache.' She heard him chuckle and turned to look at him. 'What's so funny about that?'

'It's the classic excuse.' His eyes were dark grey with amusement.

A strange fluttering sensation started in her stomach. 'For what?'

'For not making love,' he stated bluntly. 'Is that why your boy-friend isn't here now?'

'Jerry isn't my boy-friend. And I have a much simpler way of avoiding making love, I just say no.' Oh God, she wished she had her bathrobe on, but it was still hanging on the back of the bathroom door. She felt so—so *naked* dressed only in this towel that barely reached her thighs.

Jarrod was right behind her now, his warm breath caressing her bare nape. 'I have no intention of taking no from you tonight.' His arms moved about her waist and he pulled her back against him, his hands possessively cupping her breasts. 'I've come to collect, Brooke.'

'Not from me you haven't.' She squirmed as his lips caressed her nape. 'What's happened to your mistress tonight?' she sneered.

'Selina?' he murmured against her throat. 'She's at home with her husband, I would imagine.'

'Does he realise you were out with his wife this evening?' She gave up all effort of trying to escape him as he refused to let her go.

'Oh yes, he knows.' He continued a downward exploration of her creamy throat with his lips.

'Does he love his wife so much that he allows her to—to have men friends?' she asked in disgust, hoping to alienate him again by insulting him. She had to stop these caresses somehow.

'I have no idea of his feelings in the matter,' he appeared unmoved by her sarcasm. 'He was with us tonight, we were a party of eight. But I don't suppose you noticed that, you were too wrapped up in this Jerry.'

Every time his lips touched her skin her heart gave a strange leap, and yet still she fought for sanity. 'A party of eight,' she said thoughtfully. 'Who was your partner?'

He turned her in his arms to face him, holding her against the lean length of him and making her wholly aware of his throbbing thighs. 'A tall raven-haired beauty called Suzy.'

'So if you aren't with your mistress why aren't you with this Suzy?' Her gaze was fixed on the third button down on his white shirt front.

He pretended shock. 'Really, Brooke! I only met her for the first time this evening, even I wouldn't presume so much on such short acquaintance.'

'You surprise me!'

He laughed. 'I thought I might.' He looked at her closely. 'You look cute with your hair like that,' he said softly. 'But it's a cuteness that's totally deceptive.' He pulled the ribbon free of her hair, allowing it to fall in glowing red-brown waves about her shoulders. 'You looked like a little girl with your hair like that— and this isn't the time for me to be reminded of your youth.'

His body pressed against her own was working its usual magic and her legs felt weak. And the lighting in this room didn't help the situation, one bedside lamp that added to the mood of seduction. 'But I am young, Jarrod,' she latched on to this point with desperation. 'You can never change that.'

'At this moment I don't want to change a single damn thing about you.' He bent his head to claim her lips with his own.

Brooke couldn't fight her own emotions any more, couldn't fight the desire she felt for him. It had all been leading to this, all the arguments, all the friction. Her arms moved up about his neck and she gave up fighting him, revelling in his mastery of her.

'That was good,' he groaned against her mouth. 'I needed that. You did too. Admit it.'

'I——'

'Admit it, Brooke!'

'I needed it too,' she said softly.

He gave a triumphant laugh. As soon as he took his arms from about her body the towel fell to the floor. It seemed to Brooke that her whole body suffused with colour. She hurried to retrieve her only covering, but Jarrod stopped her.

'Leave it,' he ordered, his eyes never leaving the perfection of her body. 'God, you're more beautiful than even my imagination allowed for! Touching you isn't quite the same thing as seeing you like this.' He took her hand, leading her over to the bed. 'Undress me.'

'No!' She felt awful standing here naked, even more so because Jarrod was totally dressed. 'Let me get some clothes on, Jarrod,' she pleaded.

'Oh no,' he sat her firmly down on the bed. 'You can get under the covers if you like, but you are certainly not getting dressed, not now I've got you this far.'

She quickly did as he said, peering at him from below the safety of the sheet. He was calmly taking off his clothes as if they did this every night! Brooke looked hurriedly away as he stripped off his trousers, throwing them carelessly on the floor with his other clothes.

The next thing she knew the bed gave beside her and a pair of strong muscular arms pulled her against her first encounter with a naked male body. It felt good, really good, and she wondered if all men were as beautiful as Jarrod. She doubted it, he was just too perfect to be copied.

He was unique, and her hands caressed him of their own volition. 'This is wrong, Jarrod,' she said breathlessly once he had released her lips, gasping as he touched her breasts.

'How can anything that feels so right possibly be wrong? It can't, Brooke,' he answered his own question. 'Can you deny that you want me?'

'No, but I——'

'Then it can't be wrong.' He parted her lips with a savagery that took her breath away, his hands moving intimately across her body.

Just when she thought that full possession was the

only thing that would satisfy either of them the doorbell began to ring. It rang and rang until it finally
penetrated even Jarrod's passion-filled brain.

He looked down at her with tortured eyes. 'Are you
expecting anyone?'

'No,' she answered dazedly.

'Then who the hell is it!' He swore angrily as the
doorbell continued to ring. He swung his legs out of
the bed, pulling his trousers on before marching out
furiously to open the door. Brooke pitied whoever it
was.

She lay shivering in the bed with reaction, wondering at her own response and yet knowing she would
respond just as passionately when Jarrod returned.

She could hear the murmur of voices in the lounge
and wondered who Jarrod could possibly be talking
to. She slipped out of the bed, grabbing her robe from
the bathroom before quietly entering the lounge. Dave
stood up at her entrance and Jarrod came over to put
his arm about her shoulders, holding her protectively
against his side.

She couldn't help noticing how pale they both were.
'What's wrong?' she asked Jarrod. 'Has something
happened?'

His face was bleak. 'My father has had a heart
attack. I have to go to the hospital. Wait for me here
while I dress,' he told his brother before leaving the
room.

Dave looked embarrassed. 'Sorry to have burst in
on you like this,' he muttered.

'Is your father going to be all right?' Brooke asked
anxiously.

'They think so. Of course they can't be sure yet.
But I thought Jarrod ought to know.'

'Oh yes,' she agreed. 'I'm only relieved you thought
to come here.'

'I tried his apartment first, and then I tried a club
he occasionally goes to. It seems I just missed him at

the club, so I tried his apartment again. He still wasn't there.' Dave shrugged. 'I couldn't think of anywhere else he could be. After all, he did say he spends a lot of his nights here.'

'So he did,' she agreed dully. 'Excuse me, Dave. I have to speak to Jarrod.'

'Hey!' he stopped her exit. 'I didn't mean to be insulting, you know. I was just trying to explain my reasoning.'

She gave a wan smile. 'I realise that. Now I must see Jarrod.'

'Of course,' he acknowleged.

Brooke gently touched his arm. 'I told you how I felt about him from the beginning.'

'Yes, you did. I'm sorry I tried to cause trouble between you yesterday.'

If only he knew how much damage he had done! But he and Jarrod had enough to worry about with their father's illness without her raking up old arguments. She gave him a vague smile before rushing into her bedroom.

Jarrod was partly dressed by this time, his black leather shoes back on his feet and his shirt pulled back on over his powerful shoulders. His look darkened as Brooke came into the room and she ran into his arms, her own arms passing around his waist below the unbuttoned shirt. She rested her head on his hair-roughened chest, aware of the strong steady beat of his heart.

He shuddered as her arms went about him, holding her close, his face buried in her luxurious hair. 'God, this is a mess!' he moaned agonisingly.

She tilted her head back to look at him. 'Your father will be all right. I'm sure he will.' Her look was earnest.

'You think so?'

She smoothed away the lines of worry from his brow, for once aware of an air of uncertainty about him.

'I'm sure of it, Jarrod. He's a strong man. He'll pull through, you'll see,' she smiled bravely.

He touched her cheeks with gentle fingers. 'I wish I had your optimism.'

'You'll call me as soon as you know anything?' she asked anxiously.

He moved impatiently away from her and began to button his shirt. 'It could be any time of day or night when we know he's out of danger.'

'I want to know, Jarrod,' she said firmly.

'Look, it can't mean that much to you.' He pulled on his jacket, ready to leave. 'My family are nothing to you and neither am I.'

'Jarrod!' she said warningly, more hurt than she cared to admit. He had shown her very effectively that what had just taken place between them was no more than a physical attraction that was easily forgotten by him.

'Okay, okay, I'll call you.'

He left the bedroom without another word and by the time she had gathered her wits together enough to follow him he and Dave had already left. She sank down dejectedly on the couch. Would she ever see Jarrod again? Tonight he had been consumed with a desire so strong it couldn't be denied, but now that passion had faded and died, and so had his desire to see her for all she knew.

She didn't bother to go back to bed, dozing on the couch until about ten o'clock when she decided she might as well shower and dress. Jarrod hadn't called her yet and so she waited by the telephone all day in the hope that she would hear from him.

No call came, and as she hadn't thought to ask the name of the hospital Mr Stone had been admitted to she couldn't call and enquire after his health for herself. Not that she thought they would tell her anything anyway, she wasn't 'family'.

She was thoroughly exhausted by the time eleven

o'clock came round that evening, lack of sleep and loss of appetite were each paying their toll and she just had to go to bed. She would be fit for nothing in the morning, and she still had to go to work even if she was—had been—engaged to the boss.

The bed felt curiously lonely without Jarrod's presence and she found it difficult to fall asleep. When she finally did it was a deep drugged sleep from which she would find it difficult to awaken.

She woke part way through the night to find a strong masculine arm curved about her waist and a heavy weight resting on her breasts. Jarrod murmured in his sleep as she moved in surprise.

'Jarrod?' she muttered drowsily, looking down at the dark head resting against her.

'Mm?' He didn't move.

'Is everything all right?' her fogged-up brain formed the question.

'Mm,' he said again, a smile momentarily curving his mouth.

She was satisfied with that. Jarrod wouldn't be here and he wouldn't have smiled if his father wasn't out of danger. She drifted back off to sleep, content just to have him here.

When she woke in the morning he had gone. She couldn't believe it, and jumped out of bed and rushed into the bathroom to see if he was showering. He was nowhere to be found, making her wonder if she had dreamt the whole thing. Surely she hadn't imagined it? But there could be no other explanation.

She was still pale and tired when she arrived at work, her head throbbing with pain. 'Don't say it,' she groaned as Jean was about to speak. 'I know I look terrible.'

'Actually I was going to ask you if you would like a coffee.'

She gave a grateful smile. 'I'd love one, thank you. It might help wake me up.'

Jean returned with the steaming cup of coffee. 'I guess you had a lousy weekend.'

Brooke swallowed a couple of aspirins. 'You heard?'

'About Mr Stone?' Jean nodded. 'It was on the local radio.'

'It was terrible. Such a shock.' In more ways than one for Jarrod and herself!

'The boss looked in terrible shape when he came in,' Jean said sympathetically.

'Jarrod's in?' Brooke squeaked, scalding her mouth with the hot coffee.

Jean nodded. 'About fifteen minutes ago.'

'Oh.'

'I don't think he'll be staying, though,' Jean continued. 'He was dressed very casually,' she explained. 'Not his usual suave self. He's probably only in to read the post.'

'Probably.' Brooke looked up as one of the girls from the typing pool came over to her desk. 'Hello, Maureen. Anything wrong?' she asked at the other girl's puzzled look.

'Well, I——' Maureen looked confused. 'I thought I was supposed to be taking over for you today,' she explained.

Brooke frowned. 'For me? Why should you think that?' Maureen usually took over the reception desk for her if she was on holiday or off sick.

'Mr Stone rang to say you wouldn't be in today. I naturally assumed it was because of his father's illness.'

Before Brooke could protest Jean interrupted the conversation. 'I think that's an excellent idea. Why don't you go home and get some sleep, Brooke? You look as if you need it.'

'Thanks!'

'Look, you know you feel lousy,' Jean persisted.

It was true, she did. Her temples ached, her head was pounding and her body felt like lead. But there was really no need for Jarrod to have automatically announced she wouldn't be in today. He had no idea how she felt, so that couldn't possibly have been his reason for interfering.

'Go on,' Jean urged. 'It will do——' she broke off impatiently as her intercom buzzed. 'Yes? Yes, sir.' She glanced at Brooke. 'Right away. Goodbye.' She disconnected the line. 'You don't have any choice about it now. Apparently Mr Stone has just learnt you're in the building after all. He wants you to go up to his office.'

Brooke would have liked to protest at this, but she was too much aware of Maureen and the gossip such objections could cause. With a shrug she gathered up her jacket and handbag and walked over to the private lift.

Catherine Farraday treated her with none of the hauteur of their last meeting, smiling at her. She pressed the intercom at her side. 'Your fiancée is here to see you, Mr Stone.'

'Ask her to come in.' His voice sounded strangely hollow over the intercom.

'I'll show myself in, shall I?' Brooke asked tentatively.

'Certainly,' she smiled again.

She knocked on the door to Jarrod's office before entering. He was sitting behind the desk and he looked as terrible as she felt. His face was deathly pale, his eyes dark and heavy from the lack of sleep, and his hair was ruffled as if he had spent many hours running agitated hands through its thickness.

He was dressed just as casually as Jean had said he was, the denims fitting snugly on his hips and the matching denim shirt buttoned carelessly halfway up his chest.

He looked up at her as he sorted through the letters on his desk. 'I didn't expect you to be in to work today,' he said curtly.

'I gathered that,' she returned dryly. 'I waited all day yesterday for you to call me,' she added gently, still not sure if his father was out of danger or if things had gone drastically the other way.

He sat back with a sigh, his mind obviously not on what he was doing. 'It was late last night when my father came out of the critical stage, I didn't want to disturb you with a telephone call at two o'clock in the morning. It could have frightened you.'

'I wouldn't have minded, Jarrod. I wanted to know.'

His grey eyes flashed angrily. 'Do you think I didn't realise that?' he snapped. 'You had told me most definitely ... you wanted to know, so I came round to your flat.'

A terrible trembling started in her lower limbs. 'You —you did?'

'Yes,' he confirmed wearily. 'It must have been three o'clock by this time. You'd already gone to bed. And you'd foolishly left your door unlocked,' he added sternly.

'I—I had?' She had a terrible feeling that her 'dream' of Jarrod snuggled up against her hadn't been a dream at all, in fact she felt sure it wasn't.

'Mm,' a glimmer of a smile curved his mouth. 'I—er —let myself in.'

Brooke cleared her throat in embarrassment. 'Er—— Did you? I didn't hear you.' She couldn't meet his probing eyes.

'I'm not surprised, you were fast asleep. Lucky I wasn't a burglar. As it was, all I wanted was a bed for the night. You were still sleeping when I left at seven-thirty.'

'I—I woke once in the night.' She fidgeted with the strap of her handbag.

'Ah,' Jarrod nodded understandingly. 'Then there's no need for me to explain further.' He resumed sorting through the mail.

'I thought I'd imagined you being there.'

He looked at her sharply. 'Did you *want* to imagine it?'

Colour flared in her cheeks. 'No, I—— But I couldn't think how you came to be in my bed—in my room.'

'I told you, you left the door open,' he said absently.

'It won't happen again,' she muttered.

'Oh, I didn't mind. I was too tired to go home.' He looked up at her. 'And you do look very beautiful when you're asleep. Sleeping with you could become a habit.'

'As long as it's only sleep you have in mind,' she attempted to make light of it.

Jarrod gave her a long hard look. 'I wouldn't guarantee it.' He closed the folder containing his mail. 'Right, that's done. Are you ready to leave?'

'I was going home, yes, as you seem to have made arrangements for me not to be here.'

'I expected you to be sleeping in this morning.'

'I still have a job to do.'

'And I still happen to be the owner of this firm, and I don't consider you fit for work.' He stood up. 'Besides, I have plans for you today.'

Her eyebrows rose. 'And what plans are these?'

'My father wants to see you.' He picked up the folder in preparation of leaving. 'I'll just give these things to Catherine and then she can get the letters off in today's post.'

'Your father wants to see me?' Brooke couldn't help her surprise.

'Yes.' He opened the door for her. 'Shall we go?'

'Yes. But I—— Your father wants to see *me*?'

'I've just said so,' he told her impatiently. 'Let's go, Brooke. I only came in at all today to deal with the post. I want to get back to the hospital. Dave had to be back on duty at ten o'clock this morning, so my mother and Angie are at the hospital alone.'

'Of course.'

She followed him out to his secretary's office, standing quietly to one side as he gave her instructions for the day. It gave her a chance to look at him without being observed herself. He was his usual handsome self, but the strain of the last couple of days showed in the lines etched either side of his mouth and nose, and for the first time since she had known him he looked every one of his thirty-seven years.

Brooke's heart went out to him and she wished she could comfort him in some way. But he had made it obvious on Saturday night that he didn't want her sympathy.

They went down in the lift together, deciding to drive their respective vehicles back to Brooke's home and carry on together in Jarrod's car from there. She parked her car before joining him.

He turned in his seat to look at her. 'I noticed you're not wearing your ring. Go and get it,' he ordered coldly.

She was angered by his tone. 'I'm not longer engaged to you. I was going to return your ring and the other gifts, including the car, at the earliest opportunity.'

He leant his arms on the steering wheel. 'Get the ring, Brooke. Our personal vendetta can wait until later. My family believes us to be still getting married.'

'You haven't told them we've argued?'

He gave a taunting smile. 'The weekend was hardly the time to tell them.'

'I suppose not.' She opened the car door to get out. 'I won't be a moment.'

'I didn't intend leaving without you,' he returned dryly.

Brooke didn't respond to his sarcasm. They were both under great strain and an argument between them wouldn't help matters. She got the ring from the back of the drawer she had locked it in. Not that this little lock would stop a burglar if he were really determined, but she couldn't think what else to do with it. At least she had made sure Jarrod had the other jewellery.

He looked at her hand with satisfaction as she got back in beside him, starting the car without another word.

His silence angered Brooke. 'I'm only wearing this as a temporary measure,' she told him stiffly. 'As soon as we leave your family you can have it back.'

He gave her a cold look. 'You'll wear it for as long as my father can be hurt by the knowledge that the wedding is off.'

'I——'

'You'll wear it, Brooke! You may be a flirt and a little cheat, but for the moment I don't think it would benefit my father to know that. He likes you,' he added grimly.

'I like him too.' Tears shimmered in her eyes at the reputation she had deliberately earned herself with the man she loved.

'Then do this for him if for no one else. He just isn't strong enough to take the news, he won't be for several weeks. No shocks or disappointments, the doctor said.' Jarrod drove the car into a hospital parking space. 'And he'll be both of those things if we call off the wedding, shocked because he believes us to be genuinely in love, and disappointed because he thought I was going to settle down and give him grandchildren.'

'I told you it was a mistake from the beginning to involve your family. It was bad enough that you insisted on maintaining our engagement to your friends, but——'

'I had a reason for that,' he cut in abruptly, pulling his leather jacket out of the back seat.

'Oh, I know that, your arrogant pride! I'd played a trick on you and no one is allowed to get away with that,' Brooke said fiercely.

'Precisely.' He got out of the car and opened her door for her. 'Now forget your tantrums and act the loving fiancée.'

She shivered. 'I couldn't!' How could she put on an act when it was a reality, a reality that Jarrod must never see? How easily she had nearly fallen for his charm on Saturday night, and how Jarrod would relish the added knowledge that she loved him.

His face was a shuttered mask. 'Just try not to cringe when I touch you.'

'I'll try,' she whispered huskily.

Once inside the hospital Jarrod ordered his mother and sister back to his apartment for a shower, a change of clothes and something to eat. His mother was very reluctant to leave, but Jarrod was adamant.

Brooke couldn't help but feel shocked by just how ill his father looked. His skin was grey, his eyes sunken into his head and his body almost looking shrunken. But although he looked ill the blue eyes were keen enough, his face lighting up with pleasure as he saw the two of them.

The greetings over, they sat beside his bed, Jarrod conversing easily about everyday things. Brooke listened to them silently, a slight curve to her lips for his father's benefit.

Clifford Stone turned to look at her, smiling even in his pain. 'You're very quiet, Brooke,' he said gently. 'You mustn't let all this disturb you,' he indicated the heartbeat monitor and the trolley of instruments in one corner of the room. 'It's all for show.'

She knew it wasn't, but she returned his smile. 'I'm just glad to know you're feeling better, Mr Stone.'

'Well enough for your wedding not to be postponed next month. I may not be able to be at the actual ceremony, but the reception can be held at the house, I can enjoy that.'

'Oh, but——'

Jarrod's warning glare silenced her. 'Don't worry, Dad. We knew how you would feel about it, so we have no intention of postponing the wedding.'

CHAPTER TEN

'WHAT wedding next month?' Brooke demanded of him.

They had arrived back at her flat five minutes earlier, after spending an hour with Jarrod's father. Jarrod would be returning to the hospital shortly, but he had made it obvious her presence wasn't needed.

'Jarrod, I said what wedding?' she repeated impatiently.

He gave a taunting smile. 'Ours, of course.'

'But there isn't going to be a wedding! I already told you I have no intention of remaining engaged to you a moment longer than necessary. As for getting married!' She shook her head. 'That's totally out of the question.'

'You can't stand to be near me, is that it?'

'Exactly.'

'Funny,' he mocked her. 'You gave a totally different impression Saturday night.'

'That was Saturday night,' she said crossly, her cheeks fiery red.

'I see. And things have changed since then, in two days?'

The cynical hardness of his eyes mocked her in that way that she found so annoying, almost as if he were secretly laughing at her—again. 'Two days can sometimes seem a lifetime. And may I remind you that I wasn't engaged to you on Saturday night.'

'Exactly,' he repeated her word of a few minutes earlier, but with such sarcasm that she couldn't misunderstand his implication.

She blushed again. 'Meaning?'

'Meaning I wasn't engaged to you. As I wasn't last

night when you snuggled into my arms as if you did it every night of your life.'

'I didn't know it was you! I——' She broke off as she realised how damning that sounded.

Jarrod's mouth turned back in a sneer. 'Don't incriminate yourself any further, Brooke. I already know you for what you are. And don't ask me to explain that too.'

She looked the other way. 'That won't be necessary.'

'I didn't think it would be.'

'Your being insulting doesn't solve the problem of what we do about this expected wedding.'

'Expected is all it will be. We have plenty of time to get out of it.'

'You call four weeks plenty of time!' She looked sceptical. 'God, the whole thing will be arranged before you can call it off. Couldn't you just tell your mother the truth? She wouldn't have to tell your father, but it would save us all the embarrassment of having to cancel everything.'

'You selfish little bitch! Does nothing matter to you but your own embarrassment?' Jarrod demanded fiercely. 'No, of course it doesn't. Why should it matter to you that my mother is as worried as hell about my father? As long as you don't have any *embarrassment* to face you'll be happy. And that's all that matters to you, your own happiness.'

'That isn't true! I——'

'Don't give me that, Brooke,' he interrupted coldly. 'Your actions since we first met have all been self-centred. You involved me in this engagement because you felt insulted, announced our forthcoming marriage to Selina because of a conversation you'd taken exception to. You took a liking to my brother, so you decided to have him anyway, regardless of the consequences of such action amongst my family. Well, now you can do something for me—you can damn well behave yourself and keep your mouth shut. And you won't see Dave again until this thing has been settled.'

'You can't tell me what I can or cannot do,' she retorted angrily. 'If I want to see Dave I will.' Although she had no inclination to do any such thing. She and Dave had nothing left to say to one another.

'You'll see no one but me until I say you can.'

'Why, you arrogant——'

Jarrod came towards her, a determined glint in his eyes. 'It seems there's only one way of silencing you.' He pulled her roughly against the hard immovability of his body and she felt the first stirring of his desire against her thighs. 'And if I enjoy it too why should I give a damn that you're nothing but a lying little cheat? Why should I give a damn!' he repeated with a groan.

His dark head bent and his mouth covered hers in utter possession. Her head was forced back and he held her immovable by one hand threaded savagely in her hair. There was no tenderness in the taking of her lips, only anger and passion and a contempt she just couldn't bear from him.

She wrenched away from him. 'No, Jarrod! Stop it! I won't allow you to treat me like this!'

His hold wouldn't be broken and he grinned down at her struggles with devilish satisfaction. 'I'm not asking you to *allow* me to do anything,' he mocked her throatily. 'I'll take you any time I please.' He let her go abruptly, glancing tersely at his wrist-watch. 'But right now I don't have the time.' His eyes slid over her body with barely concealed contempt. 'Or the inclination,' he added dryly.

'Neither do I,' she choked, rubbing her hand roughly across her mouth. 'I despise you!'

'Really?' He took a threatening step forward. 'Would you like me to prove differently?'

She backed away. 'No—no, don't! I—I can't stand to have you near me.'

His only answer was a deep mocking laugh before

he turned towards the door. 'I have to get back to the hospital now, but I could be back later this evening.'

'I shouldn't bother!' she snapped.

'I only said I could be. If it's late I'll——'

'You'll go home,' she finished for him. 'Don't expect my door to be left unlocked tonight.'

He grinned. 'I couldn't wish for such luck two nights running.'

'I'll make sure you don't,' she vowed vehemently.

Jarrod opened the door in preparation of leaving. 'Don't go in to work tomorrow, I may need you during the day.'

'Then you can damn well need, because I have every intention of going in to work. I told you, I have a job to do.'

'Okay, you're fired,' he said arrogantly.

Brooke gasped. 'You can't do that!'

'I know that,' he agreed calmly. 'But by the time you've sorted it all out my father will be out of hospital and you can go back to work any time you want to.'

'But that's not——'

'Fair?' Jarrod finished. 'So, it's not fair, but it gets me what I want.'

'You're a selfish——'

He grasped her arm roughly, pulling her against him with a fierce intensity. 'If I'm selfish I hate to think what you are,' he ground out savagely. 'If my father wants to see you again I want you where I can reach you with relative ease. I don't want to have to go to the trouble of having to wait while you find yourself a replacement on the desk. Understood?'

He was shaking her so hard her teeth rattled. 'U-understood,' she quivered.

Jarrod pushed her away so suddenly she almost fell over. 'For once you aren't going to argue any more.' He shook his head. 'Amazing.'

'Goodbye, Jarrod,' she said stiffly, her eyes violet with dislike. 'I'll be here if your father asks to see me, other than that I don't want to see you.'

'Try and stop me, Brooke. I still mean to take you.'

She gave a choked laugh. 'You have the nerve and conceit of the devil if you think that I would ever let you touch me again!'

He smiled at her anger. 'You can't help yourself, Brooke,' he scorned. 'You may keep denying it, but once I touch you you don't deny it for much longer.'

'Get out of here, Jarrod,' she ordered, her hands clenched tightly at her side. 'Just go away!'

She didn't hear him move, but she knew he had left, her senses told her that much. She sank down into the nearest armchair, all fight leaving her body. She couldn't go on like this much longer, she just couldn't take much more.

The most awful thing of all was that Jarrod was right, her love for him made her weak and pliant in his arms and forgetful of all the self-respect that had been inborn in her. No man who felt about her as Jarrod did should be allowed to affect her this way. He treated her as he would treat any of his casual women, Selina Howard remaining the love of his life.

She groaned. Selina Howard had a perfectly good husband of her own, a man who was charming, handsome and very rich, so why couldn't she leave Jarrod alone? Because Jarrod had a sensuous magnetism that was completely his own and would attract women all his life, that was why. Selina Howard just happened to be the woman he had given his love to, it didn't stop him wanting other women.

Brooke pummelled the cushion in the chair, angry and frustrated at the same time. She wanted Jarrod for herself, wanted and loved him, but she wouldn't have him under the conditions he wanted her, knowing that all the time Selina Howard was the woman he would go back to when her own challenge had wained. And that was all she was to Jarrod, a challenge.

The trauma of the last couple of days took its toll with her and she fell asleep in the chair. The sleep was just as drugged as the night before and she felt sure that the person hammering loudly on her door must have been doing so for some time before they finally woke her.

She staggered as she stood up, pushing her wayward hair out of her eyes. A glance at her wrist-watch showed her it was almost seven o'clock in the evening, and the rumblings of her stomach told her that it was high time she ate. She hadn't eaten anything substantial for two days and now felt weak with hunger. Another argument with Jarrod was the last thing she felt able to handle.

But it wasn't Jarrod standing nervously outside her door, it was his brother Dave. 'Can I come in?' he asked uncertainly.

'I suppose so,' Brooke nodded dully, not feeling in the mood to be polite to him, not after what he had tried to do to her.

'Thanks.' He closed the door behind him, still looking at her for some sign of softening towards him.

Brooke swayed dizzily, putting out a hand blindly to stop herself from falling. Unfortunately there was nothing to hold on to and she sank slowly to the floor in a dead faint.

She opened deeply violet eyes a few seconds later to find herself on the sofa, blinking dazedly as Dave bent over her. She attempted to sit up, but sank back down against the cushions as Dave gently pushed her back down again. She smiled wanly, ashamed of her weakness.

'I'm sorry about this. I don't usually fall at the feet of my visitors!'

He grinned down at her. 'It's an unusual greeting, I must admit, but I didn't mind. Quite nice really.'

She couldn't resist his smile. 'I don't know what's

the matter with me. I suddenly came over faint. I feel rather silly now.'

He looked suddenly serious. 'Have you felt like this before? Feelings of sickness, dizziness?'

She shook her head. 'No. It's nothing to worry about, I——'

'Everything unusual is something to worry about. Your health isn't something to be taken lightly. There has to be a reason for you fainting. Have you——' he broke off, a ruddy hue rising in his cheeks. 'Oh!' he looked embarrassed.

'Yes?'

'Well, I—— It's none of my business.' He turned away stiffly.

Brooke frowned. 'What are you thinking now, Dave?' she sighed, sitting up but not having enough energy to stand up. 'Don't bother to tell me, I can imagine what you're thinking, especially with the impression Jarrod has tried to give you of our relationship. But I'm not pregnant, I'm just hungry. Such a lot has been happening the last couple of days that I seem to have forgotten to eat.'

His obvious relief showed in his face. 'You mean you haven't eaten at all?'

'I've drunk a lot of coffee but had no food.'

Dave threw off his jacket and rolled up the sleeves of his shirt. 'Stay right there and I'll get you an omelette and a cup of strong sweet tea.'

'I don't take sugar in my tea,' she protested.

'This time you will,' he said firmly. 'Doctor's orders,' he grinned.

'Jarrod warned me about you,' she teased. 'I thought he was joking.'

'He wasn't. I take all this very seriously. Now just stay there while I get you some food.'

Brooke laughed. 'I wasn't going to move. Will you be able to find everything?'

'I'll manage.'

And he did, within a few minutes producing her a light fluffy omelette and the promised tea. She grimaced as she drank this, but forced it down under his watchful eye. 'You certainly cook a good omelette.' She sat back, replete.

'It's nourishing, easy and quick to cook. It's usually all I have time for.'

'You're quite amazing really. I could never imagine Jarrod being able to do anything like that.' She made a face. 'He told me he has a housekeeper.'

'Oh, he does, but he can shift for himself like the rest of us. At my age Jarrod was just starting out in business, and like me he refused help from our father.'

'I didn't realise. Jarrod always gives the impression of being—well, of being——'

'I know exactly what you mean,' Dave sympathised. 'But he was just as hard up as we are once.' He took the plate from her hand. 'Feeling better now?'

'Much,' she smiled gratefully.

He came back from the kitchen. 'I really came round to ask if you've forgiven me for the other evening. I know Jarrod's temper and I'm afraid I did nothing to allay his suspicions.'

Brooke squeezed his hand reassuringly. 'Well, we're still engaged.' She held up her hand with the ring on that she had forgotten to remove after parting from Jarrod. 'So he couldn't have been that annoyed.'

'I'm glad, I'm not usually such a swine. My only excuse is that I rather like you myself.' He shrugged. 'Still, I suppose I'll get used to the fact that the closest relationship I'll ever have with you will be as your brother-in-law.' He looked at his watch. 'I have to go now. I just wanted to clear things up between us.'

'And prepare me a lovely meal.' She stood up as he did and followed him to the doorway. 'It was nice of you to come round, I appreciate it.'

He opened the door before turning to face her. 'Can

I claim a brotherly kiss?'

'As long as that's all it is—and it's only the one,' she added teasingly.

The kiss couldn't exactly be called brotherly but she didn't have the heart to protest. In fact, she didn't have the chance. Dave was pulled roughly away from her, leaving her dazed as she stared up into the lividly angry face of Jarrod.

His grey eyes were like slate as he glared at his brother. 'Get out of here, Dave,' he ordered, 'before I do something we'll both regret.'

'Jarrod, it wasn't——'

'Get out, Dave!' Jarrod repeated through gritted teeth.

Dave gave Brooke a helpless look before leaving. She turned to re-enter her flat, realising that Jarrod was angry beyond reason.

But he wasn't going to let her go so easily, swinging her round to face him. 'Can't you stay away from my brother for just a few weeks?' he demanded coldly. 'At least until my father is out of hospital. Good God, girl, are you so much in love with him that a few weeks is too much to ask?'

'I——'

'No wonder you told me not to come back here, you knew Dave was coming over. Each time I see you I become more and more disillusioned with you, and yet I——' he shook his head. 'I still find myself wanting you. What do you have that makes men want you— myself, Dave, that boy Jerry? What is it about you that we all find so attractive?' He looked at her critically, making her feel as if he stripped the very clothes from her body. 'I can't see what it is, you're not as beautiful as hundreds of other women I know.'

'Including Selina Howard,' she put in bitchily.

'Especially the lovely Selina.'

'What did you come here for, Jarrod?' she asked, angry and hurt.

'My father would like to see you tomorrow. I'll call for you about ten o'clock.'

'I'll be ready. Perhaps now you've said what you came here to say you'll leave,' she requested quietly, unable to meet the disgust in his eyes. He was right, each time they met she gave him an even worse impression of herself, mainly because of her lie that she and Dave were in love. If he should ever ask Dave about that love! But he never would, he wasn't that interested in her, and his pride wouldn't allow for it either.

'Don't worry,' he said harshly, 'I have no intention of staying any longer than I have to. Goodnight.'

After that each day progressed the same; Brooke would visit the hospital in the morning with Jarrod and spend the rest of the time alone. She was pale and growing thinner daily, but luckily Jarrod's family put this down to the strain they were all under. Jarrod himself hardly spoke to her and she lived in daily dread of him telling her that this was the day their association came to an end.

By the time Friday evening came she was in such a state of nervous tension that any change in the routine of the last few days was welcome. Consequently she welcomed Jerry's unexpected visit with open arms.

Jerry looked around suspiciously. 'No fiancé this evening?'

'Nor any other evening.'

He looked surprised. 'I heard you were back together.'

Brooke smiled. 'And where did you hear that?' She sat opposite him, her knees tucked beneath her chin as she looked at him.

'It was in the newspapers that you and your fiancé have been visiting Clifford Stone with the rest of the family. I naturally assumed the engagement was back on.'

'For the moment,' she acknowledged.

'For the moment?'

'Until Mr Stone is strong enough to take the news.'

'Oh, I see. I was a bit uncertain about coming round this evening, but I'm glad I did now. I——' Jerry broke off as the doorbell rang. 'Are you expecting someone?'

She frowned. 'No.'

'Oh God, I have a nasty feeling ... Does this Jarrod of yours get violent? I haven't forgotten his threat. I like you, honey, but I don't particularly want to have to fight over you.'

Brooke stood up with a laugh. 'It won't be Jarrod. He never comes here now, except to take me to see his father.'

The door swung open before she reached it, giving the lie to her statement. Jarrod was the only one arrogant enough to walk into her home uninvited. He was dressed quite casually in black corduroys and a black silk shirt, and her heart jumped nervously at the sight of him.

'Jarrod,' she said lamely.

He smiled easily, completely unlike the cold front he had been showing to her all week. His eyes narrowed slightly as Jerry came to stand beside her. 'Am I interrupting anything?' he asked softly.

'No! Yes—— No——' she wanted him here, but she didn't want another argument. Before he had seen Jerry there had been a softness in his gaze that she had never seen before. She looked at him sharply, a terrible feeling in the pit of her stomach. 'Your father, is he——'

'He's fine,' he reassured her quickly. He looked at Jerry and a charming smile lit up his face. 'I'm afraid I still don't know your name, but it's nice to meet you again, Mr——' he looked at him enquiringly.

'Saunders, Jerry Saunders,' he supplied, obviously bowled over by this charm.

Jarrod shook his hand. 'And I'm Jarrod Stone, but

then you already know that. Actually I came over to
discuss the wedding date with Brooke. Had you forgotten?' he asked her.

'I—— No, I—I didn't realise it would be tonight.'
Her face was paler than ever. Tonight was the night
Jarrod would sever their relationship once and for all.
Oh God, she couldn't live without him!

'I thought you were aware of our plans.'

'Yes, but I—I just didn't realise it would be so soon.'

'I can see no point in waiting any longer.'

Jerry looked a little uncomfortable. 'I—er—I think
I'll leave now. See you, Brooke, Mr Stone.' He nodded
abruptly and left.

'What was he doing here?' Jarrod demanded once
they were alone.

Brooke was taken aback at his anger, none of it
having shown a few minutes earlier. 'He——'

'No, don't bother to explain,' he rasped. 'I don't
want to know.'

'You said you wanted to discuss the wedding date,'
she reminded him. 'Or lack of it. Your mother telephoned this afternoon, she thinks it's time we did
something about the arrangements. Is that what's made
you decide to call the whole thing off?'

'But I haven't.'

'Haven't what?'

'Decided to call the whole thing off. On the con-
trary, I think my mother has the right idea. It *is* time
you did something about the arrangements. My mother
will enjoy helping you.'

Her eyes widened. 'But I—— We aren't——'

Jarrod looked amused. 'Aren't what? Before you say
any more I think I should tell you that I had a word
with Dave today. He seemed very surprised that the
two of you were supposed to be lovers. In fact, he
denied it emphatically. Not that he didn't like the
idea, he just knew it wasn't true. Why did you tell me
it was?'

He was so tall and intimidating and she unconsciously moved away from him. 'I——— It seemed to be what you wanted to hear.'

'Come on, Brooke,' he chided gently. 'You know damn well it was the last thing I wanted to hear. I've been puzzling over it ever since I spoke to Dave and I can't come up with the reason you lied to me about it.'

'You can't?' Her voice was husky, her eyes wide with the fear that he had discovered her secret.

'No, I can't, but you can tell me it in a minute. First I want to tell you something, quite a lot of things in fact. I'll begin with the day we got engaged. When I found out what you'd done I was angry, furiously angry.'

Brooke smiled as she remembered that anger. 'I know that. It was unmistakable.'

'But that anger soon faded. I became very curious about you, you're so unlike anyone else I've ever met. You don't let me bully you for a start, which I find quite intriguing.'

'I never would have thought it,' she said dryly.

'No one has ever stood up to me as you do. So I became attracted to you, mindlessly so. The attraction grew so strong that I just knew I had to have you. I know I haven't always been kind, but you've given me great provocation. I'm not used to denying myself anything, and you were denying me all the time. That day I kissed you in the woods adjoining my family home I'd been pushed almost beyond endurance, holding you in my arms all night.'

'You didn't show it. You appeared very calm and collected when you woke up the next morning.' Too much so as far as she had been concerned!

'I wasn't. I escaped out of that bedroom as quickly as I could before I let you see how much I wanted to get back in bed with you and stay there all day.'

'Jarrod!' She blushed scarlet.

He grimaced. 'I know, I know. But I couldn't help

myself, you have no idea the difficulty I had controlling myself. As it turned out I'd only dampened down the passion for as long as it took me to see you again. If Dave hadn't come along and interrupted us I think I would have taken you right then. But he did interrupt us, and after that I was frightened I might have scared you. You see, I'm not a boy who can be satisfied with a few kisses—I wanted everything from you. But my age has been a certain barrier between us.' He scowled.

Brooke didn't know where this conversation was leading too, but this certainly wasn't the arrogant Jarrod she was used to. 'Your age has never come between us. I've never even thought about it, except that it gives you a certain amount of experience I don't have.'

'That I wouldn't want you to have. But it seems to me that every time I've been to see you lately I've had to throw out one young man or another.' He moved impatiently. 'You can't realise what it's done to me to see you with them.'

She couldn't, but she knew she couldn't let him be misled about them any longer. 'The only times they've been here is when you've called. It was just pure coincidence.'

'That may be so, but it doesn't alter the fact that you have more in common with them that I can ever hope for you to have with me. I'm thirty-eight next month, seventeen years older than you.'

'It doesn't matter,' she insisted quietly.

'Of course it does,' he denied violently. 'But I've come here tonight to ask you to marry me anyway.'

Her eyes widened. 'You're *asking* me?'

'Yes, I'm asking.' His look was anxious.

She shook her head. 'But I—I don't understand. You said you'd make me beg for marriage,' she reminded him dazedly.

'And now I'm the one doing the begging,' he said bitterly. 'And I am begging, Brooke.'

'But—but why?'

'Why?' he gave a harsh laugh. 'I've just been telling you why.'

'Because you desire me. But you know I won't marry you because of that.'

'I know I've been cruel and harsh and that I've accused you of things that just aren't true. I know you've never been with a man, I knew that, and yet I still kept taunting you. I didn't want to feel this way about you, Brooke, but I can't help it.'

'What way?'

'I love you, damn you!' he said violently, noting her shocked face. 'Hard to believe, isn't it, when you consider how badly I've been treating you. But it's true, Brooke, I love you so much that I'm going insane with wanting you. That's what you'll have to put my harsh behaviour down to, temporary insanity.' He grasped her shoulders. 'But I'm sane now, sane enough to know that I love you and want to marry you. Will you have me?'

'I—I don't know what to say.' She searched his face for some sign of mockery. 'This isn't a trick to get me to admit to wanting you enough to marry you, is it?'

He frowned, but it wasn't an angry frown. 'Oh God, I've treated you worse than I thought. Telling you I love you isn't enough, is it? I've lost your trust, haven't I?'

'I don't know,' she admitted truthfully. 'It's just such a shock to hear you say you love me. You've never shown it in any way.'

'I was a man in the last throes of losing the freedom I've always thought I valued above everything else, and I could be losing it to a woman who doesn't give a damn for me. You were attracted to me, I knew that, but it wasn't what I wanted. I tried so hard to make you admit to some feelings for me that in the end you retreated from me altogether. But whether you love me or not, whether you marry me or not, I'll never be free again. You have a large part of me I'll never get back, that I don't want back.'

Brooke's face softened at the look of utter defeat on his face. She touched his cheek gently, a large emotional lump rising in her throat as he turned to bury his face in her palm, his lips caressing, his eyes pleading. 'There's freedom in love too, Jarrod. A different sort of freedom, but it is freedom.'

His look was hopeful. 'Does that mean that you— that you——'

She couldn't bear his pain a moment longer. 'I love you,' she finished for him. 'Much longer than you've loved me, ever since I came to work for you, in fact.'

His eyes were almost black with passion, a look of such intense adoration on his face. He pulled her close against him, his hands moulding her to the contours of his body, his sigh one of deep satisfaction. 'Oh God, Brooke,' he quivered against her, 'I'd given up hope. I tried for so long to make you love me and you always rejected me. I thought I'd alienated you for ever.' He looked down at her anxiously. 'Do you really love me?'

She smiled at him gently. 'Really.'

He buried his face in her throat. 'I don't deserve this,' he muttered. 'But I need you so much that I don't care how I get you.'

Brooke felt like crying with happiness. Jarrod loved her and wanted to marry her. Nothing else mattered any more, not the bitterness or the misunderstandings. 'Kiss me, Jarrod,' she pleaded. 'I promise I won't reject you this time. Or ever again!'

He proceeded to do so, with satisfying thoroughness. Their declared love for each other heightened their senses to fever pitch. They lay on the sofa, their arms about each other as they mused over the fact that they had loved each other for weeks and neither of them had realised it.

Suddenly Brooke sat up with a jerk, her face paling.

'Selina Howard,' was the only explanation she gave to his worried expression.

Jarrod pulled her back down to rest her head on his shoulder. 'Forget her.'

'But you—you love her.'

He laughed softly. 'Of course I don't. I love you, I thought I'd just proved that. Very effectively,' he added with remembered satisfaction.

'But all this time—— You said you were having an affair with her, that you loved her,' she insisted with remembered pain.

'Correction, *you* said those things, I just played along with you.'

'But why did you do that?'

'Because in the beginning, before I began to fall for you, I kept up our engagement to punish you. You've been right about me all along, I'm a selfish swine where women are concerned. And I didn't like the fact that one of them had got back at me. I didn't intend for it to last long, just long enough to put you through hell,' he admitted. 'But at Philip's party, when you accused me of being Selina's lover, I saw red. I was determined to make you suffer. I let you believe those lies about Selina and myself because I knew my denying them wouldn't help, you wouldn't have believed me.'

'You could have tried to explain,' she pouted.

Jarrod bent his head to kiss her. 'I could have, but then I realised I needed a good excuse to keep the engagement going, you weren't going to be fooled by the "having to keep it up for show" story. After I kissed you at my parents' house I knew that for the first time in my life I was in love, that I wanted a woman so badly I had to marry her. But I'm afraid patience has never been my strong point and I tried to seduce you into marrying me. When that failed I lost my temper and started accusing you of having affairs with every man you came into contact with.'

'I noticed.'

'It was a form of defence,' he insisted. 'But I've never had an affair with Selina, and I certainly don't love her. I may have been a bit of a rogue in the past, but I've never had an affair with a married woman.'

'But everyone said——'

'Everyone *thought* they knew, but they were all wrong. Now kiss me, woman, and stop saying ridiculous things.'

Brooke went into his arms with renewed eagerness, holding nothing back as she showed him just how much she loved him. Jarrod was pale and strained by the time he pulled reluctantly away from her, buttoning his shirt with shaking hands.

'I have to leave now before I forget how innocent you really are,' he said grimly. 'I haven't forgotten how you once accused me of being the type of man to take advantage of the engagement and forget about the wedding.'

Brooke stilled his movements. 'Stay with me tonight.'

He shook his head firmly, standing up to tuck his shirt back into the waistband of his corduroys. 'I can wait until we're married. Never let it be said I seduced you into marrying me.'

She moved to stand in front of him. 'I would never say that. I was angry when I made that comment about forgetting the wedding. Please, Jarrod, stay with me.'

'No. I respect and love you too much to do that. That's what makes you so special to me, Brooke, the fact that I may want you like hell, but I can wait until I have my ring on your finger.'

Tears gathered at his words. 'Oh, Jarrod!'

'Don't tempt me, woman,' he growled. 'Just make the wedding soon, I don't have much self-control left where you're concerned.'

She stood on tiptoe to kiss him. 'As soon as possible,' she promised.

'Tomorrow?' he asked hopefully.

'If you like.'

They laughed together, completely confident in their love for each other.

Give yourself and your friends a romantic Christmas.

First time in paperback, four superb romances by favourite authors, in an attractive maroon and gold gift pack. A superb present to give. And to receive.

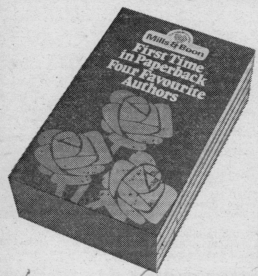

Sandstorm
Anne Mather

Man's World
Charlotte Lamb

Lord of the High Valley
Margaret Way

Enemy In Camp
Janet Dailey

United Kingdom	£2.60
Rep. of Ireland	£2.86
Publication	10th October 1980

Look for this gift pack at your local Mills & Boon stockist.

 The Mills & Boon rose is the rose of romance

The Mills & Boon Rose is the Rose of Romance

Every month there are ten new titles to choose from — ten new stories about people falling in love, people you want to read about, people in exciting, far-away places. Choose Mills & Boon. It's your way of relaxing:

December's titles are:

KING OF COPPER CANYON by *Elizabeth Graham*
Dani had gone to confront Grant King, but instead she found herself holed up with a disreputable character named Burt . . .

SEASON OF SHADOWS by *Yvonne Whittal*
Laura had become mother to her dead sister's child, but the girl also needed a father. Could Laura go through with a marriage to Anton DeVere?

THE LAST NIGHT AT PARADISE by *Anne Weale*
Arriving in the Caribbean to find her grandfather had died, Amalie was forced to accept the help of the mysterious Blake . . .

COMPULSION by *Charlotte Lamb*
Why was Lissa so reluctant to marry Chris? Shouldn't she be far more wary of the mysterious, reckless Luc Ferrier?

ENGAGED TO JARROD STONE by *Carole Mortimer*
Temper had provoked Brooke into declaring her 'engagement' to Jarrod Stone — and it suited him to make the engagement a real one!

DARK SURRENDER by *Margaret Pargeter*
The more Julie knew of Brad Hewson the more she realised that any woman who was foolish enough to love him was doomed to be hurt . . .

A DREAM OF THEE by *Mary Wibberley*
After the way Lachlan Erskine had treated her, Catriona had kept her distance from men — but now Lachlan had turned up again . . .

REUNION AT PITEREEKA by *Kerry Allyne*
Why was Rebel's brother on such bad terms with Chayne Cavanagh, the man she had come to love? She just had to find out.

THE SPANISH UNCLE by *Jane Corrie*
How could Mary give up looking after her dead sister's small son when the boy's uncle, Rafael Alvarados, made it clear that he wanted him?

SOUTHERN NIGHTS by *Janet Dailey*
When Todd Gaynor took his fiancée Barbara home to meet his family, she found herself confronted with the last man in the world she wanted to see . . .

Mills & Boon Classics

The very best of Mills & Boon
romances, brought back for those of you
who missed reading them when they
were first published

In
December
we bring back the following four
great romantic titles.

THE BEADS OF NEMESIS
by Elizabeth Hunter

Pericles Holmes had married Morag Grant as a matter of
convenience, but she had lost no time in falling in love with
him. Whereupon her beautiful stepsister Delia, who always got
everything she wanted, announced that she wanted Pericles!

HEART OF THE LION
by Roberta Leigh

When Philippa encouraged young Cathy Joyce to elope, she
didn't know the girl was the niece of her boss, the formidable
newspaper tycoon Marius Lyon — but that didn't stop him
promptly giving her the sack. But that was by no means the
last of Marius as far as Philippa was concerned!

THE IRON MAN
by Kay Thorpe

When Kim had no news of her fiancé in the Sierra Leone she
decided to go and find out what had happened to him. And
encountered opposition in the shape of the domineering Dave
Nelson who told her, 'Don't run away with the notion that
being female gives you any special immunity where I'm
concerned.'

THE RAINBOW BIRD
by Margaret Way

Paige Norton was visiting the vast Benedict cattle empire as
the guest of Joel Benedict. She had looked forward to it
immensely, although she hadn't much liked the sound of Joel's
stepbrother Ty, the boss of the station. And when she met Ty,
she liked the reality even less . . .

The Mills & Boon Rose is the Rose of Romance

AUTUMN IN BANGKOK by *Jacqueline Gilbert*
It was bad enough to have to go out to Bangkok, Alex thought.
But would Professor Nicholas Devlin allow her to stay with her
little brother?

WILD AND WONDERFUL by *Janet Dailey*
It felt like the end of everything to Glenna when the only man
who could help her father refused to do so . . .

LOVE IS A DANGEROUS GAME by *Marjorie Lewty*
What was 'a little grey mouse' like Kate doing in Hong Kong,
pretending to be the attractive Paul Caister's fiancée?

DEVIL IN COMMAND by *Helen Bianchin*
When she succeeded in diverting Paul Leandros's attention from
her sister to herself, Stacey realised, too late, that the price was
too high for her to pay.

FACE IN THE PORTRAIT by *Rosemary Carter*
Now that she had met him again, could Cindy keep from Jason
Peel the fact that her little boy was his son?

MOON OF APHRODITE by *Sara Craven*
Helen agreed unwillingly to visit her tyrannical grandfather in
Greece, but she realised too late that he had set a trap for her . . .

THE LOVING TRAP by *Daphne Clair*
The dislike that had at first sprung up between her and Marc
Nathan had soon turned into love, but would Kyla Vernon be
able to commit herself to him?

FIRE AND STEEL by *Mary Wibberley*
Millionaire tycoon Garth Vanner was quite a man, Arwenna
realised. But was it a wise thing to have got involved with him
at all?

ONLY LOVER by *Carole Mortimer*
To save her father's career, Farrah agreed to pretend to be Joel
Falcone's fiancée. But she found him too disturbingly attractive
already . . .

FIRST PASSION by *Dorothy Cork*
Why did the disagreeable Dain Legend assume that her mother's
marriage to the wealthy Walter Marshall had turned Fay into an
unscrupulous gold-digger?

If you have difficulty in obtaining any of these books from your
local paperback retailer, write to:
Mills & Boon Reader Service
P.O. Box 236, Thornton Road, Croydon, Surrey, CR9 3RU
Available January 1981

Doctor Nurse Romances

and December's
stories of romantic relationships behind the scenes
of modern medical life are:

ANGELS IN RED
by Lisa Cooper

Staff Nurse Margot Prince had been quite happy with
her career, and the brotherly attentions of Dr. Angus
Wheedon, until the arrival of Dr. Paul Laker. Why
should it all change now?

EVEN DOCTORS WEEP
by Anne Vinton

Joanna had been let down in love, and Simon Rivers'
'rational' plan — for her to marry him and forget her
heartache running a clinic in Tanzania — appealed to
her bruised pride. Then she fell in love again ... with
Simon!